MAIL/FAX BID SHEET

Heritage Auctions • HA.com
Direct Client Service Line—Toll Free:
866-835-3243
3500 Maple Avenue
Dallas, Texas 75219-3941

ALL INFORMATION MUST BE COMPLETED AND FORM SIGNED

KW-483-695

Rare Books Auction #6064
Submit Your Bids By Fax | FAX HOTLINE: 214-409-1425

NAME _____

ADDRESS _____

CITY/STATE/ZIP _____

DAYTIME PHONE (_____) _____

CLIENT # (if known) _____ BIDDER # _____

E-MAIL ADDRESS _____

CELL PHONE _____

EVENING PHONE (_____) _____

Would you like a FAX or e-mail confirming receipt of your bids? If so,

please print your FAX # _____

or e-mail address here: _____

I would like to limit my bidding to a total of $ _____

at the hammer amount for all lots listed on this bid sheet. I am aware
that by utilizing the Budget Bidding feature all bids on this sheet will be
affected. If I intend to have regular bidding on other lots I will need to
use a separate bid sheet.

Payment by check may result in your property not being released until
purchase funds clear our bank. Checks must be drawn on a U.S. bank.
(Bid in whole dollar amounts only.)

All bids are subject to the applicable Buyer's Premium. See HA.com for details.

Non-Internet bids (including but not limited to, podium, fax, phone and mail
bids) may be submitted at any time and are treated similar to floor bids. These
types of bids must be on-increment or at a half increment (called a cut bid). Any
podium, fax, phone or mail bids that do not conform to a full or half increment
will be rounded up or down to the nearest full or half increment and will be
considered your high bid.

Current Bid .... Bid Increment	
< - $10 ....$1	$10,000 - $19,999.....................$1,000
$10 - $29 ....$2	$20,000 - $29,999.....................$2,000
$30 - $49 ....$3	$30,000 - $49,999.....................$2,500
$50 - $99 ....$5	$50,000 - $99,999.....................$5,000
$100 - $199 .... $10	$100,000 - $199,999...............$10,000
$200 - $299 .... $20	$200,000 - $299,999...............$20,000
$300 - $499 .... $25	$300,000 - $499,999...............$25,000
$500 - $999 .... $50	$500,000 - $999,999...............$50,000
$1,000 - $1,999 .... $100	$1,000,000 - $1,999,999 ....$100,000
$2,000 - $2,999 .... $200	$2,000,000- $2,999,999 ....$200,000
$3,000 - $4,999 .... $250	$3,000,000- $4,999,999 ....$250,000
$5,000 - $9,999 .... $500	$5,000,000 - $9,999,999 ....$500,000
	>$10,000,000 ....$1,000,000

These bids are for Auction: # _____ Auction Description _____ *(ex. See catalog spine for auction # and description)*

LOT NO.	AMOUNT	LOT NO.	AMOUNT	LOT NO.	AMOUNT	LOT NO.	AMOUNT

PLEASE COMPLETE THIS INFORMATION:

1. IF NECESSARY, PLEASE INCREASE MY BIDS BY:
    ☐ 10%   ☐ 20%   ☐ 30%
    Lots will be purchased as much below top bids as possible.

2. ☐ I HAVE PREVIOUSLY BOUGHT FROM HERITAGE

3. ☐ I HAVE A RESALE PERMIT
    (please contact 1-800-872-6467)

I have read and agree to all of the Terms and Conditions of Auction: inclusive of
paying interest at the lesser of 1.5% per month (18% per annum) or the maximum
contract interest rate under applicable state law from the date of auction.

REFERENCES: New bidders who are unknown to us must furnish satisfactory industry references or a valid credit card in advance of the auction date.

REV. 11-3-11

SUBTOTAL	
TOTAL from other side	
TOTAL BID	

_____
(Signature required) *Please make a copy of your bid sheet for your records.*

FAX HOTLINE: 214-409-1425

LOT NO.	AMOUNT	LOT NO.	AMOUNT	LOT NO.	AMOUNT	LOT NO.	AMOUNT

Please make a copy of your bid sheet for your records.

TOTAL this side

7 *easy ways to bid*

1 Bid By Internet
Simply go to www.HA.com, find the auction you are looking for and click "View Lots" or type your desired Lot # into the "Search" field. Every lot is listed with full descriptions and images. Enter your bid and click "Place Bid." Internet bids will be accepted until 10:00 PM CT the day before the live auction session takes place.

2 Bid By e-Mail
You can also e-mail your bids to us at Bid@HA.com. List lot numbers and bids, and include your name, address, phone, and customer # (if known) as well as a statement of your acceptance of the Terms and Conditions of Sale. Email bids will be accepted up to 24 hours before the live auction.

3 Bid By Postal Mail
Simply complete the Bid Sheet on the reverse side of this page with your bids on the lots you want, sign it and mail it in. If yours is the high bid on any lot, we act as your representative at the auction and buy the lot as cheaply as competition permits.

4 Bid In Person
Come to the auction and view the lots in person and bid live on the floor.

5 Bid By FAX
Follow the instructions for completing your mail bid, but this time FAX it to (214) 409-1425. FAX bids will be accepted until 3:00 p.m. CT the day prior to the auction date.

6 Bid Live By Phone
Call 1-800-872-6467 Ext. 1150 and ask for phone bidding assistance at least 24 hours prior to the auction.

7 Bid Live using Heritage Live!™
Auctions designated as "Heritage Live Enabled" have continuous bidding from the time the auction is posted on our site through the live event. When normal Internet bidding ends, visit HA.com/Live and continue to place Live Proxy bids. When the item hits the auction block, you can continue to bid live against the floor and other live bidders.

Because of the many avenues by which bids may be submitted, there is the real possibility of a tie for the high bid. In the event of a tie, Internet bidders, within their credit limit, will win by default

THE AWARD-WINNING MAGAZINE FOR THE WORLD'S MOST PASSIONATE COLLECTORS

SUBSCRIBE NOW!

HERITAGE MAGAZINE FOR THE
INTELLIGENT COLLECTOR

RECEIVE THE NEXT 3 ISSUES
FOR ONLY $21
— A SAVINGS OF $8.85 OFF THE COVER PRICE

SUBSCRIBE TODAY TO LOCK IN THIS SPECIAL PRICE

"Heritage Magazine for the Intelligent Collector is a big, beautiful publication with writing that is both entertaining and informative and photos that are glorious to behold."
—Tony Isabella, Comics Buyer's Guide

With each issue, *Heritage Magazine for the Intelligent Collector* gives readers priceless insights into the vintage collectibles and fine art that matter most to the world's most passionate collectors.

▶INSIGHTFUL INTERVIEWS & FEATURES
Each issue includes exclusive interviews with world-class collectors who share their wisdom and knowledge about collecting.

▶FULL-COLOR PHOTOGRAPHY
Eye-popping photography gives you a detailed look at the world's top collectibles and fine art. *A Free Pull-Out Poster* is included in each issue.

▶COLUMNS BY TOP EXPERTS
Some of the top collecting experts tackle topics such as intelligent collecting, trusts and estates, and collecting with kids, and focus on specific categories such as coins, fine and rare wines, vintage jewelry and comics and comic art.

▶AUCTION PREVIEWS & PRICES REALIZED
Get a sneak peek at upcoming blockbuster auctions, in addition to prices realized for some of the world's most sought-after treasures.

▶COLLECTING CATEGORIES COVERED
Decorative arts, fine art, illustration art, Texas art, firearms and militaria, U.S. coins, world and ancient coins, comics and comic art, currency, entertainment memorabilia, American Indian art, Americana and political, rare books, Civil War, manuscripts, natural history, photography, space exploration, jewelry and timepieces, movie posters, pop culture, sports collectibles, fine and rare wine, silver and vertu.

SUBSCRIBE NOW!
▶Just $7.00 an issue
(3 issues for $21)
▶Order the next 6 issues for
only $36 and save even more

HOW TO ORDER
▶Subscribe online at
IntelligentCollector.com
▶Call Customer Service at
1-866-835-3243

NO RISK MONEY BACK GUARANTEE
If you are not delighted with your **Heritage Magazine for the Intelligent Collector** subscription, let us know. We will promptly refund 100% of payment for all un-mailed issues – no questions asked

Heritage Magazine for the Intelligent Collector is published three times a year. The cover price is $9.95. Offer good is U.S. and Canada only. All payments in U.S. funds. For orders outside the U.S., call Customer Service at 866-835-3243. Your first issue will mail 8-12 weeks from receipt of order. We never sell our mailing list to third parties.

Subscribe online at **IntelligentCollector.com** or call **1-866-835-3243**

22732 10-31-11

Heritage Signature® Auction #6064

Rare Books

Featuring: Selections from the Jack Cordes Collection of Science Fiction and Fantasy

February 8, 2012 | Beverly Hills

LIVE AUCTION Signature® Floor Session
(Floor, Telephone, HERITAGE Live!,™ Internet, Fax, and Mail)

Heritage Auctions, Beverly Hills
9478 W. Olympic Blvd. • Beverly Hills, CA 90212

Session 1
Wednesday, February 8 • 10:00 AM PT • Lots 36001–36168

HERITAGE Live!™ Internet, Fax, & Mail only Session
Session 2
Wednesday, February 8 • 4:00 PM CT • Lots 36169–36685

LOT SETTLEMENT AND PICK-UP
Immediately following session 1, or Thursday, February 9, 9:00 AM- 12:00 PM PT. Unless special arrangements are made in Beverly Hills by 12:00 PM PT Thursday, February 9, all lots will be returned to Dallas where they will be available starting Monday, February 13, by appointment only.

Extended Payment Terms available. Email: Credit@HA.com

Lots are sold at an approximate rate of 100 lots per hour, but it is not uncommon to sell 75 lots or 125 lots in any given hour.

This auction is subject to a 25% Buyer's Premium.

Heritage Numismatic Auctions, Inc.: CA Bond #RSB2004175; CA Auctioneer Bonds: Samuel Foose #RSB2004178; Robert Korver #RSB2004179; Bob Merrill #RSB2004177; Jeff Engelken #RSB2004180; Jacob Walker #RSB2005394; Scott Peterson #RSB2005395; Shaunda Fry #RSB2005396; Mike Sadler #RSB2005412; Andrea Voss #RSB2004676; Teia Baber #RSB2005525; Cori Mikeals #RSB2005645; Carolyn Mani #RSB2005661; Ed Beardsley #RSB2005694; Chris Dykstra #RSB2005738; Alissa Ford #RSB2005920; Kathleen Guzman #RSB2005966; Tim Rigdon #RSB2006164..

LOT VIEWING
Heritage Auctions, Beverly Hills
9478 W. Olympic Blvd. • Beverly Hills, CA 90212

Tuesday, February 7 • 9:00AM – 5:00 PM PT

View lots & auction results online at HA.com/6064

BIDDING METHODS:
HERITAGE Live!™ Bidding
Bid live on your computer or mobile, anywhere in the world, during the Auction using our HERITAGE Live!™ program at HA.com/Live

Live Floor Bidding
Bid in person during the floor sessions.

Live Telephone Bidding (floor sessions only)
Phone bidding must be arranged on or before Tuesday, February 7, by 12:00 PM CT.
Client Service: 866-835-3243.

Internet Bidding
Internet absentee bidding ends at 10:00 PM CT the evening before each session. HA.com/6064

Fax Bidding
Fax bids must be received on or before Tuesday, February 7, by 12:00 PM CT. Fax: 214-409-1425

Mail Bidding
Mail bids must be received on or before Tuesday, February 7.
Phone: 214.528.3500 • 800.872.6467

Fax: 214.409.1425
Direct Client Service Line: 866.835.3243
Email: Bid@HA.com

HERITAGE HA.com
AUCTIONS

Steve Ivy
CEO
Co-Chairman of the Board

Jim Halperin
Co-Chairman of the Board

Greg Rohan
President

Paul Minshull
Chief Operating Officer

Todd Imhof
Executive Vice President

Rare Books Specialists

James Gannon
Director, Rare Books

Joe Fay
Manager, Rare Books

3500 Maple Avenue • Dallas, Texas 75219
Phone 214-528-3500 • 800-872-6467
HA.com/Books

Consignment Directors: James Gannon, Joe Fay

Cataloged by: Paula Bosse, Joe Fay, James Gannon, Dave Golemon,
Brandon Kennedy, Harlan Kidd, Chad Reingold

Auction Highlights

[Incunabula]. Guillelmus Duranti. *Rationale divinorum officiorum.* [Paris: Ulrich [Gering], Martin [Crantz], and Michael [Friburger], 13 April 1475]. Large folio. [318] leaves. Bound in eighteenth-century mottled calf over thick boards. The greatest work from Guillelmus Duranti, or William Durandus (ca. 1237-1296), "canonist and one of the most important medieval liturgical writers." Estimate: $15,000 and up HA.com/6064-42001

Ian Fleming. *Goldfinger.* London: Jonathan Cape, [1959]. First edition. **Inscribed by Fleming** on the front free endpaper, "To Gerald Micklem, This piece - of homework! from Ian Fleming". Estimate: $15,000 and up HA.com/6064-51001

Charles Dickens. Christmas Books, Including: *A Christmas Carol; The Chimes; The Cricket on the Hearth; The Battle of Life; The Haunted Man* and the *Ghost's Bargain.* A handsome and complete first edition set of Dickens' time-honored Christmas stories, with the first issue of *A Christmas Carol*, all in original cloth. Estimate: $15,000 and up HA.com/6064-28001

[Pony Express Bible]. *The Holy Bible,* Containing the Old and New Testaments... New York: American Bible Society, 1857. Thick pocket-sized volume bound in eights. In the original custom leather binding, with "PRESENTED BY / RUSSELL, MAJORS & WADDELL / 1858" in gilt at the center of the front board. Estimate: $10,000 and up HA.com/6064-95001

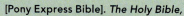 

Thomas Hardy. *Desperate Remedies.* London: Tinsley Brothers, 1871. First edition of Hardy's rare first book, one of only about 500 copies printed. **Inscribed by Hardy on a slip of paper mounted on the recto of the front free endpaper of volume I: "Autographed as requested- / Thomas Hardy."** Estimate: $7,000 and up HA.com/6064-93001

Edgar Allan Poe. *Tales of the Grotesque and Arabesque.* Philadelphia: Lea and Blanchard, 1840. First edition, one of 750 printed, and "the culmination of Poe's effort, beginning as early as 1834 to get his prose tales into volume form...[and] a milestone in his career as a prose writer." Two twelvemo volumes in the publisher's purple muslin with printed paper spine labels. Estimate: $15,000 and up HA.com/6064-84001

Maurice Sendak. *Where the Wild Things Are* (Prints). [N.p., 1971]. **Complete set of four art prints, each printed in 1971 from the original drawings for this classic and influential picture book,** each printed on a single sheet, measuring 15 x 24 inches, and **signed by Sendak in the lower right-hand corner.** Estimate: $3,000 and up HA.com/6064-73025

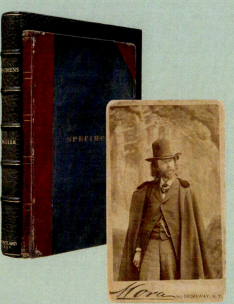

[Joaquin Miller]. C. H. Miller. *Specimens.* [*A Tale of the Rogue River War*]. [Portland: Printed by George Himes, 1868]. First edition of Miller's first book and one of the rarest of all books to emanate from the west (only about ten copies exist).
Estimate: $7,500 and up
HA.com/6064-74007

William Everson, printer. Robinson Jeffers. *Granite & Cypress: Rubbings from the Rock.* Santa Cruz: The Lime Kiln Press, 1975. First edition, **number 74 of 100 copies signed by Everson** on the limitation page. Publisher's German linen lined with Japanese Uwa paper, with the spine open-laced with deerskin rawhide with a strip of cypress on the spine. Housed in a slipcase made of Monterey Cypress with a window of granite from Jeffers' own stoneyard.
Estimate: $3,000 and up
HA.com/6064-87001

Henry M. Stanley. *In Darkest Africa or the Quest, Rescue, and Retreat of Emin, Governor of Equatoria.* New York: Charles Scribner's Sons, 1890. Demy Quarto Edition de Luxe. Limited to 250 numbered copies, of which this is number 3, **signed by the author on a special limitation page.** With two interesting autograph letters signed laid in from Stanley and his wife, Dorothy, each on the letterhead of the Plaza Hotel in New York, each dated April 11, 1891.
Estimate: $4,000 and up
HA.com/6064-83001

AN AUTO-BIOGRAPHY RICHARD AVEDON

Richard Avedon. *An Autobiography.* [New York: Random House, 1993]. First edition, one of 250 numbered copies, this being number 73, **signed boldly by Avedon** on the front free endpaper, **issued with an engraver's proof of Avedon's portrait of Marilyn Monroe.**
Estimate: $3,000 and up
HA.com/6064-59001

[Salvador Dali, Illustrator]. Lewis Carroll. *Alice's Adventures in Wonderland. Twelve Illustrations with Original Woodcuts and an Original Etching by Salvador Dali.* New York: Maecenas Press-Random House, 1969. **One of 2,500 numbered portfolios printed on Mandeure paper, signed by the artist on the title-page.**
Estimate: $4,000 and up
HA.com/6064-75001

Table of Contents

SESSION ONE

Floor, Telephone, Heritage Live!™, Internet, Fax, and Mail Signature® Auction # 6064
Wednesday, February 8, 2012 | 10:00AM PT | Beverly Hills | Lots 36001 - 36168

To view full descriptions, enlargeable images and bid online, visit HA.com/6064

Adair's Rare Book on the History of the American Indians

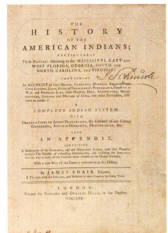

36001   James Adair. *The History of the American Indians;* *Particularly Those Nations adjoining to the Mississippi, East and West Florida, Georgia, South and North Carolina, and Virginia: Containing An Account of their Origin, Language, Manners, Religious and Civil Customs, Laws, Form of Government...* London: Printed for Edward and Charles Dilly, 1775. First edition of this history of the Indians, written by a trader who had traded with the Indian tribes for forty years. Approximately 10.75 x 8.5 inches. [10], 464 pages. With folding engraved map at front, but lacking half-title. Bound in modern half red cloth over gray pebbled cloth, spine ruled and lettered in gilt. Binding worn, with part of spine missing, previous owner's neat ink signature on title page, map with repairs to verso, worm damage to upper and lower margin of text, first several and last several pages of text with marginal paper repair with some loss of text, some ink notes and black and red pencil notes throughout, text toned. Good.

This book is somewhat unusual in its main argument: "...in proof of the American Indians being descended from the Jews" (p. ix). "Mr. Adair points out various customs of the Indians, having a striking resemblance to those of the Jews; and the great object of his work appears to be, to prove that the aborigines of America are descended from that race. Some distrust appears to have fallen upon his statements, although he himself says that his account is neither disfigured by fable nor prejudice" (Allen, as quoted by Sabin). Whatever the outcome of this argument made by the author, Howes refers to this book as the "Best 18th century English source on the Southern tribes, written by one who traded forty years with them." Howes A38. Sabin, pp. 23-24.
Estimate: $3,000-up
Starting Bid: $1,500

Caricatures, Prose and Poetry From a Gifted Early Nineteenth-Century Century Amateur

36002   [Anonymous]. Extraordinary New England Album of Original Prose, Poetry, and Sketches, Circa 1826-1830. Approximately 105 pages in manuscript written in a 6 x 8-inch album. The album was published by Durrie & Peck & N. & S. S. Jocelyn of New Haven, Connecticut in 1826. The title page features a romantic vignette engraved by S. S. Jocelyn. The album is bound in three-quarter calf and marbled boards.

Contained within are numerous pages of poetry and prose, typically with romantic or religious themes, written by an unknown, albeit talented amateur. Of particular note are eleven pages featuring twenty-two humorous sketches with captions. A fair number of the cartoons deal with African-American subjects and situations. The potential for research abounds in this intriguing and historic literary find. Fine condition.
Estimate: $1,500-up
Starting Bid: $750

Extraordinary Lithographs of New York, Circa 1877

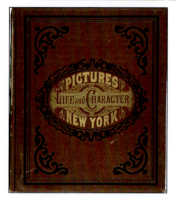

36003   G. W. Averell, lithographer. *Pictures of Life and Character in New York.* New York: Geo. W. Averell & Co., [n. d., advertisements dated 1877]. First edition. Quarto. [20] pages. Includes nineteen tinted lithographed plates on the recto with advertisements on the verso. Publisher's brick red cloth over beveled boards with decoration and titles embossed in black and gilt. Boards worn at the corners; four-inch split on the spine; contemporary hotel ownership label mounted to the front pastedown; front hinge broken, else internally a fine copy.

A quaint look at the social life and customs of New York in the late nineteenth century. The plates cover a wide range of subjects, including Fulton Ferry, Chatham Street, Castle Garden, "Mrs. McHash Private Boarding House," Chinese quarters including two men smoking opium, horse racing, unsavory characters, beggars, and street vendors throughout the city, military scenes, and more. The advertisements are equally interesting and offer goods and services such as tobacco, music boxes, optical instruments, suspenders, pianos, varnishes, hair tonic, printing materials, kid gloves, steam boat voyages, perfumery, champagne, chocolate, billiard tables, carriages, and much more. This is a scarce book with wonderful plates.

Estimate: $2,500-up
Starting Bid: $1,250

Early Account of Florida Under Spanish Rule

36004   Don Gabriel de Cardenas Z Cano [pseudonym for Andres Gonzalez de Barcia]. *Ensayo Cronologico, Para La Historia General De La Florida.* Madrid: Nicolas Rodriguez Franco, 1723. First edition. Folio. [40], 366, [56] pages. Title page printed in red and black. Folding table. Period vellum, spine lettered in manuscript. Some toning to the endpapers but otherwise a most handsome and clean copy of this very scarce work. About fine condition.

"The principal authority on Florida itself during its two centuries of undisputed Spanish supremacy, 1567-1763" (Howes). European Americana 723/10. Howes B130. Palau 105049. Sabin 3349. Wagner, *Spanish Southwest*, 84.

Estimate: $1,500-up
Starting Bid: $750

From the Library of Edgar Rice Burroughs

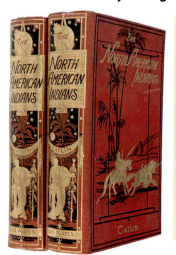 

36005   George Catlin. *The North American Indians.* Being Letters and Notes on Their Manners, Customs, and Conditions, Written During Eight Years' Travel Amongst the Wildest Tribes of Indians in North America, 1832-1839. Edinburgh: John Grant, 1926. **With the bookplate of fantasy author and Tarzan creator, Edgar Rice Burroughs affixed to each pastedown.** Two octavo volumes. With 320 illustrations (most color), engraved from the author's paintings. Publisher's decorative maroon cloth, elaborately titled and stamped in gilt and black. Both volumes a bit over-opened in a few places, else a near fine copy.

Estimate: $1,500-up
Starting Bid: $750

Salem Poet and Artist's Handmade Collection

36006   [Americana Folk Illustration]. [Rev. William Cook]. *The Eucleia, Works by*... [Salem: William Cook, 1861]. First bound edition of ten pamphlets bound into one volume. Twelvemo. Illustrated with woodcuts by the author. Period binding of cloth over boards with adhered patterned fabric laid over, with printed titles and decoration. Covers and extremities well-worn with abraded edges and moderate loss. Boards are warped, possibly due to dampstaining. Some soiling, light staining, and writing present. Ex-library markings, blind-stamping and removed bookplate. Preliminaries before printed title page of *Eucleia*, possibly including illustrated title, are excised. Original pamphlet wrappers bound in. Light toning, foxing and offsetting present throughout. Some hand-colored

graphite and ink additions. Occasional small tears, rubbing, and bumping to page edges.

Each pamphlet has illustrated colored paper wrappers with several similar illustrations within. Cook illustrates each text with charming, amateurish scenes of civic, natural and domestic life. Generally a very good copy of a scarce and charming item. "These pamphlets were printed by the author, at Salem, are illustrated with woodcuts, also by the author, and are amusing for their absurdity" Sabin 16297.

Estimate: $1,500-up
Starting Bid: $750

Rare Early Virginia Imprint on Bookbinding

36007   [Peter Cottom]. *The Whole Art of Book-Binding, Containing Valuable Receipts for Sprinkling, Marbling, Colouring, &c.* Richmond: Published by Peter Cottom, 1824. The first American edition, from the third London edition with considerable additions. Twelvemo. iv, [5]-60 pages. Large folding plate bound at back giving the list of prices of the New York Friendly Association Master Bookbinders. Lower portion of the plate missing but a copy of the same sheet from the Huntington Library has been photocopied and included. Publisher's original blue paper over boards with calf backstrip. Titles lettered in gilt on the spine. Boards moderately worn with some soiling. Hinges fragile but boards remain securely attached. The contents are sound but are uniformly toned with scattered light foxing. Still, a nice copy of this scarce work in very good condition, housed in a beautifully constructed modern clamshell case.

Accompanying the book is a one-page typed letter dated May 21, 1969 on Dawson's Book Shop letterhead, Los Angeles, and signed by Muir Dawson which was sent as an inducement to a noted collector to buy this very same copy. It reads, in part: "I have what I feel is almost certainly the first book printed in the United States on how to bind books...No author is given, but a reference I have to an English edition of 1811 gives the author as Oswestry." This is a rare, very early Virginia imprint.

Estimate: $2,500-up
Starting Bid: $1,250

Southern Stories Beautifully Illustrated by Darley

36008   [F. O. C. Darley, illustrator]. [Thomas B. Thorpe]. William T. Porter, editor. *The Big Bear of Arkansas and Other Sketches, Illustrative of Characters and Incidents in the South and South-West.* Philadelphia: Carey & Hart, 1845. First edition. Howes T238. Sabin 95662. [bound with:] **[F. O. C. Darley, illustrator]. [Johnson J. Hooper]. By a Country Editor.** *Some Adventures of Captain Simon Suggs, Late of The Tallapoosa Volunteers; together with "Taking the Census," and Other Alabama Sketches.* Philadelphia: Carey & Hart, 1845. First edition. Twelvemo. 181, 201 pages. Illustrated with several full-page engravings by Darley. Howes H612. Bound in half leather over marbled boards with gilt ruling and titles to spine. Covers and extremities rubbed with abrading to spine and corners. Minor toning to endpapers and page edges. Some offsetting to engravings. Otherwise, a very good copy of a scarce and wonderfully illustrated title.

Estimate: $1,500-up
Starting Bid: $750

The True First Appearance of Benjamin Franklin's *Autobiography*

36009 **Benjamin Franklin. *Mémoires de la vie privée de Benjamin Franklin,* ecrits par lui-meme, et adressés a son fils...** Paris: Chez Buisson..., 1791. First edition of Franklin's *Autobiography*, comprising a French translation of his 1771 manuscript for the years 1706-1731, and a translation from Wilmer's *Memoirs of Franklin* for the period after 1731. Approximately 7.25 x 4.5 inches. Octavo. [2], vi, 156, 207, [1, blank] pages (pages 204-207 misnumbered 360-363). Contemporary half brown calf over boards, spine ruled in gilt, with tan brown morocco gilt lettering label. Minor wear to binding, some foxing in text, some early ink underlining and small marginal notes throughout. Overall, a near fine copy.

"The most widely read of all American autobiographies, the gift to adolescents of countless parents, godparents and well-wishers, this book holds the essence of the American way of life..." (Grolier, *100 American*). The English edition first appeared in 1793. Ford 383. Grolier, 100 American, 21. Howes F-323. Sabin 25549. Streeter, VII, 4171.

Estimate: $2,000-up
Starting Bid: $1,000

Rare Early Account of California's "Daniel Boone"

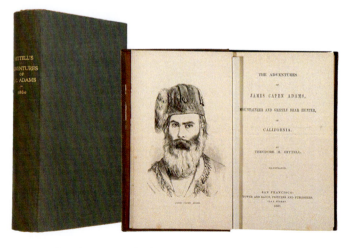

36010 **Theodore H. Hittell. *The Adventures of James Capen Adams, Mountaineer and Grizzly Bear Hunter, of California.*** San Francisco: Towne and Bacon, Printers and Publishers, 1860. First edition. Octavo. 378 pages. Twelve plates under tissue guards (including frontispiece) from drawings by Charles Nahl transformed into woodcuts by Eastman and Loomis. Publisher's original embossed brown cloth with titles stamped in gilt on the spine. Small bookplate and old bookshop sticker on the front

pastedown, else a remarkable copy in fine condition housed in a modern protective slipcase.

Though another edition of the book was published in the same year in Boston, extensive research by noted bibliographer Francis P. Farquhar determined that the San Francisco imprint is the true first edition. James Capen Adams might be described as "the California Daniel Boone" as his adventures certainly rival those of the more well-known outdoorsman. Graff 1912. Greenwood 1274. Howes H543. Wagner-Camp 348:1.

Estimate: $1,500-up
Starting Bid: $750

Inscribed by Jacqueline Kennedy

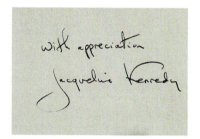

36011 **John F. Kennedy. *The Burden and the Glory.*** *The Hopes and Purposes of President Kennedy's Second and Third Years in Office as Revealed in His Public Statements and Addresses.* Edited by Allan Nevins. Foreword by President Lyndon B. Johnson. New York: Harper & Row, Publishers, [1964]. First edition. **Inscribed by Jacqueline Kennedy on the first blank: "with appreciation / Jacqueline Kennedy."** Octavo. [xx], 293, [1, blank], [1, colophon], [5, blank] pages. Publisher's special presentation issue binding of full blue crushed morocco, front cover double-ruled in gilt, with gilt central presidential seal, spine ruled in blind and stamped and lettered in gilt in compartments, all edges gilt, marbled endleaves, slipcase. Spine sunned and a bit worn, with front joint just starting (yet still solid), some rubbing to corners, previous owner's bookplate with his ink inscription. Overall, very good.

Estimate: $1,500-up
Starting Bid: $750

With a Bold Martin Luther King, Jr. Signature

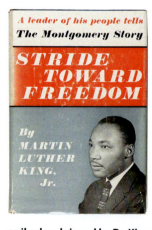

36012 **Martin Luther King, Jr. *Stride Toward Freedom*.** *The Montgomery Story.* New York: Harper & Brothers, Publishers, 1960. Early edition ("K-I"), **boldly inscribed and signed by Dr. King, "Best Wishes / Martin L King Jr."** on the front free endpaper. Octavo. 230 pages. Publisher's black buckram over blue cloth boards with silver titles. Original pictorial dust jacket. Deckled fore-edge. Moderate wear to the binding. Minor soiling to the top third of the covers. Some rubbing to the jacket panels, with a few small nicks to the edges. Spine sunned. Offsetting to endpapers. Overall, a very good copy with a strong King signature.

Dr. King's first book, with its primary focus on Rosa Parks and the Montgomery bus boycott that inspired the non-violent resistance employed by Civil Rights leaders throughout the American South.

Estimate: $2,000-up
Starting Bid: $1,000

One of the Rarest Books of Western Americana

36013   **[Joaquin Miller]. C. H. Miller. *Specimens.*** [*A Tale of the Rogue River War*]. [Portland: Printed by George Himes, 1868]. First edition of Miller's first book and one of the rarest of all books to emanate from the West (only about ten copies exist). Approximately 5.75 x 4 inches. 54 pages. Contemporary half red morocco over blue cloth boards, spine ruled in gilt. Some wear to binding, some mild soiling and wrinkling in text. Still, a fine copy of this very rare item. With a cabinet photo of Miller (approximately 4 x 2.5 inches) laid in. Chemised in blue morocco slipcase.

"With the exception of a few copies that had been distributed, the whole edition was destroyed by a fire in a bookseller's establishment" (Oregon Imprints Inventory, 453). When added to the fact that Miller himself destroyed any copy that he could find later in his life, one can see how rare this book truly is. Miller wrote it at Canyon City, Oregon and George H. Himes printed it in Portland, making it one of the first books printed in Oregon. BAL 13746.

Estimate: $7,500-up
Starting Bid: $6,000

With an Excellent Example of the Rare 1849 "New Map of Texas Oregon and California..."

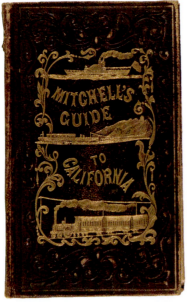

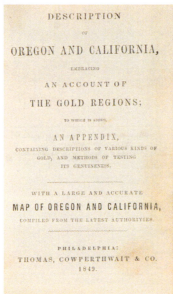

36014 **Samuel Augustus Mitchell.** *Description of Oregon and California, Embracing an Account of the Gold Regions...* With a Large and Accurate Map of Oregon and California, Compiled from the Latest Authorities. Philadelphia: Thomas, Cowperthwait & Co., 1849. Second edition. Twelvemo. 76 pages. With eleven wood-engraved text illustrations and the large hand-colored folding map (struck from the same plate used to print Mitchell's 1846 map by the same title, but with additional detail). Original dark brown morocco decoratively embossed in gilt and blind. Marbled wrappers to text. White front endpapers; salmon rear endpapers. Housed in a custom cloth box. Spine and edges rubbed. Corners bumped. Minor foxing to text. Mild toning to the map, with two very small instances of fold separation, and verso toning from the brown coloring. A clean copy in very good condition. Graff 2839. Holliday 833. Howell, *California* 50:173. Howes M687 ("b"). Sabin 19712. Smith 6889. Streeter Sale 2579. Wheat, *Books of the California Gold Rush* 143. Wheat, *Maps of the California Gold Region* 108 & pp. xxvi-xxvii.

Estimate: $7,500-up
Starting Bid: $3,750

A Satirical Look at American College Life Circa 1850

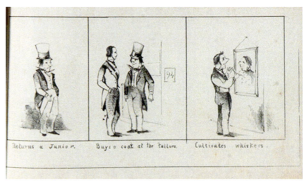

36015 **William T. Peters, illustrator.** *The College Experience of Ichabod Academicus; Illustrated by William T. Peters and Dedicated to Their Brother Collegians by the Editors, H.F.P. & G.M.* [New Haven]: [n.p.], [n.d., circa 1849-1850]. First edition. Oblong octavo. Unpaginated. Printed wrappers. String-bound. Wrappers toned with foxing and tatty along the edges. Contents with occasional scattered foxing. A few pages loose, but taken on balance a very good copy of this scarce work.

Peters' cartoons follow college students from the freshman year through senior year in serialized form.

Estimate: $1,500-up
Starting Bid: $750

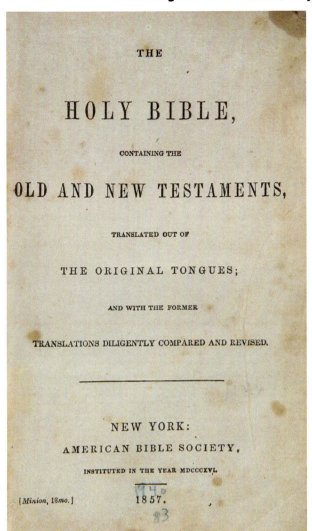

36016   **[Pony Express Bible].** *The Holy Bible*, *Containing the Old and New Testaments*, Translated Out of the Original Tongues; and With the Former Translations Diligently Compared and Revised. New York: American Bible Society, 1857 (New Testament title page dated 1857). Thick pocket-sized volume (5.5 x 3.5 inches, 139 x 89 mm.), bound in eights. 1,278 double-columned pages. In original custom leather binding, with a series of decorative borders and ovoid shapes blind-stamped to boards, and with decorative blind-stamping and gilt lettering on spine. "PRESENTED BY / RUSSELL, MAJORS & WADDELL / 1858" in gilt at center of front board. Leather binding quite rubbed with some loss of leather at spine ends and extremities. Gilt lettering rubbed. Repairs to joints. Intermittent foxing. Over-opened at page 590/591 and quite tender. Biblical notations in pencil to verso of New Testament title page. Ink numbers on rear pastedown. With names of three owners on front free endpaper: Hettie Jane Bruce, W. D. Fletcher, and Clara Fletcher. At bottom of page is written "Hettie Jane Bruce's book / 1858." A complete copy of a "Pony Express Bible" in its original, though worn, binding. In generally very good condition. Very rare, with very few extant copies located.

William Russell, Alexander Majors, and William Waddell — the three founders of the Pony Express — began their partnership in 1854 with the formation of Russell, Majors & Waddell, a large freighting and stage business which crisscrossed the Western frontier, providing freight, mail, and passenger service. In 1860, the company was contracted by the U.S. government to begin a fast mail delivery service between St. Joseph, Missouri and Sacramento. This service was The Pony Express, the legendary Wild West mail service with individual mounted horsemen riding in relays to cover vast distances in a short time, operating under the slogan "The mail must go through." The Pony Express service lasted a mere nineteen months, but it has become a mainstay in the lore and legend of the American West.

Partner Alexander Majors was a staunchly religious man who not only decreed that the Sabbath be observed as a day of rest for his employees, but who also insisted that his workers take an oath promising to abstain from using profane language, from drinking to excess, and from gambling. He presented his employees — including the Pony Express riders — with a custom-bound Bible. Over the years, this Bible has come to be known as the "Pony Express Bible." Each Bible had the words "Presented by Russell, Majors & Waddell 1858" stamped in gilt on its front cover. The Bible offered here is one of those "Pony Express Bibles," a rare and sought-after artifact of the Old West.

The first owner's name in the Bible is that of Hettie Jane Bruce. Census records show that Hetty [*sic*] Bruce was born in 1846 in Missouri, making her 12 years old in 1858. The Bible appears to have been passed from her to her son, William Dean ("W. D.") Fletcher, then to his sister Clara Fletcher. The Bible has remained in the family descended from Hettie Jane Bruce until now. A historic, if well-worn, copy of the supremely rare 1858 Russell, Majors & Waddell "Pony Express Bible," passed down through generations and kept in the family of its original owner for over a century and a half.

Estimate: $10,000-up
Starting Bid: $5,000

Following the Forty-Niners for Naught

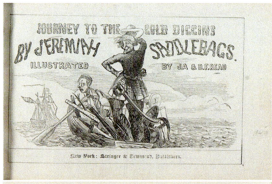

36017 **[California Gold Rush]. J. A. & D. F. Read, illustrators.** *Journey to the Gold Diggins by Jeremiah Saddlebags.* New York: Stringer and Townsend, [1849]. First American edition, simultaneous with Cincinnati. Oblong twelvemo. 63 pages. With pictorial title and 112 illustrations. Half morocco over cloth boards with gilt spine titles. Corners quite rubbed with boards exposed. Some loss to spine ends and extremities. New endpapers, lacking original wrappers. Preliminary has stain to top corner. Some light toning and foxing throughout, particularly to rear of text. A better than very good copy of this scarce title.

"Of the American comic books on the subject of the gold rush, the best known, although it is scarce, is this." This is the story of an "Argonaut who risked the hard journey to the gold fields, found that it was all a good deal more difficult than he had thought, avoided death by a hair's breadth time and again, and came home poorer than he went. It is the best of the American comic books on this theme" (Cowan). Cowan, p. 523. Howes R-92. Kurutz 524b. Murrell 170. Randall 404. Sabin 68157.

Estimate: $4,000-up
Starting Bid: $2,000

An Important Early Book About the Gold Rush Written by Paul Revere's Grandson, and Signed by Him

36018 **Joseph Warren Revere.** *A Tour of Duty in California; Including a Description of the Gold Region: and an Account of the Voyage Around Cape Horn; with Notices of Lower California, the Gulf and Pacific Coasts, and the Principal Events Attending the Conquest of the Californias.* **Edited by Joseph E. Balestier.** New York: C. S. Francis & Co, 1849. First edition of "one of the most important books on the Gold Rush [which] figures on most selected lists" (Streeter 2492). **Signed by Revere on the front free endpaper.** Octavo. [2, blank], [xii], 305, [1, blank], [6, publisher's ads], [1, blank] pages. With folding map ("The Harbor of San Francisco") inserted at front, and five full-page plates based on Revere's designs inserted throughout. On page [xi], there is an engraving entitled "Design for the Arms of California" also based on Revere's design. Publisher's full brown cloth, ruled and stamped in blind on covers, ruled and lettered in gilt on spine. Yellow-coated endpapers. Spine and board edges sunned and rubbed, a few leaves somewhat roughly opened (not affecting text), some minor wear to map at right edge just below the point where it is affixed to the text, pages 134-135 are browned, possibly due to offset from a newspaper article that may have been put there. Still, a near fine copy of this important book, with a rare signature.

"Revere was the grandson of American revolutionary Paul Revere. His book is one of the outstanding authorities on the period of the conquest, and his descriptions of California and the gold regions are among the best. The book contains valuable chapters on land law and land titles, as well as the complete report of Colonel Mason on the gold fields" (Hill 1439). "One of the most valuable works of the period" (Cowan I, pp. 189-90).

Cowan II, p. 530. Graff 3474 & 3475. Hill 1439. Howes R222. Kurutz, *The California Gold Rush* 529a.

Estimate: $1,500-up
Starting Bid: $750

Muster of the Missouri Militia

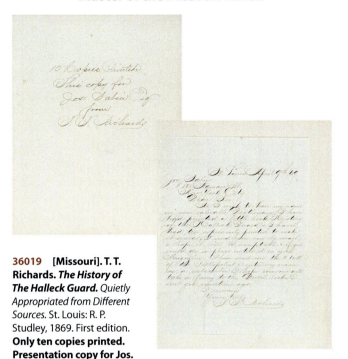

36019 **[Missouri]. T. T. Richards.** *The History of The Halleck Guard.* *Quietly Appropriated from Different Sources.* St. Louis: R. P. Studley, 1869. First edition. **Only ten copies printed. Presentation copy for Jos. Sabin Esq. from T. T. Richards. With a tipped-in one-page ALS from Richards to Sabin.** Quarto. 30 pages. Frontispiece by Mallory. Half leather over boards with gilt ruling and spine titles. Covers and extremities rubbed with small stain on front board. Both hinges lightly broken but intact. Some light toning and foxing. Catalog entry tipped in at rear. Otherwise, a better than very good copy.

"An immediate organization of all the militia of Missouri is hereby ordered, for the purpose of exterminating the guerillas that infest the State" (Sabin 70970).
Estimate: $1,500-up
Starting Bid: $750

A Rare New Orleans Printing of Washington's Farewell Address

36020 **[George Washington].** *Farewell Address of Gen. George Washington, to the People of the United States.* September 17, 1796. [New Orleans: Bradford & Anderson, 1807]. Quarto (19.5 cm x 12 cm). 47 pages. Half-title imprinted "Published by order of the Legislature." English and French texts on opposite pages. Type and printers' ornaments conform to those used by Bradford & Anderson, printers to the Territory, on the half-title pages of Acts passed at the sessions of the first-second Legislature of the Territory of Orleans. Modern dark blue morocco over blue cloth with gilt spine titles. Minor foxing. Some creasing to text. Bookplate to front pastedown. Near fine. Howes W143.
Estimate: $1,500-up
Starting Bid: $750

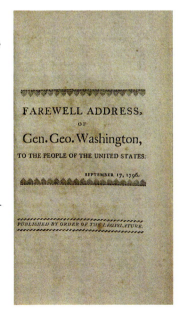

George Washington's *Official Letters to the Honorable American Congress,* Signed by His Grand-Nephew

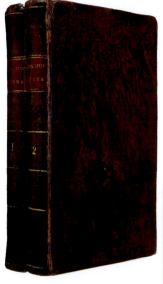

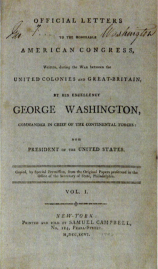

36021 **George Washington.** *Official Letters to the Honorable American Congress, Written, during the War between the United Colonies and Great-Britain, by His Excellency George Washington, Commander in Chief of the Continental Forces: now President of the United States. Copied, by Special Permission, from the Original Papers preserved in the Office of the Secretary of State, Philadelphia.* New York: Samuel Campbell, 1796. First New York edition (previously published in Boston in 1795). **Signed by George F[ayette] Washington on both title pages.** Two small octavo volumes. 296; [ii], 311, [1, blank] pages. Issued without portraits. Contemporary full tree calf, spines ruled in gilt, with burgundy gilt morocco lettering labels. Some rubbing to joints and edges, bookseller's plates on both front pastedowns, near contemporary neat ink price on front pastedown of Volume I, previous owner's ink signature (mostly erased) on front free endpapers. Some soiling, foxing to text, upper corner of page 183/184 in Volume II lacking (not affecting text), hinges just starting, yet solid. Overall, a fine copy.

George Fayette Washington (1811-1871) was President George Washington's grand-nephew, being the grandson of his brother Charles. Howes W142
Estimate: $1,500-up
Starting Bid: $750

One of 500 First Edition Copies with Separate Pagination

36022 **John Wise.** ***A Vindication of the Government of New-England Churches*** [and:] ***The Churches Quarrel Espoused: or, a Reply.*** [and:] ***A Platform of Church-Discipline...*** Boston: Printed and sold by John Boyles, 1772. First edition, one of 500 copies with separate pagination. Quarto. 80, 96, 68, [2, advertisement leaf] pages. Modern crushed morocco with gilt spine titles inside five raised bands. Minor wear to the binding. Spine sunned. Some toning and scattered foxing to text. Bookplate to front pastedown and ownership stamp to title page. Minor loss to the bottom edge of the first and last leaves. Very good condition.

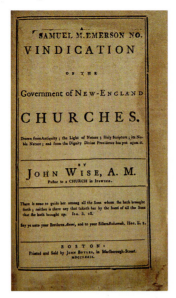

"The most authoritative defense of Congregational polity, recognized as such even in law courts" (Howes W-595). Evans 12625. Sabin 104901.

Estimate: $1,500-up
Starting Bid: $750

On the Front Lines of the Fight for the Freedom of the American Press

 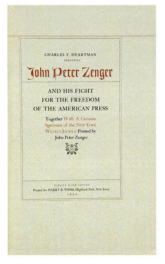

36023 **[John Peter Zenger].** ***Charles F. Heartman Presents John Peter Zenger and His Fight for the Freedom of the American Press.*** Together With A Genuine Specimen of the New York Weekly Journal Printed by John Peter Zenger. Highland Park, New Jersey: Harry B. Weiss, 1937. First edition, one of 99 copies, this being copy number 11. Approximately 13.5 x 8 inches. Folio. [iv], 60, [2, blank] pages. Text lined in red and printed in double-columns. Publisher's binding of full marbled paper, with printed labels on front board and spine. Some rubbing to edges, some wear to spine and corners. Overall, very good. With spare labels tipped in at rear. Bound-in is: **[John Peter Zenger, printer].** ***The New York Weekly Journal. Containing the freshest Advices, Foreign, and Domestick.*** **Numb. LVI.** [New York:] Munday [sic] December 2d, 1734. First edition of this newspaper. Approximately 11.75 x 7.5 inches. [4] pages.

This issue details the orders by the New York Assembly and Governor William Cosby for the burning of numbers 7, 47, 48, and 49 of Zenger's

New-York Weekly Journal on charges of Sedition against the British Crown. Zenger, a New York printer born in Germany, affected the course of American journalistic freedom when he was found not guilty of criminal libel for publishing articles and doggerel verse critical of William Cosby, then governor of New York, in the *New-York Weekly Journal,* a newspaper that he edited and printed. "Zenger's acquittal received wide attention in Europe for its revolutionary aspects, which apparently raised popular interest" (Streeter).

Estimate: $2,000-up
Starting Bid: $1,000

A Complete Copy of The Aldine Edition of Caesar's *Commentaries*

36024 **[Aldine Press]. Gaius Julius Caesar. [Opera].** *Hoc volumine continentur haec. Commentariorum de bello Gallico libri VIII. Be bello civili pompeiano. libri IIII. De bello Alexandrino. liber I. De bello Africano. liber I. De bello Hispaniensi. liber I. Pictura totius Galliæ, & Hispani... secundum C. Cæsaris Comentarios. Nomina locorum, urbiniumq[ue], & populorum Galliæ, & Hispaniæ, ut olim dicebantur latine, & nunc dicantur, secundum ordinem alphabeti. Pictura Pontis in Rehno. Item Avarici. Alexiæ. Uxelloduni. Massiliæ.* [Venice: In aedibus Aldi, et Andreae soceri, January 1518-November 1519]. Second Aldine edition, after the first of 1513 (although the date given on the title page is 1513, the Index is dated 1519, indicating the second edition of 1518-1519). Approximately 6.5 x 3.5 inches. Small octavo. [16], 296 leaves. Italic type. Two double-page woodcut maps, five full-page woodcut illustrations. These woodcuts have been partially hand-colored at a later date. Anchor and dolphin device (Fletcher 6 and 3) on title and each colophon. Capital spaces with guide letters. Near contemporary pigskin over boards (binding stamped "1537"). Binding elaborately stamped in blind on boards, spine lettered and ruled in one compartment on spine with three raised bands, "1518" written in ink on spine and "Caesar" written in ink on fore-edge. A few leaves unopened.

The first forty-six leaves bear early manuscript notes (and two small neat drawings). Some typical age-toning and wear to binding, front joint cracking (yet still quite solid), previous owner's ink inscription on front free endpaper, very light damp marking to lower edge of text. Still, an attractive and complete copy. The text reproduces the same preface by Aldus and the architect J. Jucundus, and the same woodcuts are used. Adams C29. Murphy 185. Renouard, Alde, p. 88.

Estimate: $2,000-up
Starting Bid: $1,000

The First Work Published on the Formation of the Italian Language

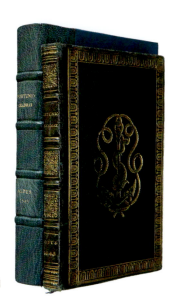

36025   [Aldine Press]. Giovanni Francesco Fortunio. *Regole grammaticalli della volgar lingua.* [Venice:] Aldine Press, 1545. First edition. Approximately 5.5 x 3.5 inches. Small octavo. [4], [48] leaves. With woodcut anchor and dolphin device on title page and recto of final leaf. Bound in eighteenth-century full turquoise crushed levant morocco, covers elaborately ruled in gilt, and with gilt central anchor and dolphin devices, spine ruled, tooled, and lettered in gilt in compartments, four raised bands, gilt board edges and turn-ins, lavender coated endpapers. Spine slightly sunned and rubbed. A fine copy. With the bookplates of famed nineteenth-century book collector Sir John H. Thorold (of Syston Park, two bookplates), and Henry William Poor. Chemised in quarter turquoise levant morocco slipcase.

Estimate: $1,500-up
Starting Bid: $750

The Complete Hunting in Africa Series by Safari Press, Each Signed by the Editor and Artist

36026   [Hunting in Africa]. [Tony Sanchez-Arino, editor]. [Hunting in Africa Series]. Long Beach: Safari Press, Inc. [1991-2000]. **First edition, one of 1,000 copes signed by the editor and the artist of each volume.** Complete in eight quarto volumes. Bound in publisher's full harlequin cloth, front cover and spine decoratively stamped and lettered in gilt and black, rear cover with publisher's symbol stamped in black, matching slipcases. A fine set. Although set is complete and numbered by the publisher on the spine as Volumes I through VIII, the limitation page states that these books are the seventh through the fourteenth volumes in the Classics in African Hunting Series. **The artists who have signed this set include: Alan James Robinson, Larry Norton, Joseph Vance (who illustrated and signed two volumes), Dino Paravano, Elise van der Heijden, Paul Bosman, and Clive Kay.**

Estimate: $2,000-up
Starting Bid: $1,000

German Edition of Buffon's Monumental Work on Natural History, with Over 2,000 Hand-Colored Plates

36027 **Georges Louis Leclerc, Comte de Buffon and Bernard-Germain-Étienne, Comte de Lacepede.** *Naturgeschichte [Histoire naturelle, générale et particulière].* Berlin: Joachim Pauli and others, 1771-1809. Sixty-nine octavo volumes (over seven linear feet). With over 2,000 hand-colored frontispieces, natural history plates, maps, and charts, some fold-out. Numerous additional plates are present but uncolored. Most volumes with hand-colored scenes on the title page. The voluminous number of colored plates include deer, rabbits, owls, turkeys, chickens, wolves, minks, rodents, tigers and other cats,

elephants, squirrels, porcupines, armadillos, horned animals, zebras, bats, skunks and other furred animals, monkeys, whales, seals, polar bears, fish, insects, snakes, turtles, frogs, lizards, and hundreds upon hundreds of birds of every stripe, including swans, cranes, ducks, and almost two entire volumes devoted to parrots. Contemporary sheep with gilt spine labels. Marbled endpapers. Overall fairly heavy wear to the bindings. Some boards detached. Some spines and title labels perished or perishing. All with the same unobtrusive ex-library label, sticker, and stamps from the Bibliotheca Mt. St. Alphonsus in Esopus, New York. Light offsetting to some volumes, but overall clean text and plates. A number of the later volumes, after 1800, are attributed to Lacepede. A monumental set in very good condition, better if not for the bindings.

Estimate: $7,500-up
Starting Bid: $3,750

"Masterpiece of Historical Penetration and Literary Style"

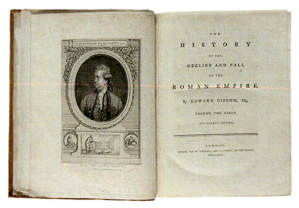

36028 **Edward Gibbon.** *The History of the Decline and Fall of the Roman Empire.* London: Printed for A. Strahan; and T. Cadell, 1781-1788. Fourth edition of Volume I, first editions of the five remaining quarto volumes. Engraved portrait of Gibbon by Hall after Reynolds in Volume I. Three engraved folding maps. With the half titles in Volumes II through VI, and the called-for errata leaves in Volumes II, III, and VI (this last volume has the errata for the final three volumes); maps, and errata leaves as issued. The following issue points which are listed in Sterling and Rothschild, are noted here: Volume II has G1 as a cancel and L1 not cancelled. Volume III is an early state with the misprint "Honorious" on page 179 and with page 177 correctly numbered; Volume IV with H3, so signed and L2 signed as *L2. Contemporary brown calf, spines ruled in gilt with red and green gilt morocco lettering labels. Spines worn, joints cracking, some rubbing to panels, front free endpaper of Volume I is loose. Bookplates. Generally, a very good copy of the scarce first edition of the majority of the work.

Gibbon's *Decline and Fall* brought to the subject a width of vision and a critical mastery of the available sources which have not been equalled to this day. "This masterpiece of historical penetration and literary style has remained one of the ageless historical works which, like the writings of Macaulay and Mommsen, maintain their hold upon the layman and continue to stimulate the scholar although they have been superseded in many, if not most, details by subsequent advance of research and changes in the climate of opinion. Whereas other eighteenth-century writers in this field, such as Voltaire, are still quoted with respect, the *Decline and Fall* is the only historical narrative prior to Macaulay which continues to be reprinted and actually read" (*Printing and the Mind of Man*).

Grolier, *100 English*, 58. Norton 20, 23, and 29. *Printing and the Mind of Man* 222. Rothschild 942-944. Sterling, Part I, 382.

Estimate: $3,000-up
Starting Bid: $2,500

Illustrations by French Painter Louis-François Cassas
from his Travels in Istria and Dalmatie

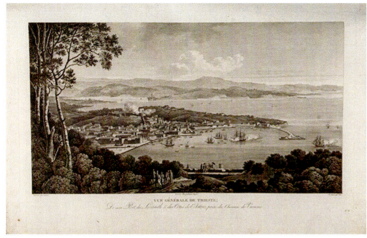  

36029   **Joseph Lavallée (Louis-François Cassas).** *Voyage Pittoresque et Historique de l'Istrie et de la Dalmatie. Rédigé d'Après L'Itinéraire de L. F. Cassas*, Par Joseph Lavallée... Ouvrage orné d'Estampes, Cartes et Plans, dessinés et levés sur les lieux par Cassas, peintre et architecte, auteur et éditeur du Voyage pittoresque de la Syrie, de la Phénicie, de la Palestine et de la basse Égypte, et graves par les meilleurs artistes en ce genre, sous la direction de Née.... Paris: Pierre Didot l'Aine, 1802. First edition. [4, half-title, engraved title, letterpress title, engraved frontispiece], viii, 190, [1] pages and sixty-seven engraved plates (many folding, including two double-page maps and one double-page plan). Complete. Elephant folio. Contemporary quarter parchment or vellum over pastepaper boards. Binding heavily worn, scuffed and bumped, and in fair condition only. Internally very good or better condition, and generally very bright and clean. One double-page map is neatly detached and partially split along the fold, else in very good condition.
Estimate: $4,000-up
Starting Bid: $2,000

One of the Best Commentaries of a Work of Classical Literature

36030   **Titus Lucretius Carus.** *De Rarum Natura Libri Sex.* A Dionysio Lambino Monstroliensi Litterarum Graecarum in Urbe Lutetia Doctore Regio... Paris et Lugduni: G. Rouillij and P. G. Rouillij, 1564. First edition, second state of the first of the renowned scholarly editions edited, and with notes by, one of the greatest classical scholars of the sixteenth century, Denys Lambin. Although this edition is a second state of the first edition, Gordon notes that despite the different dates on the title pages, the states are "alike in all other respects." Approximately 9.25 x 5.5 inches. Quarto. [xxiv], 559, [1, blank] pages. With engraved title page. Full sixteenth-century mottled, paneled calf, with the arms of James Stuart, the First Earl of Bute stamped in blind in the center of both covers (also with his bookplate on the front pastedown), spine ruled and lettered in gilt, five raised bands. Some wear and chipping to spine, panels and corners rubbed. A fine copy.

"It has learned commentaries which evince the wonderful erudition of Lambinus... [the commentary] is not only one of the very best upon Lucretius, but there are few commentaries on any classical author that excel it" (Thomas Dibdin). Laid into this copy is an Autograph Letter Signed by noted British surgeon and bibliophile Geoffrey Keynes who describes this book as "one of the better editions of Lucretius (Lambinus) — an atheistical book, I'm afraid..." Gordon 102. STC of French Books, p. 291. Graesse IV-287.
Estimate: $1,500-up
Starting Bid: $750

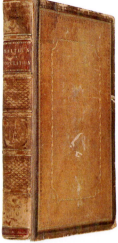 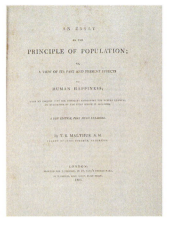

36031   Thomas Robert Malthus. *An Essay on the Principle of Population; or, a View of Its Past and Present Effects on Human Happiness... a New Edition, Very Much Enlarged.* London: Printed for J. Johnson by T. Bensley, 1803. Second edition. Quarto. viii, [ix-xi, Contents], [xii, Errata], [1]-610 pages. Contemporary sheep with gilt border and frame and floral blind-stamping on the covers. Red leather title label affixed to the spine, lettered in gilt. Gilt inner dentelles. Marbled endpapers and text edges. Binding rubbed and worn, with corners exposed. Boards recently re-attached along the hinges. Bookplate to front pastedown. Two small ink stains to fore-edge. Scattered foxing to text. Small area of corner loss to 3O2. A mostly very clean copy in very good condition.

"In 1803, Malthus published a greatly expanded second edition of the *Essay*, incorporating details of the population checks that had been in operation in many different countries and periods. Although nominally a second edition, it was regarded by Malthus as a substantially new work" (*Oxford Dictionary of National Biography*).

Estimate: $2,000-up
Starting Bid: $1,000

First Edition of Chairman Mao's "Little Red Book"

36032   Mao Zedong. *Mao zhuxi yulu.* [*Quotations of Chairman Mao*]. [N.p. (probably Beijing): Central Intelligence Bureau of the Chinese People's Liberation Army, [May 1964]. First edition, first state, of Chairman Mao's "Little Red Book," after the Bible the most printed text in the world. Twelvemo. Approximately 5.5 x 4 inches. [iii, i], [2, preface], [2, table of contents, with thirty chapters], 250, [2, blank] pages. Complete with the frontispiece portrait of Mao and Lin Biao's calligraphic endorsement leaf. Half-title printed in red, title in red and green. Wire-stitched in the original printed wrappers. Wrappers a little soiled and creased, joints rubbed. Some very minor rubbing and wear, lower edge of spine rubbed and mildly chipped,

some inoffensive ink underlining and markings throughout (mostly in red ink). Still, a fine copy of this rare and fragile item.

This first state, of which around 50,000-60,0000 copies were printed, was never intended for sale, but issued to members of the military as inspirational reading. It is only in the second state that the well-known red vinyl plastic cover first appeared. By 1967, the book had been translated into more that thirty-six languages and an estimated 720 million copies had been printed. Now, thirty-five years later, almost certainly more than one billion copies have been printed worldwide.

The printing history of Mao's "Little Red Book" (actually entitled "Quotations from the Chairman Mao") is partially obscured due to its great rarity and the fact that the very earliest printing is undated. This original first printing of selections from Mao Zedong's (1893-1976) writings and speeches was originally conceived and produced in May 1964 for military use as a pocket handbook of inspirational reading, intended by army General Lin Biao (1907-1971) to flatter Chairman Mao and improve his own advancement within the Party. Clearly even he never realized the popularity and impact of this anthology. The initial demand proved so popular that it was reprinted several times in 1965: with two additional chapters added to the second edition (March 1965) and a final thirty-third chapter added to the third edition (August 1965). By 1966, it was decided that every citizen must possess a copy (as a symbol of loyalty to the Party) and a massive printing project was created to translate the text in every language where there would be Communist followers or sympathizers.

This first edition is slightly taller in height than all the later editions and collates with fewer letterpress pages. The book originally included a calligraphic endorsement in facsimile of Lin Biao's handwriting and also has a two-page introductory preface by Lin, telling of the book's importance as a guide for daily life and moral precept. But, following Lin's alleged unsuccessful attempt to assassinate Mao in September 1971, an effort was made to obliterate his existence from recent memory, and everyone was instructed to tear out this endorsement page (and sometimes also the preface). Neither was included in copies printed from the end of 1971 onwards. Remarkably, our copy retains the endorsement leaf, a fact which would certainly have jeopardized the safety of its owner.

Estimate: $2,500-up
Starting Bid: $1,750

"The Loveliest and Grandest Island
of the Caribbean Archipelago"

36033   Dr. H. A. Alford Nicholls. *Dominica, Illustrated and Described.* Antigua: José Anjo, n.d. [ca. 1905]. First edition. Oblong twelvemo (4.625 x 7 inches). 32 pages. Twelve full-page black and white photographs by José Anjo. Front pastedown contains map of the Island of Dominica by W. A. Miller, dated 1904, with island's main roads outlined in red. Publisher's green morocco-patterned paper boards, with lettering and island motifs stamped in gilt on front board. Some fading around edges of both boards; minor rubbing to gilt. Chip to

The Very Scarce First English Edition of Rousseau's Landmark *Treatise on the Social Compact*

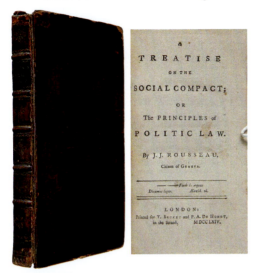

36038   **Jean Jacques Rousseau.** *A Treatise on the Social Compact; or The Principles of Politic Law.* London: Printed for T. Becket and P. A. De Hondt, 1764. First edition in English. Approximately 6.75 x 4 inches. Twelvemo. [xii], 249, [3, publisher's catalogue] pages. Contemporary full brown calf, spine ruled and tooled in gilt in compartments, black gilt morocco lettering label, five raised bands. Both boards rehinged, some wear to boards and spine, a tear in the text of page 79 with a marginal paper tape repair (which does not address the tear in the text). Bookplate. Overall, a very good copy of this very scarce title. Only two other copies have been at auction in the last sixty years.

"The *Contrat Social* remains Rousseau's greatest work... Rousseau believed passionately in what he wrote, and when in 1789 a similar emotion was released on a national scale, the *Contrat Social* came into its own as the bible of the revolutionaries in building their ideal state. Still in print, translated into every language in cheap editions and paperbacks, it remains a crucial document of egalitarian government" (*Printing and the Mind of Man,* 270, discussing the 1762 first edition).

Estimate: $2,000-up
Starting Bid: $1,000

With the Rare "Index Morborum"

36039   **William Salmon.** *Botanologia. The English Herbal: or, History of Plants...* London: Printed by I. Dawkes, for H. Rhodes and J. Taylor, 1710. First edition. Large folio in fours. vi, xvi, 1,296, [44, Index Plantarum and Index Latinus], [6, Index Morborum] pages. With

engraved title frontispiece by van der Gucht after Eloas Knight, and a voluminous number of text woodcuts. Title page printed in red and black. Text printed in two columns. Contemporary blind-tooled calf boards, rebacked and recornered in modern light brown vinyl with gilt spine titles. Significant wear and abrading to the boards. New endpapers. Uneven toning and foxing throughout. A few corner chips and marginal tears. Gatherings 2N and 5F2 are repeated where 3N and 5E2 are lacking and should be, respectively. A good copy, wanting the two gatherings, but with the excessively rare "Index Morborum." Henrey 1308.

Estimate: $1,500-up
Starting Bid: $750

The First Dublin Edition of Smith's *Wealth of Nations*

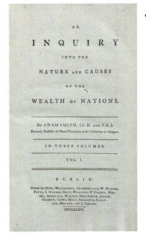

36040   **Adam Smith.** *An Inquiry into the Nature and Causes of the Wealth of Nations.* In Three Volumes. Dublin: Printed for Messrs. Whitestone, Chamberlaine, W. Watson, [et. al.]: 1776. First Dublin edition, published the same year as the true first edition (London). Approximately 8.25 x 5.25 inches. Three octavo volumes. [viii], 391, [1, blank]; [viii], 524, [3, publisher's catalogue], [1, blank], 412 pages. With the half-title in Volume I and the publisher's catalogue in Volume II as called for. Bound in contemporary full brown calf, possibly later gilt lettering on spine and red morocco gilt lettering labels. Some wear to binding, some cracking near joints at the top of Volumes II and III, and a short crack on spine of Volume I, worm damage to the text of Volume I, with some minor loss of text between pages 235 and 303. Some minor thumbsoiling in text. Overall, a very good copy.

There were only three editions published in 1776 (the English, the Irish, and the German); there wouldn't be a second edition until 1778. *The Wealth of Nations* is the fundamental work of Adam Smith (1723-1790). Smith spent ten years writing and perfecting it. It was an immediate success, the first edition selling out in six months. D.N.B. states: "...it is probable that no book can be mentioned which so rapidly became an authority both with statesmen and philosophers." It became the Bible of *laissez faire* for generations of economists and political theorists—"the certainty of its criticism and its grasp of human nature have made it the first and greatest classic of modern economic thought" (*Printing and the Mind of Man* 221, referring to the London edition).

Estimate: $4,000-up
Starting Bid: $2,000

Deluxe Quarto Edition, One of 250 Copies Signed By Stanley;
With Autograph Letters Signed by Stanley and by Lady Stanley

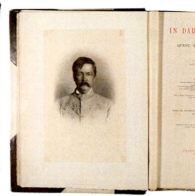

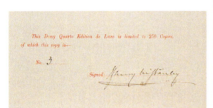

36041   **Henry M. Stanley.** *In Darkest Africa or the Quest, Rescue, and Retreat of Emin, Governor of Equatoria.* New York: Charles Scribner's Sons, 1890. Demy Quarto Edition de Luxe. Limited to 250 numbered copies, of which this is number 3, **signed by the author on a special limitation page** bound in front. Two quarto volumes. [i]-xv, 529; [i]-xv, 472 pages. With **six etched plates signed in pencil by G. Montbard**, and 150 woodcut illustrations. Four maps, three of which are folding; two are linen-backed. Titles printed in red and black. Engraved portrait frontispiece of Stanley printed on India paper. Satin book marks. Original dark brown half morocco over vellum boards with title, flag of Emin Pasha, and Stanley's signature stamped in gilt on boards and spines. Top edges gilt, others untrimmed. Moderate edge wear to boards, spine, and corners. Minor spotting, soiling and rubbing to vellum. Some slight offsetting to the preliminary pages, etchings uniformly toned, and moderate browning to the untrimmed edges. First gathering in Volume I slightly sprung at the top, tissue guard separating the frontispiece portrait and title in Volume I with a couple of tears and some creasing. Altogether, a handsome set in very good condition.

With two interesting Autograph Letters Signed laid in from Stanley and his wife, Dorothy, each on the letterhead of the Plaza Hotel in New York, each dated April 11, 1891, and each addressed to George W. Childs, newspaper publisher, philanthropist, and author of *Recollections of General Grant.*
Estimate: $4,000-up
Starting Bid: $2,000

Thirty-Two Color Plates of Norwegian Costumes

36042   **Nils Christian Tonsberg.** *Norske Nationaldragter tegnede af forskjellige norske kunstnere og ledsagede med oplÿsende text.* [Norwegian National Costumes illustrated by the best Norwegian artists with explanatory text]. Christiania: Udgiverens forlag, 1852. Folio. 6, 54, 6 pages. Title page decorated in colors plus thirty-two full-page color plates. 13.5 x 10 inches. The fifty-four pages of text consist of Norwegian, German and English text in parallel columns. There are six pages of music at the end starting with works of the celebrated Norwegian violinist Ole Bull and continuing with Norwegian folk songs. Contemporary calf backstrip (now renewed with red cloth and paper label) and corners considerably discolored and worn. Boards covered with textured floral and foliated paper. Decorated endpapers with a repeating pattern showing the Norwegian National Arms. Light foxing and finger soiling, heavier on some of the text leaves. Plates mostly clean but several with light dampstains around the margins and some with light foxing. Altogether an attractive and pleasing copy, housed in a cloth slipcase.

There was one prior Norwegian costume book by Joachim Frich, issued in 1847. It contained only ten costume plates. Plates 1-4 and 6 in the present volume were taken from Frich's book which was printed in Berlin. The remaining plates were drawn for this publication by Eckersberg. They include plates of Lapps and of Finns. The decorative title page includes five symbols and devices of the Norwegian monarchy.

Estimate: $1,500-up
Starting Bid: $750

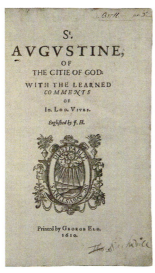

First Edition in English of
Saint Augustine's Great Work

36043 **Saint Augustine.** *Of the Citie of God.* *With the Learned Comments of Jo. Lod. Vives.* Englished by J. H. [London]: Printed by George Eld, 1610. First edition in English of Saint Augustine's *De civitate Dei* (first published in Subiaco in 1467). Approximately 11.75 x 7.5 inches. Folio in sixes. [18], 921, [1, blank], [8, index and errata] pages. Bound without the first blank leaf but with the final blank leaf. Large woodcut printer's device on title (McKerrow 375a). Decorative woodcut head-pieces and decorative and historiated woodcut initials, including three twelve-line historiated initials. Translated by John Healey. Contemporary vellum backstrip over marbled boards, spine ruled in blind with black gilt morocco lettering label. Some soiling and wear to binding, front hinge cracking, one small burn hole on pages 646 and 665 with minor loss to text. Two neat contemporary ink signatures on the title page. Still, a handsome copy of this rare and important work.

"Aurelius Augustinus, Bishop of Hippo in North Africa, was one of the four great Fathers of the Latin Church. In his Confessions he described the influence of God's action on the individual. In *'The City of God'* theology is shown in relation to the history of mankind and God's action in the world is explained...The first five books deal with the polytheism of Rome, the second five with Greek philosophy, particularly Platonism and Neo-Platonism...and the last twelve books with the history of time and eternity as set out in the Bible. History is conceived as the struggle between two communities-the Civitas coelestis of those inspired by the love of God, leading to contempt of self, and the Civitas terrena or diaboli of those living according to man, which may lead to contempt of God" (*Printing and the Mind of Man*). John Healey (d. 1610) "was ill, according to a statement of his friend and printer, Thomas Thorpe, in 1609, and was dead in the following year...The dedication [on A3] by Thorpe to William, earl of Pembroke, speaks of Healey as dead, and apologises for consequent imperfections in the translation. A second edition, revised, was issued in 1620, with a new dedication by William Crashaw (the father of the poet) to Pembroke and his brother Philip. Healey followed the elaborate edition of Vives, translating his commentary, and turning into English verse the numerous quotations by St. Augustine and by Vives from Greek and Latin poets. It was the only English translation of the *'City of God'* till the appearance in 1871 and following years of a translation of all Augustine's works under the editorship of Dr. Marcus Dods" (*D.N.B.*).

McAlpin Collection I, p. 232. Pforzheimer 19. STC 916. See *Printing and the Mind of Man* 3 (describing the 1467 Subiaco edition).

Estimate: $2,000-up
Starting Bid: $1,000

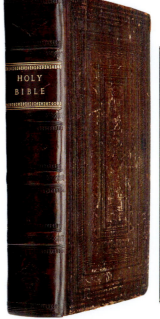
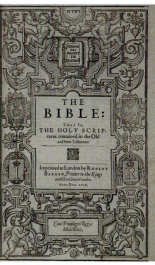

First Small Folio Edition
of the King James Bible

36044 **[King James].** *The Bible: That is, the Holy Scriptures contained in the Old and New Testament.* London: Robert Barker, 1616. [4], 444 leaves, 135 leaves New Testament, [7] leaves first and second tables, Full-page engraved title, engraved full-page Genesis frontispiece, numerous decorations and initials, several small maps, one larger illustration depicting "The Vision," and numerous smaller engravings throughout. [bound with:] *The Booke of Common Prayer, with the Psalter or Psalmes of David.* *Of that translation which is appointed to be used in Churches.* London: Robert Barker, 1616. [63] pages. Full- page engraved title, numerous ornaments and initials. [bound with:] **J.[ohn] S[peed].** *The Genealogies Recorded in the Sacred Scriptures, according to every family and tribe.* *With the line of Jesus Christ Observed from Adam, to the Blessed Virgin Mary.* [N.p.: N.p., n.d.]. 34 pages. Full-page engraved charts with numerous details and decorations. [bound with:] *The Whole Booke of Psalmes. Collected into English Meeter,* by Thomas Sternehold, John Hopkins, and others... London: Companie of Stationers, 1624. [1], 144 pages, [4] prayers, [1] table. Fifty-four engraved staves, title page seal, device, and ornaments. Spine tastefully rebacked with four raised bands, blind-stamped ruling and ornaments, morocco spine label with gilt-stamped titles and ruling. Period full leather boards with elaborate blind-tooled borders and ornaments. Covers rubbed and lightly abraded with bumped corners and shelfwear to bottom edge. Marbled endpapers. Some light foxing and toning throughout. Restoration to margins of first seven leaves, not affecting text, with last leaves showing some wear and minor wrinkling. Occasional contemporary handwriting and marginalia, most notably at title pages. Corners and fore-edges have small tears, minor holes or loss in several instances. Title page of *Psalmes* has missing torn piece across bottom margin, not affecting text. A few pages lightly dampstained in *Psalmes*. Light thumbsoiling present in places, but overall a very clean text. In two columns with sixty-four lines and shoulder notes, this volume has complementary texts, design, and wonderful illustrations. Bookplate of Frances Louisa Swayne, "lady traveller" and author of *A Woman's Pleasure Trip in Somaliland,* to the front pastedown. A very good copy. Herbert 348.

Estimate: $3,750-up
Starting Bid: $1,875

The Most Famous Work from "One of the Most Important Medieval Liturgical Writers"

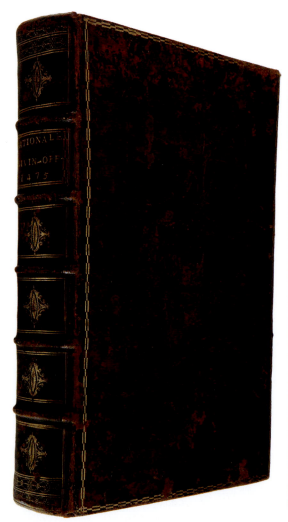

36045 **Guillelmus Duranti.** *Rationale divinorum officiorum.* [Paris: Ulrich [Gering], Martin [Crantz], and Michael [Friburger], 13 April 1475]. Large folio (12.5 x 8.875 inches; 318 x 226 mm.). [318] leaves ([16, "Tabula"], [1, blank], [301] leaves). Early ink foliation in the upper right corner of each text leaf, beginning with leaf a2 as "1". Fol. 283 supplied from another copy and inlaid to size; fol. 285 mounted on stub, but apparently original to this copy, with identical early ink foliation and headline. The first leaf of each gathering of the text signed in later pencil in the lower corner (a-u10 v10 x-z10 A-E10 F12). Gothic type. Double columns, forty-six lines, capital spaces, one with printed guide letter (the opening "P" on fol. 2v). Six-line opening initials supplied in red, sometimes extending into the margins; two- to five-line initials supplied in red or red and yellow, also sometimes extending into the margins, some with penwork decoration in black ink; paragraph marks, line fillers, and underlining in red; capitals stroked yellow. Headlines supplied in black ink, rubricated in red, in an early hand, on the recto of each leaf. The last line in the second column on fol. 129v supplied in ink in an early hand.

Bound in eighteenth-century mottled calf over thick boards (worn). Covers with decorative gilt border, spine decoratively panelled in gilt with five raised bands and red morocco label decoratively tooled and lettered in gilt, board edges ruled in gilt, turn-ins decoratively tooled in gilt, all edges gilt, marbled endpapers. Green ribbon marker. Joints and corners rubbed, front joint starting to split. Minor worming to the lower corner of the first preliminary leaf, to the lower blank corner of the last ten leaves (fols. 292-301), and to the lower gutter margin of the last seven leaves (fols. 295-301). Tiny tear and crease to the lower edge of fols. 33 and 165; short tear to the lower blank margin of fol. 99; small hole in the outer blank margin of fol. 113; short split in the text of fol. 114, just affecting four lines; a few additional minor paper flaws. Occasional very faint marginal foxing or dampstaining; a few scattered ink spots or stains. Occasional early ink and pencil marginalia, including pilcrows and drawings. Early ink inscription erased from the head of the first preliminary leaf. Overall, a very good, crisp copy. From the library of tobacco magnate and philatelist Maurice Burrus (1882-1959), with his engraved bookplate by Stern, dated 1937. Two small labels lettered in ink on the recto of the rear free endpaper. Housed in a quarter light brown calf over linen boards clamshell case, the spine decoratively tooled and lettered in gilt with five raised bands.

Guillelmus Duranti, or William Durandus (ca. 1237-1296), "canonist and one of the most important medieval liturgical writers," studied law at Bologna under Bernard of Parma and then taught it at Modena. He spent most of his life in the service of the Pope. The most famous of his works is the Rationale divinorum officiorum (first published by Fust and Schoeffer at Mainz, 1459, it was reprinted at least forty times before 1500). "It was written in 1286. Its eight books contain a detailed account of the laws, ceremonies, customs, and mystical interpretation of the Roman Rite. Book I treats of the church, altar, pictures, bells, churchyard, etc.; II of the ministers; III of vestments; IV of the Mass; V of the canonical hours; VI of the Proprium Temporis; VII of the Proprium Sanctorum; and VIII of the astronomical calendar, manner of finding Easter, Epacts, etc. Durandus's "Rationale" is the most complete medieval treatise of its kind; it is still the standard authority for the ritual of the thirteenth century and for the symbolism of rites and vestments" (Catholic Encyclopedia).

According to the British Library's ISTC, there are only ten complete copies of this edition in the world, with only two present in the United States (at Bryn Mawr College and Yale University).

BMC VIII, page 8. Goff D-409. GW 9108. ISTC id00409000. Hain-Copinger 6476. Oates 2869. Pellechet 4496. Proctor 7840.d00409000. Hain-Copinger 6476. Oates 2869. Pellechet 4496. Proctor 7840.

Estimate: $15,000-up
Starting Bid: $10,500

One of the Earliest Major Works of Greek Scholarship by a Woman

 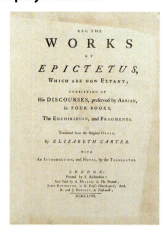

36046   [Elizabeth Carter, translator and editor]. Epictetus. *All the Works of Epictetus.* *Which Are Now Extant; Consisting of His Discourses, Preserved by Arrian, in Four Books, the Enchiridion, and Fragments. Translated from the Original Greek by Elizabeth Carter, with an Introduction and Notes, by the Translator.* London: Printed by S. Richardson, 1758. First edition. Approximately 10.75 x 8.25 inches. Quarto. [1]-[6], [12, List of Subscribers], [i]-[xlii], 505, [8, index], [4, Appendix], [2, blank] pages. Contemporary full brown calf, covers double-ruled in gilt, spine ruled and tooled in gilt, burgundy gilt morocco lettering label, gilt board edges. Some wear to spine and boards, previous owner's signature and bookplate. A fine copy of this important work.

Estimate: $2,000-up
Starting Bid: $1,000

The Complete Works of St. Jerome, Fourth-Century Translator of the Bible into Latin

36047   Hieronymus Stridonensis, Sanctus [Saint Jerome] (c. 340-420). Sancti Hieronymi Stridonensis *Opera Omnia cum notis et scholiis, variis item lectionibus,* **Desiderii Erasmi Roterodami, Mariani Victorii Reatini, Henrici Gravii, Frontonis Ducæi, Latini Latinii, aliorumque. Auctoritate et sumptibus. Domini Friderici, Ernesti Pii filii.** Frankfort: Apud Christianum Genschium, 1684. Complete in twelve volumes, bound in two folio volumes, with Appendix and four Indexes. 15.25 x 9.25 inches. Engraved title, printed title in red and black with vignette, portrait, each title with vignette, head- and tail-pieces. Full contemporary vellum, tooled in blind and with six raised bands, red morocco spine labels lettered in gilt. Binding a bit worn, with bumping at the corners, soiling and discoloring of the vellum, puckering to vellum on the boards; front joint of Volume I splitting but still sound. Altogether, still a very good copy of a beautifully printed work.

Estimate: $1,500-up
Starting Bid: $750

German Edition of the Holy Bible, 1733

36048   [The Holy Bible]. *Biblia, Das ist: Die ganze Heilige Schrift, des Alten und Neuen Testaments.* Nuremberg: Johann Andrea Endters, 1733. Folio. [74], 1,181, [1,182-1,184, Register], [1,185-1,204, Confession] pages, including two engraved titles and seven full-page engravings by Nunzer. Profusely illustrated with woodcuts in the text and woodcut initials. Contemporary pigskin over wooden boards with five raised spine bands, elaborately blind-stamped and titled on the covers, with decoratively-tooled metal cornerpieces with bosses (one cornerpiece missing), and two brass clasps attached by leather to the rear board, with one catchplate remaining on the front board. Moderate wear, soiling, and crazing to the binding. Contemporary annotations to one side, and partially on the other side, of each free endpaper. Front endpaper partially perished. Minor toning and dust-soiling to the text. Short marginal tears to a few leaves. A mostly clean copy in very good condition.

Estimate: $1,500-up
Starting Bid: $750

Seven Complete Issues of *Aspen,* "The Magazine in a Box"

36049   [Art Periodicals]. Seven Issues of *Aspen,* *The Magazine in a Box,* including: Vol. I, Nos. 1, 2, 3, 4, 5+6, 8, 9. New York: Aspen Magazine/Phyllis Johnson, 1965-1970. First editions. Four quarto hinged boxes with contents, two quarto paper folders with contents, one 8.25 x 8.25-inch boxed double-volume set with contents. All issues collated and complete. Edited, designed, illustrated, and with contributions from some of the twentieth century's most influential artists: Andy Warhol, The Velvet Underground, Marshall McLuhan, Jack Smith, John Cage, Dan Graham, George Maciunas, and numerous others. All issues housed in publisher's original box or folder. Covers rubbed and lightly soiled, with some boxes lightly split at seams; paper folders with lightly bumped corners, small tears, and rubbing. All contents generally clean and mostly appear unread or unplayed. Some occasional toning and small folds. All issues are in better than very good condition.

Though *Aspen* initially focused on the snowy regions around its namesake for the first two issues, they enlisted the help of Andy Warhol and *Rolling Stone* founding editor David Dalton for Issue 3, The Pop Art Issue, and never looked back. Issue 4 explored the work of Marshall McLuhan and was designed by Quentin Fiore. Issues 5+6, the Minimalism issue, was edited and designed by noted artist /writer Brian O'Doherty. Artist/Writer Dan Graham edited Issue 8, The Fluxus Issue, and it was designed by George Maciunas. The Psychedelic Issue No. 9 was edited and designed by Angus and Hetty MacLise. Each issue features a number of various media including flexidisc and phonograph recordings, an 8mm artists' film compilation, paper multiples, a collection of advertisements, and numerous other texts and objects. A rare achievement of art and text in periodical form with each issue differing in scope but consistent in quality and vision. Scarce in this condition, complete and collated, and rarely seen with as many issues.

Estimate: $3,000-up
Starting Bid: $1,500

One of 250 Copies Signed by Richard Avedon, with the Engraver's Proof of His Portrait of Marilyn Monroe

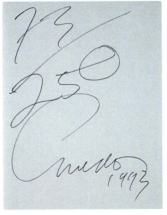

36050   **Richard Avedon.** *An Autobiography.* [New York: Random House, 1993]. First edition, one of 250 numbered copies (this being number 73) **signed boldly by Avedon** on the front free endpaper. Folio. [8], [389 unnumbered pages of black and white photographs], [31] pages. Publisher's full white cloth, lettered in gray and black on front cover, gray on spine, with mounted photo of Avedon on rear cover. Housed in white cloth embossed slipcase and original printed cardboard box. Bright and fine. This book was issued with an engraver's proof of Avedon's portrait of Marilyn Monroe (photograph #134 in the book). This proof (approximately 13 x 10.25 inches) has been matted, framed and glazed by a previous owner.

Estimate: $3,000-up
Starting Bid: $2,500

Two Limited Editions Signed by Alexander Calder

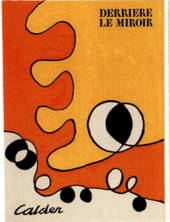

36051   **Alexander Calder.** *Fleches.* Paris: Maeght, 1968. **Number 63 of 150 copies signed by Calder** in pencil on the limitation page. Lithographed wrappers, four single-page lithographs and two double-page. [and:] *Gouaches et Totems.* Paris: Maeght, 1966. **Number 111 of 150 copies signed by Calder** in pencil on the limitation page. Sixteen pages illustrated with photographic reproductions of Calder's work, and the limitation leaf. Missing the lithographed covers and text portion of this issue. Housed together in a black cloth slipcase with a red title label lettered in black. Fine condition. Two deluxe editions of the seminal periodical, *Derriere le Miroir.*

Estimate: $1,500-up
Starting Bid: $750

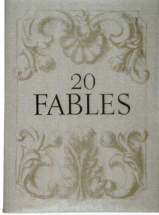

36052 **[Salvador Dali, Alexander Calder, A. M. Cassandre, et al., illustrators]. Jean de La Fontaine.** *20 Fables.* Paris: C. de Acevedo, [1966]. First edition, one of 41 Hors Commerce numbered copies out of a total edition of 440, (this being copy number H. C. 35). **Signed by the twenty participating artists, including Salvador Dali, Alexander Calder, A. M. Cassandre, Marianne Clouzot, Paul Colin, Dunoyer de Segonzac, Valentine Hugo, and others.** Approximately 15 x 11 inches. Folio. [188] pages. Issued on unbound, folded signatures, printed on Arches paper housed in printed wrappers and original glassine. This work is issued with forty full-page loose lithographic illustrations of the artwork in the book printed on Fil de Lana paper and housed in publisher's paper chemise. It is also issued with reproductions on silk of the two illustrations by Cassandre, as well as a decomposition of these two illustrations, on fourteen plates, also printed on Fil de Lana and housed in paper chemise. All housed in publisher's full terra cotta levant morocco solander box, spine lettered in gilt, and lined with blue velvet. Although the solander box is quite worn and split, the book and the illustrations inside are bright and fine.

Estimate: $3,000-up
Starting Bid: $1,500

36053 **Henri Matisse.** *Poemes de Charles d'Orleans, manuscrits et illustres par Matisse.* Paris: Teriade Editeur Verve, 1950. First edition of this book written and illustrated by Matisse, one of 1,200 numbered copies signed by Matisse (this being copy number 893). Approximately 16 x 10.25 inches. Folio. [102] pages. This copy lacking the four-page title gathering, as well as pages 37 to 40, and 53 to 56. Publisher's loose gatherings, housed in wrappers and glassine. The whole housed in publisher's gray cloth-backed chemise. Some wear and rubbing to wrappers, a few pages soiled or rubbed, one page with neat paper tape reinforcement on upper edge. Chemise is worn at joints and rubbed. Overall, a good copy.

Estimate: $1,500-up
Starting Bid: $750

Ruscha's *Nine Swimming Pools*

36054 **Edward Ruscha.** *Nine Swimming Pools and a Broken Glass.* [California]: Edward Ruscha, 1968. First edition. Small octavo. [32] leaves. Illustrated with nine full-color photographic reproductions of swimming pools and with one of a broken drinking glass. Publisher's wrappers, glassine dust jacket. Minor browning to glassine. Bright and fine. Rare. Hasselblad 198.

Estimate: $1,000-up
Starting Bid: $500

Edward Ruscha

36055   Edward Ruscha. *Real Estate Opportunities.* [California]:
Edward Ruscha, 1970. First edition. Small octavo. [24] leaves. Illustrated
with twenty-five photographic reproductions of empty lots in Los
Angeles. Publisher's original wrappers and glassine jacket. Very minor
browning to glassine. Bright and fine. Hasselblad 198.
Estimate: $1,000-up
Starting Bid: $500

Photographs of Edward Ruscha's Record Collection

**36056   Edward
Ruscha.** *Records.*
[Hollywood]: Ed
Ruscha, 1971. First
edition. Small octavo. [31], leaves. With photographs by Jerry McMillan
of thirty records (two black and white photos each, one of the album
cover, the other of the album itself, for a total of sixty photos). Original
publisher's wrappers. Very faint shadow of a price sticker on the upper
corner of the front wrapper. Very bright and fine. Hasselblad 198.
Estimate: $1,000-up
Starting Bid: $500

Original Lithographs by Chagall, Masson, Klee, Matisse, Miro, Kandinsky, and Leger

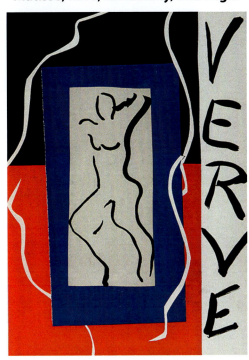

36057   [Chagall, Klee, Matisse, et al.]. *Verve. An Artistic and Literary
Quarterly.* (Volume I, Numbers 1-4). Paris: Published at 4 Rue Féror,
1937-1939. Four issues, all part of Volume I: No. 1 (December, 1937), No.
2 (March-June, 1938), No. 3 (October-December, 1938), No. 4 (January-
March, 1939). Stiff printed, illustrated wrappers. English text, black and
white and color illustrations throughout. All four issues bound together
(with wrappers) in a contemporary binding of multi-colored and -pat-
terned checkerboard cloth over boards, spine lettered in gilt. Spine
sunned and worn, some wear to corners. Still, a fine copy, with very
bright illustrations and lithography.

Verve was founded by Greek expatriate Efstatios Eleftheriades in partnership with David Smart, then publisher of "Coronet" and "Esquire" in the
United States. Smart's aim was to create "the most beautiful magazine
on earth." To this end he would provide the capital, and Tériade as managing director had *carte blanche* to provide the content. Tériade's own
aims are best explained by quoting the manifesto which appeared in
issue No. 1: "*Verve* is devoted to artistic creation in all fields and all forms...
Verve will utilize the technical methods best suited to each reproduction. It will call upon the best specialists in heliogravure in colours and in
black and white, as well as typography, and will not disdain the forgotten process of lithography."
Estimate: $1,500-up
Starting Bid: $750

A Major Eighteenth-Century Pattern Book

36058   **Isaac Ware. *A Complete Body of Architecture. Adorned with Plans and Elevations, from Original Designs by Isaac Ware, Esq....In which are interspersed Some Designs of Inigo Jones, never before published.*** London: Printed for T. Osborne and J. Shipton..., 1756. First edition, first state of plates (with plate numbers inside frame, and reading "Warwick Shire" for "Berk Shire" on plate 70/71). Folio. 16.25 x 9.75 inches. [18], 92, [2], 93-116, [2], 117-120, [2], 121-748, [4, index] pages. Engraved frontispiece, engraved title vignette of Pantheon, engraved headpiece, and 114 engraved plates (fourteen folding). Title page printed in red and black. Contemporary mottled calf, rebacked to style with a morocco lettering label on the spine. Spine double-ruled in gilt with six raised bands. Board extremities rubbed and worn. A little light foxing and offsetting, small piece torn from bottom fore-edge margin of Tt2, small hole to the top of plate 36. Dampstaining to the bottom fore-edge corners of many sheets and plates from page 609 to the end, with tidemarks sometimes faint and barely evident, and other times heavier. Stains are generally not touching text or plates, but they do extend into the frames or images on a few plates. Four index leaves at the rear are heavily worn and have been repaired and remargined (most likely supplied from another copy). Previous owner's ink signature on recto of frontispiece. A few short marginal tears. In general, a very good copy.

The *Complete Body* is a comprehensive overview of Georgian architectural theory and practice, with occasional nods to continental architects such as Daviler, Tiercelet, and Briseux. In his preface, Ware proposes "to collect all that is useful in the works of others, at whatsoever times they have been written, or in whatever language; and to add the several discoveries and improvements made since that time by the genius of others, or by our own industry...to make our work serve as a library on this subject to the gentleman and the builder; supplying the place of all other books...." The work is truly encyclopedic, covering in ten books nearly every imaginable element of architectural design, from choosing a site to ornamental detailing. Fowler 436. Park List 84.
Estimate: $3,000-up
Starting Bid: $1,500

Warhol's "Who's Who" of the 1970s, Signed Twice, and With an Original Sketch

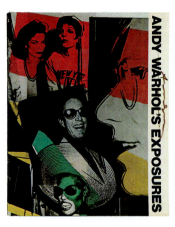 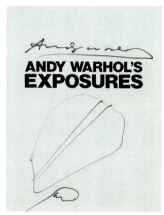

36059   **Andy Warhol and Bob Colacello. *Andy Warhol's Exposures.*** New York: Andy Warhol Books/Grosset & Dunlap, 1979. First printing. **Signed by Warhol on the dust jacket and also signed on the half-title along with an original sketch**. Quarto. 255 pages. 360 black and white photographs. Publisher's black cloth and dust jacket. Warhol's signature on the dust jacket slightly faded, as usual, else a handsome copy in near fine condition.

Warhol's book is essentially a catalog of his friends, which included the rich, famous, odd, bizarre, and forgotten cultural roadkill of the 1970s.
Estimate: $1,500-up
Starting Bid: $750

A Fascinating Collection of Unpublished Original Artwork by Thomas Worth, One of the Primary Illustrators Used by Currier & Ives

36060   Thomas Worth. A Collection of Fifteen Unpublished Drawings. [N.p., ca. 1863 or 1865]. Fifteen original drawings mounted onto the pages of a contemporary scrapbook (entitled "Scraps" on the front cover). Drawings are approximately 4.75 x 3.5 inches, and are rendered in pen and ink. Only one drawing is dated (the final number has been altered in pencil, so it is either 1863 or 1865), but all of the drawings appear to be from the same period. The first six drawings appear to tell a story of a man who falls in love with a woman on a Carte de Visite and then chronicles his misadventures in pursuit of the card; the remaining drawings are humorous (and macabre) images of young men committing suicide through various methods due to unrequited love (possibly of the same woman, whose image appears in most of these drawings). **All but five drawings are initialed by Worth** in the lower left corner, but all share his distinctive style. The scrapbook is bound in gray paper over thin boards, front and rear boards embossed in blind, brown cloth backstrip. Pages are loose, except for the final drawing which is mounted onto the rear pastedown. The scrapbook is quite worn. A fascinating collection.

Thomas Worth (1834-1917) was one of the best known artists who worked for Currier & Ives. He is perhaps best known for his humorous (and racist) *Darktown* series, which lampooned at the African-American community of his day. Perhaps what makes these original drawings so interesting is that they have no resemblance whatsoever to Worth's work for Currier & Ives.
Estimate: $2,500-up
Starting Bid: $1,250

Beautiful Examples of French Bindings, Inscribed by the Author

36061   [Bookbinding]. Henri Beraldi. *Estampes et Livres 1872-1892.* ** Paris: Librairie L. Conquet, 1892. First edition, one of 390 numbered copies, this being copy number 355. **Inscribed by the author on the title-page: "Dorme a Mr Rondeau / H Beraldi[underlined]." Approximately 10.25 x 7 inches. Quarto. [xiv], [280] pages. With engraved frontispiece and forty-one inserted plates of bindings (twelve of which are lithographed in full color on India paper, and the remainder are tinted). Beautifully bound by Taffin in contemporary full red levant morocco, spine lettered in gilt, gilt board edges and turn-ins, marbled endleaves. Spine slightly sunned and rubbed, a few soil marks to spine and rear panel, very mild wear to edges and front turn-in. Previous owner's leather or handmade-paper bookplates. A handsome, fine copy.
Estimate: $1,500-up
Starting Bid: $750

A Handsome Set of *The Writings of George Eliot*

36062   George Eliot. *The Writings of George Eliot*. Boston and New York: Houghton Mifflin, 1908. Large-Paper Edition, one of 750 numbered copies (this copy number 81). Complete in twenty-five octavo volumes. Frontispieces in two states (**frontispiece in Volume I is signed by the artist, C. E. Walmsley,** and in the final volume, there are two separate frontispieces instead of being in two states), and illustrated throughout with full-page plates. Handsomely bound by the publisher in contemporary three-quarter brown levant morocco over marbled boards, spines tooled, ruled and lettered in compartments, five raised bands, top edge gilt, others uncut, marbled endleaves. Spines lightly and uniformly sunned, minor rubbing. A fine set.

Estimate: $2,000-up
Starting Bid: $1,000

Everson's Masterpiece of Fine Printing

36063   [William Everson, printer.] Robinson Jeffers. *Granite & Cypress: Rubbings from the Rock. Poems Gathered from the Stonemason Years When Submission to the Spirit of Granite in the Building of House & Tower & Wall Focused His Imagination & Gave Massive Permanence to His Verse.* Santa Cruz: The Lime Kiln Press, 1975. First edition, **number 74 of 100 copies signed by Everson** on the limitation page. Oblong folio. Illustrated with a title page woodcut by William Prochnow. Printed on handmade Hayle paper on a double crown Acorn handpress at the McHenry Library at the University of California, Santa Cruz. Bound by San Francisco's Schuberth Bookbindery in German linen, lined with Japanese Uwa paper. The spine is open-laced with deerskin rawhide with a strip of cypress on the spine. Housed in a slipcase made of Monterey Cypress with a window of granite from Jeffers' own stoneyard. The wooden slipcase stands on a felt-lined matching cypress base. Also included are a prospectus **signed by Everson** and three proof sheets. Two horizontal hairline cracks to the slipcase (one on each side), else a superb copy in fine condition.

From the prospectus: "Readers will find here, then, four unprecedented features. In the book itself, they will read together for the first time the nuclear body of poems which Jeffers wrote under the impact of stone, the transforming symbol of his creative emergence. They will see the long Jeffers line extended to its natural outreach, like the pulse and withdrawal of the tides to which he attributed his prosody. They will find a typography in which the implication of stone is carried to the ultimate, registering a wave-worn permanence of his mood and themes. And in the incomparable case which enshrines the whole they will possess the architectonic resolution of all these elements, memorializing the achievement of a spirit intense but serene, and the passionate instinct, immoderate and fierce, by which he will always live."

Estimate: $3,000-up
Starting Bid: $1,500

The First Book of the Equinox Press

36064   **William Everson.** *A Privacy of Speech*. Berkeley: The Equinox Press, 1949. First edition limited to one hundred copies and **signed by the author** on the half-title page. Quarto. 29 pages. Block print decorations by Mary Fabilli. Quarter vellum and decorated paper over boards. Gilt titles. Printed on Tovil hand-made paper. Deckled edges. Vellum slightly toned, else fine condition.

The first book of the Equinox Press and Everson's first attempt at printing. This remarkable effort is considered to be one of the high points of modern printing. It is believed that only fifty copies were bound and issued. A perfect combination of scarcity and beauty. Bartlett & Campo A10.

Estimate: $1,500-up
Starting Bid: $750

Everson's Second Book

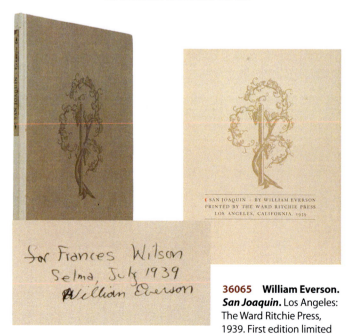

36065   **William Everson.** *San Joaquin.* Los Angeles: The Ward Ritchie Press, 1939. First edition limited to 100 copies. **Inscribed by the author on the front-free endpaper with a long, personal autograph letter from the author tipped in at the rear of the book.** Octavo. 38 pages. Title page decoration drawn by Hubert

Buel. Publisher's tan paper over boards with paper title label mounted to the cloth backstrip. Fore-edge untrimmed. A near fine copy of Everson's scarce work.

Tipped in at the rear of the book is a long, one-page autograph letter dated July 15, 1939 written by William Everson to Frances Wilson of Selma, California in which he goes into great detail about how his friend Lawrence Clarke Powell arranged to have his book published by Ward Ritchie. He writes, in part: "Dr. Powell tells me that Ritchie, who is a poetry lover himself, became very interested in this book of mine and lavished on it more attention than any of his recent work. I think it shows it. It is one of the finest books I've ever seen, I think, and I can hardly believe my own good fortune."

Estimate: $1,500-up
Starting Bid: $750

The Malmaison Edition of Napoleon's Life, One of Only Ten Numbered Copies, With a Letter by Napoleon's Minister of War Tipped In

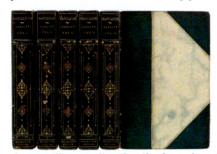

36066 **[Napoleon]. William Hazlitt.** *The Life of Napoleon.* [and:] **Louis Antoine Fauvelet de Bourrienne.** *Memoirs of Napoleon.* [and:] **Duchesse d'Arbantes.** *Memoirs of Madame Junot.* New York: Anglo-American Publishing Co., [n.d., ca. 1895-1900]. The Malmaison Edition, one of only ten numbered copies (this being copy number 10). **With a one-page letter signed by Major General Louis-Alexandre Berthier, Prince de Neuchatel** (text of letter is secretarial, signature is that of Berthier). The letter (Munich, August 17, 1806) is addressed to the Inspector General of the Grand Army and concerns Health Officers and their compensation. Together, sixteen octavo volumes. Each volume illustrated with full-page plates or facsimiles, and a hand-colored frontispiece. Publisher's three-quarter blue levant morocco over marbled boards, spines tooled and lettered in gilt in compartments, two raised bands, each with two burgundy morocco *fleur-de-lys* onlays. Top edge gilt, marbled endpapers. Some joints worn and starting, some wear and chipping to some spines and corners. Overall, very good. From the library of Circuit Court Judge E. Henry Lacombe, with his bookplate in each volume.

Estimate: $1,500-up
Starting Bid: $750

With Over 210 Color Proof Etchings and Drawings

36067 **[Bernhardt Wall, artist]. Francis J. Weber.** *Following Bernhardt Wall.* Austin: The Book Club of Texas, 1994. First edition, and copy number 2 of 195 limited edition copies **signed by Weber** on the limitation page. Large octavo. With photographic frontispiece of Wall, nine tipped-in or pasted-in etched samples or reproductions of his work (**including a signed etching** affixed to page 1), and five beautiful photogravure reproductions of Wall's etchings. Publisher's dark gray cloth over fine light gray paper boards with paper title label affixed to the upper cover. In the original paper dust jacket with paper title label affixed to the spine. Fine. Housed in the original issue matching slipcase.

This special copy is extra-illustrated with thirty fine proof etchings, ten of which are hand-signed. All are laid in and include a fine variety of Wall's work. **Also included are over 170 proof etchings, thirty-two of which are hand-signed, and ten original drawings.** All are enclosed in clear plastic protector pages and housed in a folding box binder. Among these are original drawings of a young Albert Einstein, several of Calvin Coolidge in the White House, and drawings of General Pershing, Saul Untermeyer and Sol Bloom. Included with the etchings are consecutive proofs, showing the development of a portrait, trial color inks, and proofs from some of his famous books, including: *Following Sam Houston* (twenty-six proofs), *Stephen F. Austin* (five proofs), *Washington Irving* (seven proofs), *Thomas Jefferson* (eight proofs), and *Lafayette* (three proofs). Overall, a very fine, in-depth historical record of Bernhardt Wall's artistic achievement.

Estimate: $2,500-up
Starting Bid: $1,250

An Extremely Rare Book on Scouting

36068 **Bt.-Colonel R. S. S. Baden-Powell.** *Aids to Scouting, for N.-C. Os. & Men*. London: Gale & Polden, [1899]. First edition of this rare book on scouting. Approximately 4.5 x 3.5 inches. Sixteenmo. 138, [2, publisher's ads]. Rebound in later brown cloth over limp boards. Mild rubbing, lacking three pages of ads. Still, a fine copy. [Together with:] **A copy of the revised (second) edition.** London: Gale & Polden, [1906]. Revised and enlarged (second) edition. Approximately 4.5 x 3.5 inches. Sixteenmo. [2, publisher's ads], xii, 178 pages. With fold-out diagram of Patrolling Formations. Original red cloth wrappers. Fine.

Baden-Powell wrote this book whilst preparing for the defense of Mafeking in 1899, and submitted it for publication while on leave in England. The first publishing firm refused the book and Baden-Powell had his brother, Frank, submit the manuscript to Gale & Polden. They accepted it and sent the galley proofs to Baden-Powell who was back in Mafeking. As the siege was almost upon them, Baden-Powell returned the proofs with minor revisions (on the last dispatch). In fact, the copyright page states: "The Corrected Proofs of this Book accompanied the last Despatches that got through the Boer Lines."

Estimate: $1,500-up
Starting Bid: $750

The Exceedingly Scarce First Edition

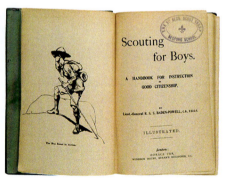

36069 **Lieut.-General R. S. S. Baden Powell C. B.** *Scouting for Boys*. *A Handbook for Instruction in Good Citizenship*. London: Published by Horace Cox, [1908]. First edition, first issue. Octavo. [ii], [398] pages. With the front and rear wrappers of each of the six parts bound in where called for. Original publisher's green cloth, front cover double-ruled in blind, with the Boy Scouts' symbol stamped in the center in blind, spine ruled in blind and lettered in gilt. Some rubbing, sunning, and mild wear to binding. Skewed. With the ink ownership stamp of the "5th Beds. Scout Troop" several times on the endleaves and in the text. A fine copy of this rare book on scouting.

Baden-Powell issued this work originally in six parts, each issued fortnightly beginning on January 15, 1908. It proved so popular that in May of that year a collected edition (containing a slightly altered text and illustrations by the author), was published both in hardcover (the present book) and in wrappers. In turn, these first editions were so popular that this title was reprinted five times that same year and has since become one of the world's best selling books.

Estimate: $1,500-up
Starting Bid: $750

Cuthbert Bede's Very Rare First Book

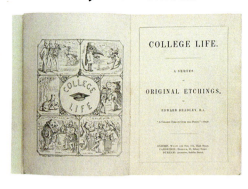

36070 **[Cuthbert Bede, pseudonym]. Edward Bradley.** *College Life*. *A Series of Original Etchings*. Oxford: Wyatt and Son; Cambridge: Dimmock; Durham: Andrews, [1849]. First edition of Bede's (Bradley's) first book. Approximately 9.25 x 6.5 inches. [iv], [24, leaves of plates, including frontispiece]. Publisher's green cloth backstrip over original boards, printed label on front cover. Some wear and chipping to spine, some rubbing and soiling to covers, one crease to lower corner of frontispiece (not affecting image). Previous owner's neat initials on front free endpaper. Still, a fine copy of this very rare item.

Cuthbert Bede (pseudonym for the Rev. Edward Bradley) was a very popular nineteenth-century English caricaturist and illustrator who was a regular contributor to *Punch Magazine* and published several humorous illustrated books.

Estimate: $1,500-up
Starting Bid: $750

The Dali Alice

36071 **[Salvador Dali, Illustrator]. Lewis Carroll.** *Alice's Adventures in Wonderland*. Twelve Illustrations with Original Woodcuts and an Original Etching by Salvador Dali. New York: Maecenas Press-Random House, 1969. One of 2,500 numbered portfolios printed on Mandeure paper, this being copy number 2,337, **signed by Salvador Dali** on the title page. Approximately 16.75 x 11.5 inches. Large folio. [4, blank], 150, [1], [1, blank], [1, limitation statement], [1, blank], [1, colophon], [5, blank] pages. Original colored frontispiece etching plus twelve full-page color illustrations, each with an original remarque. Title printed in orange and black. "The etching and remarques were printed by Ateliers Rigal. The twelve illustrations were printed by M. Nourisson. The typography was set at the press of Ateliers Rigal. Portfolios by Cartonnages Adine" (Colophon). Loose, as issued, in the publisher's brown cloth portfolio lettered in gilt on front cover. A fine copy. Housed in the publisher's quarter orange leather over linen clamshell case with leather and ivory clasps (lacking both clasps). Lovett and Lovett 383.

Estimate: $4,000-up
Starting Bid: $2,000

In the Rare Pictorial Dust Jacket

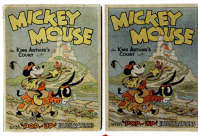

36072   **[Walt Disney Studios].** *Mickey Mouse in King Arthur's Court.* New York: Blue Ribbon Books, Inc., [1933]. First edition. Quarto. 48 pages with four amazing pop-up scenes, all in excellent condition, as well as full-page and partial-page black-and-white illustrations throughout. Publisher's glazed pictorial boards and endpapers in brilliant full color. Original pictorial dust jacket echoing the illustrated boards. Housed in a custom cloth slipcase further echoing the boards and jacket on all three sides. Very minor small stain to the top of the front board, the front free endpaper and half-title page. Small smudge to title page. Minor shelf wear and creasing to the jacket. A one-inch diagonal chip to the spine head, affecting some letters in the words "The Pop Up." Mild loss at the spine tail, and corners. Unobtrusive dampstains to the verso of the jacket. A few closed edge tears. Overall, a very good copy of a book rarely encountered in jacket. With a contemporary Disney bookmark advertising Mickey Mouse pencil boxes laid in.

Estimate: $1,500-up
Starting Bid: $750

With Forty-Eight Mounted Color Plates after Watercolor Drawings by W. Russell Flint

36073   **[Russell W. Flint, illustrator].** Sir Thomas Malory. *Le Morte Darthur. The Book of King Arthur and of His Noble Knights of the Round Table. By Sir Thomas Malory, Knt.* London: Philip Lee Warner, Publisher to the Medici Society Ltd., 1910-[19]11. One of 500 numbered copies printed on handmade Riccardi Paper, out of a total edition of 512 copies (this being number 96). Four quarto volumes. Approximately 10.5 x 7.75 inches. xx, 168, [1, colophon], [1, blank], [1, printer's device], [1, blank]; xvi, 179, [1, blank], [1, colophon], [1, blank], [1, printer's device], [1, blank]; xvi, 208, [1,

colophon], [1, blank], [1, printer's device], [1, blank]; xvi, 212, [1, colophon], [1, blank], [1, printer's device], [1, blank] pages. Forty-eight mounted color plates, after watercolor drawings by W. Russell Flint. With descriptive tissue guards printed in red. Title pages printed in blue and black, with the lettering designed by Miss M. Engall and the figures by W. Russell Flint. Original full limp vellum lettered in gilt on front covers and spines. Yapp edges. Green silk ties. Top edge gilt, others uncut. With the dust jackets and slipcases. Jacket spines a bit darkened, some chipping and wear to jacket spines, jacket of Volume IV worn with a few tears, slipcases slightly worn, with old paper tape repairs and one split seam to slipcase of Volume I, very minor occasional foxing. Fourth gutter in Volume I starting (yet solid). Still, a fine copy.

"Imprinted after the text of William Caxton as modernized, under the editorship of Alfred W. Pollard, for the Library of English Classics...in the Riccardi Press fount, by Charles T. Jacobi" (Colophon of Volume IV). Ransom, *Private Presses*, p. 395. Tomkinson, p. 149.

Estimate: $1,500-up
Starting Bid: $750

Beautiful Hand-Colored Plates of Flowers

36074   **[Hand-Colored Plates].** *Flora's Dictionary, by a Lady.* Baltimore, Fielding Lucas, Jun., [1832]. First edition. Approximately 10 x 7.5 inches. Quarto. [2], 136, 87 (Notes and Index), [1, blank] pages. With fifty-five (of fifty-six) hand-colored plates inserted throughout. Tissue guards. Near contemporary full burgundy morocco, covers ruled in black and paneled in gilt and blind, with pineapple gilt cornerpieces, and gilt central motif of palm fronds (front cover has "M. A. P." stamped in gilt in the center), spine ruled in black and tooled and lettered in gilt in compart-

ments, four raised bands, gilt board edges and turn-ins, rose-colored silk endleaves. Some wear to binding, engraved title page and title page loose (possibly supplied), tear on page 95 (no loss), text foxed, tissue guards torn and worn, mild toning to plates. Still, a very good copy. The color on the plates is still vivid and expertly done.

Estimate: $1,500-up
Starting Bid: $750

A Fantastic Association Copy with an Original Drawing by Maurice Leloir

36075 **[Maurice Leloir, illustrator]. Alexandre Dumas.** *The Three Musketeers.* Translated by William Robson with a Letter from Alexandre Dumas Fils. New York: D. Appleton and Company, 1928. First edition with 250 illustrations by Maurice Leloir. **With an original pencil sketch of one of the musketeers, presumably d'Artagnan, by Leloir, with warm presentation inscription in ink by Leloir to screenwriter Lotta Woods (who had brought Leloir to Hollywood, and worked with him on** *The Iron Mask,* **where he was the costume and production designer).** Octavo. xxiv, [358] pages. With 250 intertextual illustrations. Contemporary half blue morocco over blue cloth boards, spine tooled and lettered in gilt in compartments, five raised bands, top edge gilt, marbled endleaves. Some wear to binding, front hinge repaired. A very good copy. **Douglas Fairbanks Jr.'s copy with his bookplate.**

Laid in is a very warm and personal letter to Mrs. Douglas Fairbanks Jr. from screenwriter and family friend Lotta Woods (1869-1967) who had written several of Douglas Fairbanks Sr.'s films, including *The Three Musketeers, Son of Zorro,* and *Thief of Baghdad.* The letter states that this book is to be held for Fairbanks Jr. as her legacy to him after she dies. She quotes Ed Sullivan in saying "Up in heaven Doug Sr. is proudly telling the other angels 'That's my boy!'" (in reference to Doug Jr.'s valiant service to the United States and Britain in World War II). Overall, a charming and wonderful collection with a fantastic association.
Estimate: $1,500-up
Starting Bid: $750

With a One-Page ALS from Hugh Lofting

36076 **Hugh Lofting.** *Doctor Dolittle's Caravan.* New York: Frederick A. Stokes, [1926]. First edition. **With a December 19, 1946, one-page Autograph Letter Signed by Hugh Lofting** laid in, in which Lofting discusses the trouble of publishing horticultural books in the current climate. Octavo. xii, 342 pages, including seventy-five full-page black-and-white illustrations reckoned in the pagination. With color frontispiece and tissue guard. Publisher's blue cloth with black titles and decorative stamping and a color illustration inset into the front board. Pictorial endpapers. Minor

wear to the extremities. Spine slightly sunned and cocked. Ownership signature to front free endpaper and rear flyleaf. Light thumb-soiling to the text. Very good condition.
Estimate: $1,500-up
Starting Bid: $750

With Maxfield Parrish's Beautiful Illustrations

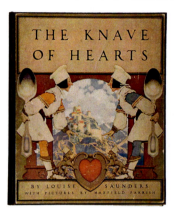

36077 **[Maxfield Parrish, illustrator]. Louise Saunders.** *The Knave of Hearts.* With Pictures by Maxfield Parrish. New York: Charles Scribner's Sons, 1925. First edition. Large quarto. [6], 46, [1], [3, blank] pages. Color frontispiece (included in pagination), with tissue guard, and fifteen full-page color illustrations by Maxfield Parrish. Original black cloth with color pictorial label on front cover. Color pictorial endpapers. Rubbing and scratches to both boards; cloth a bit faded at head of spine and corners. Front hinge cracked; binding cracked at a few openings. Lower corners of pages lightly bumped throughout; pages with occasional smudges in margins. Ink gift inscription to verso of half-title; ink name of child on the "This Is the Book of" page. Generally very good, with plates still vibrant.
Estimate: $1,500-up
Starting Bid: $750

One of 325 Copies

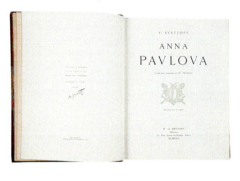

36078 **[Anna Pavlova]. V. Svetloff.** *Anna Pavlova.* Traduction française de W. Petroff. Paris: Brunoff, 1922. First edition in French, one of 325 copies signed by the publisher. Approximately 12.75 x 9.75 inches. Folio. [196] pages. With seventy-two illustrations (mostly photographic, many full page, seven designs by Leon Bakst, and the fine woodcuts by Galanis). Contemporary three-quarter brown levant morocco over marbled boards, brown morocco onlays and gilt lettering labels on spine, top edge gilt, marbled endleaves. Spine repaired, some wear and soiling to binding. Overall, a very good copy of this gorgeous work.
Estimate: $1,500-up
Starting Bid: $750

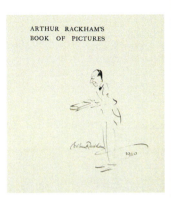

36079 **[Arthur Rackham, illustrator].** *Arthur Rackham's Book of Pictures.* With an Introduction by Sir Arthur Quiller-Couch. London: William Heinemann, [1913]. First trade edition. **With a delightful, original self-portrait drawing by the famed illustrator, signed "Arthur Rackham" and dated "1920"** on the half-title page. Quarto. 43 pages of text. With forty-four color plates (including the frontispiece) mounted on tan paper. Publisher's gray-green cloth with gilt titles. Housed in a custom cloth drop-down box with a paper spine title label lettered in black and featuring a facsimile of the original drawing. Moderate wear to the cloth. Bumped and rubbed corners. Spine cocked and bumped. Spine gilt completely rubbed away. Very good. Latimore & Haskell, p. 42.

Estimate: $1,500-up
Starting Bid: $750

Inscribed and Signed by Rowling at the "Moonlight Signing" Event

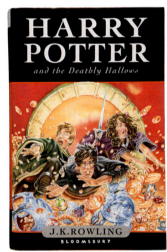

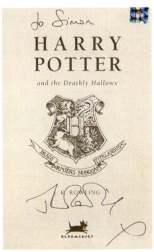

36080 **J. K. Rowling.** *Harry Potter and the Deathly Hallows.* [London]: Bloomsbury, [2007]. First edition. **Inscribed by the author, "To Simon / J K Rowling"** on the title page, with the square holographic sticker related to the autograph session affixed at the top. Octavo. 607 pages. Publisher's pictorial boards. Original pictorial dust jacket. Thumb-soiling to the title page, which is a touch over-opened. Minor rubbing to the jacket. Light crease to jacket spine. Very light dampstain to the verso of the spine head of the jacket. Near fine condition. Accompanied by a selection of Bloomsbury promotional materials related to the release of *Harry Potter and the Deathly Hallows*, including: a ticket to the "Moonlight Signing" of the book at the London Natural History Museum; a numbered ticket for the signing; a col-

orful quad-fold promotional poster; a small orange paper bag; a children's activity sheet with Harry Potter word games; three balloons; a red pencil; and three pages of instructions for the signing event.

Estimate: $1,500-up
Starting Bid: $750

The First Three Harry Potter Books, All Signed by J. K. Rowling

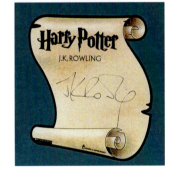

36081 **J. K. Rowling. American Editions of the First Three Harry Potter Books, Each Signed by the Author,** including: *Harry Potter and the Sorcerer's Stone; Harry Potter and the Chamber of Secrets; Harry Potter and the Prisoner of Azkaban.* [New York:] Scholastic Press, [1998-1999]. Later printings. **Each book is signed by the author** (*Harry Potter and the Sorcerer's Stone* is signed on a specially-designed bookplate, the other volumes are signed directly on the title page). Three octavo volumes. Publisher's cloth backstrips over embossed boards. Dust jackets. Minor rubbing to spines of jackets and bindings, else fine.

Proceeds from the sale of this lot will benefit the Fountain Hills Library Association. The library received the books as an anonymous donation placed in their overnight returns slot. Coincidentally, Rowling had been in town at a book signing when the donation was received.

Estimate: $1,500-up
Starting Bid: $750

First Edition in the Scarce First Issue Dust Jacket

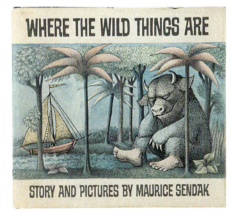

36082 **Maurice Sendak.** *Where the Wild Things Are.* New York: Harper & Row, 1963. First edition, first issue jacket (with $3.50 price intact and no mention of the Caldecott Award on the jacket flaps, nor with the metallic medal sticker on the front of the jacket). Oblong quarto. [40] pages. Illustrated in color by the author. Original green cloth-backed pictorial boards, patterned endpapers, dust jacket. Jacket slightly toned, with some rubbing and minor wear, and a small circular tear on the spine; price crossed out in pencil, but still legible. Light rubbing to book. Near fine.

The first issue jacket for this book is exceedingly scarce. When the book won the Caldecott Award very soon after publication, the books were immediately issued new jackets emblazoned with the award medal and new blurbs.

Estimate: $2,500-up
Starting Bid: $1,250

Complete Set of Four Art Prints from *Where the Wild Things Are*, Signed by Maurice Sendak

36083   Maurice Sendak. *Where the Wild Things Are* **(Prints).** [N.p., 1971]. Complete set of four art prints, each printed in 1971 from the original drawings for this classic and influential picture book (1963) which won the ALA 1964 Caldecott Medal. Each printed on a single sheet, measuring 15 x 24 inches, and **signed by Sendak in the lower right-hand corner.** Fine.

This series of prints was published in order that collectors, friends, and family of the artist could frame individual pictures without mutilating the books. All were originally published unsigned, but over the years Sendak has autographed a small quantity. The edition size of these prints is not known. A signed set of all four "Wild Things" prints is scarce.

Estimate: $3,000-up
Starting Bid: $1,500

Rare Sendak — Never Published For Sale

William Blake ∗ Sendak

36084   [Maurice Sendak, illustrator]. William Blake. *Poems from William Blake's Songs of Innocence.* London: The Bodley Head, [1967]. First and only printing. Edition limited to 275 copies for presentation at Christmas, printed for the publisher by the Stellar Press. Tall twelvemo. Original wrappers. 19 pages. Cover illustration and eight drawings by Maurice Sendak (one drawing repeated). Text reprinted from the 1957 Nonesuch Press edition of *The Complete Writings of William Blake.* Illustrated sewn wrappers. Lower corner throughout with mild bump. Laid in is an engraved slip from the publisher reading "With Compliments, Max Reinhardt." A near fine copy of a very scarce Sendak item.

Estimate: $2,000-up
Starting Bid: $1,000

A First of *The Cat in the Hat* in Dust Jacket

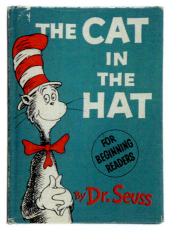

36085   Dr. Seuss [Theodor Geisel]. *The Cat in the Hat.* [New York]: Random House, [1957]. First edition, first issue, with "200/200" on front flap of dust jacket, flat rather than glazed boards, and no mention of the Beginner's Books series on back cover. Tall octavo. [62] pages. Illustrated paper boards. Illustrated endpapers. Original pictorial dust jacket. Wear to board edges and corners. A few small nicks to the board edges. Two tiny areas of discoloration to the bottom edge of the rear board. Penciled name and small stain to the verso of the front free endpaper. Light thumb-soiling to last two leaves. Light rubbing and dust-soiling to the dust jacket. One miniscule tear to the bottom edge of the rear panel. Fold lines and fold ends a bit creased, with a small area of abrasion near the spine at the top of the front panel. A wonderful copy in very good condition.

Estimate: $2,500-up
Starting Bid: $1,250

A Charming Original Watercolor Drawing by Dr. Seuss

36086   Dr. Seuss [Theodore Geisel]. Original Pen-and-Ink and Watercolor Drawing of a Dog Wearing a Scary Mask and Frightening Three Cats. [N.p., n.d., ca. 1935]. Approximately 6.5 x 10 inches. On stiff paper. **Signed in ink, "Dr. Seuss,"** at the lower left corner. Minor browning to paper, else bright and fine. This is a rare, early Dr. Seuss drawing in watercolor, a one-panel gag. We are unsure if it was ever published.

Estimate: $1,500-up
Starting Bid: $750

The Magnificent Elephant Folio of the Boydell Shakespeare

36087   [William Shakespeare]. [John and Josiah Boydell, printers]. *A Collection of Prints from pictures painted for the purpose of illustrating the dramatic works of Shakespeare.* London: John and Josiah Boydell, 1802-1803. First edition of the magnificent copper plate engravings from Boydell's Shakespeare, long regarded as the most beautiful illustrations of Shakespeare's plays. Approximately 28 x 21.5 inches. Two large folio volumes bound into one. Engraved title vignette of Volume II (engraved title-page and frontispiece of King George III both lacking from Volume I), engraved portrait of Queen Charlotte and ninety-six plates from paintings by Reynolds, Smirke, Northcote, Porter, Stothard, Hamilton, Bunbury, Opie and Westall. Contemporary full brown calf, covers elaborately ruled and paneled in gilt, spine perished. Covers detached and dried and worn. Plates slightly foxed. Plates are very good to near fine in a tattered binding.

Estimate: $1,500-up
Starting Bid: $750

A Satirical Look at Rude People with Walking Sticks and Umbrellas

36088 **[Solomon Upright, pseudonym of John Shute Duncan].** *Hints to the Bearers of Walking-Sticks and Umbrellas.* London: Printed by C. Squire, for J. Murray, 1809. Third edition (only the second is earlier, as the first doesn't appear to be extant). Approximately 8.25 x 5.25 inches. Octavo. 32 pages, 8 (publisher's catalogue). With eight hand-colored engravings inserted throughout, as well as additional woodcuts in the text. Original printed wrappers. Some wear and chipping to spine. A fine copy of this extremely rare and fragile item.

John Shute Duncan (1769-1844) was the keeper of the Ashmolean Museum in Oxford. He wrote serious scholarly works on natural history, theology, and sociology; but this strange little book is his only foray into satire, as he skewers rude people who fail to use their walking sticks or umbrellas with care. Rare.

Estimate: $1,500-up
Starting Bid: $750

With an Original Signed Drawing by Chris Van Allsburg

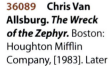

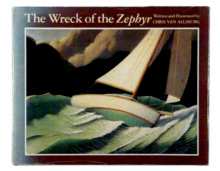

36089 **Chris Van Allsburg.** *The Wreck of the Zephyr.* Boston: Houghton Mifflin Company, [1983]. Later printing. **With an original pen and ink drawing of a sailboat floating over water by Van Allsburg and inscribed by him: "For Jo Ann / Chris Van Allsburg" on the front free endpaper.** Oblong quarto. [32] pages. Publisher's full burgundy cloth, front cover decoratively stamped in gilt (with the image of a sailboat floating over water - similar to that of the original drawing), spine lettered in gilt. Original pictorial dust jacket. Jacket spine and panel areas near joint sunned, some rubbing and mild wear to jacket edges. A fine copy in a very good jacket.

Estimate: $1,500-up
Starting Bid: $750

John Sebastian's Script for an Unproduced Musical Version of *Charlotte's Web* with Annotations by Garth Williams

36090 **[E. B. White].** **John Sebastian.** *Charlotte's Web,* **[Musical] Based on the Book by E. B. White.** Music and Lyrics by John Sebastian. Adaptation by John Sebastian. Original script for proposed musical version of *Charlotte's Web.* N.p., n.d. [circa 1980s]. **Garth Williams' copy, with his handwritten notes throughout.** 55 pages of letter-sized paper, in an unmarked brown three-ring report binder. Contains book of the musical, without lyrics or music. Contents near fine, in a lightly worn binder.

Musician John Sebastian, best known as the singer for The Lovin' Spoonful, wrote the book, the music, and the lyrics for a proposed Broadway musical based on *Charlotte's Web.* Sebastian apparently consulted with Garth Williams — not only the original illustrator of E. B. White's book, but also a close family friend and John Sebastian's godfather — and this script is filled with Williams' notes and suggestions. The musical was never produced.

Estimate: $1,500-up
Starting Bid: $750

First Complete Latin Translation of *Beowulf*

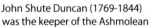

36091 **[Beowulf].** **Grimur Johnson Thorkelin.** *De Danorum Rebus Gestis Secul. III & IV. Poema Danicum Dialecto AngloSaxonica.* Havniae: Typis Th. E. Rangel, 1815. First edition. Quarto. xx, 299, [300, blank], [301-304, Addenda and corrections] pages. Blue pebbled cloth with gilt spine titles. All edges sprinkled red. Light fraying to the spine ends and corners. Minor soiling to boards. Some puckering to front cover. Offsetting to endpapers. Minor foxing. Occasional toning and creasing to text, but overall a clean copy in very good condition. The first known full translation of *Beowulf,* from Old English to Latin.

Estimate: $1,500-up
Starting Bid: $1,000

The First English Language Edition of the *Decameron*

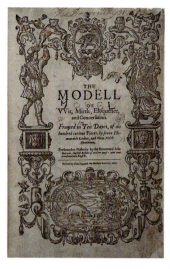 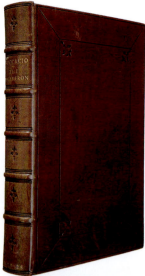

36092 Giovanni Boccaccio. *The Modell of Wit, Mirth, Eloquence and Conversation, Framed in Ten Dayes, of an Hundred Curious Pieces, by Seven Honourable Ladies, and Three Noble Gentlemen.* [Bound Together With:]. **Giovanni Boccaccio. *The Decameron, Containing an Hundred Pleasant Novels. Wittily Discoursed Betweene Seven Honourable Ladies, and Three Noble Gentlemen. The Last Five Days.*** London: Printed by Isaac Jaggard, 1620, 1625. First editions, second printing of the first title, and first printing of the second title. Approximately 10.25 x 6.5 inches. Folio. [5], 193, [1]; [14], 187 pages. Finely bound by Sangorski and Sutcliffe to style in modern full brown morocco, covers stamped in black, spine ruled and tooled in black and lettered in gilt, five raised bands, blind turn-ins. Some very minor rubbing to binding, preliminary leaves of first book have marginal restoration, some margins a bit close, some scattered soiling or foxing in text. Overall a near fine copy of these desirable titles.

The first translation into English, sometimes ascribed to John Florio, of one of the greatest books in all literature, and a work to which countless authors are indebted. These works were printed on the same presses and are contemporary with Shakespeare's First Folio. The five year delay in the issuance of the second volume has never been completely explained, but by the time it was ready, the first printing of the first volume had been exhausted, and a new printing produced. There was no comparable second printing of the second volume. Pforzheimer 72, 71b. STC 3172, 3173.

Estimate: $3,000-up
Starting Bid: $1,500

The Greatest Biography in the English Language

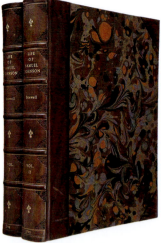 

36093 [Samuel Johnson]. James Boswell. *The Life of Samuel Johnson, LL.D.* *Comprehending an Account of his Studies and Numerous Works, in Chronological Order; A Series of his Epistolary Correspondence and Conversations with many Eminent Persons; and Various Pieces of his Composition, never before Published...* London: Henry Baldwin, for Charles Dilly, 1791. First edition, the "give" issue, regarded by Pottle to be later and a mixture of first and second issue points listed for Volume II. Two quarto volumes. xii, [16], 516; [2], 588, [i.e. 586] pages. Without the engraved frontispiece portrait by James Heath from a portrait of Johnson by Sir Joshua Reynolds, and only one of two engraved facsimile plates in Volume II. Bound to style in modern half brown calf over marbled boards, spine ruled, tooled, and lettered in gilt, and tooled in blind, five raised bands. Mild rubbing to bindings, one marginal tear in Volume II on page 361. Text is quite bright. Overall, a near fine set.

Boswell's biography of Johnson is a classic of the genre—a full, candid account of the life of one of the most famous eighteenth-century writers and thinkers by another. "The Life of Johnson was no single book miraculously produced by an inexperienced author. It was the crowning achievement of an artist who for more than twenty-five years had been deliberately disciplining himself for such a task" (Pottle, p. xxi). English, 65. Grolier, 100. Pottle 79. Rothschild 463. Sterling 71. Tinker 338.

Estimate: $2,500-up
Starting Bid: $1,250

British Find Fascination with Their Own Eccentricity

36094 [J. Arnett, publisher]. Portraits and Lives of Remarkable & Eccentric Characters. Westminster, London: J. Arnett, **[n.d., 1819].** First edition. Paper watermarked 1819. Two octavo volumes. viii, 204; viii, 203 pages. Fine engraved portraits of each subject. Early maroon leather spines over marbled paper boards. Bindings worn, with tape repairs. Gutter repair to prelims in volume one. Paper repair to page 15 of volume one. Light occasional foxing. Very good. A rare work that includes engraved portraits and biographies on a number of unusual personalities in early 19th-century Britain.

Estimate: $1,500-up
Starting Bid: $750

First Edition of Truman Capote's *Breakfast at Tiffany's*

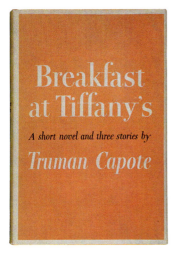

36095   **Truman Capote.** *Breakfast at Tiffany's. A Short Novel and Three Stories.* New York: Random House, [1958]. First edition. Octavo. [viii], 179, [5, blank] pages. Publisher's full yellow cloth, spine stamped in black and gilt, dust jacket. Jacket spine sunned (as is common with this title), some rubbing, mild wrinkling and thumb-soiling to panels, some offset from yellow binding to jacket verso. Still, a very good copy of this collection, the basis of the 1961 film starring Audrey Hepburn.

Estimate: $1,500-up
Starting Bid: $750

The Rarest Edition of Cather's Masterpiece

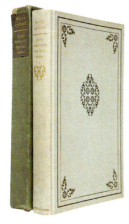

36096   **Willa Cather.** *Death Comes for the Archbishop.* New York: Alfred A. Knopf, 1927. First edition. **Number 40 of 50 specially-bound copies printed on Japan vellum and signed by Cather** on the limitation page. Octavo. [x], 303, [304, Note on the Type] pages. Publisher's decorative vellum gilt. Top edge gilt. Housed in the original green paper slipcase with black spine label lettered in gilt, somewhat worn with a bump to the spine head and label and a portion of the top side missing. Minimal edge wear to the binding. Minor spotting to boards. Spine a bit darkened. Bookplate removed from front pastedown. A very clean text, mostly unopened at the fore-edges. Near fine condition. Leather bookplate of renowned musician, Efrem Zimbalist affixed to the front pastedown, which has offset on the front free endpaper. A beautiful copy of one of the rarest finds in the Cather canon.

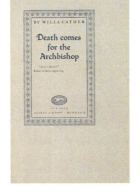

Estimate: $3,000-up
Starting Bid: $2,000

The Rare First Edition of Chaucer Issued by Stowe

36097   **Geoffrey Chaucer.** *The woorkes of Geffrey Chaucer,* newly printed, with divers addicions, whiche were never in printe before: With the siege and destruccion of the worthy citee of Thebes, compiled by Jhon Lidgate, Monke of Berie. As in the table more plainly dooeth appere. [London: Imprinted...by Jhon Kyngston, for Jhon Wight, 1561]. Fifth edition, second issue, and the first edition edited by John Stowe. Approximately 11.75 x 8 inches. Folio in sixes. [9], 378 leaves. Black letter. Fifty-six lines, double columns. Large woodcut of Chaucer's arms on title, lacks divisional title on A1 ("The Caunterburie tales") but has divisional title on Aa1 ("The Romaunt of the Rose") each within a broad woodcut border showing the genealogy of the Houses of York and Lancaster down to Henry VIII (McKerrow and Ferguson 75), woodcut of a knight on horseback on the recto of B1. Decorative woodcut initials throughout. Eighteenth-century full mottled calf, covers double-ruled in gilt, spine expertly rebacked and double-ruled in gilt, with burgundy morocco gilt lettering label. Some wear to binding, especially at spine and corners. Title-page mounted with loss of publication information, marginal repairs and some tears and chipping to first eight leaves (there is a long tear on folio seven). Trimmed a bit close at the top margin, the final leaf of text transcribed in ink by an early hand onto the first binding black. Still, a very good copy of one of Western civilization's chief contributions to world literature.

"John Stowe, born 1525?, died 1605, was a London tailor. From 1560 on he devoted himself 'to the search of our famous antiquities,' and was an ardent book collector and copyist. His first publication was the Chaucer just described...The rest of his work was historical and antiquarian" (Hammond, pp. 121-22).

The majority of pieces added by Stowe to this work are spurious. There is an earlier issue of the same date (STC 5075), which differs as follows: the title is within a woodcut border, the top of which represents a king sitting in council, and in the Prologue there are twenty-two woodcuts of the Pilgrims (thus there are fourteen preliminary leaves instead of ten). Probably because the blocks were so worn, the preliminary leaves were reprinted in the second issue without any illustrations.

Grolier, *Langland to Wither,* 42. Hammond, pp. 119-122. Pforzheimer 176 note. STC 5076.

Estimate: $4,000-up
Starting Bid: $2,000

Significantly Enlarged and Extensively Revised by Coleridge

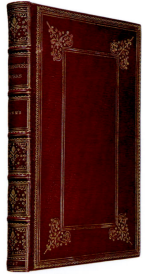

36098 Samuel Taylor Coleridge. *Poems, by S. T. Coleridge, Second Edition.* *To Which Are Now to be Added Poems by Charles Lamb, and Charles Lloyd.* London: Printed by N. Biggs, for J. Cottle and Messrs. Robinsons, 1797. Second edition. Octavo (167 x 102 mm). xx, [1]-278 pages. Sumptuous full red morocco elaborately tooled in gilt with gilt spine titles inside five raised bands. Gilt inner dentelles. Marbled endpapers. Top edge gilt, others uncut. Minor wear and soiling to the binding. Bookplate and bookseller's ticket affixed to the front pastedown. A mostly clean text, with only occasional toning and spotting. Near fine. A very important Coleridge title, practically a new edition, significantly enlarged and extensively revised by the author. Ashley I, p. 199. Wise 11.

Estimate: $2,000-up
Starting Bid: $1,000

Example of Mid-19th Century Self Publishing

THE BROAD STREET CLASSIC SCENE, SALEM.

36099 Rev. William Cook. *The Olive Grove: Poems.* Salem: [privately printed by the author], 1853. First edition. Twelvemo. 26 pages. Six plates and numerous decorations, engraved and printed by the author. Original printed yellow wrappers. Backstrip frayed a bit with some toning to the edges of the pages. One page number corrected in ink (by the author?). Remarkably fine, untrimmed copy housed in a custom green cloth clamshell case.

The author was a penniless clergyman and tutor who supplemented his income by selling his pamphlets of religious poetry and prose on the streets of Salem, Massachusetts. Not only was he the author, but the illustrator, engraver, printer, publisher and distributor as well. Accompanying Cook's poem is a small pamphlet, apparently one in a series entitled "The Ploughboy's Harrow", this being listed as "Number Three", self-published

by Cook in 1860. The pamphlet is string bound and printed in Cook's typical crude style. The four pages contain Cook's remarks made at a meeting "for the discussion of Home Education held at the First Baptist Church, Salem, November 16 and 28, 1859" and an original poem entitled "The Schoolhouse". Bound within are two original engravings, one titled "The Broad Street Classic Scene Salem" and "A District Schoolhouse Central St. South Danvers". Sabin 16297.

Estimate: $1,500-up
Starting Bid: $750

The First English Edition of *The Last of the Mohicans*

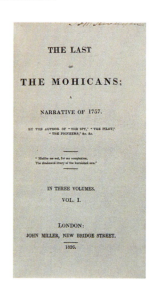

36100 [James Fenimore Cooper]. *The Last of the Mohicans.* *A Narrative of 1757. By the Author of "The Spy," "The Pioneers." &c. &c.* In Three Volumes. London: John Miller, 1826. First English edition, issued about a month after the first American edition. Approximately 6.75 x 4 inches. Three twelvemo volumes. xi, [1, blank], 287, [1, blank]; [4], 276; [4], 295, [1, blank] pages. With half-titles in Volume II and III as issued (Volume I was not issued with half-title, so this copy collates complete). Contemporary half brown calf over marbled boards, spines ruled, tooled, and lettered in gilt, additionally tooled in blind. Spines uniformly sunned, some rubbing to edges, previous owner's small bookplate on front pastedown of each volume. Text is quite clean. A fine copy. Housed in slipcase.

This is the second and most famous of the Leatherstocking Tales, and the first in which the scout Natty Bumppo was made the symbol of all that was wise, heroic and romantic in the lives and characters of the white men who lived in the American wilderness. This novel glorified for many generations of readers, both in America and abroad, some aspects of American life that were unique to our cultural history.

BAL 3833. Grolier, 100 American, 34. Spiller & Blackburn, 7.

Estimate: $2,000-up
Starting Bid: $1,000

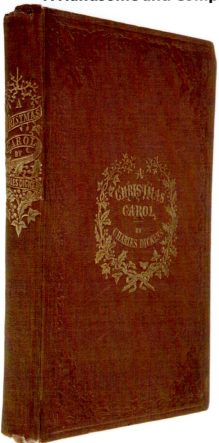

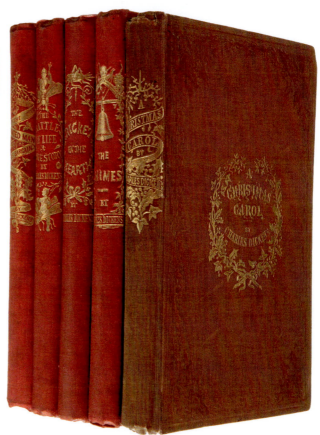

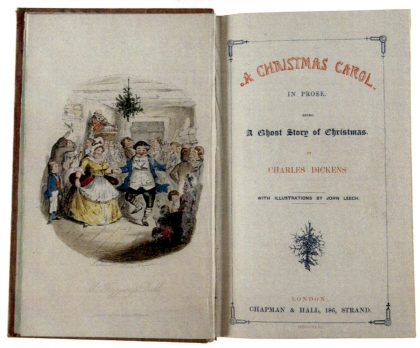

36101 **Charles Dickens. Christmas Books,** Including: ***A Christmas Carol.*** In Prose. Being a Ghost Story of Christmas. With Illustrations by John Leech. London: Chapman and Hall, 1843. First edition, first issue (i.e., "Stave I"), Todd first impression, first issue. Red and blue title-page, original green-coated endpapers (second state). Foolscap octavo. [i-viii], [1]2-166[-168] (blank). Eight illustrations by Leech, including the four hand-colored plates. [and:] **Charles Dickens. *The Chimes.*** A Goblin Story of Some Bells that Rang an Old Year Out and a New Year In. London: Chapman and Hall, 1845 [i.e., December 1844]. First edition. Foolscap octavo. [i-viii], [1]2-175[176]. First state engraved title and frontispiece by Daniel Maclise; intertextuals by Doyle, Leech, and Stanfield. [and:] **Charles Dickens. *The Cricket on the Hearth.*** A Fairy Tale of Home. London: Bradbury and Evans, 1846 [i.e., December 1845]. First edition. Foolscap octavo. [i-viii], [1]2-174. Engraved title and frontispiece by Daniel Maclise. Twelve intertextual illustrations by various artists, chiefly John Leech. [and:] **Charles Dickens. *The Battle of Life.*** A Love Story. London: Bradbury and Evans, 1846. First edition. Foolscap octavo. [i-viii], [1]2-175[176]. Engraved title (fourth state, Todd E1, Eckel 4) and frontispiece by Maclise; intertextuals by Maclise, Doyle, Stanfield and Leech. [and:] **Charles Dickens. *The Haunted Man and the Ghost's Bargain.*** A Fancy for Christmas-Time. London: Bradbury and Evans, 1848. First edition. Foolscap octavo. [i-viii], [1]2-188. Lithographic frontispiece and title, plus additional text illustrations by Leech, Stone, Stanfield and Tenniel. Together, five volumes. In the original cloth. Some chipping to the spine of *A Christmas Carol*, with a small bookseller's sticker and a slightly skewed spine. Bookplates. Still, a near fine set of these five charming books, housed together in a blue morocco box with folding cover.

The first edition of *A Christmas Carol* went on sale December 19, 1843 and by Christmas Eve every copy had sold out. Dickens had written a hugely popular work and, in so doing, created an instant classic. Within weeks of publication eight different stage adaptations of *A Christmas Carol* were playing in London theatres (*Charles Dickens at 200*, The Morgan Library & Museum, 2011). Smith II, 4, 5, 6, 8 and 9.

Estimate: $15,000-up
Starting Bid: $11,000

Peter Ackroyd's Manuscript Archive For *Dickens* and *First Light*

36102   Charles Dickens [subject]. Peter Ackroyd. Manuscript and Related Materials for *Dickens*, including: **Copy of author's corrected typescript. Signed by Ackroyd** on title page. Quarto. 2,324 pages. Pages 1,148-1,174 paper-clipped together with a note from Sinclair-Stevenson's secretary as replacement pages accidentally left blank [blanks not present]. Minor wrinkles and creases to some page edges with a one-inch closed tear and six-inch crease to title page. Three-quarter inch closed tear to page 726. Overall near fine. [and:] *Dickens.* Unbound uncorrected printer's proof of Mandarin abridged paperback edition. [1994]. 298 sheets with 2 book pages per sheet. Fine. [and:] *London Luminaries and Cockney Visionaries.* [London]: [London Weekly Television], 1993. **Signed by Ackroyd.** Quarto. 12 legal-size pages, stapled in top left corner and held in publisher's folder. Minor wrinkling and fold lines to folder, otherwise fine. [and:] *Dickens.* [New York]: HarperCollins, [1990]. First American edition, first printing. **Signed by Ackroyd** on title page. Octavo. 1,195 pages. Publisher's binding and dust jacket. Fine. [and:] **This lot also includes a printer's copy of author's corrected typescript for *First Light*. Signed by Ackroyd** on title page and with editor's typographical notations throughout. Quarto. 521 pages. Minor wrinkling and wear to some edges with a one-inch tear to title page. Page 521 shows wear with chipping, tears, and several fold lines. Overall near fine condition.

Estimate: $1,500-up
Starting Bid: $750

A Crisp First Edition in the Scarce Dust Jacket

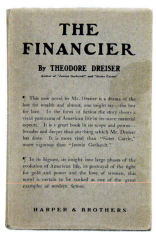

36103   Theodore Dreiser. *The Financier*. New York: Harper & Brothers, 1912. First edition. Octavo. 779 pages. Publisher's light blue cloth, stamped in gold and blue. Original printed dust jacket. A bright, crisp copy with very light rubbing to foot of cloth spine. Dust jacket is toned along the edges and spine, with light edge wear and chipping at the corners and spine ends. Jacket lightly toned with minor wear along edges and an area of discoloration to right side of front panel; quarter-sized area of surface loss to spine panel above publisher's name. A sharp, square copy in better than very good condition.

Estimate: $4,000-up
Starting Bid: $2,000

"April is the cruellest month..."

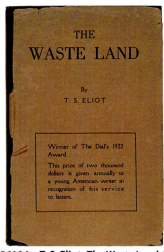

36104   T. S. Eliot. *The Waste Land*. New York: Boni and Liveright, 1922. First edition, limited to 1,000 copies, of which this is number 724. Second issue, with stiff cloth boards, the limitation number measuring 2 mm high, and with the "a" dropped in "mountain" on page 41. 64 pages. Laid in is a small advertisement listing forthcoming and backlist Modern Library titles, presumably issued contemporaneously with *The Waste Land*. Publisher's stiff black cloth boards with gilt lettering on front board and spine, and salmon-colored dust jacket, lacking the rare inner glassine jacket called for by Gallup. Mild mottling to lower corner of front board. Rear board with some mottling at lower corner, faint cup ring, and a small area of surface loss measuring approximately 1 by 8 mm. Spine lightly faded, with mottling to cloth at foot; gilt on spine a bit dulled. Pages toned around edges. Short closed tear to fore-edge of leaf containing pages 55 and 56, measuring one-half inch. Dust jacket mostly all accounted for, but in pieces, most cleanly split along folds, with only a little over half the spine missing: front panel and front flap still intact; rear panel with piece of spine panel containing "Land" and "T. S. Eliot"; rear flap; and small part of spine panel with partial price printed on it. Altogether a very good copy in the rare dust jacket.

The modernist classic, considered by many to be the single most important and influential poetic work of the twentieth century. On its publication, an unsigned reviewer in the *Times Literary Supplement* wrote: "we know of no other modern poet who can more adequately and movingly reveal to us the inextricable tangle of the sordid and the beautiful that make up life." Ezra Pound — to whom Eliot owed much — wrote that this "series of poems" was "possibly the finest that the modern movement in English has produced, at any rate as good as anything that has been done since 1900, and which certainly loses nothing by comparison with the best work of Keats, Browning, or Shelley" (Paige, p. 175).

Though no ownership markings appear in this book, it is from the collection of Margaret Anderson — publisher of *The Little Review*, the extremely important arts journal of the 1920s to which Eliot contributed — coming directly from the family of Dorothy Caruso, Miss Anderson's longtime companion and widow of the great Italian opera singer, Enrico Caruso. *From the Letters, Books, and Papers of Margaret C. Anderson and Dorothy Caruso, Collected by Eric Murray*.

Gallup A6a. D. D. Paige, *The Letters of Ezra Pound*, 1907-1941.

Estimate: $4,000-up
Starting Bid: $2,000

The True First Edition of *Tom Jones*

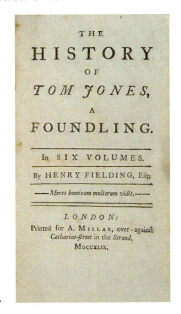

36105 Henry Fielding. *The History of Tom Jones, a Foundling.* *In six volumes.* London: Printed for A. Millar, 1749. First edition, mixed early state, without the list of errata in Volume I and with some errata still uncorrected throughout. Six twelvemo volumes. With both final blanks present in Volumes I and III. Contemporary full calf, boards double-ruled in gilt, spines double-ruled in gilt in compartments, burgundy morocco gilt lettering labels. Spines and joints chipped and worn (some boards nearly detached), boards worn, bookplates of Ham Court (common name of Brampton Castle). A very good set. The Jean Hersholt copy, with his bookplate inside the lined book-backed clamshell case which houses the set. "One of the three most perfect plots ever penned" (Coleridge). Cross III, pages. 316-317. Grolier, *100 English*, 48. Rothschild 850-851. Sterling 360.
Estimate: $1,500-up
Starting Bid: $750

Paramount Pictures' Copy of the First Edition, First Printing of *The Great Gatsby*

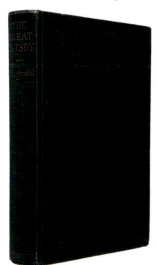 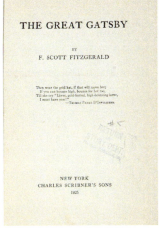

36106 F. Scott Fitzgerald. *The Great Gatsby.* New York: Charles Scribner's Sons, 1925. First edition, first printing, meeting all six points in Bruccoli. Octavo. 218 pages. Publisher's linen-grained green cloth with titles stamped in gilt on spine and in blind on front board. Minor rubbing to extremities; binding slightly cocked. A few spots of foxing to fore-edge, some intruding very slightly to fore-edge margin; minor foxing to bottom edge. Bookstore ticket to rear pastedown ("Hollywood Book Store, Opposite Hollywood Hotel, Hollywood California"), with some offsetting to facing page. Rubber stamp on front free endpaper and title page reading "RETURN TO STORY DEPT. Paramount Productions, Inc." with "#5" in pencil beneath. A very good copy.

This copy of Fitzgerald's most enduring work belonged to the Paramount movie studio which, in 1926, released the Famous Players-Lasky Corporation's film version of *The Great Gatsby*, the first such adaptation of the novel. Fitzgerald was paid $13,500 for the film rights, and the resulting

eighty-minute silent film starred Warner Baxter as Jay Gatsby, Lois Wilson as Daisy Buchanan, Neil Hamilton as Nick Carraway, and William Powell as George Wilson.

This first film production of *The Great Gatsby* is notable, not only for being the only one of the three feature films thus far produced (with another currently in pre-production) to be filmed during the Jazz Age of the 1920s when the story actually takes place, but it is also one of the most famous "lost films" in cinema history. No prints of this film are known to survive — a poster for the film and a one-minute trailer which has been preserved by the Library of Congress is the only evidence that the film was made. An appealing copy of the first printing of *The Great Gatsby* with an interesting Hollywood association.

Bruccoli A11.1.a.
Estimate: $1,500-up
Starting Bid: $750

Rare First Edition, First Issue, of *Madame Bovary*

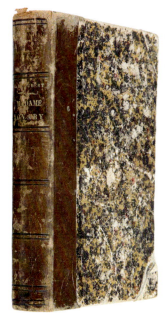 

36107 Gustave Flaubert. *Madame Bovary. Mœurs de Province.* Paris: Michel Lévy Frères, Libraires-Éditeurs, 1857. First edition, first issue, with the misspelling of the name "Senart" on the dedication leaf (later issues have the dedicatee's name spelled "Senard"). Two twelvemo volumes bound into one. Approximately 7 x 4.25 inches. [4], 232; [4], [233]-490 pages. Bound without the sixteen-page publisher's catalogue from Volume I and the two preliminary leaves and final blank of Volume II. Bound in nineteenth-century quarter brown calf over marbled boards (remnants of cornerpieces of boards in vellum, but covered in the same marbled paper, possibly indicating an attempt to reinforce the corners), spine double-ruled in black and lettered in gilt. Some rubbing and wear to spine and boards, crease to lower front board, neat inkstamp on half-title, title page with a small smudge and damage to publication date, obscuring the final two digits, later ink note on title-page indicating the incorrect date "1856," some light creasing in text, short tear to upper margin of page 115 of the first part. Still, a very good copy.

"*Madame Bovary* was first published in 1856 in the *Revue de Paris*, and upset readers' susceptibilities even though cuts had been made by the editor. Flaubert was prosecuted, together with the part-proprietor and the editor of the journal, for offences against public morals, but after a trial which was a literary sensation of the day he was acquitted" (*The Oxford Companion to French Literature*). Vicaire III, col. 721.
Estimate: $1,500-up
Starting Bid: $750

With an Original Pencil Drawing of Brer Rabbit by A. B. Frost

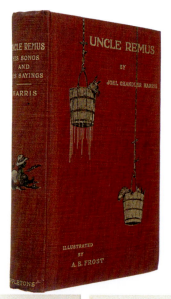

The First in the Alphabet Franchise, Inscribed and Signed by Grafton

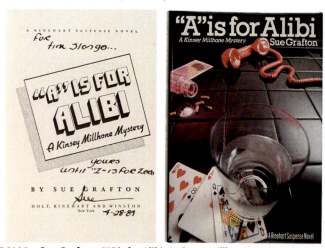

36109 **Sue Grafton.** *"A" is for Alibi. A Kinsey Millhone Mystery.* New York: Holt, Rinehart and Winston, 1982. First edition. **Inscribed by the author on the title page: "For Tim Slongo / Yours until "Z" is for Zero / Sue / 4-28-89".** Octavo. 274 pages. Publisher's cloth and dust jacket. Trivial shelf wear, else a fine copy.
Estimate: $1,500-up
Starting Bid: $750

36108 **[A. B. Frost, illustrator].** Joel Chandler Harris. *Uncle Remus. His Songs and His Sayings.* **New and Revised Edition, with One Hundred and Twelve Illustrations by A. B. Frost.** New York: D. Appleton and Company, 1910. New and revised edition. **With a lovely, full-page original pencil drawing of Brer Rabbit inscribed by A. B. Frost ("Drawn for Ms. Poole / by A. B. Frost. / Mch [sic] 1925.").** Additionally, this book is **inscribed by a J. C. Harris,** who could either be Harris' son, Joel Chandler Harris, Jr. or Julia Collier Harris, who wrote the *Life and Letters of Joel Chandler Harris*, Houghton Mifflin, 1918: **"To Billy Tripp - Christmas 1910 / I think I prove my faith / in your versatility when I / send you this dialect story. / A merry Christmas, Billy Tripp, to you and Mrs. Tripp, and / a Happy New Year, too. / Sincerely / JC Harris[underlined]."** Octavo. [xxiv], 265, [4, publisher's ads] pages. With numerous black and white plates and illustrations in the text. Original decorated red cloth lettered in gilt. Spine slightly sunned, else fine. A wonderful item with a nice association and a lovely, large drawing of one of the main characters in these classic stories.
Estimate: $1,500-up
Starting Bid: $750

First Edition of Thomas Hardy's Extremely Rare First Book, Inscribed by Him

 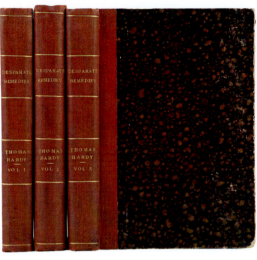 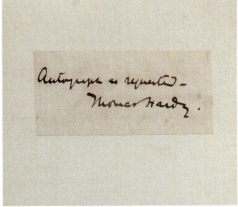

36110 **Thomas Hardy.** *Desperate Remedies.* A Novel. London: Tinsley Brothers, 1871. First edition of Hardy's scarce first book, one of only about 500 copies printed. **Inscribed by Hardy on a slip of paper mounted on the recto of the front free endpaper of Volume I: "Autographed as requested- / Thomas Hardy."** Three octavo volumes. vi, 304; vi, 291, [1, blank]; vi, 274 pages. Complete with half-titles. Volumes trimmed to different sizes: Volume I is 6.75 x 4.25 inches, Volume II is 7.25 x 4.75 inches, and Volume II is 7 x 4.5 inches. Boards are same size, however. Contemporary marbled boards, rebacked in later red cloth, spines ruled and lettered in gilt. Some wear to bindings, some soiling in text, overopened in a few places; in Volume II pages 37 and 227 have ink blots on them, obscuring small portions of text, and page 95 has a short tear at the margin. Still, a very good set of this very rare item. Purdy, pp. 2-5. Not in Sadleir (number two on his List of Comparative Scarcities).

Estimate: $7,000-up
Starting Bid: $3,500

One of 500 First Editions of Hardy's Second Book

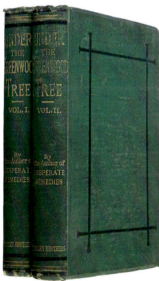 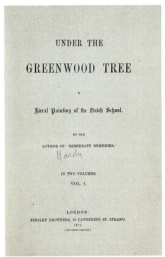

36111 **[Thomas Hardy].** *Under the Greenwood Tree.* A Rural Painting of the Dutch School. By the Author of 'Desperate Remedies.' In Two Volumes. London: Tinsley Brothers, 1872. First edition, one of 500 printed. Two octavo volumes. [vi], 215; [vi], 216 pages. Publisher's green, beveled, sand-grain cloth with gilt spine titles, rules in gilt and black on the spine, and black Oxford frame stamping on the covers. Moderate wear to the cloth, with noticeable rubbing to the spine gilt, especially to volume two. Spines cocked. Corners rubbed and some exposed. Bindings shaken, and cracked in several places in volume one and after page 64 of volume two. Some gatherings standing proud, with one or two almost loose in volume two. Hinges tender and starting. Ownership signatures to the front pastedowns. A complete copy of Hardy's rare second book, published anonymously, in very good condition. Purdy, pp. 6-8. Sadleir 1117. Webb, pp. 5-6.

Estimate: $1,500-up
Starting Bid: $750

One of 634 First Edition Copies of Hardy's *Wessex Tales*

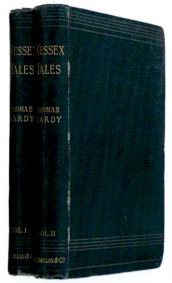
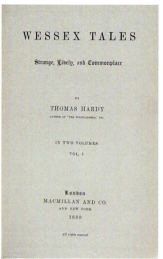

36112 **Thomas Hardy. *Wessex Tales*.** *Strange, Lively, and Commonplace.* London: Macmillan and Co., 1888. First edition, one of 634 copies bound by the publisher. Two octavo volumes. [viii], 247; [viii], 212, [4, publisher's advertisements] pages. Illustrated frontispiece in volume one. Publisher's green cloth with gilt spine titles; blocked in pale green on front and spine with bands at top and bottom, and publisher's monogram device on rear covers. Edges uncut. Housed together in a green half-leather slipcase and chemise. Moderate edge wear to the cloth, with some abrading along the joints. Light rubbing and minimal soiling to the boards. Bumped corners and bottom edges. Spines a bit cocked. Bookplate of collector, Arthur M. Brown affixed to each front pastedown, which has offset to the front free endpapers. A clean text. Very good condition. Purdy, pp. 58-60.

Estimate: $2,000-up
Starting Bid: $1,000

First Edition, First Printing in the First Issue Dust Jacket

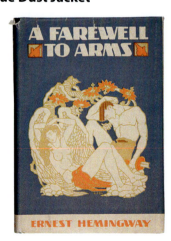

36113 **Ernest Hemingway. *A Farewell To Arms*.** New York: Charles Scribner's Sons, 1929. First trade edition, first printing, without the legal disclaimer on page [x]. Octavo. 355 pages. Publisher's smooth black cloth with gold paper labels, lettered and ruled in black. Top and bottom edges trimmed; fore-edge untrimmed. In the first issue dust jacket, with the "Katharine Barclay" misspelling on the front inner flap. Minor wear to the edges and corners. Some whitish soiling and rubbing to boards. Light rubbing to spine label. Light foxing to text edges, endpapers, and first & last few leaves. Minor rubbing to jacket, especially along the spine. Noticeable dust-soiling, mainly to the panels and spine. Small fingernail-sized stain to bottom edge of rear jacket panel. Very minor chips to the fold ends. Spine head lightly tattered, with two short closed tears, not touching any text. Overall, a bright copy in an unrestored example of the scarce first issue dust jacket, better than typically offered. Hanneman 8A.

Estimate: $2,000-up
Starting Bid: $1,000

First Edition, First Printing in the Scarce First Issue Dust Jacket

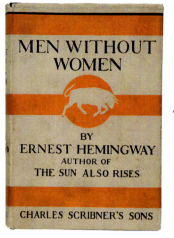

36114 **Ernest Hemingway. *Men Without Women*.** New York: Charles Scribner's Sons, 1927. First edition, first printing, with a perfect "3" on page 3. Octavo. 232 pages. Publisher's black cloth with gold paper labels on front board and spine, stamped in black. Top edge red. In the first issue dust jacket, with no reviews. Light rubbing to the extremities, with mildly worn corners. Minor soiling to cloth. Light spotting to the first few leaves and text edges. Creasing to a few terminal leaves. Very minor chipping at the fold ends of the jacket, with light bumping to the top edge. Noticeable dust-soiling to the jacket panels and spine. Pencil notation of the number "70" and four small-to-tiny dark ink stains on the jacket spine. Overall, a tight, square copy in very good condition, in a great, unrestored example of the rare first issue jacket.

"There were fine and important stories among the fourteen collected in the volume [*Men Without Women*], some of them certified masterpieces: 'The Undefeated,' 'Hills Like White Elephants' and 'In Another Country'" (James R. Mellow: *Hemingway: A Life Without Consequences*, p. 353). Hanneman 7A.

Estimate: $3,000-up
Starting Bid: $1,500

Inscribed by Ernest Hemingway

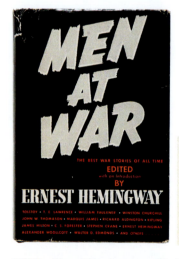

36115 **[Ernest Hemingway, editor]. *Men At War*.** *The Best War Stories of All Time.* New York: Crown Publishers, [1942]. First edition, first issue in first issue dust jacket. **Inscribed by Hemingway on the front free endpaper: "To Bob Spencer / from his friend / Ernest Hemingway".** Octavo. [xxxii], 1,072 pages. Publisher's full black cloth, spine lettered in gilt. Original printed dust jacket with $3.00 price, and with "First Edition" on the front flap. Jacket spine lightly worn, a few short creased tears to upper edge, some additional rubbing to jacket, cloth spine and corners a bit rubbed, lettering on spine dull. Still, a near fine copy, better than generally seen, with an excellent inscription by Hemingway. Hanneman A19a.

Estimate: $1,500-up
Starting Bid: $750

A Stunning Presentation Copy of Hemingway's First Book, Warmly Inscribed to Margaret Anderson and Jane Heap, the Editors of "The Little Review" Who Published His First Prose Work

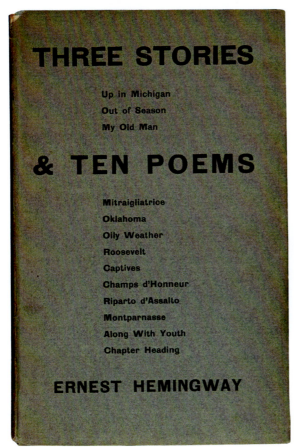

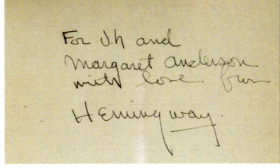

36116   Ernest Hemingway. *Three Stories & Ten Poems.* [Paris]: Contact Publishing Co., 1923. First (and only) edition of Hemingway's first book, one of only 300 copies printed, this copy **with a warm inscription from the author to the editors of** *The Little Review,* **the "little magazine" in Paris that had published his first mature prose work the same year:** "For j.h. and Margaret Anderson with love from Hemingway" ("j.h." being Jane Heap). Twelvemo. 58 pages plus printer's imprint. Printed at Dijon by Maurice Darantière, who also printed James Joyce's *Ulysses.* Original grayish-blue wrappers. Top edges of three leaves (including the title leaf) unopened. Small white spot to rear wrapper. Some toning to backstrip and along edges; wear to head of spine measuring approximately one-half inch. Else, a beautiful, clean, tight copy in near fine condition.

In 1923 Ernest Hemingway was a 23-year old unpublished writer living in Paris, working as a journalist. Upon his arrival in the city, he wasted little time becoming acquainted with the expatriate *avant-garde* writers and artists who frequented the Left Bank bars and cafés, and he quickly became a favorite of Gertrude Stein and was a fixture at her famed *salons.*

That year he met Margaret C. Anderson and Jane Heap (who was known professionally by her initials, "j.h."). They were the somewhat radical American co-editors of *The Little Review,* one of the most popular and influential of the "little magazines." Margaret Anderson was a flamboyant and impulsive force of nature who, with the equally unconventional Jane Heap (for a while her romantic partner as well as her business partner) edited the publication that introduced modernist writers and artists to America, publishing works by everyone from Joyce and Yeats to Eliot and Pound to Picasso, Gris, and Brancusi.

The Little Review was founded by Anderson in 1914 with the lofty desire to, as she wrote in the first issue, "make no compromise with the public taste."

In its early days it featured on its pages not only literary works and criticism, but also extremist social commentary for the time, including Anderson's own writing in defense of homosexuality and feminism. It became a publication of much notoriety when Ezra Pound joined on as foreign editor in 1917 and began to send Anderson pieces that were "too unconventional for the *Dial,* too risqué for the *Transatlantic Review,* and too bizarre to receive serious consideration anywhere else" (Green). Such an offering was James Joyce's *Ulysses,* which Anderson and Heap insisted on publishing, even though they knew they were treading on dangerous ground in publishing Joyce's scandalous work. It ran for three years, published as a work-in-progress, in serialized installments. Much-discussed because of what was considered its lewd and blasphemous content, it was no surprise when the United States Post Office seized and destroyed copies of the magazine and Anderson and Heap were charged with obscenity. "The publication of *Ulysses* would, alone, gain Miss Anderson a place in the annals of the little magazine; her standing trial because of that publication gained her martyrdom" (Joost, p. 49). The trial was an international *cause célèbre,* and, in the end, Anderson and Heap were found guilty, and each was fined fifty dollars. In 1923, not long after the famous trial, *The Little Review* relocated from New York to Paris, and Margaret Anderson and Jane Heap became major figures in the world of literary "exiles."

It was there in Paris, in 1923, where the "martyred" editors met the young, unpublished Hemingway. In her memoirs, Anderson wrote of their first dinner with Hemingway and his wife Hadley: "Jane Heap and I went to dine with them and Hemingway read us a story. It was one of the first stories he had written - he had not yet found a publisher. I took it immediately for the *Little Review...* A few months after his first appearance in the *Little Review* we printed the second story of his to be accepted anywhere - 'Mr. and Mrs. Eliot [*sic*]' - a gem of a story " (Anderson, p. 258).

Hemingway's vignettes - short prose pieces collectively titled "In Our Time" - led off the May 1923 *Little Review* issue which was called the "Exiles' Number" because, as Anderson wrote, "all of the contributors are at present pleasantly exiled in Europe." Contributors to the issue from the expatriate community included Gertrude Stein, E. E. Cummings, Mina Loy, and George Antheil; European contributors included Fernand Léger, Joan Miró, and Jean Cocteau. "That Hemingway's Imagist vignettes led off such a company is evidence enough of the impression he made on Margaret Anderson and Jane Heap" (Joost, p. 53). *Poetry* magazine had published a sample of Hemingway's poetry a few months earlier, but "he achieved his métier as a writer in the short prose vignettes he published in *The Little Review*" (Joost, p. 32). Several of these vignettes appeared a few months later in *Three Stories & Ten Poems*, Hemingway's first book which quickly established him as a major new talent.

When *Three Stories & Ten Poems* was published, publisher Robert McAlmon allowed him four author's copies, which he picked up from Sylvia Beach at her legendary book shop, Shakespeare and Company, mere days before he left Paris for a newspaper job in Toronto. One of these copies was inscribed by Hemingway to Miss Beach that day, and it seems likely that the copy offered here which he warmly inscribed for Anderson and Heap is also one of those author's copies - not only did the very small limitation sell out almost immediately, but Hemingway's financial state at the time did not allow for his buying up copies of his own book for presentation. It is fitting that he presented one of his few, precious copies to the two women to whom he owed a debt of gratitude for having enthusiastically published his first mature prose work in the pages of their *Little Review*. Not only had they granted him what amounted to an official *entrée* into the world of the literary elite of the sizzling *Rive Gauche*, but more importantly, they had introduced him to receptive audiences in America and the wider world beyond.

The Little Review, though hugely influential and always much-discussed, was never really on stable financial footing. It required an enormous amount of Margaret's and Jane's time and effort to produce, and eventually the grind wore them both down. Publication ceased in 1929 after fifteen years in operation, and Margaret and Jane went their separate ways: Jane

to London to teach the spiritual philosophy of G. I. Gurdjieff, and Margaret, ultimately, after the heart-breaking death of her beloved Georgette LeBlanc, back to the United States.

Margaret Anderson and Hemingway had had their ups and downs with each other, but Hemingway remained fond of her ("I never met a nicer or more flutter brained legendary woman, or a prettier one in my life than Margaret Anderson," he wrote to Janet Flanner in 1933) (Baker, p. 388), and when word reached him in 1941 that she was unable to afford the ticket for the ocean passage home, he sent a check for $400 to her friend Solita Solano with a note: "Here is the check for Margaret. I hope so [much that] she has good luck getting over. Greet her for me will you? ... Much love Solita and take good care of yourself and don't ever worry because as long as any of us have any money we all have money" (Baker, p. 522).

It was on the ocean voyage to the U.S. that Margaret met Dorothy Caruso, widow of the internationally-acclaimed Italian tenor Enrico Caruso. They fell in love and spent the next 13 years together until Dorothy's death in 1955, after which Margaret returned to France. She died there of heart failure in 1973 at the age of 86. Jane died in London in 1964 at the age of 80. They had both outlived Hemingway who committed suicide in 1961, one day after his 61st birthday.

We know of no other presentation copy of a book inscribed to both editors of *The Little Review*. This, Ernest Hemingway's first book, inscribed by him to the two women who published his first important work and whose magazine helped to define and popularize modernism during the years when the "Lost Generation" was coming of age, is an incredible association item. This unique presentation copy of *Three Stories & Ten Poems* comes directly from the estate of Dorothy Caruso, widow of Enrico Caruso and longtime companion of Margaret Anderson. It has never been offered for sale. *From the Letters, Books, and Papers of Margaret C. Anderson and Dorothy Caruso, Collected by Eric Murray*.

Hanneman A1. Margaret Anderson, *My Thirty Years' War*. Carlos Baker, editor, *Ernest Hemingway: Selected Letters, 1917-1961*. Michelle Erica Green, "Making No Compromises with Critical Taste: The War for *The Little Review*." Frederick J. Hoffman, Charles Allen, and Carolyn F. Ulrich, *The Little Magazine, A History and a Bibliography*. Nicholas Joost, *Ernest Hemingway and the Little Magazines: the Paris Years*.

Estimate: $75,000-up
Starting Bid: $55,000

Margaret Anderson

Jane Heap

In the Scarce, Unrestored Dust Jacket

36117 **Ernest Hemingway.** *The Torrents of Spring.* New York: Charles Scribner's Sons, 1926. First edition. Octavo. [viii], [1]-143 pages. Publisher's smooth dark green cloth with red titles stamped on the front cover and spine. Original pictorial dust jacket printed in orange, black, and tan, with the front cover drawing by "M. F." depicting a lunch counter scene. Light rubbing and a few instances of soiling to the boards. Top, rear corner bumped. Small area at the top edge of each board bumped. Small bump to spine head. Almost imperceptible nick to the top edge of the first three leaves. Faint binding glue offsetting to endpapers, otherwise a very clean text. Some rubbing and noticeable dust-soiling to the panels and spine of the dust jacket. Very minimal nicks to the fold ends, with a tiny area of loss to the top edge of the front flap. Small areas of biopredation to the top fold ends, most noticeable at the spine head, where it affects some letters in the title. A very good copy in a handsome example of the original dust jacket. Hanneman A4a.

Estimate: $1,500-up
Starting Bid: $750

With a Page of Manuscript and Two Pages of Corrected Page Proofs by William Cullen Bryant

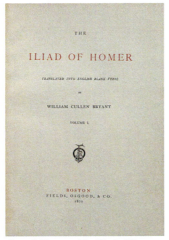

36118 **[William Cullen Bryant, translator]. Homer.** *The Iliad of Homer.* Boston: Fields, Osgood & Co., 1870. First edition of Bryant's translation. **Volume I has two pages of hand-corrected proofs by Bryant bound-in (pages 63 and 64) and Volume II has three pages of manuscript of this translation, also in Bryant's hand.** Two quarto volumes. [2], [xx], 398; [viii], 426 pages. Bound in contemporary half plum morocco over marbled paper boards. Spines ruled and tooled in blind. Ruled, tooled, and lettered in gilt in compartments with five raised bands. Marbled endleaves. Spines and edges of binding sunned to brown with some rubbing and mild wear to binding. Overall, a near fine copy. Bound for politician and author Whitelaw Reid, with his name stamped in gilt on the spines.

Estimate: $1,500-up
Starting Bid: $750

Inscribed by Langston Hughes

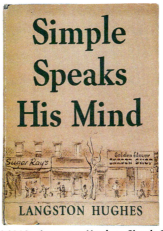

36119 **Langston Hughes.** *Simple Speaks His Mind.* [New York]: Simon and Schuster, [1950]. First edition. **Inscribed by Langston Hughes: "For my friends, / Dr. and Mrs. / "Tex" Burnett, / from an "ole Lincoln- / ite" / Langston / New York, / November 27, / 1950."** With original mailing label laid in from Hughes in New York to "Dr. J.M. Burnett" in Fort Worth, Texas. Octavo. Viii, 231, [1] pages. Publisher's green cloth stamped in black and gilt. Original pictorial dust jacket. Top edge stained gray-green. Jacket with minor chipping and browning, and starting to split along the lower front joint. Page edges slightly browned. Altogether, a very good copy with a nice Hughes inscription.

Estimate: $1,500-up
Starting Bid: $750

A Fine Copy of Irving's First Book

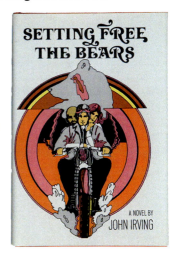

36120 **John Irving.** *Setting Free the Bears.* New York: Random House, [1968]. First edition, first printing. Octavo. 335 pages. Publisher's gilt-stamped red cloth over blind-stamped red paper boards, top edge stained red, and dust jacket with $5.95 price on front flap and "1/69" on rear flap. Tiny nick to paper on front board; minor crease to corner of rear jacket flap. An otherwise exceptional copy in fine condition.

Irving's first novel, an expanded and revised version of the manuscript he originally submitted as his Master's thesis at the University of Iowa's Writer's Workshop in 1967.

Estimate: $1,500-up
Starting Bid: $750

One of 750 Copies Signed by Kerouac

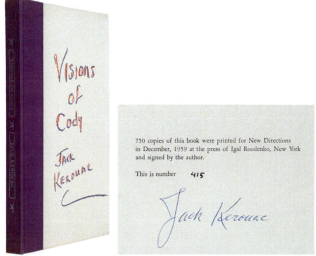

36121   **Jack Kerouac. *Excerpts From Visions of Cody.*** [New York: New Directions, 1960]. First edition, **one of 750 copies signed by Kerouac.** Octavo. 128 pages. Purple cloth backstrip, lettered and decorated in silver on the spine, over cream boards, front board lettered in lavender and red. Original publisher's glassine, chipped slightly at the top of the spine, not affecting book. Cloth backstrip slightly faded. A very clean copy of a book normally seen quite rubbed. *Visions of Cody* was not published in its entirety until 1972, after Kerouac's death. This limited edition has become quite scarce.

Estimate: $1,500-up
Starting Bid: $1,000

A Beautiful First Edition of Kerouac's Masterpiece

36122   **Jack Kerouac. *On the Road.*** New York: The Viking Press, 1957. First edition. Octavo. [vi], [1]-310, [4, blank] pages. Publisher's full black cloth, front board and spine lettered in white. Original pictorial dust jacket. Jacket has slight rubbing to extremities, one short closed tear to lower margin of rear jacket panel, minor foxing to jacket verso, and very light rubbing to jacket spine. A bright, fine copy of this cornerstone of Beat Literature.

Estimate: $1,500-up
Starting Bid: $1,000

One of Fifty Hand-Printed on Cartridge Paper

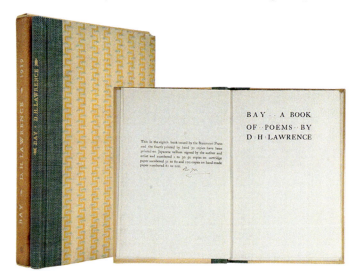

36123   **D. H. Lawrence. *Bay. A Book of Poems.*** [Westminster: Printed by Cyril W. Beaumont, 1919]. First edition, first issue. **Number seventy of 200 hand-numbered copies printed by hand at Beaumont's press on Charing Cross Road, and one of fifty copies printed on cartridge paper.** Octavo. 46, [2, flyleaf] pages. Publisher's green backstrip over decorative yellow and green paper boards. Housed in a custom, half-leather folding box by Atmore Beach with gilt titles on the spine and front cover. Trivial wear to the boards. Beach's bookplate to the front pastedown. A fine copy.

Estimate: $1,500-up
Starting Bid: $750

With Two Limited Editions Signed by D. H. Lawrence

36124   **D. H. Lawrence. Three First Editions of *Pansies*,** including: *Pansies.* London: Martin Secker, [1929]. **Number five of 250 copies, with a bold signature by Lawrence** on the limitation page. Minor foxing. Noticeable tape repairs to the spine ends of the verso of the jacket. [and:] *Pansies.* The first, unexpurgated edition, which includes fourteen poems omitted from the earlier Secker edition, **number 249 of 500 copies signed by Lawrence.** Publisher's white wrappers and slipcase (heavily worn). [and:] *Pansies.* London: Martin Secker, [1929]. First trade edition. Publisher's cloth. Foxing. All volumes in very good condition.

Estimate: $1,500-up
Starting Bid: $750

One of 100 Copies of D. H. Lawrence's *Sun*

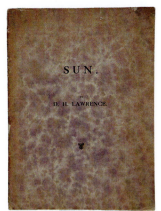 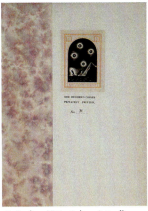

36125   D. H. Lawrence. *Sun.* London: E. Archer [Privately printed], September, 1926. First edition, privately printed and **limited to 100 hand-numbered copies, of which this in number 71.** Octavo. 20 pages. Decorative paper wrappers. Rockwell Kent-designed bookplate neatly mounted on the inside cover. With modest chipping at the extremities, toning along the edges of the wrappers and pages, else a near fine copy.
Estimate: $1,200-up
Starting Bid: $600

Inscribed Frieda Lawrence Book, Issue of *The Laughing Horse*, and the Red Baron's Horn Snuff Container.

 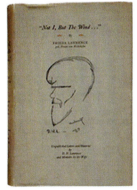

36126   Frieda Lawrence. Fantastic Frieda and D. H. Lawrence Lot, including: ***Not I, But the Wind...***" Santa Fe: The Rydal Press, 1934. First edition limited to 1,000 hand-numbered copies of which this is copy number 106. **Inscribed by the author in red ink, and with an undated Christmas card laid in which is also inscribed by her.** Octavo. 311 pages. Illustrated. Grey cloth boards with natural cloth backstrip, printed paper label on spine, original dust jacket. Minor rubbing and wear, else fine. [and:] **Willard Johnson, editor. *The Laughing Horse*, May - 1924.** Santa Fe: James T. Van Rensselaer, et. al. Octavo. Unpaginated. Red wrappers printed in black, housed in a half-morocco folded box with titles stamped in gilt on the spine. Includes a letter from D. H. Lawrence titled "Dear Old Horse" on pages three through six. The issue also includes a poem by Mabel Dodge Luhan titled "The Ballad of a Bad Girl" with an illustration by D. H. Lawrence captioned "The Bad Girl in the Pansy Bed." [and:] **Horn Snuff Container Given to Willard Johnson by Frieda Lawrence.** Willard Johnson was the editor of *The Laughing Horse*, a literary magazine published in Santa Fe, New Mexico. He was a close friend of the Lawrences and helped Frieda, in particular with many of her publishing projects after her husband's death. This horn snuff box measures about 3" in length and is pictured on an included photograph. The horn snuff container has a fancy script "R" carved below a crown. It is said that it had been given to Frieda by her distant cousin, Baron Manfred von Richthofen, the famous "Red Baron." Fine condition.
Estimate: $1,200-up
Starting Bid: $600

First Edition of Mailer's First Book

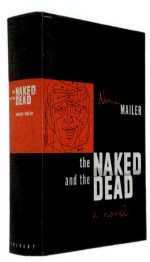

36127   Norman Mailer. *The Naked and the Dead.* New York: Rinehart and Company, [1948]. First edition, first state with dust jacket blurb by Stanley Rinehart. Octavo. 721 pages. Publisher's black cloth with white titles on spine, and dust jacket with $4.00 price. Tiny spot of foxing to fore-edge. A few brown streaks to rear panel of jacket. A beautiful copy in a remarkably crisp dust jacket. Fine condition. Mailer's first book.
Estimate: $3,000-up
Starting Bid: $1,500

Cormac McCarthy's Epic Trilogy, All Signed

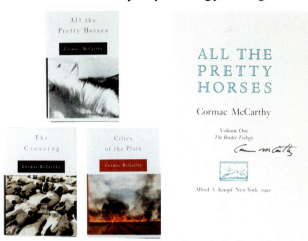

36128   Cormac McCarthy. The Border Trilogy, including: *All the Pretty Horses; The Crossing; Cities of the Plain.* New York: Alfred A. Knopf, 1992, 1994, 1998. First editions. **Each volume signed by the author,** *All the Pretty Horses* signed on the title-page, *The Crossing* and *Cities of the Plain* are signed on special tipped-in sheets stating that they are one of one thousand copies signed by the author on the special tipped-in sheet. Three octavo volumes. Publisher's black cloth over black paper boards with front covers and spines stamped in gilt. Original pictorial dust jackets. Light rubbing to jackets. Fine copies.

Cormac McCarthy's almost mythic trilogy — a startling and powerful modern classic of the Southwest that propelled McCarthy to international mainstream literary acclaim — is comprised of three stand-alone novels. *All the Pretty Horses*, the National Book Award-winning first novel in the trilogy, is now a staple on high school reading lists, and is, perhaps, McCarthy's most popular work. A beautiful first edition set of the trilogy, rarely found with all volumes signed.
Estimate: $3,000-up
Starting Bid: $1,500

A Fine Copy of McMurtry's First Book

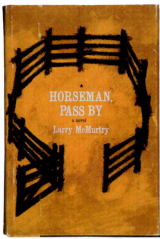

36129 **Larry McMurtry.** *Horseman, Pass By.* New York: Harper & Brothers Publishers, 1961. First edition. Octavo. 179 pages. Original mustard cloth backstrip and black paper over boards with titles stamped in black on the spine, and dust jacket with "0461" on front flap. Minor bump to front joint at base of spine; front board a trifle dusty. Price-clipped jacket. A near fine copy of McMurtry's first book, later adapted into the Academy Award-winning film *Hud*.

Estimate: $1,500-up
Starting Bid: $750

A Beautiful Signed First Edition

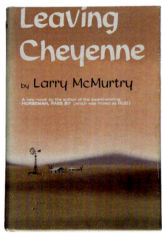

36130 **Larry McMurtry.** *Leaving Cheyenne.* New York: Harper & Row, 1963. First edition. **Signed by McMurtry** on front free endpaper. Octavo. 298 pages. Publisher's beige cloth stamped in orange and black, and dust jacket with "0963" on front flap. Jacket is price-clipped, as usual, with a circular ghost sticker in bottom corner of front flap. A beautiful copy in near fine condition. The author's sentimental second book.

Estimate: $2,000-up
Starting Bid: $1,000

The True First Edition of *Moby-Dick*

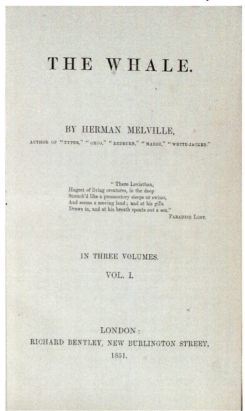

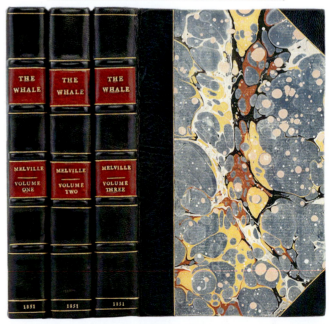

36131 **Herman Melville.** *The Whale.* In Three Volumes. London: Richard Bentley, 1851. The true first edition of *Moby-Dick*, preceding the New York (Harper & Brothers) one-volume edition by about four weeks. Three twelve-mo volumes (7.3125 x 4.5625 inches; 185 x 115 mm.). vi (no half-title), 312; iv, 303; iv, 328 pages. Uniformly bound in sumptuous three-quarter blue morocco over marbled boards, with gilt spine titles in compartments with five raised bands. Volume I has minor, scattered spotting, noticeably from D4-D9. Small blotch to M4v and M5r, affecting the first four lines of text. Light areas of spotting to volume II, noticeably from the beginning through B9, from C10-C12, D5-D9, E3, and L8-L9. Small area of bottom margin of E4 torn away. Volume III shows minor spotting, more noticeable at D9-D10, E2-E3, G6-G12, I7-I8, K11-12, L11-L12, and M2. Small blotch to I5, affecting nine lines of text. Otherwise, mostly light, marginal thumbsoiling, with very mild foxing, in all volumes. A few corners creased in each volume. Overall, a cleaner-than-usual copy in very good condition.

"The English edition, *The Whale*, Bentley, London, 3 vols....was published October 18 against the American November 19. This edition was set up from Harper proof-sheets, which were edited to some extent by Bentley, without Melville's knowledge. The editing consisted of toning down profanity and some alleged irreverent references; also, the 'Epilogue' was omitted, which caused at least one English review to comment on the impossibility of a first-person narrative, when everyone on the *Pequod* was killed by the white whale's attack...*Moby Dick* is the great conundrum-book. Is it a profound allegory with the white whale the embodiment of moral evil, or merely the finest story of the sea ever written? Whichever it is, now rediscovered, it stirs and stimulates each succeeding generation, whether reading it for pleasure or with a scalpel. Within its pages can be found the sound and scents, the very flavor, of the maritime life of our whaling ancestors" (Grolier, *100 American*).

"This book was expurgated for publication in England, the American text containing thirty-five passages not included in Bentley's edition" (Sadleir, *Excursions in Victorian Bibliography*, p. 339).

BAL 13663. Grolier, *100 American*, 60. Sadleir 1685 ("one of the rarest of three-deckers").

Estimate: $40,000-up
Starting Bid: $20,000

One of 100 Copies Signed by Henry Miller

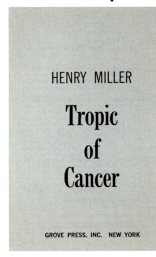
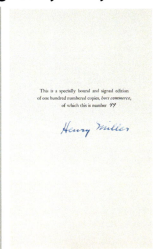

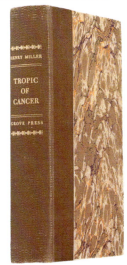

36132   Henry Miller. *Tropic of Cancer*. New York: Grove Press, Inc., [1961]. First edition, first printing. **Number 99 of 100 specially-bound copies *hors commerce*, signed by Miller** on the limitation page. Octavo. xxxiv, 318 pages. Publisher's brown buckram over marbled paper boards with gilt spine titles. Gray endpapers. Edge wear and bumps to boards. Spine cloth lightly rubbed, but gilt still fresh. Corners bumped and exposed. Minor thumbsoiling to text edges. Internally, a bright copy. Very good condition. Contains the introduction by Karl Shapiro, a critical assessment which Miller felt served his work well.

Estimate: $2,000-up
Starting Bid: $1,000

The First Complete Edition of Petronius' Novel, *Satyricon*

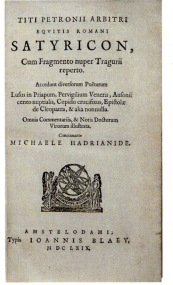

36133   Titus Petronius Arbiter. *Satyricon*, *Cum Fragmento Nuper Tragurii reperto.* Amsterdam: Joannes Blaeu, 1669. [bound with:] **Titus Petronius Arbiter. *Integrum Fragmentum*,** *Ex antiquo codice Tragvriensi Romae exscriptum cum Apologia Marini Statilli I. V. D.* Amsterdam: Joannes Blaeu, 1670. Approximately 7.5 x 4.25 inches. Octavo. [xxxiv], 558, [42, Index], 168, [8, Index], [viii], 70, [32] pages. With the engraved title by Romeyn de Hooghe. Complete. Nineteenth-century full brown calf, covers triple-ruled in gilt, spine tooled and ruled in gilt in compartments, burgundy morocco gilt lettering label, five raised bands, gilt board edges, blind turn-ins, marbled endleaves. Spine slightly sunned and worn, some wear to corners, panels rubbed, two small bookplates from previous owners, some light occasional thumbsoiling in text. Overall, a near fine copy. *Satyricon* is not always bound with the *Fragmentum*. This novel, one of the few surviving Roman novels, and a very rare look into the lives of the lower classes of Rome. Many consider this to be the earliest extant novel of Western civilization. Brunet IV, 574. Schweiger II, p. 723.

Estimate: $3,000-up
Starting Bid: $1,500

First Complete English Translation of Plato

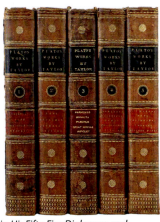

36134   Plato. The Works of Plato, *viz. His Fifty-Five Dialogues, and Twelve Epistles, Translated from the Greek; Nine of the Dialogues by the late Floyer Sydenham, and the Remainder by Thomas Taylor: with Occasional Annotations on the Nine Dialogues Translated by Sydenham, and Copious Notes by the Latter Translator; in Which is Given the Substance of Nearly all the Existing Greek MS. Commentaries on the Philosophy of Plato, and a Considerable Portion of Such as are Already Published. In Five Volumes.* London: Printed for Thomas Taylor, by R. Wilks..., 1804. First edition of the first complete translation into English of Plato, with Greek commentaries, and the extended notes of Thomas Taylor. Approximately 11.5 x 8.75 inches. Five quarto volumes. [12], cxxiii, [1, blank], 544; [4], 657, [1, blank], [1], [1, blank]; [4], 600; [4], 614; [4], 720 pages. Complete with half-titles and the plate of diagrams (bound into Volume V between pages 62 and 63). Bound without the errata slip. Contemporary full calf. Covers double ruled in gilt, spines ruled and tooled in gilt in compartments, black, dark green and burgundy gilt morocco lettering labels, gilt board edges and turn-ins, marbled endpapers. Joints starting (joints of Volume I nearly detached), some wear to bindings, one small marginal tear on p. 57 in Volume I, and a few pages neatly creased in the upper corner of Volume II. Overall, a very good set of these rare volumes.

From the library of Platonic scholar John Athawes, with his bookplates and extensive notes (both in English and Greek), underlinings, and marginalia (virtually every page has neat and intricate markings or writing, presumably by Athawes - some pages have very little, some pages are nearly covered in his neat, thoughtful and fascinating notes).

Taylor's 1804 edition was the first complete English translation of the works of Plato. It includes copious notes which contain the substance of the surviving commentaries of the later Platonists (Damascius, Olympiodorus, Hermias and especially Proclus), making it not only an important translation, but also a source of insightful elucidation of the dialogues. Taylor himself translates Plato's Dialogues from within the ancient Greek Tradition, and many believe his translation to still be the finest available. Thomas Taylor, 1758-1835, was an English scholar and translator known for his translations of Plato and the Neoplatonists, especially his translation of the complete works of Plato, published in five volumes in London in 1804. Taylor's translations are distinctive for their esoteric and Neoplatonic perspective: Taylor was more a devotee than an "objective" presenter, and therefore more a disciple than a pure scholar. Like the New England Transcendentalists who enjoyed his writings, such as Amos Bronson Alcott and Ralph Waldo Emerson, he was self-styled, self-taught, working independently outside the walls and sanctions of academe. Emerson, during his second trip to England in 1848, was astonished that Taylor was not better known and respected in his own country.

Estimate: $3,000-up
Starting Bid: $1,500

A Remarkable Collection of Over One Thousand Pocket Books, Encompassing the Imprint's First Twenty-One Years

36135   [Pocket Books]. A Very Large Group of Pocket Books, Including a Complete Run of the First 1,257 Titles. New York: Pocket Books, in association with Simon and Schuster, [1939-1960]. Mixed printings throughout (title #1, *Lost Horizon*, is a fourth printing). All mass market paperbacks. Numbers 1-1257 are all present; this collection also with numbers 1258-1278 (missing six numbers). 1,272 total books in this lot, all in very good or better condition.

Pocket Books was the brainchild of Robert Fair de Graff whose dream was to offer "the widest variety of books at the lowest price to the greatest number of people." Pocket Books, the first mass-market "pocket-sized" paperbacks issued in America, revolutionized the publishing industry with its low-priced editions of popular fiction, mysteries, and non-fiction titles. Not only was Pocket Books known for its affordable editions of classics and recent bestsellers, it was also a godsend for artists who were commissioned to do the eye-catching original cover art for the imprint's incredibly diverse selection of titles. The books were immensely popular — at the end of the first year, 1.5 million books had been sold. A collection this complete is almost unheard of, and the remarkable condition of these books is truly astounding. A wonderful opportunity to acquire an instant collection of one of the most important achievements in twentieth-century publishing history.

Estimate: $1,500-up
Starting Bid: $750

The First Appearance of Poe's Seminal Poem, "The Raven"

36136   [Edgar Allan Poe]. *The American Review: A Whig Journal of Politics, Literature, Art and Science.* New York: Wiley and Putnam, February 1845. First edition, first printing, of one of the most celebrated poems in American literature. Octavo. The February issue only, being volume I, number II of *The American Review* for 1845. [ii, title leaf], [113]-220 pages. Later smooth brown leather with gilt spine titles inside two raised bands with black borders and rules. Minor wear to the boards. Spine and board edges sunned. Marginal tear to page 159-160, not affecting text. Minor foxing. A few creased corners. Very good condition.

Published under the pseudonym "Quarles," *The Raven* (pages 143-145) brought Poe instant literary fame, quickly becoming one of the most discussed and recited poems in the country. The appearance in the *American Review* is the accepted first edition - the publication in the *New York Mirror* on January 29, 1845 was printed from advance sheets of *The American Review*.

Estimate: $2,000-up
Starting Bid: $1,000

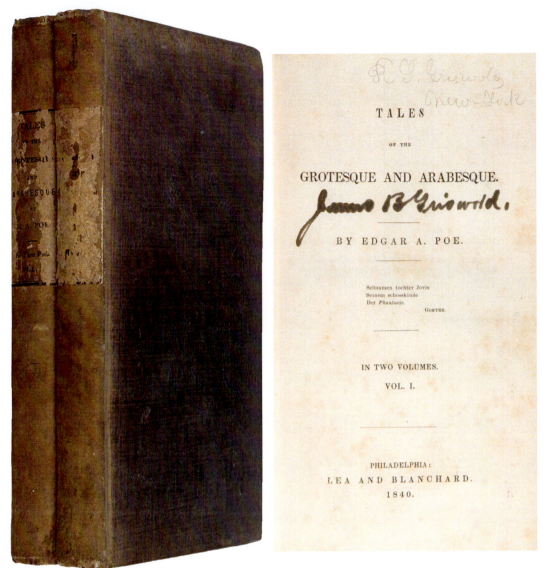

36137   Edgar Allan Poe. *Tales of the Grotesque and Arabesque.* Philadelphia: Lea and Blanchard, 1840. First edition, one of 750 printed, with the following points: volume II, page 213 correctly numbered; "i" and hyphen on page 219 of volume II are below the line; four pages of critical notices serving as advertisements bound in before the title page in Volume II. Two twelvemo volumes. [ii, blank], [1]-243, [2, blank] pages; [ii, blank], i-iv (advertisements), [1]-228, [2, blank] pages. Publisher's purple muslin with printed paper spine labels. Moderate wear and soiling to the cloth. Spines and top edges sunned. Spine labels worn, with about half of the label for volume I remaining, and much less of volume II surviving. Corners bumped. Uneven foxing throughout. Penciled signature to title page and first page of text in each volume. Inked signature to each title page. All of these signatures bear the last name Griswold (Rufus Griswold's family?). Overall, a very good, complete copy, quite rare in the original cloth and with the original critical notices and flyleaves present.

"These volumes mark the culmination of Poe's effort, beginning as early as 1834 to get his prose tales into volume form. It is a milestone in his career as a prose writer, but was a failure commercially" (Heartman & Canny, *A Bibliography of First Printings of the Writings of Edgar Allan Poe*, page 53).

BAL 16133. Heartman & Canny, pp. 49-54.
Estimate: $15,000-up
Starting Bid: $7,500

Polidori's Classic Novel, Conceived the Same Night as Shelley's *Frankenstein*

 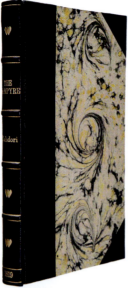

36138 **[John William Polidori].** ***The Vampyre; A Tale.*** London: Sherwood, Neely, and Jones, 1819. First edition, second issue (Viets III), with the original text of the "Extract of a Letter from Geneva" set in twenty-four lines. The first word of the last line on page 36 corrected to "almost." Octavo. xxv, [xxvi, blank], [27]-84 pages. Modern three-quarter black morocco over marbled boards, with decorative gilt spine stamping inside four raised bands. All edges untrimmed. Marbled endpapers. Original front wrapper bound in. Minimal wear to the binding. Minor dust-soiling and toning to the text. Two small marginal chips to E7, E8, and the last page of text. Ink stains to E4. A handsome copy in very good condition.

The Vampyre was conceived during the same competitive story-telling evening as Mary Shelley's *Frankenstein*, and was written by Byron's doctor, John William Polidori (1795-1821). Originally published under Byron's name, Polidori sought an injunction against the printer and Byron disowned it altogether. Although the book was successful, Polidori made little from it; he committed suicide two years later.

Henry R. Viets, "The London Editions of Polidori's 'The Vampyre'", Papers of the Bibliographical Society of America, Volume 63, 1969.

Estimate: $2,000-up
Starting Bid: $1,000

First Edition of Pope's Homer, With a Subscription Slip Signed by Pope

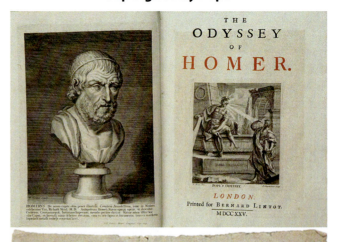

36139 **[Alexander Pope, translator].** **Homer.** ***The Iliad of Homer,*** *Translated by Mr. Pope.* London: Printed by W. Bowyer for Bernard Lintott, 1715-1720. [Together With:] **[Alexander Pope, translator].** **Homer.** ***The Odyssey of Homer.*** London: Printed for Bernard Lintott, 1725-1726. Each volume a first edition, subscriber's issue (presumably issued before other issues of the first edition). Approximately 11 x 8 inches. Complete in eleven quarto volumes. *Iliad* with half-title, portrait of Homer, folding map of Greece in Volume I, folding plate of the Siege of Troy in Volume II, and the Shield of Achilles plate in Volume V; *Odyssey* with portrait of Homer, engraved title page. Each volume has privilege leaf, as issued. This edition is embellished with ornamental initials and devices not used in the trade editions. **Laid-in is the original subscription slip of "Colonel Hara" (he is named on the List of Subscribers), and signed "A Pope".** All volumes uniformly bound in contemporary full mottled calf, covers ruled in gilt, spines ruled and tooled in gilt, with brown morocco lettering labels. Minor wear to bindings, a few joints starting, previous owner's royal (with crown) and noble (with arms) bookplates. A near fine set. Lintott gave approximately 750 specially-bound copies of this work to Pope to sell directly to subscribers. Samuel Johnson referred to Pope's translation of the *The Iliad* as the greatest ever produced in English or any other language.

Estimate: $6,000-up
Starting Bid: $5,000

The First Faithful Facsimile of the First Folio of Shakespeare

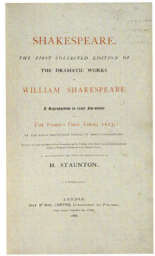

36140   William Shakespeare. *The First Collected Edition of the Dramatic Works of William Shakespeare. A Reproduction in exact fac-simile of the Famous First Folio, 1623, by the newly-discovered Process of Photo-Lithography. Under the Superintendence of H. Staunton.* London: Day & Son, Limited, 1866. First edition of first lithographed facsimile of the First Folio. Approximately 15.75 x 9.75 inches. [xix], 399 pages. With the facsimile of the original title-page with Droeshout's famous engraving of Shakespeare. Publisher's original full brown cloth over beveled boards, covers decoratively ruled and paneled in blind, gilt central stamp of the Shakespearian arms, spine ruled, tooled, and lettered in gilt. Some wear to binding, some of which has been professionally repaired, hinges starting, a few very minor tears in text (not affecting printed material). "The first faithful reproduction of the Jaggard canon. It was executed (from the originals at Bridgewater House and the British Museum) at H. M. ordinance survey office (Jaggard, p. 539).

Estimate: $1,500-up
Starting Bid: $750

Signed Limited Edition of *East of Eden*

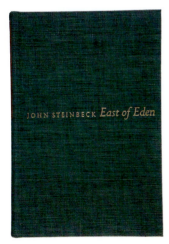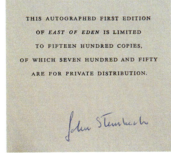

36141   John Steinbeck. *East of Eden.* New York: The Viking Press, 1952. First edition, **limited to 1,500 numbered copies signed by Steinbeck.** Octavo. [vi]; [1-2] 3-602 pages. Publisher's green cloth, lettered in gilt on front board, stamped in brown and lettered in gilt on spine. Edges stained salmon. Publisher's cardboard slipcase, original acetate dust jacket. Acetate jacket spine with a small tear near the top and a bit soiled, slipcase worn and split at several seams. Still, a fine copy of the book. Goldstone & Payne A32a.

Estimate: $1,500-up
Starting Bid: $750

Inscribed and Signed by John Steinbeck

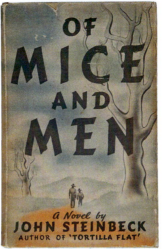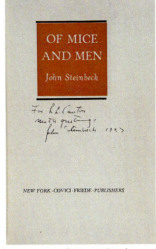

36142   John Steinbeck. *Of Mice and Men.* New York: Covici-Friede, [1937]. First edition, first issue, with the correct issue points per Goldstone & Payne. **Inscribed and signed in the year of publication by Steinbeck, "For L. H.(?) Cantor / with greetings / John Steinbeck 1937"** on the title page. Small octavo. 186, [6, blank] pages. Publisher's beige cloth, front cover and spine stamped in black and orange. Original later-issue pictorial dust jacket. Housed in a brown half-leather slipcase with marbled boards and cloth chemise. Minor dustsoiling to the boards. Spine a bit sunned. Tape scars and offsetting to front endpapers. Newspaper clippings pasted to the page opposite of the first page of text, all of the rear flyleaves, and the rear endpapers. Front free endpaper removed. Minor wear and light chipping to the jacket edges. Spine sunned. Six strips of tape reinforcement to the verso of the jacket. Very good. Goldstone & Payne A7a.

Estimate: $2,000-up
Starting Bid: $1,000

One of 100 Proof Copies, Signed by Alfred, Lord Tennyson

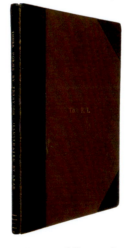

36143   Alfred, Lord Tennyson. *Poems. Illustrated by Edward Lear.* London: Boussod, Valadon & Co., 1889. First edition, **one of 100 copies signed by Tennyson,** this being number 58. Printed on Japan Paper. Large quarto. Approximately 12.5 x 9.25 inches. [8], [vi], 51, [1, blank], [1, colophon], [1, blank] pages. With portrait frontispiece of Tennyson after Watts and sixteen full-page plates after Lear inserted. Six head- and tail-pieces after Lear and one head-piece portrait of Lear. All illustrations with printed tissue guards. Publisher's half brown levant morocco over brown cloth boards, spine lettered in gilt, with gilt central lettering ("To E. L.") on the front board. Joints lightly worn (yet still solid), some wear to edges. Overall, a near fine copy of this rare item. From the collection of prominent Bay area book collectors Babette and Herbert Clayburgh with their bookplate. Tennyson and Lear greatly admired each other's work, and this mutual respect eventually grew into friendship. Lear died in 1888, and this work was published as a memorial by Tennyson for his friend.

Estimate: $1,500-up
Starting Bid: $750

First Edition of John Updike's First Book, Inscribed to an Editor at *The Reader's Digest*

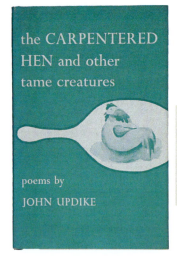

36144 **John Updike.** ***The Carpentered Hen and other tame creatures.*** **Poems by John Updike.** New York: Harper & Brothers, [1958]. First edition of the author's first book. **Inscribed by Updike on the rear free endpaper (upside-down!): "for Caroline Rogers/Best wishes/John Updike". Laid-in is a Typed Letter Signed by Ms. Rogers, on Reader's Digest stationery and dated "May 21, 1970" requesting that Updike sign her book. Below her signature, Updike has responded in holograph: "happy to - if you send it with/stamped return book envelope/J. U." Also laid-in is the original envelope for the letter, addressed in Updike's hand.** Octavo. [xii], 82, [2, blank] pages. Publisher's black cloth backstrip over paper-covered boards, front cover and spine stamped in gilt. Original pictorial dust jacket. Very minor rubbing to jacket. Fine. A wonderful book and letter, of the highest interest to the modern first collector.

Estimate: $1,500-up
Starting Bid: $750

First Book in Updike's Famous Rabbit Series

36145 **John Updike.** ***Rabbit, Run.*** New York: Knopf, 1960. First edition, first printing. Octavo. 307 pages. Publisher's quarter green cloth over blue boards. Top edge stained green. Spine slightly cocked with sunning and foxing along top edge. A bit of faint offsetting and foxing to endpapers. Price clipped jacket shows light rubbing and wear to edges. A few tiny chips and tear to extremities. Mild sunning to spine with two light folds to front inner flap. Very good.

Estimate: $2,000-up
Starting Bid: $1,000

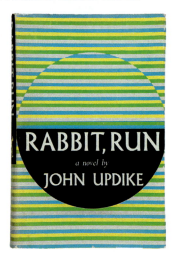

With Charlie Chaplin's Copy of Rudolph Valentino's *Day Dreams*

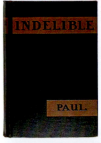

36146 **[Hollywood]. [Rudolph Valentino, Charlie Chaplin, et al.]. Three Association Copies of First Editions,** including: **Rudolph Valentino.** ***Day Dreams.*** New York: Macfadden Publications, Inc., 1923. Octavo. 143 pages. Publisher's orange cloth with gilt titles on the front board. **Charlie Chaplin's copy,** with his "Tramp" bookplate affixed to the front pastedown and a promotional photo laid in. A stamp-signed Valentino TLS and a period cigar label are tipped in to the front flyleaf and half-title page, respectively. [and:] **Elliot H. Paul.** ***Indelible.*** Boston and New York: Houghton Mifflin Company, [1922]. Octavo. 297 pages. Publisher's black cloth. **Louise Dresser's copy, inscribed by her** on the front free endpaper, and with her large "Flapper" bookplate affixed to the front pastedown. Spine noticeably cocked. [and:] **William S. Hart.** ***Injun and Whitey Strike Out for Themselves.*** New York: Grosset and Dunlap Publishers, [1921]. **Signed by Hart** on the front free endpaper. Octavo. 280 pages. Publisher's tan cloth decoratively stamped in red and black. With a first day cover honoring Hart laid in and the cowboy bookplate of Myles Standish Slocum affixed to the front pastedown. All volumes in very good condition.

Estimate: $1,500-up
Starting Bid: $750

Asbestos "451", Signed and/or Inscribed by Bradbury Four Times in Four Different Decades

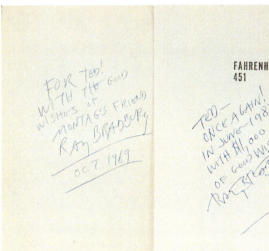

36147   Ray Bradbury. *Fahrenheit 451.* New York: Ballantine Books, [1953]. First edition. Number 33 of 200 limited edition copies, **signed by Bradbury** on the limitation page. **Additionally inscribed and signed by Bradbury on the verso of the front free endpaper (in 1969), on the half-title page (in 1982) and on the title page (in 1990)**, all to the same owner, whose bookplate is affixed to the front pastedown. Octavo. 199 pages. Illustrated by Joe Mugnaini. Publisher's binding of Johns-Manville Quinterra, "an asbestos material with exceptional resistance to pyrolysis." Lettering in red on spine and cover. No dust jacket, as issued. Significant wear and soiling to the boards. Spine completely perished. Corners exposed. Minor toning to the endpapers. A good copy.

Estimate: $3,000-up
Starting Bid: $1,500

Signed Copy of Bradbury's Third Book

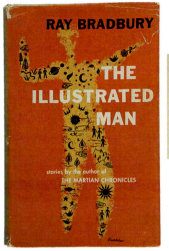

36148   Ray Bradbury. *The Illustrated Man.* Garden City: Doubleday, 1951. First edition, first printing. **Signed by Bradbury with a wonderful early signature** on front free endpaper. Octavo. 251 pages. Publisher's light brown cloth with dark brown spine titles. Original pictorial dust jacket. Light rubbing and toning to cloth extremities with a slightly cocked spine. Minor offsetting to endpapers. Jacket shows light rubbing and wear to edges with a few chips and tears, and some sunning along spine. A bright, very good copy with a fantastic early signature.

Estimate: $1,500-up
Starting Bid: $750

Inscribed by Burroughs

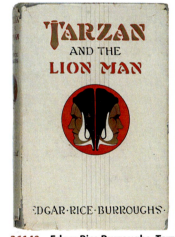

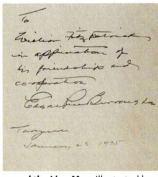

36149   Edgar Rice Burroughs. *Tarzan and the Lion Man*. Illustrated by J. Allen St. John. Tarzana, California: Edgar Rice Burroughs, Inc. Publishers, [1934]. First edition. **Inscribed by Burroughs on the front free endpaper: "To / William Fitzpatrick / in appreciation of / his friendship and / co-operation / Edgar Rice Burroughs / Tarzana / January 23 1935."** Octavo. 318 pages plus one-page publisher's advertisement. Publisher's gray cloth with black titles and red Janus figure on the front board and spine. Top edge stained red. Original first issue pictorial dust jacket with Janus figure and *Pirates of Venus* on the rear panel. Minor rubbing to extremities, light soiling to cloth especially at spine, internally very clean. Dust jacket with chipping at corners and folds with some loss at the top and bottom of spine. Jacket splitting along bottom of front joint, and starting on the flap folds. Altogether a very good copy in a good jacket and with a nice inscription. Zeuschner 627.

Estimate: $1,500-up
Starting Bid: $750

A Superb Copy of Tom Clancy's
The Hunt for Red October

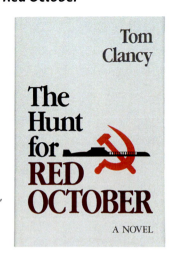

36150 **Tom Clancy.** *The Hunt for Red October.* Annapolis: Naval Institute Press, [1984]. First edition, first printing, in the first issue jacket (with six blurbs on the rear panel instead of eight). Octavo. [viii], 387, [1, blank], [1, acknowledgments], [3, blank] pages. Publisher's full red cloth with front cover decoratively stamped in blind, spine lettered in silver, and ISBN number stamped in silver on rear. Dust jacket. Fine. Best-selling author Tom Clancy's first book, basis for the 1990 film starring Sean Connery.
Estimate: $1,500-up
Starting Bid: $750

"Cosmos" Complete in Seventeen Issues

36151 **John W. Campbell, Jr., Otis Adelbert Flagg, Lloyd Arthur Eshbach, Edmond Hamilton, A. Merritt, Edward E. Smith, et al. Rare "Cosmos" Serial 17 Issues Complete.** Jamaica [New York]: Science Fiction Digest Company, [1934]. 5.5" x 7.75". Pamphlet format. Staple holes present in all issues but no staples are present. All issues have some toning; some issues have lightly bent corners and edge wear but overall the condition is near fine.

This extremely scarce set of science-fiction serials is presented here in its complete, original form. All seventeen issues, as well as the introductory pamphlet and loose card, are included. Collectors have long considered this a set that is incredibly difficult to assemble. Published by the legendary sci-fi fanzine that began life as *The Time Traveller* and later published under the names *Fantasy Magazine* and *Science Fiction Digest*, "Cosmos" is a round-robin serial, with each installment written by a different writer. The first installment came out in July 1933; the serial wrapped up in November 1934. Installments were written by the leading science fiction writers of the time. The lineup was as follows: Ralph Milne Farley, David H. Keller, Arthur J. Burks, Bob Olsen, Francis Flagg, John W. Campbell Jr., Rae Winters, Otis Adelbert Kline, E. Hoffman Price, Abner J. Gelula, Raymond A. Palmer, A. Merritt, J. Harvey Haggard, Edward E. Smith, P. Schuyler Miller, L. A. Eshbach, Eando Binder and Edmond Hamilton. The introductory pamphlet has a two-color woodblock print illustration by Hannes Bok, one of the legendary artist's earliest known published works. Each installment is about 16 pages. A rare and marvelous treasure of early science fiction.
Estimate: $2,000-up
Starting Bid: $1,000

A Near Fine Copy, Inscribed by Ian Fleming

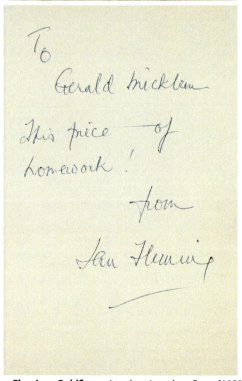

36152 **Ian Fleming.** *Goldfinger.* London: Jonathan Cape, [1959]. First edition. **Inscribed by Fleming, "To / Gerald Micklem, / This piece - of / homework! / from / Ian Fleming"** on the front free endpaper. Octavo. 318 pages. Publisher's black cloth with blind and gilt stamped front and gilt stamped spine. Spine has a very slight lean and the mildest of bumping to the extremities. Dust jacket has minor darkening along edges and a light stain at top edge of spine. Housed in a beautiful custom clamshell box by The Dragonfly Bindery. The box front reproduces an image of skull with rose from front panel of the jacket in intricate, multicolored leathers. A near fine copy of the seventh Bond novel. The Gerald Micklem in the inscription is quite possibly the famed British amateur golfer and golf administrator.
Estimate: $15,000-up
Starting Bid: $12,000

First Edition James Bond, Inscribed by Ian Fleming

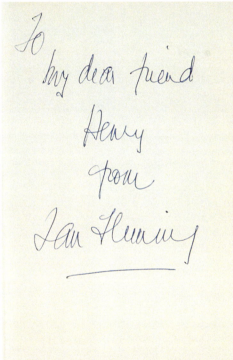

36153   Ian Fleming. *On Her Majesty's Secret Service.* London: Jonathan Cape, [1963]. First edition. **Inscribed by Fleming, "To / my dear friend / Henry / from / Ian Fleming"** on the front free endpaper. Octavo. 288 pages. Publisher's black cloth with white stamped design on front and silver stamped titles on spine. Moderate rubbing to the extremities. Dust jacket has some darkening along edges and spine. Modest soiling to rear panel. There are two one-eighth-inch tears on bottom edge of rear panel. Housed in a beautiful custom clamshell box by The Dragonfly Bindery. The box front reproduces an image of a shield from front panel of dust jacket in intricate, multicolored leathers. A near fine copy of the eleventh Bond novel.
Estimate: $10,000-up
Starting Bid: $8,500

Rare First Printing of John Grisham's First Book

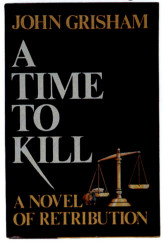

36154   John Grisham. *A Time to Kill.* New York: Wynwood Press, [1989]. First edition, first printing. Octavo. 415 pages. Publisher's maroon cloth over orange paper boards, and dust jacket with $18.95 price. Slight to bump to each corner of both boards. Shallow crease to rear jacket panel at foot of spine. Else, a fine copy of Grisham's first book.
Estimate: $1,500-up
Starting Bid: $750

All Work and No Play...

36155   Stephen King. *The Shining.* Garden City: Doubleday, 1977. First edition, with "R49" in the gutter on page 447. **Inscribed and dated by the author, "To Ross - / Best, / Stephen King / 9/8/79"** on the front free endpaper. Octavo. 447 pages. Publisher's black cloth over tan paper boards with gilt spine titles. Original pictorial dust jacket. Extremities somewhat worn, with light soiling to the cloth. Corners lightly rubbed. Very minor spotting to text edges, with the bottom edge sprinkled red. Otherwise, textblock very clean. Light spotting and a few small areas of discoloration to the jacket. A very good copy.
Estimate: $1,500-up
Starting Bid: $750

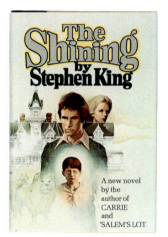

Unique Copy of "The Witching Hour" Screenplay, Signed Three Times by Anne Rice and Inscribed by Her to a Close Friend

36156   Anne Rice. "The Witching Hour" Screenplay. Unpublished, dated June 13, 1995, with "Copyright Warners & Geffen" in black felt tip marker at lower left corner of title page. **Signed three times by Anne Rice, with two warm inscriptions.** Front red cover has, in the author's hand, "The Witching Hour Script Anne Rice" in ink and "For Brian Robertson, With love, Anne Rice" in black felt tip; title page has "For Brian, All blessings - this is it before Warner's strikes - Love, Anne" in black felt tip. 163 pages of 8.5 x 11-inch paper, printed recto only. Brad-bound photocopied screenplay, in textured red paper covers. Some minor small tears along fore-edge of covers; small puncture by brad through rear cover. In near fine condition.

The film rights for *The Witching Hour*, Anne Rice's novel originally published in 1990, were optioned by producer David Geffen, and in early 1992, it was reported to be in pre-production, with Richard Donner attached as director. But as often happens in the mercurial world of Hollywood, the film was never made, and twenty-one years after the publication of the book, Anne Rice still lives in hope of an eventual film or television miniseries being made.

This 163-page unproduced screenplay by Anne Rice, adapted from her novels *The Witching Hour* and *Lasher*, has never been published. A 124-page version attributed to Rice is available online, but it is not the same as this screenplay. It is unclear if that online version was actually written by Rice, especially in light of her comments about the script that she wrote to her fans in 1996: "I am adamant that I won't touch this *Witching Hour* script, until there is a director attached (pray the guy doesn't want me around, and I have no contractual obligation to touch it anyway) because I feel the narrative links of this script are utterly tight, it is a powerfully coherent story, and I'm not about to start hacking at it in Hollywood committee style just to make it 'short.'"

The screenplay is inscribed by Anne Rice to Brian Robertson, a young fan who became a friend of Rice and whom she describes on her website as "a very dear friend of mine [...] Brian has had quite an influence on my work the last two years. [...] Brian is one of the most brilliant people I've ever met. I'm very devoted to Brian — I consider him my nephew!"

A singular copy of a truly unique, unpublished Anne Rice item which has never been offered for sale and has never been offered at auction.
Estimate: $1,500-up
Starting Bid: $750

A Handsome Lot of Books About Robin Hood

36157 **[Robin Hood]. A Lot of Eight Titles Related to Robin Hood**, including: *The Celebrated History of the Renowned Robin Hood. Captain of the Merry Outlaws of Sherwood Forest.* Bocking: Printed by J. F. Shearcroft, [n.d., ca. 1820]. First edition of this charming chapbook. Sixteenmo. 26 pages. Self-wrappered. [and:] **Spencer T. Hall. *The Forester's Offering.*** London: Whitaker and Co., 1841. First edition. **Presentation copy, inscribed by the author on the front pastedown.** Small octavo. [2], 142 pages. Inserted frontispiece. Publisher's green cloth. Covers embossed in blind, front cover lettered in gilt. [and:] **Stephen Percy. *Robin Hood and His Merry Foresters.*** London: Tilt and Bogue, 1841. First edition. Small octavo. [vi], 154 pages. With eight hand-color plates inserted throughout. Publisher's green cloth, covers stamped in blind, front cover and spine stamped and lettered in gilt. [and:] **Another copy.** London: Joseph Cundall, 1843. Second edition. Small octavo. [vi], 154 pages. With eight tinted plates inserted throughout. Publisher's light green cloth, covers stamped in blind, front cover and spine

stamped and lettered in gilt. [and:] **George Emmett. *Robin Hood and the Archers of Merrie Sherwood.*** London: Hogarth House, [1890]. Later edition. Volume I only. Octavo. 156 pages. Publisher's wrappers (front wrapper is hand-colored. [and:] **[Frederick Warne]. *The Marriage of Allan-a-Dale.*** London: Frederick Warne & Co., [n.d., ca. 1890]. First edition. Small quarto. [16] pages. Illustrated with tinted and full-color plates. Publisher's full-color wrappers, self-wrappered. [and:] ***The Robin Hood Library. With Bow and Blade or, The Outlaws of Sherwood Forest.*** [London: The Amalgamated Press, 1919]. First edition. Twelvemo. 33 pages. Publisher's wrappers, self-wrappered. [and:] **[Thriller Picture Library]. *Robin Hood - The Magnificent.*** [London: Fleetway Publications, n.d., ca. 1950]. First edition. Octavo. 64 pages. Publisher's full-color wrappers. Forester's Offering is quite worn, tape repairs to hinges (partially obscuring the author's inscription), pencil marks throughout. Good. The rest of the items are generally very good or better. An interesting lot of Robin Hood material.
Estimate: $1,500-up
Starting Bid: $750

Eighty-Five Volumes of the "King of the British Pulps"

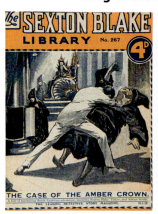 

36158 ***Sexton Blake Library* Bound Volumes.** London: Amalgamated Press Ltd., 1926-'60s. Original file copies of issues of the digest-sized British "penny dreadfuls" that have been trimmed and uniformly bound into a set of approximately 85 hardcover volumes (plus plus about 40 loose '60s-era issues), representing the bulk of the long-running series. The digests are in very nice condition with bright covers, supple pages, and mild tanning and wear. Many volumes with labels on front boards reading "This File Volume must not be mutilated, and should be returned at the earliest possible moment"; also with rubber stamps reading "Property of the Stock Room, Bear Alley. Please Return." Very good or better. Not currently in Bookery's.

The character Sexton Blake, sometimes called "the poor man's Sherlock Holmes," was an enormously popular figure in British popular culture, appearing in over 4,000 stories by more than 200 different authors. He starred in his own long-running title, *The Sexton Blake Library*, which ran from 1915 to 1968 and was published in five "series." A fabulous collection.
Estimate: $1,500-up
Starting Bid: $750

Jack Cordes, First Fan of Science Fiction

When I traveled to Peoria, Illinois this past autumn to pick up a science fiction book collection from a man named Jack Cordes, I had some idea of the collection through photos and documents. It looked like a few thousand books, pulps, vintage paperbacks, paintings, and the like, and there was a good measure of hope that this collection was good, which it certainly is. But even more impressive than the collection is the man behind it.

Jack Cordes. The name sounded familiar, and after doing a bit of research, I realized that I had probably seen his name in a fanzine or two over the years. Or perhaps I remembered him from reading one of the two books dedicated to him by Philip Jose Farmer (The Mad Goblin and Behind the Walls of Terra). Knowing that Mr. Cordes was intimately involved in first fandom, I was excited to meet him, and to see his collection. It proved to be one of the real pleasures of my life.

Mr. Cordes invited me into his house. We talked about science fiction and his friend, Philip Jose Farmer, and about Ray Bradbury and H. P. Lovecraft and movies and art and Hollywood, and I knew from the start that I had met a blithe, and kindred, spirit. Mr. Cordes directed me to his attic library and showed me around the stacks with the ease of a friend, relating with casual conviction that he cherished his collection, but that his books were now meant to fire their engines and fly to other places. The memory of the books would sustain him from this moment forward.

I found out very quickly that Mr. Cordes is not only an energetic book collector, and a wonderful conversationalist, but also a devoted father and grandfather, a decorated World War II veteran with a Purple Heart earned at Normandy, an A-V-I-D reader, a true first fan of science fiction, and just the spryest 86 year-old man you can imagine, with the smile and heart of someone a fraction his age. He is surely one of the only men his age who can honestly profess a love for the film, Repo Man! And when he tells you something, you know it's true. Mr. Cordes claims to have read everything in his library, and he's not lying. He smiles like he knows a wonderful secret that you don't, but one that you might find buried in one of his books, or that you might find after decades of reading stories of wonder and daydreaming of the outer limits.

He has wonderful stories about the aforementioned Philip Jose Farmer, a close friend of his for many years, and of his interactions with the likes of his friends Vernell Coriell and Hannes Bok (with whom he carried on a brief but very friendly correspondence), and correspondence with luminaries such as Charles Addams, Keith Laumer, Anthony Burgess, and many others, many of whom you will find represented in the pages that follow and throughout the next year in our weekly rare books auctions, our March 31 Entertainment auction (the part of his book collection signed by classic Hollywood stars), various Comics auctions (his pulp collection), and our March 1 Illustration Art auction (for his small but impressive collection of paintings).

Mr. Cordes didn't collect to invest. He didn't collect to wow anyone. He didn't mail his books to the four winds in order to rub his friends' noses in it when the books returned signed by somebody they all admired. He bought books to read. He subscribed to Fantasy Press and Gnome and other publishers because he wanted to make sure he got a copy of the books to read. He sent them away for inscriptions and signatures because he valued the personal connection involved with, if only for a moment, having one of his books in the hands of a hero, and getting that book back signed, and often inscribed to him, and then he'd read them. He collected, but as an avid reader, the collection happened almost by accident, and now he wants to pass this serendipitous assortment of fantastic literature to you. It's going to be a fun year or so bringing Mr. Cordes's collection out of his attic reading room in Peoria and into your libraries and lives.

An Archive of Sixteen Typed Letters Signed, and More, from Hannes Bok

36159   Hannes Bok. Archive of Correspondence with His Friend and Fellow Science Fiction Fan, Jack Cordes. Contents include sixteen fascinating Typed Letters Signed from Hannes Bok to Jack Cordes, dated between 1959 and 1962, all featuring a quick drawing by Bok, and most, if not all, from Bok's New York residence. Please visit our website at HA.com/6064-77065 for a complete listing of the letters, including sizes.

At least two of Bok's letters mention the sale of Bok's *Girl and Dino* painting (to be offered in our March 1 Heritage Illustration Art auction) to Cordes for the sum of $100 in late 1960-early 1961. Bok refers to Cordes by a number of names in the letters, including Jack, Jacques, Bo, Beaubeau Cattyfeller, and would sometimes playfully address the letters to Cordes and his wife, Edna, as "Cordesesesesesesetc" or "JackEdna or Jedanack," among others. In the letters, Bok mentions a number of names and titles important to science fiction and fantasy fans, including Vernell Coriell, Tarzan, *MAD* magazine, Gerry de la Ree, Ray Bradbury, Martin Greenberg, Lester del Rey, Ray Palmer, *Destination Moon, The Invisible Man Returns, Journey to the Center of the Earth*, and more. In one letter, Bok makes mention of his idolization of Norman Rockwell, and often includes information about what he's reading or watching or working on at the moment. The letters are occasionally annotated with handwritten comments by Bok.

In addition to the sixteen letters, there are five Christmas cards designed by Bok from 1957-1962 (no card from 1958), four signed "Hannes" and one with a short note in blue ink. This unique archive also includes fourteen of Bok's original typed mailing envelopes, a two-page typed appreciation by Ray Bradbury (likely transcribed from a previous source) and Emil Petaja's *Bokanalia* Memorial Portfolio.

The letters are in generally fine condition, having been preserved by Jack Cordes in a three-ring binder for decades. An intimate archive, testament to a wonderful and obvious friendship between Bok and Jack Cordes, two of science fiction's first fans. *From the collection of first fan, Jack Cordes.*

Estimate: $800-up
Starting Bid: $400

Bradbury's First Collection, Signed by Him in 1948

36160 **Ray Bradbury.** *Dark Carnival.* Sauk City: Arkham House, 1947. First edition. **Signed and dated, "Ray Bradbury / January 6, 1948"** on the front free endpaper. Octavo. 313 pages. Publisher's black cloth boards with gilt spine titles. Original pictorial dust jacket by George Barrows. Minor wear to boards, with lightly bumped corners. Dust jacket noticeably rubbed, and a bit tattered at the spine ends. A very good copy, with a contemporary Bradbury signature, of what Jack Chalker described as Bradbury's "first book and his most representative story collection. Similar but not identical to the later collection *The October Country*." *From the collection of first fan, Jack Cordes.*

Estimate: $1,500-up
Starting Bid: $750

Inscribed by Bradbury to Jack Cordes in the Year of Publication

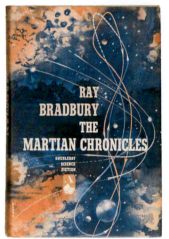

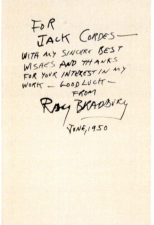

36161 **Ray Bradbury.** *The Martian Chronicles.* Garden City: Doubleday & Company, 1950. First edition. **Inscribed and signed by Bradbury in the year of publication to Jack Cordes, "For / Jack Cordes - / With my sincere best / wishes and thanks / for your interest in my / work - good luck - / from / Ray Bradbury / June, 1950"** on the front free endpaper. Octavo. 222 pages. Publisher's green cloth with maroon spine titles. Original first issue pictorial dust jacket. Minor shelf wear to boards. Spine cloth and dust jacket spine a bit sunned. Minimal wear to the spine ends. All in all, an excellent copy with a wonderful inscription. *From the collection of first fan, Jack Cordes.*

Estimate: $1,500-up
Starting Bid: $750

An Early Clarke Masterpiece

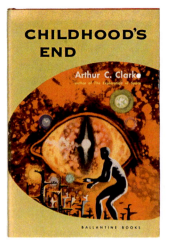

36162 **Arthur C. Clarke.** *Childhood's End.* New York: Ballantine, [1953]. First edition, first printing. Octavo. 214 pages. Publisher's red cloth with black spine titles. Original pictorial dust jacket. Modest rubbing to cloth extremities. Jacket spine sunned. Panels lightly toned. Short splits along the spine folds and flap folds of the dust jacket. Very good. *From the collection of first fan, Jack Cordes.*

Estimate: $1,500-up
Starting Bid: $750

First Edition, First Printing of Clarke's Second Story Collection

36163 **Arthur C. Clarke.** *Reach for Tomorrow.* New York: Ballantine Books, [1956]. First edition, first printing. Twelvemo. 166 pages. Publisher's red cloth with blue spine titles. Original pictorial dust jacket. Uniform toning to the text, as usual. Minor toning to the jacket. A near fine copy of a rare Clarke title. *From the collection of first fan, Jack Cordes.*

Estimate: $1,500-up
Starting Bid: $750

NOT an Ex-Library Copy, and Inscribed from Farmer to His Friend, Jack Cordes as a Wedding Present

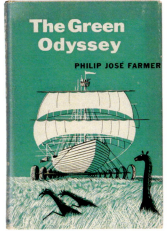

36164   **Philip Jose Farmer.** *The Green Odyssey.* New York: Ballantine Books, [1957]. First edition, first printing. **With a delightful inscription signed by the author to friend and fellow Peoria resident and first fan, Jack Cordes on the verso of the dedication leaf, as follows: "Jack, / I know you'll have / a pleasant voyage on your / green odyssey through the / matrimonial sea, because / you'll not be wanting to escape / your own personal Amra. / Philip Jose Farmer."** Octavo. [vi], 152 pages. Publisher's tan-gray cloth with green spine titles. Original pictorial dust jacket. Minor wear to extremities. Light rubbing to the dust jacket, with a noticeably sunned spine. Short closed tear to top edge of front panel of the jacket. Very minor loss to spine ends and flap fold ends. Overall, a near fine copy. Not an ex-library copy or book club, as usually found. *From the collection of first fan, Jack Cordes.*

Estimate: $2,000-up
Starting Bid: $1,000

Inscribed from Farmer to His Friend, Jack Cordes

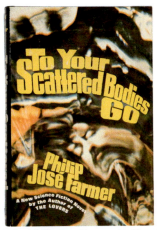

36165   **Philip Jose Farmer.** *To Your Scattered Bodies Go.* New York: G. P. Putnam's Sons, [1971]. First edition, first printing. **With a warm and lengthy inscription signed from Farmer, reading: "For Jack Cordes, who puts / it all together, from / Philip Jose Farmer, / whose body may not be / scattered but is certainly / spreading & whose mind / is scattered & maybe / even shattered but / what the hell as long / as the Cutty Sark / holds out?"** on the front free endpaper. Octavo. 221 pages plus Postscript. Publisher's black cloth with gilt spine titles. Original pictorial dust jacket. Minor rubbing to the jacket, with a small nick at the spine head and a small stain at the spine tail, and light dust-soiling, else a near fine copy. *From the collection of first fan, Jack Cordes.*

Estimate: $1,500-up
Starting Bid: $750

Rare Signed Subscriber's Copy

36166   **L. Ron Hubbard.** *Slaves of Sleep.* Chicago: Shasta Publishers, 1948. First edition. **One of 250 subscriber's copies signed by Hubbard** on the front free endpaper. Twelvemo. [x], 206, [2, About the Author leaf] pages. Publisher's gray buckram with gilt spine titles. Original pictorial dust jacket by Hannes Bok. Minor abrasion and small bump to the front board. Light soiling to boards. Mild rubbing to corners. Minor toning to the spine and edges of the dust jacket. Very small abraded area near the spine tail. A few tiny closed tears to the jacket edges. Overall, a bright copy in very good condition. *From the collection of first fan, Jack Cordes.*

Estimate: $1,500-up
Starting Bid: $750

One of 500 Deluxe Limited Edition Copies
Signed by King and Whelan

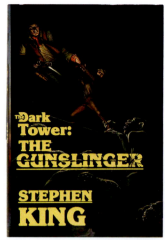

36167 **Stephen King.** *The Dark Tower: The Gunslinger.* [West Kingston, Rhode Island]: Donald M. Grant Publisher, Inc., [1982]. First edition, **number 196 of 500 deluxe limited edition copies signed by Stephen King and Michael Whelan** on the limitation page. Octavo. 224 pages. Publisher's luxurious beige cloth with brown titles. Original pictorial dust jacket. Pictorial endpapers. Housed in the original olive cloth slipcase. Light rubbing to the jacket, with mild sunning to the spine. Minor crease to front flap of dust jacket. Soiling to slipcase. A near fine copy of an exceedingly scarce King title. *From the collection of first fan, Jack Cordes.*

Estimate: $1,500-up
Starting Bid: $750

The First Arkham House Book

36168 **H. P. Lovecraft.** *The Outsider and Others.* Collected by August Derleth and Donald Wandrei. Sauk City: Arkham House, 1939. First edition, one of only 1,200 copies. Octavo. xiv, 553 pages. Publisher's black cloth with gilt spine titles. Original pictorial dust jacket designed by Virgil Finlay. Minor soiling and edge wear to the boards. A somewhat tattered dust jacket, with creasing and some areas of loss along the folds and the fold ends. Small tape reinforcements to the verso of the dust jacket. Flap folds a bit off-center. Overall, a very good book in a somewhat worn dust jack-

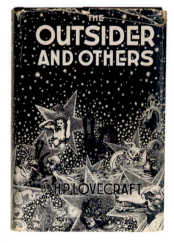

et. Barron, *Horror Literature,* 3-132. Bleiler. *The Guide to Supernatural Fiction,* 1040. *From the collection of first fan, Jack Cordes.*

Estimate: $1,500-up
Starting Bid: $750

End of Session One

SESSION TWO

Heritage Live!™, Internet, Fax, and Mail Only Session
Wednesday, February 8, 2012 | 4:00PM CT | Dallas, Texas | Lots 36139 - 36685

To view full descriptions, enlargeable images and bid online, visit HA.com/6064

SPECIAL INTERNET BIDDING FEATURE

Online proxy bidding ends at HA.com two hours prior to the opening of the live auction. Check the Time Remaining on individual lots for details. After Internet proxy bidding closes, live bidding will take place through Heritage Live™, our bidding software that lets you bid live during the actual auction. Your secret maximum will compete against those bids, and win all ties. To maximize your chances of winning, enter realistic secret maximum bids before live bidding begins. (Important note: Due to software and Internet latency, bids placed through Live Internet Bidding may not register in time and those bidders could lose lots they would otherwise have won, so be sure to place your proxy bids in advance.)

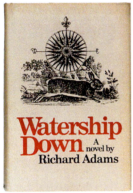

36169   Richard Adams. Watership Down. New York: Macmillan Publishing Co., Inc., [1972]. First edition, first printing. **With a signed card inscribed and signed by Adams** affixed to the front free endpaper. Octavo. [xii], 430 pages. Publisher's light brown cloth over tan paper boards with gilt titles. Original pictorial dust jacket. Light soiling and some biopredation to the dust jacket at the top of the panels and at the spine tail. Minor sunning to spine. Overall, a very good copy. *From the collection of first fan, Jack Cordes.*
Est.: $400-up
Start Bid: $200

36170   [Original Drawing]. Charles Addams. *Favorite Haunts.* New York: Simon and Schuster,

[1976]. Book club edition. **Signed and inscribed by Addams to Jack Cordes and with an original full page illustration.** Quarto. 96 pages. Publisher's binding and dust jacket. Minor edge wear and bumping. Very good. *From the collection of first fan, Jack Cordes.*
Est.: $600-up
Start Bid: $300

36171   Isaac Asimov. *Foundation.* New York: Gnome Press Publishers, [1951]. First edition, first issue (Currey priority A binding). Octavo. 255 pages. Publisher's dark blue cloth with red titles. Original first issue dust jacket with three titles advertised on the rear panel and two on the rear flap. Minor soiling to the spine cloth. Bumped corners. Minor wear, dust-soiling, and rubbing to the dust jacket. Spine a touch sunned. Spine ends and flap fold ends a bit wrinkled. A few tiny dampstains to the verso of the jacket. Verso of spine stained, but unobtrusive. Very good. *From the collection of first fan, Jack Cordes.*
Est.: $800-up
Start Bid: $400

36172   Isaac Asimov. *Foundation and Empire.* New York: Gnome Press Publishers, [1952]. First edition, first state (Currey binding A). Octavo. 247 pages. Publisher's red cloth with black titles, with the publisher's imprint on the spine measuring 2.2 cm. First state dust jacket designed by Edd Cartier. Noticeable rubbing and some minor chipping to the dust jacket. Spine sunned. A very good copy. *From the collection of first fan, Jack Cordes.*
Est.: $600-up
Start Bid: $300

36173   Isaac Asimov. *I, Robot.* New York: Gnome Press, Inc. Publishers, [1950]. First edition. Octavo. 253 pages. Publisher's red

cloth with black titles. Original pictorial dust jacket by Edd Cartier. Moderate rubbing to the dust jacket. Spine sunned to gray. Minor creasing at the spine ends. Very good. *From the collection of first fan, Jack Cordes.*
Est.: $400-up
Start Bid: $200

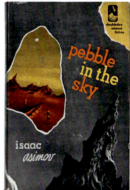

36174   Isaac Asimov. *Pebble in the Sky.* Garden City: Doubleday & Company, 1950. First edition. Octavo. 223 pages. Publisher's tan cloth with orange spine titles. Original pictorial dust jacket. Light rubbing and dust-soiling to the jacket. Minor chipping and sunning to the spine. Near fine. *From the collection of first fan, Jack Cordes.*
Est.: $600-up
Start Bid: $300

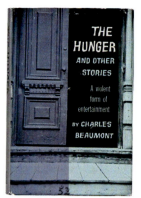

36175   Charles Beaumont. *The Hunger and Other Stories.* New York: Putnam, [1957]. First edition, first printing. **Inscribed and signed by the author, "10/13/65 / For Jack Cordes, / with best wishes - / Chuck Beaumont"** on the front free endpaper. Octavo. 234 pages. Publisher's gray buckram with spine titles in white and baby blue. Original pictorial dust jacket. Minor wear to board edges and corners. Mild bump to top corner of text. Minor tape(?) abrasion to the inscription. Light rubbing and tiny areas of loss to the spine and flap fold ends of the dust jacket. Spine lightly sunned. One small one-inch by one-inch closed abrasion to the rear panel of the jacket, flattened out. Overall, a very good copy of a book rarely found signed. Beaumont died of a mysterious illness at the early age of 38 just over two years after this inscription was penned. *From the collection of first fan, Jack Cordes.*

Est.: $600-up
Start Bid: $300

36176   Hannes Bok. *The Sorcerer's Ship.* Extracted from the December 1942 issue of *Unknown Worlds.* Paginated 9-70. Custom black pebbled cloth boards by the Peoria Book Bindery with gilt titles to the spine and front board. **With a wonderful, original colored-pencil drawing by Bok on the front free endpaper, inscribed to Jack Cordes as follows: "A Youuk[?] for / Jack Cordes / who liked this story / enough to have

it put / in hard covers - / Hannes Bok / 1953."** Text uniformly toned, as usual. Fine condition. *From the collection of first fan, Jack Cordes.*

Est.: $600-up
Start Bid: $300

36177   Ray Bradbury. *Fahrenheit 451.* New York: The Limited Editions Club, 1982. First edition, **number 1,773 of 2,000 copies signed by the author and the illustrator** on the limitation page. Quarto. xx, 152 pages. Illustrated by Joseph Mugnaini with one full-page original lithograph and three fold-out color plates. Hand-bound in aluminum over boards. Silkscreened in red, white and black. All page edges silvered. Housed in the original silver paper slipcase lettered in black. Minor edge wear. Some minor nail impressions to the boards. Light shelf wear to the slipcase. Near fine. Limited Edition Club's "Monthly Letter" laid in. *From the collection of first fan, Jack Cordes.*

Est.: $300-up
Start Bid: $150

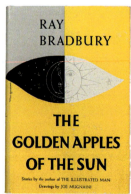

36178   Ray Bradbury. *The Golden Apples of the Sun.* Garden City: Doubleday & Company, Inc., 1953. First edition. **Inscribed by Bradbury, in the year of publication, "For / Jack Cordes - / With the good / wishes of / Ray Bradbury / March, 1953"** on the

front free endpaper. Octavo. 250 pages. Publisher's dark brown textured cloth with yellow stamping. Original pictorial dust jacket. Minor fading to the cloth edges. Light rubbing to jacket. Near fine. *From the collection of first fan, Jack Cordes.*

Est.: $300-up
Start Bid: $150

36179   Ray Bradbury. *The Halloween Tree.* New York: Alfred A. Knopf, 1972. First edition. **Signed by the author** on a label affixed to the front pastedown. Octavo. 145 pages. Illustrated by Joseph Mugnaini. Publisher's black cloth with orange and silver stamping. Original pictorial dust jacket. Minor rubbing to the jacket, else a fine copy. *From the collection of first fan, Jack Cordes.*

Est.: $300-up
Start Bid: $150

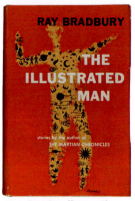

36180   Ray Bradbury. *The Illustrated Man.* Garden City: Doubleday & Company, Inc., 1951. First edition. Octavo. 252 pages. Publisher's light brown cloth with dark brown spine titles. Original pictorial dust jacket. A somewhat brittle dust jacket, split almost entirely along the front flap fold and about halfway along the rear flap fold. Spine a bit sunned. Very good condition, otherwise. *From the collection of first fan, Jack Cordes.*

Est.: $300-up
Start Bid: $150

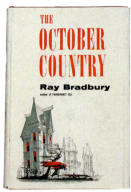

36181   Ray Bradbury. *The October Country.* New York: Ballantine Books, [1955]. First edition, first state. Octavo. 306 pages. Illustrated by Joe Mugnaini. Publisher's red cloth covers with the spine lettered in black. Upside-down monogram on the spine signifying the first state. Original pictorial dust jacket. Minor edge wear to the boards. A few tiny areas of loss to the jacket edges. Spine sunned. Light rubbing to panels. Short split along the rear flap fold. Very good. *From the collection of first fan, Jack Cordes.*

Est.: $300-up
Start Bid: $150

36182   Edgar Rice Burroughs. *Tarzan and the Lost Empire.* New York: Grosset & Dunlap Publishers, [1940]. Later edition. **Inscribed and signed by the author, "To Monte (last name?) / Merry Christmas / Edgar Rice Burroughs"** on the front free endpaper. Octavo. 313 pages plus one-page ad at rear. Publisher's red cloth with black titles. Top edge stained green. Original pictorial dust jacket. Spine cocked. Moderate edge wear to the jacket, with some minor loss at the spine ends and flap fold ends. Flap folds and panels rubbed. Very good. *From the collection of first fan, Jack Cordes.*

Est.: $300-up
Start Bid: $150

36183   John W. Campbell, Jr. *The Black Star Passes.* Reading: Fantasy Press, [1953]. First edition, **number 153 of 500 copies signed by Campbell** on the limitation page. Publisher's purple cloth with gilt spine titles. Original pictorial dust jacket. Minor chipping at the spine head. Light rubbing to jacket. A near fine copy. *From the collection of first fan, Jack Cordes.*

Est.: $300-up
Start Bid: $150

36184   John W. Campbell, Jr. *The Moon Is Hell!* Reading: Fantasy Press, [1951]. First edition, **limited to 500 numbered copies of which this is number 208. Signed by Campbell.** Octavo. 256 pages. Publisher's binding and dust jacket. Overall near fine with some light rubbing. *From the collection of first fan, Jack Cordes.*

Est.: $300-up
Start Bid: $150

36185   John W. Campbell, Jr. *Who Goes There? Seven Tales of Science-Fiction.* Chicago: Shasta Publishers, 1948. First edition, **one of 200 subscriber's copies signed by Campbell** on the front flyleaf. Octavo. 230 pages. Publisher's blue cloth with gilt spine titles. Original pictorial dust jacket by Hannes Bok. Minor edge wear to the jacket, with minimal loss at the spine ends and corners. Spine sunned. A near fine copy. *From the collection of first fan, Jack Cordes.*

Est.: $500-up
Start Bid: $250

36186   Arthur C. Clarke. *Childhood's End.* London: Sidgwick and Jackson, [1954]. First British edition. **Inscribed and signed by Clarke, "To Jack Cordes, / with all good wishes / from / Arthur C Clarke / 7 Apr '68"** on the front free endpaper. Octavo. 253 pages. Publisher's yellow cloth with black spine titles. Original pictorial dust jacket. Minor edge wear and dust-soiling to the boards. Light off-setting to the endpapers. Jacket noticeably wrinkled, with mild fraying at the spine ends. Minimal loss at the corners and one short closed tear to the bottom edge of the front panel. A very good copy. *From the collection of first fan, Jack Cordes.*

Est.: $300-up
Start Bid: $150

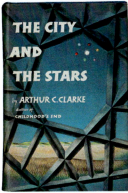

36187   Arthur C. Clarke. *The City and the Stars.* New York: Harcourt, Brace and Company, [1956]. First edition. Octavo. viii, 310 pages. Publisher's blue marbled paper boards with silver spine titles and colored star designs. Original pictorial dust jacket by George Salter. Minor dust-soiling to text edges. Jacket spine somewhat wrinkled and sunned. Two areas of black soiling to the rear jacket panel. Very good condition. *From the collection of first fan, Jack Cordes.*

Est.: $300-up
Start Bid: $150

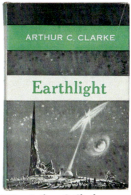

36188   Arthur C. Clarke. *Earthlight.* New York: Ballantine, [1955]. First edition. Octavo. [vi], 186 pages. Publisher's light brown cloth with blue spine titles. Original pictorial dust jacket. Minor wear to the jacket edges, with minimal wear to the spine ends and corners. Light rubbing and creasing. Sunned spine. Very good. *From the collection of first fan, Jack Cordes.*

Est.: $300-up
Start Bid: $150

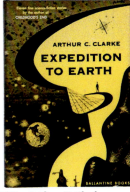

36189   Arthur C. Clarke. *Expedition to Earth.* New York: Ballantine Books, Inc., [1953]. First edition. Twelvemo. 165 pages. Publisher's black cloth with silver spine titles. Original pictorial dust jacket. Minor rubbing to the jacket. Light sunning to the jacket spine. Small bump to top edge of the front flap of the jacket. Overall, a near fine copy. A wondrous collection of eleven short stories with the first book appearance of "The Sentinel," the precursor to *2001: A Space Odyssey. From the collection of first fan, Jack Cordes.*

Est.: $300-up
Start Bid: $150

36190   Arthur C. Clarke. *Sands of Mars.* New York: Gnome Press, [1952]. First American edition. **Inscribed by Clarke, "To Miss Annette Funicello, / with good wishes from / Arthur C Clarke / Xmas 1961"** on a slip of paper tipped-in to the front free endpaper. Octavo. 216 pages. Publisher's gray cloth with red spine titles. Original pictorial dust jacket by Ric Binkley. Minor shelf wear to the boards. Bumped corners. Glue discoloration to the paper holding the inscription. Noticeable wear to the jacket, with two square tape stains to the spine and each flap. Two long tears to the rear flap and panel inexpertly repaired with paper tape to the verso. Spine sunned. About very good condition. *From the collection of first fan, Jack Cordes.*

Est.: $300-up
Start Bid: $150

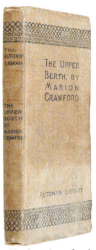

36191   Marion Crawford. *The Upper Berth.* London: T. Fisher Unwin, 1894. First edition. Tall octavo. [1-4], 5-189, [2, printer's imprint and advertisement leaf] pages. Publisher's oatmeal linen cloth with titles and decorations in black. Moderate soiling and bumping to boards. Spine cocked. Light, scattered foxing, mostly to the text edges. Missing the front free endpaper. Otherwise, very good. Volume one of Unwin's Autonym Library. Bleiler, page 52. *From the collection of first fan, Jack Cordes.*

Est.: $300-up
Start Bid: $150

36192   L. Sprague de Camp. *The Wheels of If and Other Science-Fiction.* Chicago: Shasta Publishers, 1948. First edition, first printing. **Signed by de Camp** on front free endpaper. Publisher's binding and dust jacket. Wrap-around dust jacket illustrated by Hannes Bok. Minor rubbing and toning to extremities. Very good. *From the collection of first fan, Jack Cordes.*

Est.: $400-up
Start Bid: $200

36193   Lester del Rey. *Marooned on Mars.* Philadelphia: Winston, [1952]. First edition, first printing. **Inscribed and signed by del Rey to Jack Cordes** on half-title page. Illustrated endpapers. Publisher's binding and dust jacket. Dust jacket illustration by Paul Orban. Minor rubbing and toning, with bumping to extremities. Very good. *From the collection of first fan, Jack Cordes.*

Est.: $400-up
Start Bid: $200

36194   August Derleth. *Something Near.* Sauk City: Arkham House, 1945. First edition, first printing. **Inscribed and signed by Derleth, "For Jack Cordes / a book of ghosts / Spectrally, / August Derleth"** on the front free endpaper. Twelvemo. 274 pages. Publisher's black cloth with gilt spine titles. Original pictorial dust jacket by Ronald Clyne. Minimal edge wear to the book and jacket. Light toning to the jacket edges and spine. Otherwise, a near fine copy. *From the collection of first fan, Jack Cordes.*

Est.: $300-up
Start Bid: $150

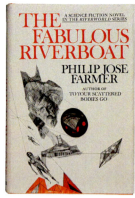

36195   Philip Jose Farmer. *The Fabulous Riverboat.* New York: Putnam, [1971]. First edition, first printing. **Inscribed and signed by Farmer to his friend and fellow Peoria resident, Jack Cordes, "For Jack, / No. 2X2Z580 / from / Philip Jose Farmer"** on the front free endpaper. Octavo. 253 pages. Publisher's orange buckram with black spine titles. Original pictorial dust jacket. Minor rubbing to the jacket, with one short closed tear to the top edge of the rear panel. Dustsoiling to the spine. Overall, a near fine copy. *From the collection of first fan, Jack Cordes.*

Est.: $400-up
Start Bid: $200

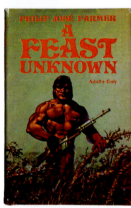

36196   Philip Jose Farmer. *A Feast Unknown.* [Kansas City]: Fokker D-LXIX Press, [1975]. First hardcover edition, first printing. **Inscribed by Farmer to Jack Cordes and signed by Richard Corben, illustrator.** Publisher's binding and dust jacket. Near fine. *From the collection of first fan, Jack Cordes.*

Est.: $300-up
Start Bid: $150

36197   Philip Jose Farmer. Two Inscribed and Signed First Editions of *Flesh,* including: *Flesh.* Garden City: Doubleday & Company, Inc., 1968. First American edition. Octavo. 212 pages. Publisher's yellow cloth with silver spine titles. Original pictorial dust jacket. [and:] *Flesh.* [London]: Rapp & Whiting, [1969]. First British edition. Octavo. 212 pages. Publisher's maroon cloth with silver spine titles. Original pictorial dust jacket. **Both copies inscribed and signed by the author, "To Jack Cordes from Philip Jose Farmer & Bette Farmer,"** with the latter name in the author's wife's hand. Noticeable rubbing and some edge loss to the jackets. Both in very good condition. *From the collection of first fan, Jack Cordes.*

Est.: $300-up
Start Bid: $150

36198   Philip Jose Farmer. Group of Two Signed Subterranean Press First Editions, including: *Pearls from Peoria.* 2006. First trade edition, first printing. **Signed and inscribed by Farmer to Jack Cordes.** [and:] *Up from the Bottomless Pit.* 2007. First edition, **limited to 250 copies. Signed and additionally inscribed by Farmer to Cordes.** [Burton]: Subterranean Press. Two octavo volumes. Publisher's binding and dust jackets. Fine. *From the collection of first fan, Jack Cordes.*

Est.: $300-up
Start Bid: $150

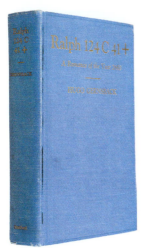

36199 Hugo Gernsback. *Ralph 124 C 41 +, A Romance of the Year 2660.* Boston: The Stratford Company, 1925. First edition. Octavo. 293 pages. Frontispiece plus ten black and white plates illustrated by Frank R. Paul. Publisher's blue cloth with gilt lettering to front cover and spine (Currey's binding state A, with "Stratford" at base of spine measuring 1.5 cm). Spine somewhat darkened. Ink stains in the joints. A couple of small smudges to the boards. Lightly bumped and rubbed corners and spine ends. Minor paper abrasion to the front free endpaper. Short marginal tear to page 239. Very good. *From the collection of first fan, Jack Cordes.*

Est.: $300-up
Start Bid: $150

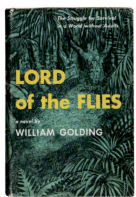

36200 William Golding. *Lord of the Flies.* New York: Coward-McCann, Inc., [1955]. First American edition. Octavo. [x], 243, [2, flyleaf] pages. Publisher's tan buckram over textured green cloth boards with green spine titles. Original pictorial dust jacket. Some fading to cloth. Spine slightly cocked. Very minor loss at jacket corners and along the rear flap fold. Spine ends a bit worn. Lightly sunned spine. Very good condition. *From the collection of first fan, Jack Cordes.*

Est.: $300-up
Start Bid: $150

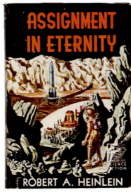

36201 Robert A. Heinlein. *Assignment in Eternity.* Reading, Pennsylvania: Fantasy Press, [1953]. First edition. **Number 140 of 500 numbered copies inscribed and signed by Heinlein to Jack Cordes** on the limitation page. Publisher's brick red cloth with gilt spine titles. Original pictorial dust jacket illustrated by Ric Binkley. Light fading to spine cloth. Minimal loss at spine head and one corner. Some rubbing, most noticeable at the top of the rear panel. Near fine. *From the collection of first fan, Jack Cordes.*

Est.: $600-up
Start Bid: $300

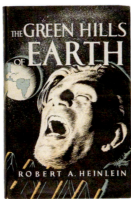

36202 Robert A. Heinlein. *The Green Hills of Earth.* Chicago: Shasta Publishers, [1951]. First edition. **One of 250 subscriber's copies signed by Heinlein** on the half-title page. Octavo. 256 pages. Publisher's black cloth over green buckram boards. Original pictorial dust jacket by Hubert Rogers. Minor shelf wear to the edges and corners of the book and jacket. Some rubbing to the rear panel of the jacket. Mild sunning to the jacket spine and edges. A near fine copy. *From the collection of first fan, Jack Cordes.*

Est.: $600-up
Start Bid: $300

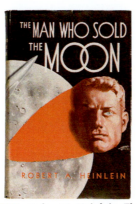

36203 Robert A. Heinlein. *The Man Who Sold the Moon.* Chicago: Shasta Publishers, [1950]. First edition. **One of 250 subscriber's copies signed by Heinlein** on a tipped-in front flyleaf. Octavo. 288 pages. Publisher's black cloth over tan buckram with gilt spine titles. Original pictorial dust jacket by Hubert Rogers. Minor shelf wear to the boards. Small bump to the bottom edges of the boards. Minor wear to the spine ends and corners of the jacket. A few tiny closed tears along the top and bottom edges of the jacket. Light rubbing to the rear panel. Spine a bit sunned. A very good copy. *From the collection of first fan, Jack Cordes.*

Est.: $600-up
Start Bid: $300

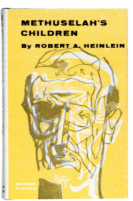

36204 Robert A. Heinlein. *Methuselah's Children.* Hicksville, New York: Gnome Press, [1958]. First edition, first state (Currey priority A). Octavo. 188 pages. Publisher's black cloth with red spine titles. Original first state dust jacket. Moderate edge wear to the boards. Minor rubbing to the jacket. Jacket spine somewhat browned, with a small abrasion affecting only the "N" in Heinlein's name. Text uniformly toned, as usual. Very good. *From the collection of first fan, Jack Cordes.*

Est.: $300-up
Start Bid: $150

36205 Robert A. Heinlein. *Revolt in 2100.* Chicago, Shasta Publishers, [1953]. First edition, first printing, one of approximately 200 subscriber's copies **signed by the author** on an inserted flyleaf. Octavo. 317 pages. Publisher's black cloth over red boards with gilt spine titles. Original pictorial dust jacket. Minimal wear to board edges. Light rubbing to the jacket. Sunned spine. A near fine copy. *From the collection of first fan, Jack Cordes.*

Est.: $400-up
Start Bid: $200

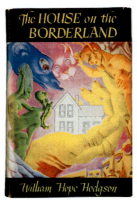

36206 William Hope Hodgson. *The House on the Borderland, and Other Novels.* Sauk City: Arkham House, 1946. First omnibus edition, one of 3,024 copies printed. Octavo. xi, 639 pages. Publisher's black cloth with gilt titles. Original pictorial dust jacket by Hannes Bok. Minor shelf wear to the boards, with lightly bumped corners. Mild dust-soiling to the jacket and some toning to the edges and spine. A one-and-a-half inch split to the front spine fold near the spine head, light chipping to the jacket edges, with minimal loss at the corners. Overall, a very good copy. *From the collection of first fan, Jack Cordes.*

Est.: $300-up
Start Bid: $150

36207   Robert E. Howard.
Skull-Face and Others. Sauk City: Arkham House, 1946. First edition. Publisher's black cloth stamped in gilt on the spine. Original pictorial dust jacket by Hannes Bok. Minor shelf wear to the boards. Bottom corners bumped. Light toning and rubbing to the jacket, with minor sunning to the spine and a few minor nicks to the jacket edges. Minimal loss at the spine ends of the jacket. A near fine copy. *From the collection of first fan, Jack Cordes.*

Est.: $600-up
Start Bid: $300

36208   Robert E. Howard. The Complete Eleven-Volume Deluxe Conan Series, including: ***The People of the Black Circle.*** 1974. [and:] ***Red Nails.*** 1975. [and:] ***The Tower of the Elephant.*** 1975. [and:] ***A Witch Shall Be Born.*** 1975. [and:] ***The Devil in Iron.*** 1976. [and:] ***Rogues in the House.*** 1976. [and:] ***Queen of the Black Coast.*** 1978. [and:] ***Black Colossus.*** 1979. [and:] ***Jewels of Gwahlur.*** 1979. [and:] ***The Pool of the Black One.*** 1986. [and:] ***The Hour of the Dragon.*** 1989. All titles published by Donald M. Grant in West Kingston, Rhode Island. Publisher's bindings and original dust jackets. All with sunned spines, else near fine in dust jackets. *From the collection of first fan, Jack Cordes.*

Est.: $300-up
Start Bid: $150

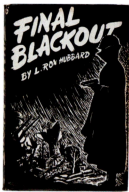

36209   L. Ron Hubbard. *Final Blackout.* Providence: Hadley Publishing, [1948]. First edition, one of 1000 copies. **Inscribed and signed by the author, "With Best Wishes / L Ron Hubbard / Hollywood 1948"** on the front free endpaper. Octavo. 154 pages. Illustrations by Halladay. Publisher's black pebbled cloth with gilt spine titles. Original pictorial dust jacket. Minor shelf wear to the book and jacket. Spine ends a bit frayed. Minor sunning to the jacket spine. Light rubbing and toning to the jacket. A near fine copy, rarely encountered with the author's signature. *From the collection of first fan, Jack Cordes.*

Est.: $600-up
Start Bid: $300

36210   Stephen King and Peter Straub. *Black House.* Hampton Falls: Donald M. Grant, 2002. First edition, **limited to 1520 copies of which this is number 240. Signed by King, Straub, and Rick Berry [illustrator].** Publisher's black cloth with silver titles. Original matching clamshell box. Box with modest rubbing. Fine. *From the collection of first fan, Jack Cordes.*

Est.: $300-up
Start Bid: $150

36211   Stephen King. *Christine.* West Kingston, Rhode Island: Donald M. Grant, Publisher Inc., [1983]. First edition, **number 466 of 1,000 limited edition copies signed by the author and illustrator, Stephen Gervais** on the limitation page. Octavo. 544 pages. Publisher's red cloth with silver titles and decoration on the spine and front board. Original pictorial dust jacket. Housed in the original red cloth slipcase. Tiny chip at the spine tail, otherwise a fine copy. *From the collection of first fan, Jack Cordes.*

Est.: $600-up
Start Bid: $300

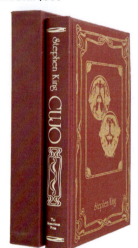

36212   Stephen King. *Cujo.* New York: The Mysterious Press, 1981. First edition, **number 126 of 750 limited edition copies signed by the author** on the limitation page. Octavo. 319 pages. Publisher's maroon cloth with titles in gilt on the spine and extensive decoration in gilt on the front and rear boards. Housed in the publisher's clear plastic dust jacket and matching maroon cloth slipcase. Small crease to plastic dust jacket at one corner, else an exceptional copy in fine condition. *From the collection of first fan, Jack Cordes.*

Est.: $600-up
Start Bid: $300

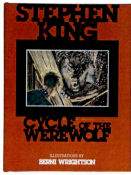

36213   [Bernie Wrightson, illustrator]. Stephen King. *Cycle of the Werewolf.* [Westland]: Land of Enchantment, [1983]. First edition, **limited to 350 copies of which this is number 239. Signed by King and Wrightson on limitation page.** Publisher's binding, dust jacket, and slipcase. Modest rubbing to extremities with some sunning along spine. Near fine. *From the collection of first fan, Jack Cordes.*

Est.: $800-up
Start Bid: $400

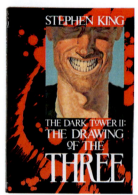

36214   Stephen King. *The Dark Tower II: The Drawing of the Three.* [West Kingston, Rhode Island]: Donald M. Grant, Publisher, Inc., [1987]. First edition, **number 369 of 850 deluxe, limited edition copies signed by King and illustrator Phil Hale** on the limitation page. Octavo. 400 pages. First edition. Publisher's beige cloth with title in copper. Original pictorial dust jacket. Housed in the original gray cloth slipcase. A fine copy. *From the collection of first fan, Jack Cordes.*

Est.: $600-up
Start Bid: $300

36215 Stephen King. *The Dark Tower III: The Waste Lands*. Hampton Falls, New Hampshire: Donald M. Grant Publisher, Inc., [1991]. First edition, **number 369 of 1,250 limited edition copies signed by King and the illustrator, Ned Dameron** on the limitation page. Octavo. 511 pages. Publisher's sumptuous white cloth with copper titles on the spine and front board. Original pictorial dust jacket and blue cloth slipcase. Fine condition. *From the collection of first fan, Jack Cordes.*

Est.: $600-up
Start Bid: $300

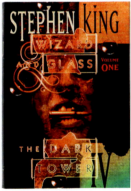

36216 Stephen King. *The Dark Tower IV: Wizard and Glass*. Hampton Falls, New Hampshire: Donald M. Grant, Publisher, Inc., [1997]. First edition, **number 369 of 1,250 limited edition copies signed by King and illustrator Dave McKean** on the limitation page. Two octavo volumes. 408; 384 pages. Publisher's white cloth with copper titles and designs. Original pictorial dust jackets. Housed together in the publisher's blue cloth slipcase. Minor rubbing to the jacket spines, else fine condition. *From the collection of first fan, Jack Cordes.*

Est.: $600-up
Start Bid: $300

36217 Stephen King. *The Dark Tower VI: Song of Susannah*. Hampton Falls: Donald M. Grant, 2004. First edition, **limited to 1400 copies of which this is number 369. Signed by King and Darrel Anderson, illustrator.** Publisher's binding, dust jacket, and slipcase. Fine. *From the collection of first fan, Jack Cordes.*

Est.: $300-up
Start Bid: $150

36218 Stephen King. *The Dark Tower VII: The Dark Tower*. Hampton Falls: Donald M. Grant, 2004. First edition, **limited to 1,500 numbered sets of which this is 369. Signed by King and Michael Whelan, illustrator.** Two octavo volumes. 432; 443 pages. Publisher's binding, dust jackets, and slipcase. Fine. *From the collection of first fan, Jack Cordes.*

Est.: $300-up
Start Bid: $150

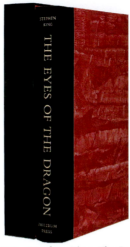

36219 Stephen King. *The Eyes of the Dragon*. Bangor: Philtrum Press, 1984. First edition, **number 698 of 1,000 copies signed by King** on the limitation page. Folio. 314, [2, flyleaf], [2, limitation] pages. Publisher's black cloth over red marbled boards. Housed in the publisher's matching slipcase. No dust jacket, as issued. Minimal threading to the spine cloth. Light rubbing to the corners, else a near fine copy. *From the collection of first fan, Jack Cordes.*

Est.: $300-up
Start Bid: $150

36220 Stephen King. *Firestarter*. Huntington Woods, Michigan: Phantasia Press, 1980. First edition, **number 99 of 725 limited edition copies signed by King** on the limitation page. Octavo. 428 pages. Publisher's blue cloth with silver titles. Original pictorial dust jacket by Michael Whelan. Minor rubbing to dust jacket. Fine condition. *From the collection of first fan, Jack Cordes.*

Est.: $600-up
Start Bid: $300

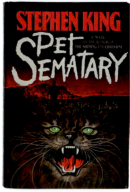

36221 Stephen King. *Pet Sematary*. Garden City: Doubleday & Company, Inc., 1983. First edition. **Inscribed and signed by King in the year of publication to Jack Cordes, "For Jack - / With all best wishes - Thanks / for the good letter! / Stephen King / 12/2/83"** on the title page. Octavo. [x], 374 pages. Publisher's black cloth with gilt titles. Original pictorial dust jacket. Minor shelf wear to the book and jacket. A near fine copy. *From the collection of first fan, Jack Cordes.*

Est.: $600-up
Start Bid: $300

36222 Stephen King. *Skeleton Crew*. Santa Cruz: Scream Press, 1985. First edition, **limited to 1000 copies of which this is number 71, signed by King and Potter.** Quarto. 545 pages. Illustrated by J. K. Potter. Publisher's binding, dust jacket, and slipcase. Fine. *From the collection of first fan, Jack Cordes.*

Est.: $600-up
Start Bid: $300

36223 **Stephen King and Peter Straub.** *The Talisman.* West Kingston and Boston: Donald M. Grant Publisher, Incorporated, 1984. First edition, **number 240 of 1,200 special illustrated copies signed by the authors** on the limitation page. Two octavo volumes. 463; 334 pages. Eleven color plates. Publisher's cream cloth with stamped decoration in blind, gilt rules and titles, with pictorial paper inlays on the front boards. Housed in the publisher's matching cloth slipcase. Minor dust-staining to the slipcase. Fine condition. *From the collection of first fan, Jack Cordes.*

Est.: $600-up
Start Bid: $300

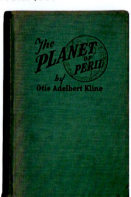

36224 **Otis Adelbert Kline.** *The Planet of Peril.* [Chicago]: A. C. McClurg & Co., 1929. First edition. **Inscribed and signed by the author to Don Moore, the future editor of** *Argosy* **magazine, "To / Don Moore / with the compliments / and sincere good wishes / of / Otis Adelbert Kline"** on the front free endpaper. Octavo. [x], 358 pages. Publisher's green cloth with black titles. Light soiling to the boards. Minor fraying of the cloth at the spine ends and corners. Tape repair and horizontal cloth gouge at the spine head. Binding cracked at page 198. Overall, an about very good copy of a title rarely found signed. *From the collection of first fan, Jack Cordes.*

Est.: $300-up
Start Bid: $150

36225 **Nigel Kneale.** *The Year of the Sex Olympics and Other TV Plays.* [London]: Ferret Fantasy Ltd., 1976. First edition, **number 73 of 100 specially-bound copies signed by the author** on the limitation page. Octavo. 144 pages. Publisher's black buckram with gilt spine titles. Original printed dust jacket. Minimal biopredation to the jacket edges. Near fine. *From the collection of first fan, Jack Cordes.*

Est.: $300-up
Start Bid: $150

36226 **Murray Leinster.** *Sidewise in Time.* Chicago: Shasta Publishers, 1950. First edition, **signed by the author both as Jenkins and Leinster** on the front free endpaper. Octavo. 211 pages. Publisher's red cloth with silver spine titles. Original pictorial dust jacket by Hannes Bok. Minor edge wear to the book and jacket. Two tiny closed tears to the jacket edges. Light toning to the jacket edges and spine. Very minor bumping to the corners. Otherwise, a near fine copy. *From the collection of first fan, Jack Cordes.*

Est.: $300-up
Start Bid: $150

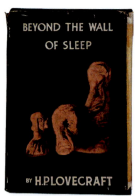

36227 **H. P. Lovecraft.** *Beyond the Wall of Sleep.* Sauk City: Arkham House, 1943. First edition. Octavo. [xxx], 458, [2, colophon] pages. Publisher's black cloth with gilt spine titles. Original pictorial dust jacket. Noticeable wear and some soiling to the book cloth and dust jacket. Portion of spine head missing, affecting most or all of the words "Beyond the Wall." Minor loss at the corners. Creasing and short, closed tears to the jacket. One tiny puncture to the rear panel of the jacket. A few brown tape repairs to the front of the jacket. A good copy overall. *From the collection of first fan, Jack Cordes.*

Est.: $400-up
Start Bid: $200

36228 **[H. P. Lovecraft, Robert E. Howard, et al.].** *Fanciful Tales of Time and Space.* Oakman, Alabama: Shepherd & Wollheim, 1936. First edition. Octavo. 45 pages plus three pages of advertising. Original paper wrappers bound into custom black cloth boards with gilt titles to the spine and front board. Small abrasion to front wrapper. Text uniformly toned, as usual. Overall, a near fine copy. Contains Lovecraft's "The Nameless City" and Howard's "Solomon Kane's Homecoming" among

other stories by Derleth, Keller, and Wollheim. *From the collection of first fan, Jack Cordes.*

Est.: $300-up
Start Bid: $150

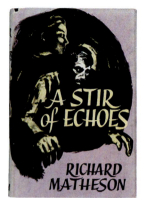

36229 **Richard Matheson.** *A Stir of Echoes.* London: Cassell & Company, Ltd., 1958. First British edition. **Inscribed and signed by Matheson, "To Jack Cordes, / with best wishes, / Richard Matheson"** on the front free endpaper. Small octavo. 220 pages. Publisher's black cloth with silver spine titles. Original pictorial dust jacket. News agent stamp to bottom of the front free endpaper. Some edge wear, rubbing and light soiling to the price-clipped jacket. Spine sunned. Two small chips at the spine ends. Very good. *From the collection of first fan, Jack Cordes.*

Est.: $300-up
Start Bid: $150

36230 **Talbot Mundy.** *Queen Cleopatra.* Indianapolis: The Bobbs-Merrill Company Publishers, [1929]. First edition, **number 144 of 265 special edition copies signed by the author** on the limitation page. Large octavo. [xvi], 426, [6, flyleaves] pages. Photographic frontispiece of the author. Publisher's black cloth over brown paper boards with paper title label affixed to the spine. Minor rubbing to the boards. Light soiling to the spine label. Top corner of the front free endpaper clipped. Short fore-edge marginal tears and slight wrinkling to pages 17-20. Very good. *From the collection of first fan, Jack Cordes.*

Est.: $300-up
Start Bid: $150

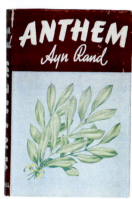

36231   Ayn Rand. *Anthem.* London: Cassell and Company, Limited, [1953]. Second edition. **Inscribed and signed by Rand, "To Jack Cordes - / - Cordially - / 12/4/67 Ayn Rand"** on the front free endpaper. Small octavo. 147 pages. Publisher's maroon cloth with gilt spine titles. Original pictorial dust jacket. Very light dustsoiling to cloth. Spine slightly cocked. Minor rubbing to the jacket, with very minimal loss at the spine ends. Very good. *From the collection of first fan, Jack Cordes.*

Est.: $300-up
Start Bid: $150

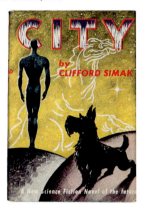

36232   Clifford D. Simak. *City.* [New York]: Gnome Press, [1952]. First edition. Octavo. 224 pages. Publisher's light green cloth with blue spine titles. Original pictorial dust jacket. Lightly rubbed corners. Rubbing and light soiling to dust jacket. Small chip at the spine tail. Two small frayed areas to top edge of jacket. Very good. *From the collection of first fan, Jack Cordes.*

Est.: $300-up
Start Bid: $150

36233   Clark Ashton Smith. *Lost Worlds.* Sauk City: Arkham House, 1944. First edition. Octavo. 419 pages. Publisher's black cloth with gilt spine titles. Original pictorial dust jacket. Minor wear to the board and jacket edges. Corners bumped. Some biopredation to the jacket, with minor loss to the spine and at the spine ends. Spine sunned. Very good. *From the collection of first fan, Jack Cordes.*

Est.: $300-up
Start Bid: $150

36234   Clark Ashton Smith. *Out of Space and Time.* Sauk City: Arkham House, 1942. First edition, one of 1,054 copies printed. Octavo. xii, 370 pages. Introduction by August Derleth and Donald Wandrei. Publisher's black cloth with gilt spine titles. Original pictorial dust jacket by Hannes Bok. Minor edge wear to the boards. Some biopredation to the text edges and dust jacket. Light soiling to the panels. and spine. Spine toned. Jack Cordes's Hannes Bok-designed bookplate to front free endpaper. A very good copy. *From the collection of first fan, Jack Cordes.*

Est.: $400-up
Start Bid: $200

36235   Edward E. Smith, Ph.D. Six Fantasy Press First Editions of the Lensman Series, Five of the Six Signed, Limited Editions Inscribed to Jack Cordes, including: *Triplanetary.* First trade edition (Currey priority B). Publisher's blue cloth with gilt spine titles. Original first edition dust jacket with *Triplanetary* in red on the front cover. [and:] *First Lensman.* Publisher's blue cloth with gilt spine titles. First issue dust jacket (Currey priority A) advertising four Smith titles on the rear panel. [and:] *Galactic Patrol.* Publisher's blue cloth with gilt spine titles (Currey priority A). [and:] *Grey Lensman.* Publisher's blue cloth with gilt spine titles. First issue dust jacket (Currey priority A) advertising three Smith Lensman titles on the rear panel. [and:] *Second Stage Lensman.* Publisher's blue cloth with gilt spine titles (Currey priority A). [and:] *Children of the Lens.* Publisher's blue cloth with gilt spine titles (Currey priority A). **All titles (except *Triplanetary*) are one of 500 numbered copies inscribed and signed by the author to Jack Cordes.** Reading: Fantasy Press, 1948-54. Original pictorial dust jackets. Minor rubbing, chipping, and biopredation to the jackets. Spines slightly sunned. Overall, a very good set. *From the collection of first fan, Jack Cordes.*

Est.: $600-up
Start Bid: $300

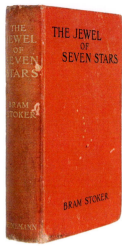

36236   Bram Stoker. *The Jewel of the Seven Stars.* London: William Heinemann, 1903. First edition. **With a signed card from Stoker to his theater colleague, Genevieve Ward, reading: "Genevieve Ward / from her old friend / Bram Stoker / 1903"** pasted to the front free endpaper. Octavo. [viii], 337 pages. Publisher's red cloth with black and gilt titles and a blind-stamped scarab design on each board, and the seven stars in gilt on the front cover only. Noticeable wear, soiling and abrading to the boards. Minor staining to text. Binding cracked in a few places. A good copy. Ward was a famous American-born soprano and actress in Europe, and must surely have met Stoker during his days at the Lyceum Theatre. Described by Richard Dalby, in his Stoker bibliography, as "Stoker's best supernatural novel after *Dracula.*" Dalby 14(a). *From the collection of first fan, Jack Cordes.*

Est.: $600-up
Start Bid: $300

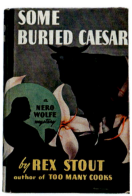

36237   Rex Stout. *Some Buried Caesar.* New York: Triangle Books, [1941]. Later edition. **Inscribed by Stout, "For / Jack Cordes - / with best wishes - / Rex Stout / February 3 - 1973 -"** on the half-title page. Octavo. [vi], 296, [2, flyleaf] pages. Publisher's aqua cloth with yellow titles. Original pictorial dust jacket. Light wear to the boards, with two bumped corners. Text uniformly toned throughout. Minor wear and wrinkling to the jacket edges, with minimal loss at the spine ends and corners. Very good. *From the collection of first fan, Jack Cordes.*

Est.: $300-up
Start Bid: $150

36238   A. E. van Vogt. *Slan.* Sauk City: Arkham House, 1946. First edition, first printing. **Signed by van Vogt on front free endpaper.** Publisher's binding and dust jacket. Lightly rubbed and toned with some insect nibbling to extremities. Very good. *From the collection of first fan, Jack Cordes.*

Est.: $300-up
Start Bid: $150

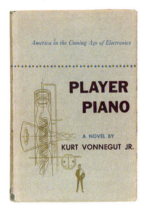

36239   Kurt Vonnegut, Jr. *Player Piano.* New York: Charles Scribner's Sons, 1952. First edition. **Delightfully inscribed and signed by the author to Jack Cordes,** "Warmest possible greetings / to Jack Cordes, who this / day, God love him, asked me / to autograph a book which, / unloved, went out of print / thirteen years ago / Kurt Vonnegut Jr. / Iowa City / Sept. 29, 1966" on the front free endpaper. Octavo. [viii], 295 pages. Publisher's green cloth with silver spine titles. Original pictorial dust jacket. Minor wear to board edges. Light soiling, bumping and fading to spine cloth. Corners bumped and rubbed. Dust jacket spine

sunned. Overall, the price-clipped jacket is a bit tired, with some biopredation to the rear panel and spine tail, resulting in some loss. Minor loss to spine head and other fold ends. A nice copy, with a wonderful inscription. *From the collection of first fan, Jack Cordes.*

Est.: $800-up
Start Bid: $400

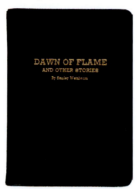

36240   Stanley Weinbaum. *Dawn of Flame and Other Stories.* [Jamaica, New York: Printed by Ruppert Printing Service, 1936]. First edition, second issue (Currey priority B). Not a Palmer copy, but **signed by Raymond Palmer** on the sponsors' page. Octavo. 313 pages plus colophon leaf. Photographic frontispiece of the author bound after the sponsors' page. Publisher's black Fabrikoid with gilt titles on the front cover. All edges red. No dust jacket, as issued. Minor wear around the edges of the binding. Short tear to spine cloth near the head measuring about 1.5 cm. Top edge and fore-edge of textblock a bit faded. Very good condition. *From the collection of first fan, Jack Cordes.*

Est.: $600-up
Start Bid: $300

36241   [Stephen King, et al.]. Douglas E. Winter [editor]. *Prime Evil.* West Kingston: Donald M. Grant, [1988]. First edition, **limited to 1000 copies of which this is number 232. Signed by all con-**

tributors. Publisher's binding and slipcase. Fine. *From the collection of first fan, Jack Cordes.*

Est.: $300-up
Start Bid: $150

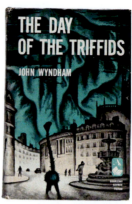

36242   John Wyndham [pseudonym of John Wyndham Parkes Lucas Beynon Harris]. *The Day of the Triffids.* Garden City: Doubleday & Company, 1951. First American edition. Octavo. 222 pages. Publisher's blue cloth with green spine titles. Original pictorial dust jacket by Whitney Bender. Minor edge wear to the book and jacket. Light creasing and minimal loss to the spine ends and corners of the jacket. Jacket spine a bit sunned. Very good condition. *From the collection of first fan, Jack Cordes.*

Est.: $300-up
Start Bid: $150

36243   The New Black Mask Quarterly, Complete Run, Signed by Numerous Contributors. New York: Harcourt Brace Jovanovich, [1985-197]. First editions, **each issue containing signatures of some of the contributors.** Eight small octavo wrappers. Trade paperback originals. Occasional minor wear to edges. All very good or better. Complete run of the publication that featured interviews and stories from the top crime writers of the past few decades. **Signatures of approximately twenty authors, including Robert B. Parker, Elmore Leonard, John Le Carré, Donald**

Westlake, James Ellroy, Georges Simenon (signed bookplate), and Joyce Carol Oates.

Est.: $600-up
Start Bid: $300

36244   Ray Bradbury. *The Golden Apples of the Sun.* Garden City: Doubleday, 1953. First edition, first printing. **Signed by Bradbury** on front free endpaper. Octavo. 250 pages. Publisher's binding and dust jacket. Minor rubbing and toning to cloth extremities with a few tiny splits at head of spine. Jacket shows light rubbing and wear to edges with a few small chips and tears. Internal tape to verso of jacket. Very good.

Est.: $500-up
Start Bid: $250

36245   Ray Bradbury. *The Martian Chronicles.* Avon: Limited Editions Club, 1974. **Number 705 of 2,000 numbered copies signed by Bradbury and illustrator, Joseph Mugnaini.** Quarto. 309 pages. Publisher's binding, glassine dust jacket, and slipcase. A fine copy in a lightly rubbed slipcase.

Est.: $300-up
Start Bid: $150

36246 Edgar Rice Burroughs.
Jungle Tales of Tarzan. Chicago:
McClurg, 1919. First edition, first
printing. Octavo. 319 pages.
Publisher's bright orange cloth
with black titles to the front
cover and spine. Minor rubbing
and soiling to cloth extremities.
Spine slightly cocked. Names to
front endpapers. Staining to fore-
edge, lightly affecting textblock.
Illustrated. About very good.
Zeuschner 214.
Est.: $400-up
Start Bid: $200

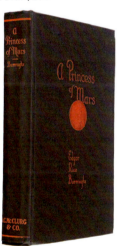

36247 Edgar Rice Burroughs.
A Princess of Mars. Chicago:
McClurg, 1917. First edition, first
printing. Octavo. 326 pages.
Publisher's dark brown cloth with
red titles on the front cover and
spine. Modest rubbing. Hinges
cracking and owner name
cleaned from front free endpaper.
Illustrated. Housed in a custom
cloth chemise and slipcase. A
bright copy in near fine condition.
Zeuschner 423.
Est.: $400-up
Start Bid: $200

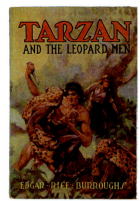

36248 Edgar Rice Burroughs.
Tarzan and the Leopard Men.
Tarzana: Edgar Rice Burroughs,
1940. Burroughs, Inc. reprint.
Octavo. 332 pages. Publisher's
red cloth with blue lettering.
Laminated state of the original
pictorial dust jacket. Jacket is price
clipped, otherwise a fine, fresh
copy. Zeuschner 621.
Est.: $300-up
Start Bid: $150

36249 Edgar Rice Burroughs.
Tarzan and the Lion Man. Tarzana:
Edgar Rice Burroughs, [1934].
First edition. Octavo. 318 pages.
Publisher's gray cloth with black
lettering and red Janus figure on
the front cover. Original pictorial
dust jacket. Minor rubbing and
toning to cloth extremities with
lower corner bumped, also affecting textblock. Front hinge cracked.
Small stain to top page edges,
slightly bleeding into textblock.
Jacket shows light rubbing and
wear to edges with a few tiny chips
and tears. Very good. Zeuschner
627.
Est.: $500-up
Start Bid: $250

36250 Edgar Rice Burroughs.
Tarzan, Lord of the Jungle.
Chicago: A. C. McClurg, 1928. First
edition. **Inscribed and signed
by the author, "To / R E Carr /
with all good wishes / from his
friend / Edgar Rice Burroughs
/ Tarzana / Nov 8, 1928"** on the
front free endpaper. Octavo. 377
pages. Four (of five) plates, including the frontispiece, by J. Allen
St. John. Publisher's green cloth
with black lettering on the front
cover and spine. Moderate wear
and some rubbing to the boards.
Spine sunned and a bit frayed at
the spine tail. Mild thumbsoiling to
text. Very good. Zeuschner 682.
Est.: $600-up
Start Bid: $300

36251 Edgar Rice Burroughs.
Tarzan of the Apes. Chicago: A. C.
McClurg, 1914. **First edition of the
first Tarzan book, first state (no
acorn device on spine).** Octavo.
400 pages. Publisher's dark red
cloth with gilt titles to the front
cover and spine. Spine sunned
and slightly worn, some rubbing
and light soiling to boards, hinges
starting, previous owner's neat
signature, text a bit skewed. Good.
Zeuschner 696.
Est.: $1,000-up
Start Bid: $500

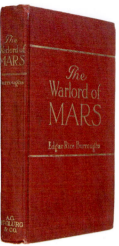

36252 Edgar Rice Burroughs.
The Warlord of Mars. Chicago:
McClurg, 1919. First edition, first
printing. Octavo. 296 pages.
Publisher's dark red cloth with gilt
titles to the front cover and spine.
Minor rubbing. Spine slightly
cocked and bumped. Small crack
to front hinge. Illustrated. Housed
in a lightly worn custom cloth
chemise and slipcase. Very good.
Zeuschner 829.
Est.: $400-up
Start Bid: $200

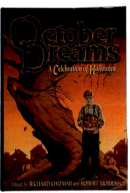

**36253 Richard Chizmar
and Robert Morrish [editors].**
October Dreams. Baltimore:
Cemetery Dance, 2000. First edition, **limited to 450 numbered
copies of which this is 24. Signed
by 45 contributors.** Quarto. 660
pages. Publisher's binding, dust
jacket, and slipcase. Fine.
Est.: $300-up
Start Bid: $150

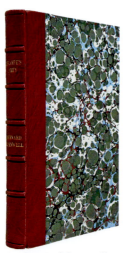

36254 **Bernard Cornwell.**
Sharpe's Prey with an appreciation by Anthony Price. Blakeney, Glos., Scorpion Press, [2001]. **Limited Edition, one of 16 de luxe lettered copies signed by Cornwell and Price in a special binding.** Octavo. [viii], [261], [3, blank] pages. Publisher's quarter burgundy morocco over marbled boards. Acetate jacket. Fine.

Est.: $600-up
Start Bid: $300

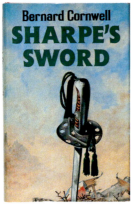

36255 **Bernard Cornwell.**
Sharpe's Sword. London: Collins, [1983]. First edition. **Signed by Cornwell** on the title page. Octavo. 319, [1, blank] pages. Publisher's binding and dust jacket. Very mild rubbing to jacket, gutter facing title page just barely overopened (possibly done by Cornwell when he signed it). A near fine copy.

Est.: $800-up
Start Bid: $400

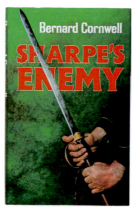

36256 **Bernard Cornwell.**
Sharpe's Enemy. London: Collins, [1984]. First edition. **Signed by Cornwell** on the title page. Octavo. 351, [1, blank] pages. Publisher's binding and dust jacket. Mild rubbing to jacket, else fine.

Est.: $600-up
Start Bid: $300

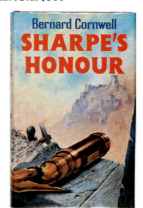

36257 **Bernard Cornwell.**
Sharpe's Honour. London: Collins, 1985. First edition. **Signed by Cornwell** on the title page. Octavo. 320 pages. Publisher's binding and dust jacket. Very mild rubbing, browning to jacket. Near fine.

Est.: $600-up
Start Bid: $300

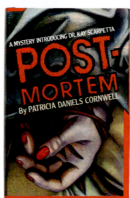

36258 **Patricia Daniels Cornwell.** *Post-Mortem*. New York: Charles Scribner's Sons, [1990]. First edition, first printing. Octavo. 293 pages. Publisher's silver-stamped black cloth over red paper boards and dust jacket with $16.95 price. Fine. Cornwell's first book (she soon dropped the "Daniels"), the first to feature Dr. Kay Scarpetta.

Est.: $600-up
Start Bid: $300

36259 **August Derleth.**
Something Near. Sauk City: Arkham House, 1945. First edition of a printing of two thousand copies. **Signed by the author** on the front free endpaper. Octavo. 274 pages. Publisher's black cloth with gilt titles. Original pictorial dust jacket by Ronald Clyne. Contents uniformly toned, as usual. Dust jacket toned and slightly worn at the edges, else very good condition.

Est.: $300-up
Start Bid: $150

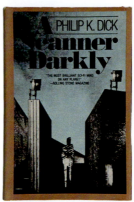

36260 **Philip K. Dick.** *A Scanner Darkly*. Garden City: Doubleday, 1977. First edition, first printing. Octavo. 220 pages. Publisher's binding and dust jacket. Only modest rubbing to cloth extremities. Faint foxing to top page edges. Toned jacket shows light wear to edges with a few small chips and tears. A near fine book in a very good jacket.

Est.: $300-up
Start Bid: $150

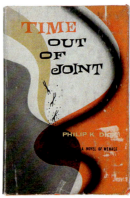

36261 **Philip K. Dick.** *Time Out of Joint*. Philadelphia: Lippincott, [1959]. First edition, first printing. Octavo. 221 pages. Publisher's binding and dust jacket. Cloth is lightly rubbed with several spots of abrading to extremities. Bumping to spine ends and corners. Jacket shows rubbing and wear to edges with small chips and tears. One-inch wrinkled tear to bottom edge of front panel with mild sunning along spine. A scarce title in about very good condition.

Est.: $600-up
Start Bid: $300

36262 **Leah Bodine Drake.** *A Hornbook for Witches. Poems of Fantasy*. Sauk City: Arkham House, 1950. First edition of 553 copies printed. Octavo. 70 pages. Publisher's black cloth and dust jacket designed by Frank Utpatel. Contents slightly toned at the edges, else a fine copy.

Est.: $800-up
Start Bid: $400

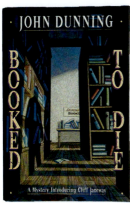

36263 **John Dunning.** *Booked to Die.* New York: Charles Scribner's Sons, [1992]. First edition, first printing. **Signed by Dunning** on half-title page. Octavo. 324 pages. Publisher's binding and dust jacket. Touch of rubbing to front board with a modest bump to lower corner of rear, otherwise a fine copy.

Est.: $400-up
Start Bid: $200

36264 **Lord Dunsany. [Edward Plunkett].** *The Gods of Pegana.* [N.p.]: The Pegana Press, 1911. Second edition. Octavo. 94 pages. With illustrations in photogravure by S. H. Sime. Cloth spine with stamped titles and paper boards with Illustration and titles stamped in dark blue to front. Page edges uncut. Tissues present for all eight engravings. Covers very lightly sunned and slightly bowed. Minor abrasion to rear board and a hint of dampstaining. Some light toning and foxing to page edges, endpapers, and lightly throughout. Otherwise, a better than very good copy of the author's first book and the only publication by The Pegana Press.

Est.: $600-up
Start Bid: $300

36265 **Lord Dunsany.** *Time and the Gods.* London: William Heinemann, 1906. First edition. Large octavo. [xii], 179, [1, colophon] pages. With 10 full-page illustrations by S. H. Sime inserted throughout. Publisher's binding of paper-covered boards, front cover with mounted illustration and lettered in gilt. Mild rubbing, previous owner's neat ink inscription on front free endpaper, some foxing to edges of text block (not appearing on leaves). A fine copy. "His rich language, his cosmic point of view, his remote dream-worlds, and his exquisite sense of the fantastic, all appeal to me more than anything else in modern literature" (H. P. Lovecraft).

Est.: $600-up
Start Bid: $300

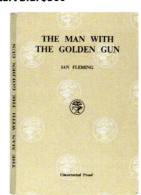

36266 **Ian Fleming.** *The Man With the Golden Gun.* London: Jonathan Cape, [1965]. Uncorrected proof of the first edition. Twelvemo. 221 pages. Publisher's green printed wrappers. Spine cocked, as usual. Otherwise, a near fine copy.

Est.: $600-up
Start Bid: $300

36267 **Ian Fleming.** *Thunderball.* London: Jonathan Cape, [1961]. Uncorrected proof of the first edition. Twelvemo. 254 pages. Publisher's green printed wrappers. **In the rare proof state dust jacket**, with "PROOF ONLY, Publication date: March 27th" and price 15s. net on front flap**. Spine cocked, as usual. Stain to bottom corner of front wrapper; stains to bottom margin of most pages, intruding upon only one or two word of text on two leaves. Crease to rear wrapper. Jacket is worn and chipped at spine ends, affecting "Ian" at head of spine; wear along folds and a few minor creases. Generally a very good copy of a scarce James Bond proof copy, in the scarcer proof state dust jacket.

Est.: $1,000-up
Start Bid: $500

36268 **[Ian Fleming]. [Kingsley Amis]. Robert Markham.** *Colonel Sun, A James Bond Adventure.* London: Jonathan Cape, [1968]. **Uncorrected proof.** Twelvemo. Original wrappers; also **with original proof dust jacket** with "21s. net" price on front flap, and "PROOF ONLY / Provisional publication date 4 April, 1968" stamped notice on rear flap. 255 pages. Yellow-green printed wrappers. Binding slightly cocked, as is common for these advance review copies. Very minor toning to title page; slight wear along folds of jacket, most notably at head of spine. A near fine copy. The first James Bond novel to be issued after Ian Fleming's death. "Robert Markham" was the pseudonym of novelist Kingsley Amis.

Est.: $600-up
Start Bid: $300

36269 **Sue Grafton.** *"A" is for Alibi.* New York: Holt, Rinehart and Winston, [1982]. First edition, first printing. Octavo. 274 pages. Publisher's red-stamped gray cloth and dust jacket with $12.95 price and "0482" on front flap. Fine.

Grafton's first installment in her enormously popular "alphabet series" of crime novels.

Est.: $800-up
Start Bid: $400

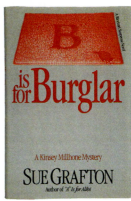

36270 **Sue Grafton.** *"B" is for Burglar.* New York: Holt, Rinehart and Winston [1985]. First edition, first printing. Octavo. 229 pages. Publisher's quarter red cloth over gray boards and silver spine titles. Faint sunning to top board edges. Jacket shows minor edge toning. Overall fine condition.

Est.: $800-up
Start Bid: $400

36271 **Sue Grafton.** *"C" is for Corpse.* New York: Henry Holt, [1986]. First edition, first printing. Octavo. 243 pages. Publisher's gray boards and silver spine titles. Faint foxing to top page edges. Jacket shows minor edge toning. Overall fine condition.

Est.: $600-up
Start Bid: $300

36272   Sue Grafton. *Keziah Dane.* New York: Macmillan, [1967]. First edition, first printing. Octavo. 220 pages. Publisher's red cloth with gilt lettering to spine. Publisher's blue stain to top edge. Slightly leaning spine. Two tiny folds to upper corner of jacket front inner flap. A bright, near fine copy.

Est.: $800-up
Start Bid: $400

36273   Sue Grafton. *Kinsey and Me. A Collection of Short Stories.* Santa Barbara, California, 1991. First edition, **number 39 of 300 copies signed by the author** on the limitation page. Publisher's maroon cloth over gray paper boards with gilt spine titles. Housed in the matching maroon cloth slipcase. Laid in is the publisher's prospectus for *Kinsey & Me* **signed by Sue Grafton.** Fine condition.

Est.: $400-up
Start Bid: $200

36274   Tony Hillerman. *Dance Hall of the Dead.* New York: Harper & Row, [1973]. First edition, first printing. **Signed by Hillerman** on title page. Octavo. 166 pages. Publisher's binding and dust jacket. Mild rubbing and wear to extremities. Near fine.

Est.: $300-up
Start Bid: $150

36275   No Lot.

36276   Tony Hillerman. *The Fly on the Wall.* New York: Harper & Row, [1971]. First edition, first printing. Octavo. 212 pages. Publisher's binding and dust jacket with $5.95 price and "0971" at bottom of front flap. Minor abrading to board extremities. Jacket shows light edge wear and sunning. Very good.

Est.: $300-up
Start Bid: $150

36277   Tony Hillerman. *The Fly on the Wall.* New York: Harper & Row, [1971]. First edition, first printing. **Inscribed and signed**

by Tony Hillerman on the front free endpaper. Octavo. 212 pages. Publisher's blue cloth binding, and dust jacket with $5.95 price and "0971" at bottom of front flap. Spine of jacket lightly faded; a few shallow creases to front flap. A fine copy of Hillerman's second novel.

Est.: $1,000-up
Start Bid: $500

36278   Robert E. Howard. *Always Comes Evening.* Sauk City: Arkham House, 1957. First edition of 636 copies printed. This copy is one of the first 536 printed with titles stamped in gilt on the spine. Octavo. 86 pages. Publisher's black cloth and dust jacket designed by Frank Utpatel. Modest toning to the endpapers. Former owner's name in ink on the verso of the half-title page and ownership ink stamp at the top of the contents page. Jacket scuffed and slightly tatty along the edges with old adhesive tape reinforcement at the corners and spine. Still a generally very good copy.

Est.: $300-up
Start Bid: $150

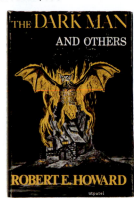

36279   Robert E. Howard. *The Dark Man and Others.* Sauk City: Arkham House, 1963. First edition of a printing of two thousand copies. Octavo. 284 pages. Publisher's black cloth with titles stamped in gilt. Complete with the Frank Utpatel designed dust jacket.

Trivial tape stains on the rear panel of the dust jacket, else a solid copy in fine condition.

Est.: $300-up
Start Bid: $150

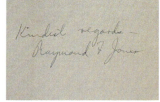

36280   Raymond F. Jones. *This Island Earth.* Chicago: Shasta, [1952]. **Signed by Jones** on front free endpaper. Octavo. 220 pages. Publisher's binding and dust jacket. Minor rubbing and toning to extremities of boards. Mild soiling and offsetting to endpapers. Jacket shows light rubbing and wear to edges with a few small chips and tears, with sunning to spine and front panel. Very good.

Est.: $300-up
Start Bid: $150

36281   Stephen Jones, editor. *The Very Best of Best New Horror.* With an Introduction by Ramsey Campbell. [Northborough, MA]: Earthling Publications, 2010. First edition, **number 144 of 200 special edition copies signed by all contributors** on three limitation pages bound in front. Large octavo. 617 pages plus a note about the editor. Publisher's full black leatherette with silver titles. Original pictorial dust jacket and black cloth slipcase. A fine copy. Contributors include Stephen King, Harlan Ellison, Neil Gaiman, Joe Hill, and many other greats of the genre.

Est.: $400-up
Start Bid: $200

36282 **Stephen King.** *Firestarter.* New York: The Viking Press, [1980]. First trade edition. **Inscribed and signed by the author in the year of publication, "For Fred - / With all best - / Stephen King / 8/19/80"** on the front free endpaper. Octavo. 428 pages. Publisher's orange cloth over black paper boards with gilt and black titles. Original pictorial dust jacket. Some age toning and very minor creasing to the jacket. Minor bumps and dustsoiling to the text edges. Otherwise, a very good copy.
Est.: $600-up
Start Bid: $300

36283 **Stephen King.** *Gerald's Game.* [New York]: Viking, [1992]. First edition, first printing. **Signed by King** on half-title page. Octavo. 332 pages. Publisher's binding and dust jacket. Fine.
Est.: $400-up
Start Bid: $200

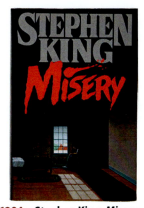

36284 **Stephen King.** *Misery.* [New York]: Viking, [1987]. First edition. **Inscribed and signed by the author, "For Brian - / From your #1 fan - / Stephen King"** on the half-title page. Octavo. 310 pages. Publisher's black cloth spine over gray paper boards with red titles. Original pictorial dust jacket. Minor edge wear overall, with some abrading to the bottom edge. Small bump to front board near the fore-edge. Tiny pressure gouge on rear board. Minor bumping and fingernail abrasions to textblock edges. Tape remnant on front pastedown. Minor edge wear and creasing to jacket edges. A few short scuffs to the jacket panels. Overall, a very good copy. A concert ticket for a 2001 show and VIP reception for the author-centric rock and roll band, the Rock Bottom Remainders (for whom King plays rhythm guitar) laid in.
Est.: $600-up
Start Bid: $300

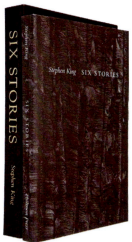

36285 **Stephen King.** *Six Stories.* Bangor: Philtrum Press, 1997. First edition, **number 862 of 1,100 limited edition copies signed by King** on a special limitation page. Octavo. 197 pages. Publisher's plain white wrappers, with a crimson paper dust jacket attached along the spine. Housed in the publisher's matching crimson cloth

36286 **Stephen King.** *The Stand.* Garden City: Doubleday & Company, 1978. First edition (with code "T39" present in the gutter of page 823). **Inscribed and signed by King on the front free endpaper, "To Ross - / All best, / Stephen King / 9/8/79."** Octavo. [xii], 823 pages. Publisher's black cloth over tan paper boards with gilt spine titles. Original pictorial dust jacket. Minor soiling and rubbing to cloth. Edges a bit worn, with a few noticeable bumps to the edges. Spine slightly bowed and creased, seen often with this title. Very minor spotting to text edges and endpapers, otherwise the text is very clean. A couple of small areas of discoloration to the jacket. Spine a touch creased. The jacket appears to be slightly misfolded. Overall, a very good copy of the first publication of King's epic.
Est.: $800-up
Start Bid: $400

36287 **Stephen King. Two Signed** *Dark Tower* **First Editions,** including: *The Dark Tower IV: Wizard and Glass.* Hampton Falls, New Hampshire: Donald M. Grant, Publisher, Inc., [1997]. First trade edition. **Signed by King** on the front free endpaper. Octavo. 787 pages. Publisher's black cloth with gilt spine titles. Original pictorial dust jacket. Fine. [and:] *The Dark Tower V: Wolves of the Calla.* Hampton Falls, New Hampshire:

slipcase. Wear along the flap folds of the jacket. Two insignificant fingernail marks to the text edges, else a fine copy.
Est.: $800-up
Start Bid: $400

Donald M. Grant, Publisher, Inc., In Association with Scribner, [2003]. First trade edition. **Signed by King** on the half-title page. Octavo. 714 pages. Publisher's black cloth with gilt spine titles. Original pictorial dust jacket. Fine. Both volumes housed together in the publisher's slipcase.
Est.: $400-up
Start Bid: $200

36288 **Stephen King. Two Signed** *Dark Tower* **First Editions,** including: *The Dark Tower VI: Song of Susannah.* Hampton Falls, New Hampshire: Donald M. Grant, Inc., In Association with Scribner, [2004]. First trade edition. **Signed by King on the title page.** Octavo. 413 pages. Publisher's black cloth with gilt spine titles. Original pictorial dust jacket. Fine. [and:] *The Dark Tower VII: The Dark Tower.* Hampton Falls, New Hampshire: Donald M. Grant, Inc., In Association with Scribner, [2004]. First trade edition. **Signed and dated by King, and signed by illustrator Michael Whelan on the title page.** Octavo. 845 pages. Publisher's black cloth with gilt spine titles. Original pictorial dust jacket. Fine. Both volumes housed together in the publisher's slipcase.
Est.: $400-up
Start Bid: $200

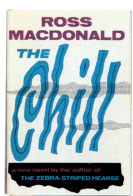

36289 **Ross Macdonald.** *The Chill.* New York: Alfred A. Knopf, 1964. First edition, first printing. **Inscribed and signed by Ross Macdonald** on front free endpaper. Octavo. 279 pages. Publisher's red cloth-backed blue paper boards, with red stain to top edge; dust jacket with $3.95 price and "1/64"

at bottom corner of front flap. Very minor shallow bend to bottom corner of several leaves. Neat bookstore sticker to rear pastedown. Slight toning along top edge of jacket. Fine. The eleventh appearance of Macdonald's Lew Archer detective.

Est.: $600-up
Start Bid: $300

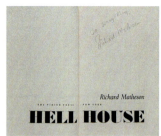

36290   Richard Matheson. *Hell House.* New York: Viking, [1971]. First edition, first printing. **Signed and inscribed by Matheson** on title page. Octavo. 279 pages. Publisher's binding and dust jacket. Slightly cocked spine with modest rubbing to boards and a bit of faint soiling to fore-edge. Light rubbing and wear to jacket extremities. Very good.

Est.: $300-up
Start Bid: $150

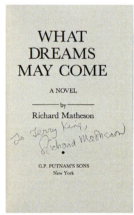

36291   Richard Matheson. *What Dreams May Come.* New York: Putnam, [1978]. First edition, first printing. **Signed and inscribed by Matheson** on title page. Octavo. 304 pages. Publisher's binding and dust jacket. Lower corner of rear board with soft bump. Jacket shows a bit of light rubbing to extremities. Overall fine.

Est.: $300-up
Start Bid: $150

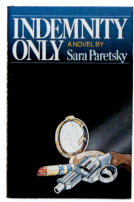

36292   Sara Paretsky. *Indemnity Only.* New York: Dial Press, [1982]. First edition, first printing. Octavo. 244 pages. Publisher's silver-stamped black cloth over pale blue paper boards and dust jacket with $14.95 price. Fine. Paretsky's first book, introducing the reader to detective V. I. Warshawski.

Est.: $400-up
Start Bid: $200

36293   George Pelecanos. Five Signed Limited First Editions, Each Being Limited to 52 Lettered Copies, including: *The Sweet Forever; Shame the Devil; Hell to Pay; Hard Revolution; Drama City.* Tucson: Dennis McMillan, 1998-2005. First editions, each volume is one of 52 lettered copies (unknown what letter each is, due to the fact that **each is still in the original shrinkwrap**). Five octavo volumes. Publisher's bindings, dust jackets and slipcases. Fine.

Est.: $600-up
Start Bid: $300

36294   Ellery Queen. *The Detective Short Story, A Bibliography by Ellery Queen.* Boston: Little, Brown and Company,

1942. First edition, limited to 1,060 copies, of which 1,000 copies were for sale. This copy is **inscribed by Ellery Queen (the pseudonym of Fred Dannay) to Gertrude E. Larson, secretary of famed collector Ned Guymon, with Guymon's well-known "skull and claw" bookplate**. Octavo. 145 pages. Publisher's red cloth binding and dust jacket with $4.00 price. Jacket has a few tiny nicks and a darkened spine. Else, a fine copy of, as the blurb on the front cover states, "the first bibliography of the detective short story ever written...the *only* work of its kind in the world."

Est.: $600-up
Start Bid: $300

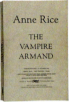

36295   Anne Rice. Two Inscribed Dedication Copies of *The Vampire Armand*, including: **Photocopy of the Final Version of the Manuscript, inscribed and signed by Anne Rice to one of the dedicatees, a young friend, Brian Robertson.** Fine condition. [and:] **Advance Review Copy.** New York: Alfred A. Knopf, 1998. **Signed by Anne Rice on the title page and also warmly inscribed by her on the dedication page to dedicatee Brian Robertson.** Original printed wrappers, with light thumbsoiling; binding skewed. Otherwise near fine. A pair of unique association items.

Est.: $600-up
Start Bid: $300

36296   Sax Rohmer. "The Invisible President," A Fu Manchu Series, Complete in Twelve Parts in *Collier's* Magazine. Springfield, Ohio: Crowell Publishing Company, 1936. Complete in twelve issues published weekly from February 29, 1936 to May 16, 1936. Illustrated by C. C. Beall. Light coffee splash to first issue, else, colors, covers, and contents bright. Original subscriber's mailing label

to front covers. Original large format magazines in overall near fine condition.

Est.: $600-up
Start Bid: $300

36297   Henry St. Clair, compiler. *Tales of Terror, or the Mysteries of Magic: A Selection of Wonderful and Supernatural Stories.* Boston: Printed and Published by Charles Gaylord, 1833. First edition. Two octavo volumes in one. vi, 7-178, [2, blank], 119 pages. Engraved frontispiece. Publisher's tan backstrip over printed paper boards. Paper spine label. Housed in a custom half leather slipcase and chemise. Heavy wear to the binding, with one noticeable gouge to the rear board, and the paper covering the boards about half-perished. A third of the worn spine label perished. Corners of the binding and text heavily worn. Bottom corner of the front free endpaper torn away. Foxing throughout. A good copy of a rare title. Wright 2266.

Est.: $400-up
Start Bid: $200

36298   Robert Silverberg, editor. *Legends. Short Novels by the Masters of Modern Fantasy.* New York: TOR Fantasy / A Tom Doherty Associates Book, [1998]. First edition, number 158 of 200 limited edition copies **signed by the editor and all contributors on the limitation page, including Silverberg, Stephen King, Terry Goodkind, Ursula K. Le Guin, George R. R. Martin, Raymond E. Feist, Terry Pratchett, Orson Scott Card, Tad Williams, Anne McCaffrey, and Robert Jordan.**

Octavo. 715 pages. Publisher's full green leather with gilt spine titles. Illustrated endpapers. Housed in the publisher's matching green buckram slipcase. Fine condition.

Est.: $600-up
Start Bid: $300

36299   Dan Simmons. *Hyperion.* New York: Doubleday, [1989]. First edition, first printing. **Signed by Simmons on title page, dated in year of publication, and with a charming drawing by the author.** Octavo. 482 pages. Publisher's binding and dust jacket. Fine.

Est.: $300-up
Start Bid: $150

36300   Clark Ashton Smith. *The Dark Chateau and Other Poems.* Sauk City: Arkham House, 1951. First edition, one of 563 copies printed. Octavo. 63 pages. Publisher's black cloth and dust jacket designed by Frank Utpatel. Some modest toning to the preliminary and terminal pages. Corners trivially bumped. Jacket toned on the spine panel and slightly worn at the corners, else a near fine copy.

Est.: $300-up
Start Bid: $150

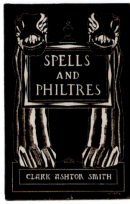

36301   Clark Ashton Smith. *Spells and Philtres.* Sauk City: Arkham House, 1958. First edition, one of 519 copies printed. Octavo. 54 pages. Publisher's black cloth and dust jacket designed by Frank Utpatel. Modest toning to the endpapers. Corners slightly bumped. Jacket trivially toned on the rear panel with one small closed tear at the lower edge of the front panel. Otherwise a near fine copy.

Est.: $300-up
Start Bid: $150

36302   [Clark Ashton Smith, Jack Williamson, et al.]. *Science Fiction Series.* New York: Stellar Publishing, [1929-1932]. First editions of the first eighteen issues of this short story magazine. Eighteen octavo volumes, the first twelve issues have an illustrated frontispiece. Original publisher's wraps. Some minor rubbing and light soiling. Fine. Authors include Jack Williamson (his first book) and Clark Ashton Smith.

Est.: $600-up
Start Bid: $300

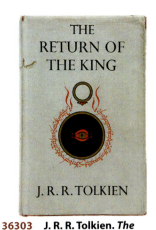

36303   J. R. R. Tolkien. *The Return of the King. Being the Third Part of the Lord of the Rings.* London: George Allen & Unwin, 1955. First edition, first issue per Hammond, with signature mark "4" at the base of page 49 and all lines on the page sagging in the middle. Octavo. 416 pages. Large folding map tipped in back. Publisher's red cloth with gilt spine. Top edge stained red. Two examples of the original pictorial dust jacket. Minor shelf wear to the cloth, with one bottom corner bumped. Interior jacket worn and soiled, with a four-inch smile-shaped closed tear to the spine and rear panel. Spine sunned. Minimal loss at the spine tail. Outer jacket with minor rubbing and a bit wrinkled along the edges, with a very short closed tear to the top edge of the front panel. Overall, a very good copy. Hammond A5iii.

Est.: $600-up
Start Bid: $300

36304   Jules Verne. *Le Superbe Orénoque.* Paris: J. Hetzel et Cie, [n.d., circa 1898]. First illustrated edition in the original French. Collection Hetzel edition consolidating the serialized issues. Quarto. 411, [8] publisher's ads pages. Illustrated by George Roux. Stunning pictorial boards accented in gilt, red, green and blues. All edges gilt. Text block slightly slanted. Modest shelf wear to boards. Contents with occasional light scattered foxing, else very

good condition. This is one of the handful of Verne titles that were not translated into English until recently, published in 2003 as *The Mighty Orinoco.*

Est.: $600-up
Start Bid: $300

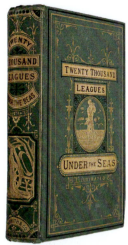

36305   Jules Verne. *Twenty Thousand Leagues Under the Seas; The Marvelous and Exciting Adventures of Pierre Aronnax, Conseil His Servant, and Ned Land, A Canadian Harpooner.* Boston: George M. Smith & Company, 1874. Second American printing, sold by subscription. Octavo. xiii, [3], [1]-303 pages. One hundred and ten illustrations from the James R. Osgood & Company edition. Original green pictorial cloth with lavish gilt decoration. A rather nice copy with modest wear to the boards, mainly at the spine ends. Contents bright with a former owner's name in ink on the fly-leaf and small ownership stamps on the title page and tissue guard of the frontispiece. A very good copy.

Est.: $600-up
Start Bid: $300

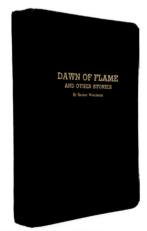

36306   Stanley Weinbaum. *Dawn of Flame and Other Stories.* Jamaica, NY: Ruppert Printing Service, 1936. First edition, Currey priority B. Twelvemo. 313 pages.

Original black Fabrikoid with gilt titles on the front panel. All edges stained red. Light shelfwear to covers. Owner's signature to front pastedown. Otherwise, near fine.

Est.: $1,000-up
Start Bid: $500

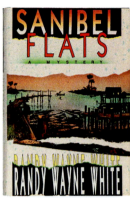

36307   Randy Wayne White. *Sanibel Flats.* New York: St. Martin's Press, [1990]. First edition, first printing. Octavo. 307 pages. Publisher's silver-stamped black cloth binding and dust jacket with $17.95 price. Fine. Author's first book.

Est.: $600-up
Start Bid: $300

36308   [John H. Amory]. *Alnomuc: or the Golden Rule, A Tale of the Sea.* Boston: Published for Weeks, Jordan and Company, 1837. First edition. Sixteenmo. 144 pages. Illustrated with twenty-four wood engraved plates. Contemporary embossed brown cloth. Spine elaborately decorated in gilt. Modest shelf wear to boards. Contents with some light scattered foxing. A single library discard stamp on the front pastedown and a contemporary owner's name in ink on the front free endpaper, else a very good copy. This edition not mentioned in Wright.

Est.: $600-up
Start Bid: $300

36309   Richard Brautigan. *A Confederate General from Big Sur.* New York: Grove Press, [1964]. First edition. Octavo. 159 pages. Publisher's binding and dust jacket. A touch of fading to board edges. Matching light toning to jacket edges, spine and flaps. Minute tear to the head of the title page. Otherwise, near fine.

Est.: $600-up
Start Bid: $300

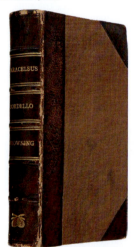

36310   Robert Browning. *Paracelsus.* London: Published by Effingham Wilson, 1835. First edition of Browning's second separately-published work. xii, 216 pages [and:] *Sordello.* London: Edward Moxon, 1840. First edition. [iv], 253, [254, printer's imprint], [255-256, publisher's advertisement leaf] pages. Two octavo volumes bound in one. Three-quarter brown morocco over brown cloth boards with gilt titles and decorative stamping on the spine with five raised bands. Noticeable abrading at the spine ends and corners and along the joints. Bookplate of the Oxford and Cambridge University Club Library on the front pastedown, with this organization's circular library stamp to several leaves. Short closed tear to the top edge of the half-title page of *Sordello.* Very good. Broughton A4; A14.

Est.: $1,000-up
Start Bid: $500

36311   [Sir Richard F. Burton, translator]. *The Perfumed Garden of the Sheik Nefzaoui. Or, The Arab Art of Love.* XVIth Century. Translated from the French Version of the Arabian MS. Cosmopoli: For Private Circulation Only, 1886. Pirated edition (from the second edition). Printed in purple and red ink. Full vellum, now rebacked. Vellum a bit soiled and spotted, some light intermittent foxing to the sheets, and a few soiled spots. Bookplate. Very good.

Est.: $600-up
Start Bid: $300

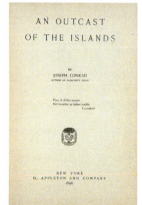

36312   Joseph Conrad. *An Outcast of the Islands.* New York: D. Appleton and Company, 1896. First American edition. Twelvemo. 335 pages, 10 pages of publisher's ads. Publisher's full green cloth with gilt spine titles, black designs and titles to front. Some rubbing and wear to covers with slight fading to spine. Endpapers somewhat foxed with light abrasions, ink notes, and erasures. Slight ghosting of marks to preliminaries. Ownership signature to title page. Toning to page edges and light foxing. Few very minor abrasions to text block. Otherwise, generally very good.

Est.: $600-up
Start Bid: $300

36313   Joseph Conrad. *The Secret Agent*, *A Drama in Three Acts.* London: Privately Published for Subscribers Only by T. Werner Laurie Ltd., 1923. First edition, **number 955 of 1,000 copies signed by Conrad** on the limitation page. Octavo. [xii], 185, [3, blank] pages. With frontispiece and limitation page inserted. Publisher's binding, with the plain paper dust jacket with paper label on spine. Jacket has long tape repair to verso (front joint is torn), some browning and rubbing to spine and edges, parchment spine very slightly browned. Previous owner's bookplate (designed by Rockwell Kent) on the front pastedown. Still, a near fine copy.

Est.: $600-up
Start Bid: $300

36314   Bernard Cornwell. Two Signed Richard Sharpe First Editions, including: *Sharpe's Regiment: Richard Sharpe and the Invasion of France, June to November 1813.* [and:]*Sharpe's Siege: Richard Sharpe and the Winter Campaign, 1814.* London: Collins, 1986-1987. First British hardcover editions, first printings. **Both volumes signed by the author on the title page.** Two octavo volumes. Publisher's bindings and dust jackets. Light wear to books and jackets. Toning to pages of *Sharpe's Regiment.* Otherwise, near fine.

Est.: $600-up
Start Bid: $300

36315   Bernard Cornwell. Three Signed Richard Sharpe First Editions, including: *Sharpe's Eagle: Richard Sharpe and the Talavera Campaign, July 1809.* [and:] *Sharpe's Gold: Richard Sharpe and the Destruction of Almeida, August 1810* [and:] *Sharpe's Company: Richard Sharpe and Siege of Badajoz, January to April 1812.* London: Collins, 1981-1982. First British hardcover editions, first printings. **All three volumes signed by the author on the title page.** Three octavo volumes. Publisher's bindings and dust jackets. Light wear to all books and jackets. *Sharpe's Company* has a slight lean and some occasional folding to the bottom corner of the somewhat scuffed text block. Otherwise, all very good or better copies.

Est.: $800-up
Start Bid: $400

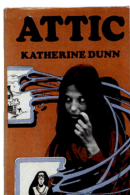

36316   Katherine Dunn. *Attic.* New York: Harper & Row, [1970]. First edition, first printing. **Signed by Dunn** on the title page. Octavo. 134 pages. Publisher's binding and dust jacket. Sunning to extremities with spotting along top page edges, lightly affecting text block. Hinges cracked. Jacket shows light rubbing and wear to edges with a few small chips and tears, and a

staining to top margin of rear panel. A very good copy, rarely found signed by the author.

Est.: $600-up
Start Bid: $300

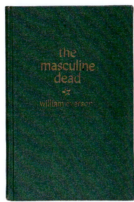

36317   William Everson. *The Masculine Dead. Poems, 1938-1940.* Prairie City [Illinois]: The Press of James A. Decker, 1942. First edition. **Inscribed by the author on the front free endpaper and with holographic corrections by Everson in text.** Octavo. 44 pages. Publisher's green cloth with titles stamped in gilt on the front board. Modest shelf wear to the boards with a slight warp to the front board. Endpapers toned, else a near fine copy housed in a custom clamshell case.

Est.: $600-up
Start Bid: $300

36318   William Everson. *River-Root. A Syzygy for the Bicentennial of These States.* Berkeley: Oyez Press, 1976. Limited to 250 copies of which 200 were for sale, this being **a presentation copy marked "D" and signed by the author** on a special limitation bound in back. **Also inscribed by the author on the half-title page: "To Bob Hawley / Whose faith and friendship / snatched this poem from manuscript / and made it a realized book- / with deepest gratitude / Bill Everson/**

July 25, 1976 / San Francisco / The Gleeson Library". Quarto. 51 pages. Illustrated by Patrick Kennedy. Half calf and decorated boards. Fine.

Est.: $600-up
Start Bid: $300

36319   William Everson. *These Are the Ravens.* San Leandro: Greater Western Publishing Company, 1935. First edition of the author's first work. From the Pamphlet Series of Western Poets. 11 pages. Printed wrappers, pamphlet format, stapled. Paper ever-so-slightly toned, else fine. Accompanied by a printed 4.5" x 2.75" card reading "With the Director's Compliments/ William Andrews Clark Memorial Library/ University of California, Los Angeles/ Lawrence Clark Powell/ Director".

Est.: $600-up
Start Bid: $300

36320   William Faulkner. *A Fable.* New York: Random House, [1954]. First edition, **number 37 of 1,000 limited edition copies signed by Faulkner** on limitation page. Octavo. 437 pages. Publisher's blue cloth beveled boards with blue and silver stamping and original glassine dust jacket. Housed in a custom cloth chemise and matching book-

backed slipcase with gilt spine titles and ruling. Glassine jacket has a few small tears and chips. Otherwise, fine.

Est.: $1,200-up
Start Bid: $600

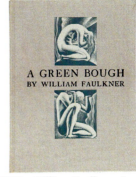

36321   William Faulkner. *A Green Bough.* New York: Harrison Smith and Robert Haas, 1933. Limited edition, one of 360 copies, of which 350 are for sale, this being number 293, **signed by William Faulkner.** Square octavo. 67 pages. With wood engravings by Lynd Ward. Publisher's tan cloth binding with mounted illustrations to front board. A beautiful copy in fine condition. Faulkner's last collection of poetry published during his lifetime.

Est.: $1,200-up
Start Bid: $600

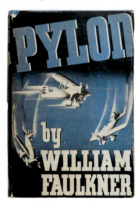

36322   William Faulkner. *Pylon.* New York: Harrison Smith and Robert Haas, Inc., 1935. First edition, first printing. Octavo. 315 pages. Publisher's blue and black cloth over boards with gilt titles. Original pictorial dust jacket. Very minor edge wear and soiling to boards. Spine cloth a bit faded and the gilt titles noticeably rubbed. Loss to spine ends of jacket, namely the spine head, touching the extreme tops of the letters in "WILLIAM." Minor areas of loss to jacket at flap fold ends. Front flap fold split a couple inches at top and bottom. Spine a bit sunned. A very good copy.

Est.: $600-up
Start Bid: $300

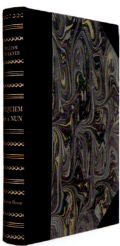

36323 **William Faulkner.** *Requiem For a Nun.* New York: Random House, [1951]. First edition, **number 84 of a limited edition of 750 copies signed by the author** on a special limitation page bound in front. Octavo. 286 pages. Publisher's three quarter cloth and marbled boards. Titles stamped in gilt on the spine. Fine.

Est.: $600-up
Start Bid: $300

36324 **Eugene Field.** *The Tribune Primer.* Chicago: Reilly & Britton Co., 1916. First edition. **Personal copy of Edgar Rice Burroughs.** Octavo. 63 pages. Pictorial boards with the original protective glassine wrapper and housed in the original box of issue. Card with "Mr. Burroughs" laid-in. Fine condition. This volume was given to attendees of the Sixteenth Annual Banquet of the American Booksellers' Association in Chicago, May 18, 1916 as a souvenir from The Reilly & Britton Company. Fine condition.

Est.: $600-up
Start Bid: $300

36325 **Jonathan Fisher.** *Short Poems: Including a Sketch of the Scriptures to the Book of Ruth: Satan's Great Devise, or Lines on Intemperance: I and Conscience, or a Dialogue on Universalism: and a Few Others on Various Subjects.* Portland: A. Shirley, Printer, 1827. First edition. Eighteenmo. 143 pages. Early marbled paper over boards with leather backstrip. Titles lettered in gilt on the spine. Wear to the edges of the boards and spine with some scattered foxing throughout, else a sound copy of this scarce work in very good condition.

Est.: $800-up
Start Bid: $400

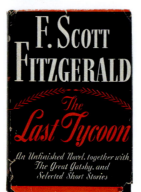

36326 **F. Scott Fitzgerald.** *The Last Tycoon. An Unfinished Novel,* together with **The Great Gatsby and Selected Stories**. New York: Charles Scribner's Sons, 1941. First edition. Octavo. 476 pages. Publisher's binding and dust jacket. Boards and extremities somewhat worn. Top front corner bumped. Shelfwear to bottom edge and spine. Faint spots of dampstaining to tail of boards and bottom edge of text block. Spine and top edge lightly sunned. Glue bleed through pastedown. Toning to endpapers and page edges, with a few spots to fore-edge. Lightly rubbed jacket has edgewear and small tears with minor chipping to corners. Spine tail has moderate loss, as does the bottom corner of the front panel, while also missing the lower third of the front flap. Light toning to flaps, spine and rear panel. Very good.

Est.: $600-up
Start Bid: $300

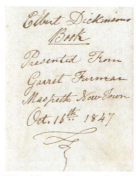

36327 **[Garret Furman].** **Rusticus [pseudonym for Garrett Furman].** *Long Island Miscellanies.* New-York: Robert, Hovey & King, Printers, 1847. First edition. Octavo. 185 pages. Six tinted lithographed plates. Publisher's green cloth with floral vignette stamped in gilt on the front board and titles in gilt on the spine. Boards worn and damp stained. Contents toned with some occasional scattered foxing, else very good and rare in any condition. A scarce privately printed volume of American fiction. All of the tales and anecdotes have a Long Island background. Garrett (also spelled Garrit) Furman was also the author of two volumes of early Long Island verse - *Rural Hours* and *Maspeth Poems*. All of his books were privately printed. Howes F424. Sabin 74425.

Est.: $600-up
Start Bid: $300

36328 **[Garrett Furman].** *The Maspeth Poems.* New York: Conner & Cooke, 1837. First edition. Twelvemo. 128 pages. Nine engraved plates including a portrait of Garrett (sometimes spelled Garrit) Furman used as the frontispiece. Publisher's orange paper over boards. Joints weak; spine chipped at the ends; contents with light to moderate scattered foxing; a few pages with small tears. Former owner's name in ink on the flyleaf. A rare volume of poetry inspired by the author's association with Maspeth, Long Island. Sabin 26221.

Est.: $600-up
Start Bid: $300

36329 **[Edward Gorey, illustrator].** *Hauntings. Tales of the Supernatural.* Garden City: Doubleday & Company, 1968. First edition. Edited by Henry Mazzeo. Octavo. 318 pages. With illustrations in text by Edward Gorey. Publisher's cloth and dust jacket. Slight toning to the preliminary and terminal pages; dust jacket scuffed and chipped at the edges, else a very good copy.

Est.: $300-up
Start Bid: $150

36330 **Thomas Gray.** *Gray's Elegy.* London: Longman, 1846. First edition of this work illuminated in full color by Owen Jones. Small quarto. [36] pages. Publisher's full sculpted calf (in papier mâché style) binding. Some rubbing and light wear to binding, text shaken with some pages loose, yet present. Good. Housed in cloth slipcase.

Est.: $600-up
Start Bid: $300

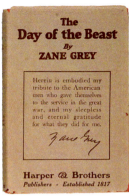

36331   Zane Grey. *The Day of the Beast.* New York and London: Harper & Brothers, 1922. First edition. Octavo. 351 pages. Publisher's binding and dust jacket. **Zane Grey library blind stamp on the front free endpaper.** A handsome copy, slightly tatty along the edges of the dust jacket and with minor toning to the endpapers, else in fine condition.

Est.: $600-up
Start Bid: $300

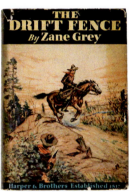

36332   Zane Grey. *The Drift Fence.* New York and London: Harper & Brothers, 1933. First edition. **Inscribed by the author to his son: "To / Romer / from / Dad / Zane Grey"** on the front free endpaper. Octavo. 314 pages. Publisher's binding and dust jacket. Modest wear at the corners and spine ends of the dust jacket, else a handsome, personal copy in near fine condition.

Est.: $800-up
Start Bid: $400

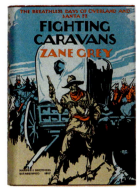

36333   Zane Grey. *Fighting Caravans.* New York and London: Harper & Brothers Publishers, 1929. First edition. **Inscribed by the author on the front free endpaper "To R. C. / from / Zane Grey".** Octavo. 361 pages. Publisher's binding and dust jacket. Illustrated endpapers. Spine panel ever-so-slightly faded, else a fine copy.

Est.: $600-up
Start Bid: $300

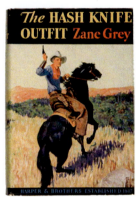

36334   Zane Grey. *The Hash Knife Outfit.* New York and London: Harper & Brothers, 1933. First edition. Octavo. 323 pages. Publisher's binding and dust jacket. **Zane Grey library blind stamp on the front free endpaper.** A bright, tight copy in fine condition.

Est.: $600-up
Start Bid: $300

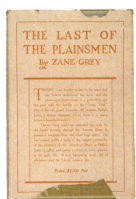

36335   Zane Grey. *The Last of the Plainsmen.* New York: The Outing Publishing Company, 1908. First edition. Octavo. 314, [4] publisher's catalog pages. **Zane Grey**

library blind stamp on the front free endpaper. With illustrations from photographs by the author. Publisher's pictorial cloth with titles stamped in gilt. A lovely copy in the original dust jacket. The jacket is missing a small section at the lower front panel and bears chips and a few closed tears along the edges. Still, a near fine copy in a good dust jacket. Housed in a custom slipcase.

Est.: $600-up
Start Bid: $300

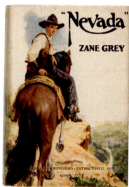

36336   Zane Grey. *"Nevada." A Romance of the West.* New York and London: Harper & Brothers, 1928. First edition. **Inscribed by the author to his son: "March 1928 / To / Romer / from / Dad / Zane Grey"** on the front free endpaper. Octavo. 365, [6, publisher's catalog] pages. Publisher's binding and dust jacket. Illustrated endpapers. A beautiful, personal copy in fine condition.

Est.: $800-up
Start Bid: $400

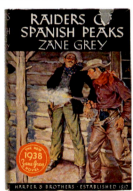

36337   Zane Grey. *Raiders of Spanish Peaks.* New York and London: Harper & Brothers, 1938. First edition. **Signed by the author** on the front free endpaper. Octavo. 332 pages. Publisher's binding and dust jacket. Illustrated endpapers. **Zane Grey library blind stamp on the front free endpaper.** A beautiful, tight copy with one small sec-

tion of the front panel of the jacket missing affecting the word "of" in the title, else in near fine condition.

Est.: $600-up
Start Bid: $300

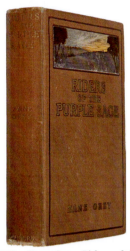

36338   Zane Grey. *Riders of the Purple Sage. A Novel.* New York and London: Harper & Brothers Publishers, 1912. First edition (January, 1912). Octavo. 335 pages. With four plates (including frontispiece) illustrated by Douglas Duer. Publisher's tan cloth with titles stamped in gilt and a small color illustration mounted to the front board, as issued. Modest wear to the edges of the boards and spine ends. Former owner's name in ink on the front free endpaper. A handsome copy in very good condition.

Est.: $300-up
Start Bid: $150

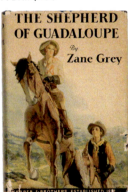

36339   Zane Grey. *The Shepherd of Guadaloupe.* New York and London: Harper & Brothers Publishers, 1930. First edition. **Inscribed by the author to his sister "To Ida / from / Zane"** on the front free endpaper. Octavo. 335 pages. Publisher's binding and dust jacket. Illustrated endpapers. Jacket slightly tatty along the edges, else a near fine copy.

Est.: $600-up
Start Bid: $300

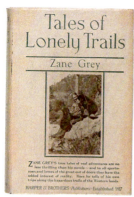

36340 **Zane Grey.** *Tales of Lonely Trails.* New York and London: Harper & Brothers, 1922. First edition. Octavo. 394 pages. Publisher's green cloth with titles stamped in gilt with photographic illustration mounted to front board as called for. Illustrated. Price-clipped dust jacket. **Zane Grey library blind stamp on the front free endpaper.** An internally bright copy with a slightly faded spine panel. Dust jacket toned. In general, a near fine copy.

Est.: $600-up
Start Bid: $300

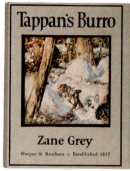

36341 **Zane Grey.** *Tappan's Burro and Other Stories.* New York and London: Harper & Brothers Publishers, 1923. First edition. **Presentation copy inscribed by the author's daughter Betty to her good friend Norma Shine: "Dear Norma / These were my favorite / stories / much love / Betty." Also signed by the author on the front free endpaper. Includes a charming birthday card envelope with a small drawing and birthday wishes by a young Betty to her father on the occasion of his fortieth birthday. Small Zane Grey library label on the front free endpaper.** Octavo. 253 pages. Publisher's cloth with color illustration by Charles S. Chapman mounted to the front board. Seven color illustrations by Charles S. Chapman and Frank

Street. Minor toning to the endpapers, else a near fine copy in a bright dust jacket.

Est.: $800-up
Start Bid: $400

36342 **Zane Grey.** *The Trail Driver.* New York and London: Harper & Brothers, 1936. First edition. Octavo. 302 pages. Publisher's binding and dust jacket. **Zane Grey library blind stamp on the front free endpaper.** A handsome copy with some smoothed folds on the front panel of the dust jacket, else in fine condition.

Est.: $600-up
Start Bid: $300

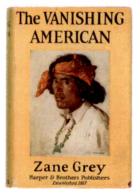

36343 **Zane Grey.** *The Vanishing American.* New York and London: Harper & Brothers Publishers, 1925. First edition. **Inscribed by the author to his sister "To / Ida / from / Brother / Zane / Nov 17, 1925"** on the front free endpaper. Octavo. 308, [4] publisher's catalog pages. Publisher's binding and price-clipped pictorial dust jacket. Some toning to the preliminary and terminal pages and the edges of the textblock, else a near fine copy.

Est.: $600-up
Start Bid: $300

36344 **Zane Grey.** *West of the Pecos.* New York and London: Harper & Brothers, 1937. First edition. Octavo. 314 pages. Publisher's binding and dust jacket. Illustrated endpapers. **Zane Grey library blind stamp on the front free endpaper.** A beautiful, bright copy in fine condition.

Est.: $600-up
Start Bid: $300

36345 **Zane Grey.** *Wild Horse Mesa.* New York and London: Harper & Brothers, 1928. First edition. Octavo. 365 pages. Publisher's binding and dust jacket. Illustrated endpapers. **Zane Grey library blind stamp on the front free endpaper.** A beautiful, bright copy with trivial wear to the dust jacket's spine ends, else in near fine condition.

Est.: $600-up
Start Bid: $300

36346 **Zane Grey.** *The Young Pitcher.* New York and London: Harper & Brothers Publishers, 1911. First edition. Octavo. 249 pages. With four plates illustrated by William F. Taylor. Publisher's pictorial green cloth. Some toning to the spine panel, else a near fine bright copy.

Est.: $600-up
Start Bid: $300

36347 **Joel Chandler Harris.** *Uncle Remus. His Songs and His Sayings. The Folk-Lore of the Old Plantation.* New York: D. Appleton and Company, 1881. First edition, first issue (with "presumptive" on the last line of page nine and no mention of the work in the publisher's catalog). Octavo. 231, [8, publisher's catalog] pages. Illustrations by Frederick S. Church and James H. Moser. Publisher's green pictorial cloth rebacked with a portion of the original spine laid down. Original endpapers illustrated with butterflies. Boards worn at the corners. Old tape repairs to the hinges. Small dampstain at the top of the text block. Scattered light foxing, else generally a very good copy.

Est.: $600-up
Start Bid: $300

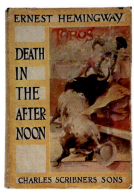

36348 **Ernest Hemingway.** *Death in the Afternoon.* New York: Scribner's, 1932. First edition. Publisher's black cloth stamped in gilt. Minor scuffing and rubbing. First issue dust jacket is slightly browned and foxed, with chipping and some small losses; some splitting along front flap fold. Old cellophane tape repairs to the verso of jacket. A very good copy.

Est.: $1,000-up
Start Bid: $500

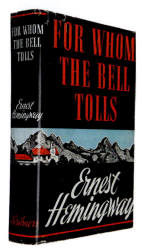

36349 **Ernest Hemingway.** *For Whom the Bell Tolls.* New York: Charles Scribner's Sons, 1940. First edition, with "A" on copyright page. Octavo. 471 pages. Publisher's binding first state jacket with no photographer's credit on the rear panel. Jacket has light wrinkling to edges, very minor chipping and a few small tears. Touch of toning to flaps. Last 30 pages of text have some crimping with minute tears to fore-edge. Otherwise, a nice, tight, clean, square copy in very good condition.

Est.: $1,000-up
Start Bid: $500

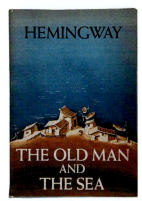

36350 **Ernest Hemingway.** *The Old Man and the Sea.* New York: Scribner's, 1952. First edition. Octavo. 140 pages. Publisher's binding and original first state dust jacket. Moderate toning to cloth with light rubbing to extremities. Minor wear to jacket edges with chipping at spine head and a one-inch folded tear to top edge of rear panel. Very good.

Est.: $600-up
Start Bid: $300

36351 **James Hilton. Two Mr. Chips First Editions,** including: *Goodbye Mr. Chips!* London: Hodder & Stoughton, 1934. [and:] *To You Mr. Chips!* London: Hodder & Stoughton, 1938. First editions. Two octavo volumes. [128]; 244 pages. Publisher's cloth and dust jackets. Some rubbing and mild wear to jackets. Near fine copies.

Est.: $600-up
Start Bid: $300

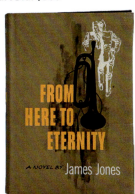

36352 **James Jones.** *From Here to Eternity.* New York: Scribners, 1951. First edition, first printing. **Signed by Jones** on front free endpaper. Octavo. 861 pages. Publisher's binding and dust jacket. Mild rubbing to cloth extremities.

Hinges slightly shaken. Minor wear to jacket with a few light wrinkles. Very good.

Est.: $600-up
Start Bid: $300

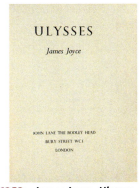

36353 **James Joyce.** *Ulysses.* London: John Lane / The Bodley Head, [1936]. **First British Limited edition, one of 900 hand-numbered copies, this copy being number 828.** Quarto. 765 pages. Publisher's full linen buckram with gilt-stamped design by Eric Gill to front cover and gilt spine titles. Top edge gilt, others uncut. Covers rubbed and somewhat worn, slight bubbling to rear. Shelfwear to bottom edge and spine. Corners turned in with top front bumped. Spine lightly faded. Lightly toned page edges with a few small spots at page edges at front. Bookplate. Generally very good.

Est.: $1,000-up
Start Bid: $500

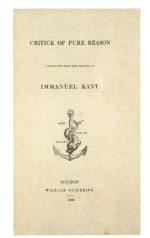

36354 **Immanuel Kant.** *Critick of Pure Reason.* London: W. Pickering, 1838. First edition in English. Octavo. xxxvi, 655, [1, errata] pages. Publisher's green cloth and paper spine label laid down over a rebacked spine with original boards. Covers worn and rubbed with bumped corners. Lightly faded spine and rubbed label. Pages somewhat toned with occasional foxing and small stain to bottom of text block. First few signatures a bit proud. Previous owner's signatures

to front pastedown. Generally very good. *Printing and the Mind of Man* 226.

Est.: $1,000-up
Start Bid: $500

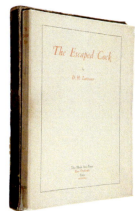

36355 **D. H. Lawrence. Two First Editions,** including: *The Escaped Cock.* Paris: The Black Sun Press, 1929. First edition, limited to 450 numbered copies, of which this is number 35. Octavo. 96 pages. Frontispiece. Publisher's wrappers and glassine. Marbled paper-covered slipcase. Very good condition. [and:] *The Man Who Died.* New York: Alfred A. Knopf, 1931. First American edition, advance reader's copy. Octavo. 103 pages. Publisher's binding. Review slip tipped in. Fine.

Est.: $600-up
Start Bid: $300

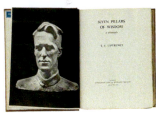

36356 **T. E. Lawrence.** *Seven Pillars of Wisdom.* London: Jonathan Cape, [1935]. First trade edition. Quarto. 672 pages. Illustrations and maps. Publisher's full cloth with gilt-stamped titles and design to front and titles to spine. Covers somewhat rubbed and darkened with light abrading to the spine ends and turned corners. Page edges lightly toned with occasional foxing. Bookplate, bookseller's ticket, and owner's signature to front. Slightly cocked. Generally very good.

Est.: $1,000-up
Start Bid: $500

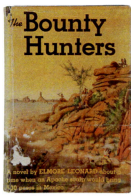

36357   Elmore Leonard.
The Bounty Hunters. Boston:
Houghton Mifflin, 1954. First edition, first printing. **Signed by
Leonard** on title page. Octavo. 180
pages. Publisher's binding and
dust jacket. Rubbing and wear to
cloth with abrading to extremities
and splitting along joints. Jacket
shows wear to edges with a few
small chips and tears. Ex-library
with minimal markings. Very good.
Est.: $600-up
Start Bid: $300

**36358   Jack London. *The Son of
the Wolf.*** Boston: Houghton Mifflin,
1900. First edition, later impression.
Octavo. 251 pages. Publisher's gray
cloth with silver titles and decoration. Mild rubbing to cloth with
a tiny bit of abrading to corners.
Slightly cocked spine. A few small
spots of soiling to endpapers. Very
good.
Est.: $800-up
Start Bid: $400

**36359   [Photoplay edition].
Faith Compton Mackenzie. *The
Sibyl of the North: The Tale of
Christina, Queen of Sweden.***
New York: Grosset & Dunlap, n.d.
Photoplay edition. Octavo. 262
pages. Endpapers with photographs from the 1933 Metro-
Goldwyn-Mayer film *Queen
Christina,* starring Greta Garbo.
Publisher's black-stamped purple
cloth and dust jacket without price
as issued. Top and bottom edges
of boards and spine faded. Gouge
and tear to fore-edge margin of
three leaves, affecting one word of
text; two facing pages with minor
stain to gutter margin. Ink gift inscription and pencil name to half-
title. Spine ends of jacket chipped;
a few other minor chips, rubbing,
and darkening of spine. A tight,
square copy in overall very good
condition. Scarce.
Est.: $600-up
Start Bid: $300

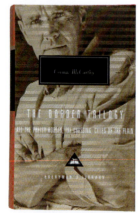

36360   Cormac McCarthy.
The Border Trilogy. New York:
Everyman's Library, [1999]. First
edition, first printing. **Signed by
McCarthy** on title page. Octavo.
Publisher's binding and dust jacket.
Includes *All the Pretty Horses, The
Crossing,* and *Cities of the Plain.* Fine.
Est.: $600-up
Start Bid: $300

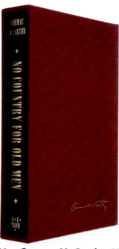

**36361   Cormac McCarthy. *No
Country For Old Men.*** [New
Orleans: Trice, 2005]. First edition,
**limited to 325 numbered copies of which this is 125. Signed
by McCarthy.** Octavo. 309 pages.
Publisher's binding and slipcase.
Fine.
Est.: $800-up
Start Bid: $400

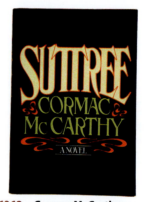

36362   Cormac McCarthy.
Suttree. New York: Random House,
[1979]. First edition, first printing.
Octavo. 471 pages. Publisher's
binding and dust jacket. Mild rubbing to jacket with a few tiny tears
at spine head. Not price clipped
or remainder marked, as is often
seen. A bright, fine copy, better
than usual.
Est.: $600-up
Start Bid: $300

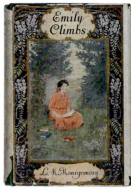

36363   L. M. Montgomery.
Emily Climbs. New York: Frederick
A. Stokes Company, 1925. First
edition. Octavo. 312 pages. Color
frontispiece illustrated by M. L.
Kirk. Publisher's green cloth with
pictorial front board illustration.
Original pictorial dust jacket. Some
toning to the preliminary and
terminal pages. Contemporary gift
inscription in pencil on the front
free endpaper. Dust jacket a bit
tatty around the edges with some
dampstaining to the spine and rear
panel. Overall, a very good copy.
Est.: $600-up
Start Bid: $300

36364   George G. W. Morgan.
***Aspiration and Realization. A
Story in Verse For Children.*** San
Francisco: Winterburn & Company,
1874. First edition. **Inscribed
by Morgan "*With the author's
compl*"** at the top of the title
page. Octavo. 18 pages. Three
plates. Beautifully bound in green
morocco with a raised central
panel bordered by three gilt rules
and containing a floral vignette
accented with red morocco inlays and gilt accents. The back
board shares a similar vignette.
Embossed gold endpapers. All
edges gilt. This copy has the name
"Mrs Winterburn" stamped in gilt on
the front board. Presumably Mrs.
Winterburn was associated with
the publisher Joseph Winterburn.
Hinges reinforced with blue cloth

tape. Spine slightly faded. Corners bumped, else a beautiful example of early California bookbinding.

Est.: $600-up
Start Bid: $300

36365   Giuseppe Pichi. *Traduzion Dal Toscan en Lengua Veneziana de Bertoldo Bertoldin e Cacasseno Con i Argomenti,* *Allegorie, Spiegazion dele parole, e frase Veneziane, che non fusse capie in ogni logo, stampae in sto caratere.* Padua: Zanbatista Conzati, 1747. First edition in Venetian of the second volume. Octavo. [vi], [209]-485, [1, blank] pages. With inserted frontispiece, and a plate. Original string-bound boards. Minor rubbing, else fine.

Est.: $600-up
Start Bid: $300

36366   Plato. *Phaedon: or, a Dialogue on the Immortality of the Soul.* New York: W. Gowan, 1833. First American edition. Octavo. 209 pages. Original muslinbacked boards with paper spine label. Covers rubbed and somewhat soiled with abraded edges and bumped bottom corners. Spine label with minor loss. Light toning to endpapers and page edges. Very minor spotting to endpapers. Bookplate. Very good.

Est.: $600-up
Start Bid: $300

36367   [Edgar Allan Poe]. First Appearance of Edgar Allan Poe In a Literary Magazine - Review of His Poem "Fairy-Land" in *The Yankee; and Boston Literary Gazette.* Boston: Wells and Lilly, 1829. Volume II, No. 3. Octavo. 55 pages. Printed wrappers. String bound. Covers detached but present. Front cover with loss at the upper right corner. The edges of the pages are tatty but on the whole it is in very good condition. John Neal reviews Poe's poem "Fairy-Land": "E. A. P. of Baltimore — whose lines about 'Heaven,' though he professes to regard them as altogether superior to anything in the whole range of American poetry, save two or three trifles referred to, are, though nonsense, rather exquisite nonsense - would but do himself justice, might make a beautiful and perhaps magnificent poem. There is a good deal to justify such a hope." An extract of "Fairy-Land" follows.

Est.: $600-up
Start Bid: $300

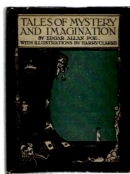

36368   Edgar Allan Poe. *Tales of Mystery and Imagination.* New York: Tudor Publishing Company, 1933. First Tudor illustrated edition. Quarto. 412 pages. With thirty-two plates and additional illustrations in text by Harry Clarke. Publisher's black cloth with paper title label mounted to the front board. Boards shelf worn at the extremities. Gilt titles on the spine faded. Contents slightly toned around the

edges of the pages, else a sound copy in very good condition complete with the original dust jacket. The jacket is worn at the edges and spine ends but remains in very good condition. Difficult to find this title with the original jacket.

Est.: $400-up
Start Bid: $200

36369   [Punch Magazine]. *A Bowl of Punch.* Philadelphia: G. B. Zieber & Co. and New York: Burgess Stringer & Co., 1844. First edition. Octavo. 216 pages. Frontispiece engraved by August Koellner. Twelve lithographs in text. Three-quarter morocco and marbled boards. Marbled endpapers. Top edge gilt. [Bound With:] **Thomas Hood.** *The Dream of Eugene Aram. The Murderer.* London: David Bogue, 1846. New edition. Octavo. 31 pages. Illustrations by W. Harvey. Front board detached. Spine panel loose. Contents generally sound and in very good condition.

Est.: $600-up
Start Bid: $300

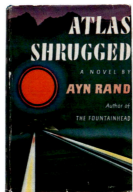

36370   Ayn Rand. *Atlas Shrugged.* New York: Random House, [1957]. First edition. Octavo. [viii], [1,174] pages. Publisher's full green cloth with front cover stamped in gilt, spine stamped in gilt and black. Top edge stained black. Original pictorial dust jacket. Minimal soiling and two small bumps to boards. Very minor thumbsoiling to text. Minor chipping to jacket edges. A 3.5 inch vertical tear, extending a half-inch horizontally across the spine to the rear spine fold of the jacket. Without the tear, it's a near fine copy. Still, an unusually bright copy in very good condition.

Est.: $600-up
Start Bid: $300

36371   [Baron Munchausen]. [Eric Rudolph Raspe]. *Gulliver Redivivus: or the Celebrated and Entertaining Travels and Adventures, of the Renowned Baron Munchausen, by Sea and Land:* *Including a Tour to the United States of America.* Philadelphia: Key & Mielke, 1832. Later edition. Thirtytwomo. 162 pages. With five full-page engravings and one large fold-out. Period quarter-leather with gilt spine titles over marbled boards. Covers and extremities rubbed and worn with abrading to edges and corners. Endpapers, pages, and edges moderately foxed and toned. Fold-out illustration has tear and minor loss at bottom right corner, mildly affecting image. A miniscule amount of nibbling to bottom of rear joint and spine. Two minute spots of dampstaining to preliminaries. Generally, a very good copy.

Est.: $600-up
Start Bid: $300

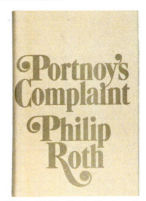

36372   Philip Roth. *Portnoy's Complaint.* New York: Random House, [1969]. First edition, **number 179 of 600 numbered copies signed by the author.** Octavo. 274 pages. Publisher's binding, dust jacket and slipcase. Previous bookseller's sticker on rear pastedown, light rubbing to slipcase. Fine.

Est.: $1,000-up
Start Bid: $500

36373   Jean Jacques Rousseau. *La Nouvelle Héloise, ou Lettres de Deux Amans, Habitans d' Une Petite Ville au Pied des Alpes.* Lausanne: Lacombe, 1792. Approximately 5.75 x 3.5 inches. Four twelvemo volumes. With twelve plates inserted throughout. Text in French. Later half green calf over marbled boards, spines ruled in gilt in compartments with four raised bands and brown morocco gilt lettering labels. Spines uniformly sunned, some rubbing to bindings, previous owner's ink inscriptions in volume I. From the library of Chief Secretary of Ireland Augustine Birrell (in office 1907-1916) with his bookplate in each volume. Near fine.
Est.: $600-up
Start Bid: $300

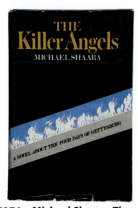

36374   Michael Shaara. *The Killer Angels.* New York: David McKay, [1974]. First edition, first printing. Octavo. 374 pages. Publisher's binding and dust jacket. General rubbing and light wear with fold lines and tiny tears to jacket. Overall very good.
Est.: $600-up
Start Bid: $300

36375   [Photoplay edition]. Mary W. Shelley. *Frankenstein or, the Modern Prometheus.* New York: Grosset & Dunlap, [n.d., circa 1931]. Photoplay edition with scenes from the Universal film directed by James Whale and starring Boris Karloff. Octavo. xiv, 240 pages. Six inserted illustrations from the movie and a frontispiece featuring Boris Karloff as Frankenstein. Publisher's red cloth with titles stamped in black. Top edge stained green. Dust jacket illustrated by Mach Tey. Boards with modest shelfwear and slightly bumped corners. Front hinge cracked but the text block and binding are tight. Contents clean with one plate loose. The jacket art remains bright with some toning to the spine and rear panel. Generally a very good copy of this desirable edition.
Est.: $400-up
Start Bid: $200

36376   Emma Smith. *Maiden's Trip.* London: Putnam & Co., 1948. First edition of the author's first book. Octavo. [iv], 208 pages. Publisher's binding, and original pictorial dust jacket. Jacket spine a bit browned, some rubbing to jacket panels, mild bumping to corners of book. Skewed. Still, near fine. **With two Autograph Letters (two pages each) by the author and an envelope addressed by her.** She answers the letters of an admirer, who has asked questions about this book and her second book, *The Far Cry.*
Est.: $600-up
Start Bid: $300

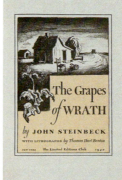

36377   [Thomas Hart Benton, illustrator]. John Steinbeck. *The Grapes of Wrath.* New York: The Limited Editions Club, 1940. **Number 391 of 1,146 copies signed by the illustrator, Thomas Hart Benton.** Two quarto volumes. Illustrated with lithographs by Thomas Hart Benton. Publisher's quarter rawhide and grass cloth over boards with silver spine titles with slipcase. Slipcase gently rubbed. Otherwise, near fine.
Est.: $1,000-up
Start Bid: $500

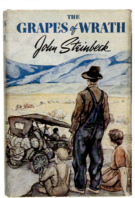

36378   John Steinbeck. *The Grapes of Wrath.* New York: Viking, [1939]. First edition. Octavo. 619 pages. Publisher's binding. Original pictorial dust jacket. Jacket spine a bit browned with some rubbing and several tears to jacket. Tape repairs to jacket verso. Minor rubbing to binding. Bookplate. Very good.
Est.: $800-up
Start Bid: $400

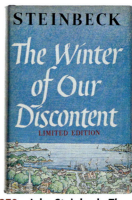

36379   John Steinbeck. *The Winter of Our Discontent.* New York: The Viking Press, 1961. First edition, **limited to 500 copies specially bound for friends of the author and publishers.** Octavo. 311 pages. Publisher's blue-gray cloth with gilt titles over beveled boards with the original pictorial dust jacket and original acetate wrapper. Very light wear to board edges. Jacket lightly toned at spine, edges and verso with rubbing at spine. Otherwise, near fine.
Est.: $1,200-up
Start Bid: $600

36380   Wallace Stevens. *Harmonium.* New York: Alfred A. Knopf, 1923. First edition, third binding state, one of 715 copies printed in 1926. Octavo. 140 pages. Original blue cloth with titles printed in red on a yellow paper label mounted to the spine. Slight toning to spine panel, with a former owner's name written neatly in ink on the front free endpaper, otherwise with trivial shelf wear and in near fine condition. Housed in a custom half-morocco slipcase with titles stamped in gilt on two labels on the spine. *Harmonium* was Stevens' first collection of poetry published at the late age of 44. Some of his most famous poems are included here, such as "The Emperor of Ice-Cream," a poem on the banality of funeral ceremonies, "The Snow Man," and "Sunday Morning." Edelstein, A1.a. Connolly, *One Hundred Modern Books*, 46.

Est.: $600-up
Start Bid: $300

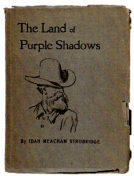

36381   Idah Meacham Strobridge. *The Land of Purple Shadows.* Los Angeles: The Artemisia Bindery, 1909. **Autograph edition limited to one thousand copies hand-numbered and signed by the author on a special limitation page in front.** Octavo. 133, [8, publisher's catalog] pages. With illustrations by Maynard Dixon. Printed wrappers. Edges of the wrappers slightly tatty and toned. Rear wrapper detached but present. Contents bright and in very good condition.

Est.: $600-up
Start Bid: $300

36382   Rodolphe Töpffer. *Monsieur Pencil.* Genève: [n.p.], 1840. Oblong format. 72 pages. Lithography by Schmid. Printed wrappers. A few creases to scattered pages; light scattered foxing, else a near fine copy. The album includes 214 pen drawings on seventy plates drawn, written and transferred in autograph by the author.

Est.: $600-up
Start Bid: $300

36383   Mark Twain. *Life on the Mississippi.* Boston: James R. Osgood and Company, 1883. First edition, second state. Octavo. 624 pages. Profusely illustrated. Publisher's brown pictorial cloth stamped in gilt and black. Modest shelf wear to boards. Former owner's book plate on the front pastedown. A clean, bright copy in very good condition.

Est.: $600-up
Start Bid: $300

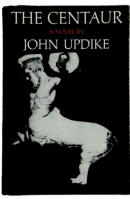

36384   John Updike. *The Centaur.* New York: Knopf, 1963. First edition. **Signed by Updike** on title page. Octavo. 302 pages. Publisher's binding and dust jacket. Slightly cocked spine with toning to board edges. Jacket shows light rubbing and wear to edges with a few tiny chips and tears. Faint sunning along spine. Very good.

Est.: $1,000-up
Start Bid: $500

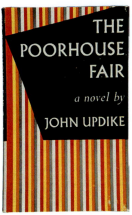

36385   John Updike. *The Poorhouse Fair.* New York: Knopf, 1959. First edition, first printing. Octavo. 185 pages. Publisher's binding and first state dust jacket. Minor sunning to top board edges. Light stain for fore-edge. Jacket shows mild rubbing to extremities with a small area of staining and a one-inch tear to rear panel. Overall, near fine.

Est.: $600-up
Start Bid: $300

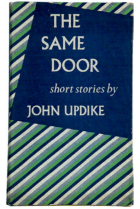

36386   John Updike. *The Same Door.* New York: Knopf, 1959. First edition, first printing. Octavo. 185 pages. Publisher's binding and dust jacket. Minor toning to board edges with one softly bumped lower corner. Jacket shows light rubbing and wear to edges with modest chipping at head of spine. Overall, near fine.

Est.: $600-up
Start Bid: $300

36387   [François-Marie Arouet de Voltaire]. *La Princesse de Babilone.* A Geneve (London), 1768. Pirated printing of the first French language edition. Octavo. 184 pages. Modern full carmine leather with five raised bands and morocco label with gilt titles. Boards lightly bowed. New endpapers, preliminaries, and terminals. Pages edges moderately toned, somewhat significantly at front and rear. Some light bumping, minor loss, and folding to bottom corner of first thirty pages. Occasional light foxing and toning throughout. Generally, very good.

Est.: $600-up
Start Bid: $300

36388   A. V. W. [Ames Van Wart]. *A Recollection of Wondrous Wanderings.* Fontainebleau [London: William Macintosh, 1864]. First edition. Quarto. 67 pages. Illustrated by Irving Van Wart. Publisher's pictorial brown cloth lavishly accented in gilt. All edges gilt. Boards worn at the extremities; binding slightly shaken, else a very good copy. A remarkable and unusual book of comic poetry.

Est.: $600-up
Start Bid: $300

36389 **Eudora Welty.** *Music from Spain.* Greenville, Mississippi: Levee Press, 1948. First edition, **number 351 of 775 copies signed by the author. Additionally inscribed by the author** opposite the title page. Publisher's brown paper covered pictorial boards with a paper spine label. Slight browning and bumps, spine a bit darkened and with small stain. A very good copy.
Est.: $600-up
Start Bid: $300

36390 **P. G. Wodehouse.** *Plum Stones - The Hidden P. G. Wodehouse,* **Complete in Twelve Volumes.** [London]: Galahad Books, [1993-1995]. First editions, **each volume limited to 250 numbered copies.** Octavo stapled wrappers. Commentary by Tony Ring. Original gold-lettered plum-colored wrappers. All fine. Collection of Wodehouse stories not previously published in book form, here in the original-issue wrappers. Scarce.
Est.: $600-up
Start Bid: $300

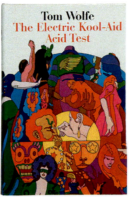

36391 **Tom Wolfe.** *The Electric Kool-Aid Acid Test.* New York: Farrar Straus and Giroux, [1968]. First edition, first printing. Octavo. 413 pages. Publisher's binding and dust jacket. Toning to board edges. Price-clipped jacket shows mild wear to extremities. Very good.
Est.: $1,000-up
Start Bid: $500

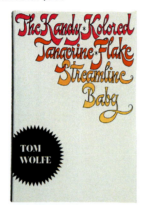

36392 **Tom Wolfe.** *The Kandy-Kolored Tangerine-Flake Streamline Baby.* New York: Farrar Straus and Giroux, [1965]. First edition, first printing. **Signed by Wolfe** on front free endpaper. Octavo. 339 pages. Publisher's binding and dust jacket. Slightly cocked spine. Softly bumped spine ends. Dust jacket shows minor rubbing with a few tiny tears along top edge. Very good.
Est.: $800-up
Start Bid: $400

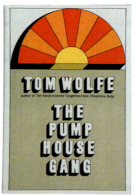

36393 **Tom Wolfe.** *The Pump House Gang.* New York: Farrar Straus and Giroux, [1968]. First edition, first printing. **Signed by Wolfe** on front free endpaper. Octavo. 309 pages. Publisher's binding and dust jacket. Fine.
Est.: $600-up
Start Bid: $300

36394 **[Henry L. Stephens, illustrator].** *The Fables of Aesop, With Fifty-Six Illustrations From Designs By Henry L. Stephens.* New York: J. W. Bouton, 1868. Early edition. Quarto. 76 pages. Fifty-six plates by Stephens. Publisher's three-quarter morocco and cloth. All edges gilt. Marbled endpapers. Corners and joints worn; front joint starting to split. Front hinge broken causing the front board to be slightly loose; rear hinge starting. Spine loose. Else a rare edition with beautiful illustrations, worthy of conservation and in internally bright and fine condition.
Est.: $600-up
Start Bid: $300

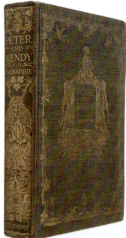

36395 **J. M. Barrie.** *Peter and Wendy.* New York: Charles Scribner's Sons, [1911]. First American edition. Octavo. 267 pages. With thirteen illustrations by F. D. Bedford. Publisher's olive green cloth with gilt titles and elaborate gilt stamping to the front cover and spine. Housed in a custom marbled slipcase. Minor wear and light soiling to the cloth. Minimal sunning to spine. Slightly bumped corners, one exposed. Bookplate and bookseller's ticket to the front free endpaper. Small stain to the verso of the plate at p. 108. Overall, a near fine copy with unusually bright gilt stamping.
Est.: $400-up
Start Bid: $200

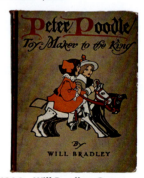

36396 **Will Bradley.** *Peter Poodle Toy Maker to the King.* New York: Dodd, Mead & Company, 1906. First edition. Quarto. 166 pages. Illustrated throughout by the author. Pictorial boards with maroon cloth backstrip. Illustrated endpapers. Edges of the boards moderately worn. Binding slightly shaken. Small ownership stamp in blind a the preliminary pages, else a sound copy of this uncommon work in very good condition.
Est.: $600-up
Start Bid: $300

36397   [Dinah Maria Craik]. *The Adventures of a Brownie As Told to My Child.* London: Sampson Low, Marston, Low and Searle, 1872. First edition, with rear ads dated 1871. Octavo. [xiv], [120], [4, ads], [32, publisher's catalogue] pages. Publisher's full red cloth, front cover and spine stamped in black and gilt, rear cover stamped in blind. Some soiling and rubbing to binding. Skewed. Very good. With the signature of Lady Wilkinson. The first edition of this work is very rare, and Sadleir only reports seeing one in his life.

Est.: $600-up
Start Bid: $300

36398   [Walter Crane, illustrator]. [Edmund] Spenser. *Spenser's Faerie Queene.* *A Poem in Six Books, with the Fragment Mutabilitie.* Edited by Thomas J. Wise. Pictured by Walter Crane. London: Published by George Allen, 1897-1896. First edition illustrated by Walter Crane, **one of 1,000 copies on handmade paper** for England and America. Approximately 10.25 x 8.25 inches. Six quarto volumes. Double-page general title, seven title-pages, and eighty-eight full-page woodcut illustrations (including one double-page). With 132 head- and tail-pieces, numerous decorative initials, and printer's and publisher's colophons. Contemporary half olive levant morocco over marbled boards, spines ruled and lettered in gilt in compartments, five raised bands, top edge gilt, marbled endleaves. Spines slightly sunned, some wear to binding, bookplates. Overall, very good. "The most important work in the whole long list of books illustrated by Walter

Crane..." (Konody, p. 71). Ashley V, p. 196. Engen, *Crane,* p. 102. Massé, pp. 47-48.

Est.: $600-up
Start Bid: $300

36399   [Cruikshank, illustrator]. Horace Mayhew. *The Tooth-Ache:* *The Origin of the Tooth-Ache.* Philadelphia: A. Hart, c. 1850. Later American edition. Twelvemo. 24 folded concertina-style pages. 43 panels of hand-colored engravings. Pictorial paper over boards with cloth spine. Boards somewhat toned and rubbed with minor loss to extremities. Pages lightly toned and creased with some reinforced seams on reverse. Some rubbing to page edges. Needs repair of main block to rear board. Otherwise, very good.

Est.: $600-up
Start Bid: $300

36400   [Walt Disney Studios]. *Mickey Mouse and His Horse Tanglefoot.* Philadelphia: David McKay Company, 1936. First edition. Octavo. 60 pages. With numerous color illustrations in text illustrated by the staff of Walt Disney Studios. Original publisher's pictorial boards and rare dust jacket. A bit of trivial toning to pages; contemporary gift inscription on the front-free endpaper; jacket soiled with some loss at the corners and spine ends; else a very good copy in the seldom seen original dust jacket.

Est.: $600-up
Start Bid: $300

36401   [Walt Disney Studios]. *The "Pop-Up" Silly Symphonies Containing Babes in the Woods and King Neptune.* New York: Blue Ribbon Books, Inc., 1933. First edition. Octavo. 48 pages. With thirty-four illustrations including four double-page pop ups illustrated by the staff of Walt Disney Studios. Publisher's color pictorial boards and original dust jacket. Pictorial endpapers. A beautiful copy of this desirable Disney pop-up with modest wear to the boards, toning to the dust jacket and some loss at the spine ends, but internally sound and in near fine condition.

Est.: $800-up
Start Bid: $400

36402   [Gustave Dore, illustrator]. Lodovico Ariosto. *Arioth's Rasender Roland.* Breslau, S. Schottlaender, [n.d., ca. 1880-1881]. First German edition. Approximately 16.75 x 11.75 inches. Two folio volumes. [vi], x, 299, [1, blank]; [iv], [301]-636 pages. With eighty-one full-page plates inserted throughout. Publisher's full red cloth, front covers elaborately stamped in decorative black, gilt, and gray, spine elaborately stamped in black and gilt. Silk endleaves. Bookplates. Despite some very minor rubbing to binding and light soiling to front

endleaves in both volumes, these volumes are exceedingly bright and in near fine condition.

Est.: $600-up
Start Bid: $300

36403   [Gustave Doré, illustrator]. Samuel Coleridge. *The Rime of the Ancient Mariner.* New York: Harper and Brothers, 1886. Early edition. Folio. Forty full-page plates, including vignette title page. Publisher's brown cloth with bevelled edges. spine and cover decoratively gilt, brown endpapers. Binding a bit rubbed and worn, especially on rear with scraping and discoloration, corners lightly worn and bumped. Internally quite clean with just light foxing in places. Very good.

Est.: $600-up
Start Bid: $300

36404   [Gustave Doré, illustrator]. Dante Alighieri. *The Vision of Hell.* Translated by the Rev. Henry Francis Cary,... London: Cassell, ... [n.d., ca. 1900]. New Edition. Folio. Inserted portrait frontispiece, title-page and seventy-five plates by Doré. Half brown morocco, maroon cloth boards, spines gilt in compartments, raised bands, all edges gilt, pale-yellow coated endpapers. Some light foxing, else very good.

Est.: $600-up
Start Bid: $300

36405   **[Gustave Doré, illustrator].** Edgar Allan Poe. *The Raven.* With comment by Edmund C. Stedman. New York: Harper & Brothers, 1884. First American edition. Large folio. Wood-engraved title vignette after Vedder and twenty-six wood-engraved plates after drawings by Doré. Original gray cloth decoratively stamped with an angel design in purple and gilt, brown endpapers, all edges gilt. Wear and bumping to corners, spine starting at joints and with small tears. Front free endpaper all but detached. Still, a very good, attractive copy of Doré's last book.

Est.: $600-up
Start Bid: $300

36406   **[F. G. Ducray-Duminil].** *Ambrose and Eleanor; or, the Adventures of Two Children Deserted on an Uninhabited Island.* Translated from the French. London: Printed for R. and L. Peacock, 1797. Second edition. Octavo. iv, 226, [2, ads] pages. With frontispiece. Contemporary full tree calf, spine ruled in gilt. Some wear to binding, joints starting. Very good. Adapted and translated by Lucy Peacock.

Est.: $600-up
Start Bid: $300

36407   **Rachel Field.** *Hitty, Her First Hundred Years.* New York: Macmillan, 1929. First edition, first printing. **Signed by Rachel Field and illustrator Dorothy P. Lathrop.** Field's copy with her bookplate and notation "First copy off the press. October 22nd, 1929." Square octavo. 207 pages. Illustrations, some in color, by Dorothy P. Lathrop. Publisher's floral-patterned cloth and printed paper label to front board. Spine sunned. A few pencil notations throughout made presumably by the author. Else, a very good copy. Housed in a custom clamshell box. Winner of the 1930 Newbery Medal.

Est.: $600-up
Start Bid: $300

36408   **[Gumuchian & Compagnie].** *Les Livres de L'Enfance du XVe au XIXe Siècle.* Paris: Gumuchian & Compagnie, [n.d., 1930]. Limited edition, **one of 900 copies on Papier Vélin.** Two large quarto volumes. [xxiv], 446, plus three pages of ads; unpaginated, with 336 plates. Preface by Paul Gavault. Text in French and English. Illustrated with color and black and white plates. Quarter red leather and cloth by Sotheran & Co., London. Top edges gilt. Wear to extremities, including corners, joints, and raised bands. Over-opened at plate 157 in Volume II. Else, a near fine set of the first major bibliography of children's books.

Est.: $600-up
Start Bid: $300

36409   **Syd Hoff.** *Julius.* New York: Harper & Row Publishers, [1959]. Later printing. **With an original pen and ink drawing by Hoff of a dog's face in profile and inscribed by him: "Love / to / Jason, / Syd / Hoff".** Octavo. 64 pages. Publisher's pictorial boards. Some rubbing to boards and spine. Near fine.

Est.: $600-up
Start Bid: $300

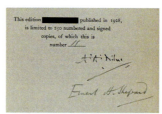

36410   **A. A. Milne.** *The House at Pooh Corner.* New York: E. P. Dutton & Co, [1928]. First edition. **Signed by Milne and artist, Ernest Shepard** on the limitation page. This copy is one of a very few wherein the limitation page from the Dutton large paper deluxe edition has been tipped in between the title and dedication pages of the first trade edition - this sheet of Japon paper is numbered 11 (of 250), trimmed for this smaller format, and the words "on Large Paper" have been inked out. Twelvemo. xi, 178 pages. Illustrations by Ernest H. Shepard. Publisher's salmon cloth, titled and pictorially stamped in gilt. All edges gilt. Pictorial endpapers. In glassine dust jacket and marbled slipcase. Very minor scuffing to spine ends and corners. Top tenth or so of the glassine missing. Otherwise, a near fine copy of a rare variant.

Est.: $600-up
Start Bid: $300

36411   **A. A. Milne.** *When We Were Very Young.* First appearance, eighteen chapters, contained in *Punch, or the London Charivari.* Volume 166, January-June, 1924. First edition. Quarto. 708 pages with Almanack at rear. Contemporary red cloth with minor rubbing to extremities. Spine sunned with a touch of fraying to head. Very good.

Est.: $600-up
Start Bid: $300

36412   **[Kay Nielsen, illustrator].** *East of the Sun and West of the Moon.* Old Tales from the North. [London]: Hodder & Stoughton, [n.d., 1914]. First edition. Quarto. 206 pages. With twenty-five tipped-in color plates protected by captioned tissue guards and several black-and-white text illustrations and chapter heading designs by Nielsen. Recently rebacked in blue cloth over the original blue cloth boards with gilt lettering and decoration to the spine and front board. Pictorial endpapers. Corners re-tipped. Minor shelf wear and rubbing to the boards. Edges and pages lightly toned with scattered foxing and thumbsoiling. Plates in excellent condition. A very good copy of a wonderfully illustrated book.

Est.: $600-up
Start Bid: $300

36413   [Willy Pogany, illustrator]. Helen von Kolzitzhyer, Muriel Smith, et al. *The Wimp and the Woodle and Other Stories.* Los Angeles: Suttonhouse, Ltd., 1935. First edition, **number 78 of 250 copies signed by Pogany and the authors.** Quarto. [xvi], [181], [1, blank] pages. With seven mounted full-color plates inserted throughout. Publisher's suede binding, front cover and spine lettered in gilt. Binding a bit dry (with some flaking) and rubbed. Overall, a near fine copy.
Est.: $600-up
Start Bid: $300

36414   **Nine Puffin Books, Including Eight First Editions**. All books published in London by Penguin Books, Limited, and all are oblong octavos in publisher's printed wrappers (except as noted), including: **Clarke Hutton. Punch & Judy.** [N.d., ca. 1945]. [28] pages. [and:] **Chiang Yee. The Story of Ming.** [N.d., ca. 1945]. [28] pages. [and:] **Kathleen Hale. Orlando's Invisible Pyjamas.** [N.d. ca. 1945]. 30 pages. [and:] **W. J. Bassett-Lowke and Paul B. Mann. Marvellous Models.** [1947]. Revised edition. 31 pages. [and:] **Enid Marx. A Book of Rigmaroles or Jungle Rhymes.** [N.d., ca. 1945]. [28] pages. [and:] **Anne Skibulits and Clarke Hutton. The Story of Tea.** 1948. 31 pages. [and:] **R. B. Serjeant and Edward Bawden. The Arabs.** [N.d., ca. 1947]. Hardcover. [36] pages. [and:] **R. B. Talbot Kelly. Paper Birds.** [N.d., ca. 1947]. 30 pages. [and:] **J. B. Priestley and Doris Zinkeisen. The High Toby.** [N.d., ca. 1948]. [16] pages. Plus sixteen leaves of scenery and dolls to cut out to perform

the play (all leaves uncut and present). Condition is generally near fine or better.
Est.: $600-up
Start Bid: $300

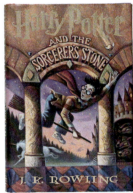

36415   J. K. Rowling. *Harry Potter and the Sorcerer's Stone.* New York: Scholastic, [1998]. First American edition, first printing. Octavo. 309 pages. Publisher's binding. Original first issue ($16.95) dust jacket with *The Guardian* blurb on the rear panel. Very minor sunning to jacket spine, some rubbing to edges. Fine.
Est.: $800-up
Start Bid: $400

36416   **Dr. Seuss. *How the Grinch Stole Christmas!*** New York: Random House, [1957]. First edition in first issue dust jacket. Octavo. Publisher's glazed paper boards, and dust jacket with "250/250" price. Moderate wear to extremities; binding slightly cocked. A couple of tears to paper along rear joint. Light indentations to bottom margin of most pages. Neat ink name to front free endpaper. Jacket with chips, particularly significant at spine ends and at bottom edge of front panel; a few tears (one measuring one inch) and creasing to rear panel. Generally very good.
Est.: $600-up
Start Bid: $300

36417   [William Steig]. Original Drawing from *Giggle Box*. A delightful original drawing for the Alfred A. Knopf children's anthology, *Giggle Box* (1950), for which Steig provided all of the illustrations. This image is for the excerpt from Glen Rounds' *Pay Dirt*. Executed on a white sheet of sketch paper measuring 7.5 x 10 inches. Beneath the inked image are blue penciled notations for the design department. On the verso is affixed an official Knopf paper shipping label with an inked note to "return to" the publisher's offices. A charming example of the work of a well-known and prolific cartoonist.
Est.: $600-up
Start Bid: $300

36418   **The Honorable Mrs. W. & Lady M (Mary Ward and Jane Mahon). *Entomology in Sport, and Entomology in Earnest.*** London: Paul Jerrard & Son, [n.d., ca. 1859]. First edition. Octavo. 68 pages. With frontispiece and engraved title page. Hand-colored plates and vignettes throughout. Publisher's brown cloth, front cover double-ruled in gilt, and decoratively stamped in gilt, and lettered in green, rear cover similarly stamped in blind, spine lettered in gilt. Some rubbing to binding. Text shaken with some loose pages. Good.
Est.: $600-up
Start Bid: $300

36419   **William Wegman with Carole Kismaric and Marvin Heiferman.** *Cinderella.* New York: Hyperion: [1993]. First edition, second printing. **With an original ink drawing by Wegman of two dogs' faces (presumably Wegman's characteristic Weimaraners) in profile and inscribed by him: "To / Taylor / William Wegman / 1993".** Quarto. [40] pages. Publisher's black cloth backstrip over black paper boards, front board lettered in blind, spine lettered in gilt. Lacking dust jacket. Some rubbing, mild bumping to binding. Very good.
Est.: $600-up
Start Bid: $300

36420   **E. B. White. *Charlotte's Web.*** Pictures by Garth Williams. New York: Harper & Brothers, Publishers, [1952]. First edition, with "I-B" on the copyright page. Octavo. 184 pages. Publisher's brown cloth with decorative blue and black titles. Original first issue dust jacket with four blurbs for *Stuart Little* on the rear panel (price-clipped). Minor abrading at the spine folds of the jacket. One small closed tear to the top of the front panel, a tiny chip at the spine head, and minimal loss at the spine tail. Otherwise, a near fine copy.
Est.: $600-up
Start Bid: $300

36421 E. B. White. *Charlotte's Web.* Pictures by Garth Williams. New York: Harper, [1952]. First edition. Publisher's cloth and first issue dust jacket. Minor toning to the dust jacket, with chipping and slight loss at corners and spine ends. A very good copy.

Est.: $400-up
Start Bid: $200

36422 Garth Williams. Original **Large Watercolor Painting of Unused Illustration for** *Baby's First Book*, **1955**, featuring a house and a family-filled car. Watercolor on thick paper board measuring 15 x 20 inches. **Signed in full by Garth Williams** in ink at bottom right, and with his notations. Also with four sheets of preliminary pencil drawings: three on opaque paper (two of which are taped together), **initialed by Williams**, and one on tracing paper, **signed in full by Williams**. A couple of pencil sketches with very minor edge wear and cellotape at corners. Else, all generally fine. *From the Estate of Garth Williams.*

Est.: $600-up
Start Bid: $300

36423 Garth Williams. Original **Large Watercolor Painting of Unused Illustration for** *Baby's First Book*, **1955**, featuring a horse and train. Watercolor on thick paper board measuring 15 x 20

inches. **Signed in full by Garth Williams** in ink at bottom left, and with his notations. Also with four sheets of preliminary pencil drawings on paper, all **initialed by Williams**, and with his notations. All generally fine. *From the Estate of Garth Williams.*

Est.: $600-up
Start Bid: $300

36424 Garth Williams. Original **Large Watercolor Painting of Unused Illustration for** *Baby's First Book*, **1955**, featuring a girl on a swing and a tree. Watercolor on thick paper board measuring 15 x 20 inches. **Signed in full by Garth Williams** in ink at lower right, and with his notations. Generally fine. *From the Estate of Garth Williams.*

Est.: $600-up
Start Bid: $300

36425 Garth Williams. Original **Large Watercolor Painting of Unused Illustration for** *Baby's First Book*, **1955**, featuring a house at night under a starry sky. Watercolor on thick paper board measuring 15 x 20 inches. **Signed in full by Garth Williams** in ink at upper left, and with his notations. Generally fine. *From the Estate of Garth Williams.*

Est.: $600-up
Start Bid: $300

36426 Garth Williams. Original **Large Watercolor Painting of Unused Illustration for** *Baby's First Book*, **1955**, featuring an airplane, a horse, a ball, a teddy bear, and a tree — proposed as the rear cover of the book. Watercolor on thick paper board measuring 20 x 15 inches. **Signed in full by Garth Williams** in ink at lower right, and with his notations. Sliver of browned tape at top margin, with a few smudges; water stain to verso which does not affect picture. Else, generally fine. *From the Estate of Garth Williams.*

Est.: $600-up
Start Bid: $300

36427 Garth Williams. Three **Original Watercolor Paintings for Unused Cover Art for** *Baby's First Book*, **1955**. Three sheets, two measuring roughly 12 x 7.35 and one, a folded sheet, measuring 12 x 15.75 inches with the image on one-half of the sheet. Expected puckering to paper. Watercolor on paper, all **signed in full by Garth Williams** in ink, with his written notations. All generally fine. *From the Estate of Garth Williams.*

Est.: $400-up
Start Bid: $200

36428 Garth Williams. Five **Original Watercolor Paintings for Unused Cover Art for** *Baby's First Book*, **1955**. Five sheets measuring 8 x 6.75 inches. Watercolor on paper, all **signed in full by Garth Williams** in ink. One with strip of paper for spine design reading "MY FIRST BOOK" stapled to top left corner of one of the sheets. Expected puckering to paper. All generally fine. All are alternate cover ideas, but two are very close to the design which was ultimately used (the baby reading the book). *From the Estate of Garth Williams.*

Est.: $400-up
Start Bid: $200

36429 Garth Williams. Five **Original Watercolor Paintings for Unused Cover Art for** *Baby's First Book*, **1955**. Five sheets, two measuring 11 x 8.5, and three measuring 8 x 6.75 inches. Watercolor on paper, all **signed in full by Garth Williams** in ink. Expected puckering to paper. All generally fine. All are alternate cover ideas, but two are very close to the design which was ultimately used (the baby reading the book). *From the Estate of Garth Williams.*

Est.: $400-up
Start Bid: $200

36430 Garth Williams. Eleven **Preliminary Drawings for Unused Cover Art for** *Baby's First Book*, **1955**. Eleven sheets, with ten measuring 11 x 8.5, and one measuring x 10.5 14.5 inches. Ten sheets contain rough pencil drawings on paper; one sheet is on a "Little Golden Book Layout Sheet" on card stock (this with cut-out pictures and words glued to sheet). Large sheet is **signed in full by Garth Williams,** with his written notations, and the other ten are **initialed by Garth Williams.** All generally fine. *From the Estate of Garth Williams.*

Est.: $400-up
Start Bid: $200

36431   Garth Williams. Three Original Watercolor Paintings Prepared for *Baby's First Book,* **1955.** Three sheets measuring 11 x 8.5 inches, some in landscape. Watercolor on paper, all **signed in full by Garth Williams** in ink, with his written notations. Expected puckering to paper. All generally fine. *From the Estate of Garth Williams.*

Est.: $400-up
Start Bid: $200

36432   Garth Williams. Three Original Watercolor Paintings Prepared for *Baby's First Book,* **1955.** Three sheets measuring 11 x 8.5 inches, some in landscape. Watercolor on paper, all **signed in full by Garth Williams** in ink, with his written notations. A few minor creases to edges. Expected puckering to paper. All generally fine. *From the Estate of Garth Williams.*

Est.: $400-up
Start Bid: $200

36433   Garth Williams. Three Original Watercolor Paintings Prepared for *Baby's First Book,* **1955.** Three sheets measuring 8.5 x 11 inches. Watercolor on paper, all **signed in full by Garth Williams** in ink, with his written notations. One with a few light creases to corner. Expected puckering to paper. All generally fine. *From the Estate of Garth Williams.*

Est.: $400-up
Start Bid: $200

36434   Garth Williams. Six Original Watercolor Paintings Prepared for *Baby's First Book,* **1955.** Six sheets, four measuring 11 x 8.5 inches and two measuring roughly 8.5 x 5.5 inches, some in landscape. Watercolor on paper, all **signed in full by Garth Williams** in ink, with his written notations. One small piece stapled to a larger one. Expected puckering to paper. All generally fine. *From the Estate of Garth Williams.*

Est.: $400-up
Start Bid: $200

36435   Garth Williams. Nine Original Watercolor Paintings Prepared for *Baby's First Book,* **1955.** Nine sheets measuring 11 x 8.5 inches, some in landscape. Watercolor on paper, all **initialed by Garth Williams,** with his written notations. Expected puckering to paper. A few shallow bends at edges. All generally fine. *From the Estate of Garth Williams.*

Est.: $400-up
Start Bid: $200

36436   Garth Williams. Ten Original Preliminary Drawings Prepared for *Baby's First Book,* **1955.** Ten sheets measuring 11 x 8.5 inches, some in landscape. Pencil on paper, all **initialed by Garth Williams.** One sheet with small area of discoloration at top right corner. Else all generally fine. *From the Estate of Garth Williams.*

Est.: $400-up
Start Bid: $200

36437   Garth Williams. Original Preliminary Drawings Prepared for *Baby's First Book,* **1955.** Eleven large sheets measuring in size from approximately 11 x 17 inches

(opaque paper) to 11.75 x 18.5 inches (tracing paper). Drawings are in pencil; several sheets have drawings on both sides. **All are signed in full by Garth Williams.** Some sheets appear to have been torn unevenly from a pad by the artist; sheets of tracing paper with occasional minor chips. Else all generally fine. *From the Estate of Garth Williams.*

Est.: $400-up
Start Bid: $200

36438   Garth Williams. Six Original Watercolor and Ink Preliminary Drawings for *The Chicken Book,* **1946,** including the preliminary cover/title page design. Six sheets of paper of various sizes measuring from 8 x 9.5 inches to 10.5 x 15.25 inches. Watercolor and ink on paper, all **signed in full by Garth Williams.** Some chips and a few creases. With the expected puckering to the sheets. All very good or better. *From the Estate of Garth Williams.*

Est.: $400-up
Start Bid: $200

36439   Garth Williams. Original Watercolored Blueline Cover Proof for *The Chicken Book,* **1946.** Cover art/title page of Garth Williams' charming little book on baby chicks, quite a bit different from the final version published. Watercolor on thick paper with printed blueline outlines, and detail, measuring 10 x 14.5 inches, mounted on a thick paper layout board measuring 12.75 x 18.75 inches. **Signed in full by Garth**

Williams on board at bottom right. Generally fine. *From the Estate of Garth Williams.*

Est.: $400-up
Start Bid: $200

36440 **Garth Williams. Original Watercolored Blueline Proof for** *The Chicken Book*, **1946.** First two-page spread. Watercolor on thick paper with printed blueline text, outlines, and detail, measuring approximately 9.25 x 22 inches. **Signed in full by Garth Williams** at bottom right. Publisher info on verso. Generally fine. *From the Estate of Garth Williams.*

Est.: $400-up
Start Bid: $200

36441 **Garth Williams. Original Watercolored Blueline Proof for** *The Chicken Book*, **1946.** Second two-page spread. Watercolor on thick paper with printed blueline text, outlines, and detail, measuring approximately 9.25 x 22 inches. **Signed in full by Garth Williams** at bottom right, with his notations. Publisher info on verso. Generally fine. *From the Estate of Garth Williams.*

Est.: $400-up
Start Bid: $200

36442 **Garth Williams. Original Watercolored Blueline Proof for** *The Chicken Book*, **1946.** Third two-page spread. Watercolor on thick paper with printed blueline text, outlines, and detail, measuring approximately 9.25 x 22 inches. **Signed in full by Garth Williams** at bottom right, with his notations. Publisher info on verso. Generally fine. *From the Estate of Garth Williams.*

Est.: $400-up
Start Bid: $200

36443 **Garth Williams. Original Watercolored Blueline Proof for** *The Chicken Book*, **1946.** Fourth two-page spread. Watercolor on thick paper with printed blueline text, outlines, and detail, measuring approximately 9.25 x 22 inches. **Signed in full by Garth Williams** at bottom right, with his notations. Publisher info on verso. Generally fine. *From the Estate of Garth Williams.*

Est.: $400-up
Start Bid: $200

36444 **Garth Williams. Original Watercolored Blueline Proof for** *The Chicken Book*, **1946.** Fifth two-page spread. Watercolor on thick paper with printed blueline text, outlines, and detail, measuring approximately 9.25 x 22 inches. **Signed in full by Garth Williams** at bottom right, with his notations. Publisher info on verso. Generally fine. *From the Estate of Garth Williams.*

Est.: $400-up
Start Bid: $200

36445 **Garth Williams. Original Watercolored Blueline Proof for** *The Chicken Book*, **1946.** Sixth two-page spread. Watercolor on thick paper with printed blueline text, outlines, and detail, measuring approximately 9.25 x 22 inches. **Signed in full by Garth Williams** at bottom right, with his notations. Publisher info on verso. This illustration with the acetate overlay containing text, outlines, and detail. Generally fine. *From the Estate of Garth Williams.*

Est.: $400-up
Start Bid: $200

36446 **Garth Williams. Original Watercolored Blueline Proof for** *The Chicken Book*, **1946.** Seventh two-page spread. Watercolor on thick paper with printed blueline text, outlines, and detail, measuring approximately 9.25 x 22 inches. **Signed in full by Garth Williams** at bottom right, with his notations. Publisher info on verso. Generally fine. *From the Estate of Garth Williams.*

Est.: $400-up
Start Bid: $200

36447 **Garth Williams. Original Watercolored Blueline Proof for** *The Chicken Book*, **1946.** Eighth two-page spread. Watercolor on thick paper with printed blueline text, outlines, and detail, measuring approximately 9.25 x 22 inches. **Signed "Garth"** at bottom right, with his notations. Publisher info on verso. Generally fine. *From the Estate of Garth Williams.*

Est.: $400-up
Start Bid: $200

36448 **Garth Williams. Original Watercolored Blueline Proof for** *The Chicken Book*, **1946.** Ninth two-page spread. Watercolor on thick paper with printed blueline text, outlines, and detail, measuring approximately 9.25 x 22 inches. **Signed in full by Garth Williams** at bottom right, with his notations. Publisher info on verso. Generally fine. *From the Estate of Garth Williams.*

Est.: $400-up
Start Bid: $200

36449 **Garth Williams. Original Watercolored Blueline Proof for** *The Chicken Book*, **1946.** Tenth two-page spread. Watercolor on thick paper with printed blueline text, outlines, and detail, measuring approximately 9.25 x 22 inches. **Signed in full by Garth Williams** at bottom right, with his notations. Publisher info on verso. Generally fine. *From the Estate of Garth Williams.*

Est.: $400-up
Start Bid: $200

36450 **Garth Williams. Original Watercolored Blueline Proof for** *The Chicken Book*, **1946.** Eleventh two-page spread. Watercolor on thick paper with printed blueline text, outlines, and detail, measuring approximately 9.25 x 22 inches. **Signed in full by Garth Williams** at bottom right, with his notations. Publisher info on verso. Generally fine. *From the Estate of Garth Williams.*

Est.: $400-up
Start Bid: $200

36451 **Garth Williams. Original Watercolored Blueline Proof for** *The Chicken Book*, **1946.** Twelfth two-page spread. Watercolor on thick paper with printed blueline text, outlines, and detail, measuring approximately 9.25 x 22 inches. **Signed in full by Garth Williams** at bottom right, with his notations. Publisher info on verso. Generally fine. *From the Estate of Garth Williams.*

Est.: $400-up
Start Bid: $200

36452 **Garth Williams. Original Watercolored Blueline Proof for** *The Chicken Book*, **1946.** Thirteenth two-page spread. Watercolor on thick paper with printed blueline text, outlines, and detail, measuring approximately 9.25 x 22 inches. **Signed in full by Garth Williams** at bottom right, with his notations. Publisher info on verso. Generally fine. *From the Estate of Garth Williams.*

Est.: $400-up
Start Bid: $200

36453 **Garth Williams. Original Watercolored Blueline Proof for** *The Chicken Book*, **1946.** Fourteenth (and last) two-page spread. Watercolor on thick paper with printed blueline text, outlines, and detail, measuring approximately 9.25 x 22 inches. **Signed in full by Garth Williams** at bottom right, with his notations. Publisher info on verso. Also with this is a less-detailed and unfinished version on slightly longer paper; this sheet is **signed in full by Garth Williams** on the reverse, with no publisher info. Both generally fine. *From the Estate of Garth Williams.*

Est.: $400-up
Start Bid: $200

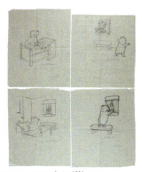

36454   Garth Williams. Preliminary Drawings for Illustrations in *Bedtime for Frances* **by Russell Hoban, 1960.** Pencil on tracing paper. Four sheets measuring roughly 17 x 14 inches, all folded twice by the artist. **Each signed in full by Garth Williams.** Includes preliminary drawing for cover. With a few shallow creases. Otherwise, in generally fine condition. *From the Estate of Garth Williams.*

Est.: $400-up
Start Bid: $200

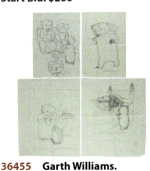

36455   Garth Williams. Preliminary Drawings for Illustrations in *Bedtime for Frances* **by Russell Hoban, 1960.** Pencil on tracing paper. Four sheets, two measuring roughly 17 x 14 inches, two measuring roughly 13.75 x 10 inches. Larger sheets folded twice by the artist, smaller sheets folded once. **Each signed in full by Garth Williams.** With a few shallow creases. Otherwise, in generally fine condition. *From the Estate of Garth Williams.*

Est.: $400-up
Start Bid: $200

36456   Garth Williams. Preliminary Drawings for Illustrations in *Bedtime for Frances* **by Russell Hoban, 1960.** Pencil on tracing paper. Five sheets, four measuring roughly 14 x 10 inches, one measuring roughly 6.25 x 14 inches. All sheets folded twice by the artist. **Four signed in full by Garth Williams, one initialed by Williams.** With a few shallow creases. Otherwise, in generally fine condition. *From the Estate of Garth Williams.*

Est.: $400-up
Start Bid: $200

36457   Garth Williams. Original Color Separation/Layout Materials for Cover Art of *Farmer Boy* **by Laura Ingalls Wilder, 1953** (artwork differs slightly from version ultimately used). Stiff cardboard measuring approximately 15 x 20 inches and four overlays, all with Garth Williams' handwritten notes and/or instructions. Tear measuring 8.25 inches to top overlay which contains the lettering. Cardboard is **initialed by Garth Williams.** Very good. *From the Estate of Garth Williams.*

Est.: $800-up
Start Bid: $400

36458   Garth Williams. Large Original Drawing for an Unused Version of the Cover Art for *Farmer Boy* **by Laura Ingalls Wilder, 1953** (a portion of which was used as an illustration in the chapter titled "Winter Evening"). Pencil on large sheet of tracing paper measuring approximately 13.5 x 16.5 inches, **signed in full by**

Garth Williams, with his notes. A couple of closed tears to left side, one measuring approximately 4.25 inches and intruding into image area above cow's head. Also with **small preliminary rough sketch of the larger drawing**, of Almanzo milking the cow, beneath the words "The Happy Book"; pencil on onionskin, measuring 9.5 x 7.75 inches, **initialed by Williams.** Also with **printed proof of the large drawing, initialed in pencil by Williams.** All very good or better. *From the Estate of Garth Williams.*

Est.: $800-up
Start Bid: $400

36459   Garth Williams. Two Preliminary Drawings for the Dust Jacket of *Farmer Boy* **by Laura Ingalls Wilder**, 1953. Pencil on tracing paper. Two sheets, measuring 11 x 13.75 inches and 10.75 x 8.75 inches. **Both signed in full by Garth Williams** in ink. Rear panel with artist's vertical fold designating jacket spine. Sheet with drawing of rear panel has a small hole at bottom margin (not affecting image area) and light creasing to lower left corner; front panel drawing has a chip to the lower right corner. Else, a few shallow bends and a couple of tiny short tears, along the edges. Very good or better condition. *From the Estate of Garth Williams.*

Est.: $600-up
Start Bid: $300

36460   Garth Williams. Nine Rough Sketches and Preliminary Drawings for Illustrations for *Farmer Boy* **by Laura Ingalls Wilder, 1953.** Pencil on tracing paper. Nine sheets, most measuring approximately 8.5 x 5.5 inches. **All initialed by Garth Williams,** a few with brief notations. All generally near fine, with the artist's own folds and occasional imprecisely cut edges. Includes several preliminary versions of the drawing of Almanzo and his father at the

workbench from the chapter "Birthday." *From the Estate of Garth Williams.*

Est.: $400-up
Start Bid: $200

36461   Garth Williams. Eight Rough Sketches and Drawings for Unused Illustrations for *Farmer Boy* **by Laura Ingalls Wilder, 1953.** Pencil on tracing paper, one on a lined sheet of paper from a spiral notebook. Eight sheets, most measuring approximately 8.5 x 11 inches. **All initialed by Garth Williams,** a few with brief notations. All very good or better, with occasional shallow creases and minor chips along edges. *From the Estate of Garth Williams.*

Est.: $400-up
Start Bid: $200

36462   Garth Williams. Original Color Separation/Layout Materials for Cover Art of *Little House in the Big Woods* **by Laura Ingalls Wilder, 1953.** Stiff cardboard measuring 12.5 x 16.75 inches, and three overlays, all with handwritten instructions. Cardboard is **signed in full by Garth Williams** and has his note: "This is NOT my original, it is a close copy. Garth Williams." This was the art used for the later Harper Crest Library edition. Very good. *From the Estate of Garth Williams.*

Est.: $800-up
Start Bid: $400

36463   Garth Williams. Three Original Pen and Ink Preliminary Drawings for the Jacket Design for *The Rescuers* **by Margery Sharp, 1959.** Ink on cardstock, with additional color wash, one with pasted on "nibbled" newsprint. Three sheets measuring roughly 7 x 6 inches. **Two signed in full by Garth Williams, all three initialed by him.** With his notations describing the design on the front, and with his opinions on each of the designs on the verso, also with an additional sketch. Also with a printed cover proof, **initialed twice by Williams**, with his note on layout. Drawings in generally fine condition. *From the Estate of Garth Williams.*

Est.: $400-up
Start Bid: $200

36464   Garth Williams. Original Crayon and Ink Drawing "C" for Preliminary Jacket Design for *The Rescuers* **by Margery Sharp, 1959.** Ink on paper, colored with crayon. One sheet measuring 8.5 x 11 inches, folded twice by the artist to resemble a dust jacket. **Signed in full by Garth Williams.** With his notations describing the design: "Scene: Bianca, Nils & Bernard looking over a map." He has drawn a second, smaller sketch at the left, adding a candle (this was the jacket design ultimately used). Paper crinkled, with some shallow bends and creases. In very good or better condition. In generally fine condition. *From the Estate of Garth Williams.*

Est.: $400-up
Start Bid: $200

36465   Garth Williams. Original Crayon and Ink Drawing "B" for Unused Jacket Design for *The Rescuers* **by Margery Sharp, 1959.** Ink on paper, colored with crayon. One sheet measuring 8.5 x 11 inches, folded twice by the artist to resemble a dust jacket. **Signed in full by Garth Williams.** With his notations describing the design: "Scene: lowering keys down to Norwegian Poet in cell below

through the grating for food." In generally fine condition. *From the Estate of Garth Williams.*

Est.: $400-up
Start Bid: $200

36466   Garth Williams. Original Crayon and Ink Drawing "A" for Unused Jacket Design for *The Rescuers* **by Margery Sharp, 1959.** Ink on paper, colored with crayon. One sheet measuring 8.5 x 11 inches, folded twice by the artist to resemble a dust jacket, with spine indicated. **Initialed three times by Garth Williams**, with his notations to the editor regarding layout and design. In generally fine condition. *From the Estate of Garth Williams.*

Est.: $400-up
Start Bid: $200

36467   Garth Williams. Two Original Preliminary Ink Drawings for Illustrations in *The Rescuers* **by Margery Sharp, 1959.** Ink on paper, one with white correction fluid. Two sheets measuring roughly 8 x 12 inches. **Both signed in full by Garth Williams.** One with toning to left edge, the other with a small area of discoloration, a small area of surface loss, and two chips to top edge (none of which affects image area). Very good or better. *From the Estate of Garth Williams.*

Est.: $400-up
Start Bid: $200

36468   Garth Williams. Three Original Preliminary Ink Drawings for Illustrations in *The Rescuers* **by Margery Sharp, 1959.** Ink on paper. Two sheets measuring 8 x 12 inches; one sheet measuring 16 x 12 inches, folded in half. **All signed in full by Garth Williams.** (Larger sheet has a second sketch, in pencil, **initialed by Williams**.) Minor toning to edges. Else, all generally fine. *From the Estate of Garth Williams.*

Est.: $400-up
Start Bid: $200

36469   Garth Williams. Two Drawings for *Harry Cat's Pet Puppy* **by George Selden, 1973. One drawing in ink** on paper measuring approximately 7 x 9 inches, **signed in full by Garth Williams** on the reverse. The other, the preliminary sketch for this drawing in pencil on paper measuring 11 x 8.5 inches, **initialed by Garth Williams**. Both fine. Also included is a manila mailing envelope from *Guitar Player Magazine* addressed to Williams in Mexico, with Williams' writing on the outside of the envelope: "'Huppy' - Harry Cat's Pet Puppy / Rough Sketches." *From the Estate of Garth Williams.*

Est.: $400-up
Start Bid: $200

36470   Garth Williams. Ten Preliminary Drawings for *Harry Cat's Pet Puppy* **by George Selden, 1973.** Pencil on paper. Ten sheets measuring 11 x 8.5 inches. **All initialed by Garth Williams** (one with "GW" printed in block letters)**.** All in generally fine condition. *From the Estate of Garth Williams.*

Est.: $400-up
Start Bid: $200

36471   Garth Williams. Eight Preliminary Drawings for *Harry Cat's Pet Puppy* **by George Selden, 1973.** Pencil on paper. Eight sheets measuring 11 x 8.5 inches. **All initialed by Garth Williams.** One sheet with a coffee stain measuring approximately 2 x 1.5 inches, stain intrudes into image area. Else, all are in generally fine condition. *From the Estate of Garth Williams.*

Est.: $400-up
Start Bid: $200

36472   Garth Williams. Twelve Preliminary Drawings for *Harry Cat's Pet Puppy* **by George Selden, 1973.** Pencil on paper. Eleven sheets measuring 11 x 8.5 inches, and one sheet of folded tracing paper measuring 8.25 x 14 inches. **All initialed by Garth Williams.** One sheet with a vertical crease running through image of a fountain, made, presumably, by the artist. Else, all are in generally fine condition. *From the Estate of Garth Williams.*

Est.: $400-up
Start Bid: $200

36473   Garth Williams. Eight Preliminary Drawings for *Harry Cat's Pet Puppy* **by George Selden, 1973.** Pencil on paper. Eight sheets of various sizes, most measuring 11 x 8.5 inches; two on blue paper. **All initialed by Garth Williams.** All in generally fine condition. *From the Estate of Garth Williams.*

Est.: $400-up
Start Bid: $200

36474   Garth Williams. Nine Preliminary Drawings for *Harry Cat's Pet Puppy* **by George Selden, 1973.** Pencil on paper. Nine sheets measuring 11 x 8.5 inches; one on blue paper. **All initialed by Garth Williams.** All in generally fine condition. *From the Estate of Garth Williams.*

Est.: $400-up
Start Bid: $200

36475   [Garth Williams.] Rosemary Wells. Four Illustrations by Garth Williams for *Stuart Little*, **With Original Application of Watercolor by Rosemary Wells.** Each illustration is on stiff watercolor paper and is **signed by Rosemary Wells**. Measurements range from approximately 8.25 x 6.25 inches to 8.25 x 9.75 inches. All generally fine. *From the Estate of Garth Williams.*

Est.: $400-up
Start Bid: $200

36476   [Garth Williams.] Rosemary Wells. Four Illustrations by Garth Williams for *Stuart Little*, **With Original Application of Watercolor by Rosemary Wells.** Each illustration is on stiff watercolor paper and is **signed by Rosemary Wells**. Measurements range from approximately 5.5 x 5.5 inches to 9.75 x 9.25 inches. All generally fine. *From the Estate of Garth Williams.*

Est.: $400-up
Start Bid: $200

36477   [Garth Williams.] Rosemary Wells. Four Illustrations by Garth Williams for *Stuart Little*, **With Original Application of Watercolor by Rosemary Wells.** Each illustration is on stiff watercolor paper and

is **signed by Rosemary Wells**. Measurements range from approximately 4.75 x 5 inches to 6.75 x 6.75 inches. All generally fine. *From the Estate of Garth Williams.*

Est.: $400-up
Start Bid: $200

36478   [Garth Williams.] Rosemary Wells. Four Illustrations by Garth Williams for *Stuart Little*, **With Original Application of Watercolor by Rosemary Wells.** Each illustration is on stiff watercolor paper and is **signed by Rosemary Wells**. Measurements range from approximately 5.75 x 6.25 inches to 8.5 x 9.25 inches. All generally fine. *From the Estate of Garth Williams.*

Est.: $400-up
Start Bid: $200

36479   [Garth Williams.] Rosemary Wells. Five Illustrations by Garth Williams for *Stuart Little*, **With Original Application of Watercolor by Rosemary Wells.** Each illustration is on stiff watercolor paper and is **signed by Rosemary Wells**. Measurements range from approximately 6.75 x 8.25 inches to 9 x 8.75 inches. All generally fine. *From the Estate of Garth Williams.*

Est.: $400-up
Start Bid: $200

36480   [Garth Williams.] Rosemary Wells. Five Illustrations by Garth Williams for *Stuart Little*, **With Original Application of Watercolor by Rosemary Wells.** Each illustration is on stiff watercolor paper and is **signed by Rosemary Wells**. Measurements range from approximately 7.25 x 6.5 inches to 11 x 10.257.75 inches. All generally fine. *From the Estate of Garth Williams.*

Est.: $400-up
Start Bid: $200

36481   [Garth Williams.] Rosemary Wells. Five Illustrations by Garth Williams for *Stuart Little*, **With Original Application of Watercolor by Rosemary Wells.** Each illustration is on stiff watercolor paper and is **signed by Rosemary Wells**. Measurements range from approximately 5.75 x 7 inches to 9.25 x 9.5 inches. All generally fine. *From the Estate of Garth Williams.*

Est.: $400-up
Start Bid: $200

36482   [Garth Williams.] Rosemary Wells. Five Illustrations by Garth Williams for *Stuart Little*, **With Original Application of Watercolor by Rosemary Wells.** Each illustration is on stiff watercolor paper and is **signed by Rosemary Wells**.

Measurements range from approximately 5.25 x 6.75 inches to 7.75 x 8.5 inches. All generally fine. *From the Estate of Garth Williams.*

Est.: $400-up
Start Bid: $200

36483 **[Garth Williams.]**
Rosemary Wells. Five Illustrations by Garth Williams for *Stuart Little*, With Original Application of Watercolor by Rosemary Wells. Each illustration is on stiff watercolor paper and is **signed by Rosemary Wells**. Measurements range from approximately 5.25 x 7.5 inches to 8.5 x 8.25 inches. All generally fine. *From the Estate of Garth Williams.*

Est.: $400-up
Start Bid: $200

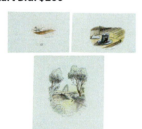

36484 **[Garth Williams.]**
Rosemary Wells. Six Illustrations by Garth Williams for *Stuart Little*, With Original Application of Watercolor by Rosemary Wells. Each illustration is on stiff watercolor paper and is **signed by Rosemary Wells.** Measurements range from approximately 5.75 x 4.25 inches to 11.75 x 9.75 inches. All generally fine. *From the Estate of Garth Williams.*

Est.: $400-up
Start Bid: $200

36485 **[Garth Williams.]**
Rosemary Wells. Six Illustrations by Garth Williams for *Stuart Little*, With Original Application of Watercolor by Rosemary Wells. Each illustration is on stiff watercolor paper and is **signed by Rosemary Wells**. Measurements

range from approximately 5.5 x 6.75 inches to 11 x 9 inches. All generally fine. *From the Estate of Garth Williams.*

Est.: $400-up
Start Bid: $200

36486 **[Garth Williams.]**
Rosemary Wells. Eight Illustrations by Garth Williams for *Stuart Little*, With Original Application of Watercolor by Rosemary Wells. Each illustration is on stiff watercolor paper and is **signed by Rosemary Wells**. Measurements range from approximately 5.5 x 7.25 inches to 10.25 x 8.75 inches. All generally fine. *From the Estate of Garth Williams.*

Est.: $400-up
Start Bid: $200

36487 **[Garth Williams.]**
Rosemary Wells. Four Illustrations by Garth Williams for *Stuart Little*, With Original Application of Watercolor by Rosemary Wells. Each illustration is on stiff watercolor paper and is **signed by Rosemary Wells**. Measurements range from approximately 6.75 x 7.25 inches to 9.25 x 11.25 inches. All generally fine. *From the Estate of Garth Williams.*

Est.: $400-up
Start Bid: $200

36488 **[Garth Williams.]**
Rosemary Wells. Four Illustrations by Garth Williams for *Stuart Little*, With Original Application of Watercolor by Rosemary Wells. Each illustration is on stiff watercolor paper and is **signed by Rosemary Wells**.

Measurements range from approximately 5.75 x 3.5 inches to 8 x 7.75 inches. All generally fine. *From the Estate of Garth Williams.*

Est.: $400-up
Start Bid: $200

36489 **Garth Williams. Original Drawing for the Laura Ingalls Wilder Award, 1954.** Original circular drawing featuring Laura Ingalls Wilder as a child, holding a doll, fashioned from three layers of paper, measuring 10 inches in diameter. Pencil on paper. **Signed "Garth" on the front, and with Mr. Williams' full signature on the reverse** with instructions to return the drawing to him in Aspen, Colorado. Drawing has a few shallow bends, a tiny nick to the edge (above the "G" in "Ingalls"), and a glue stain along the top of Laura's head. Else, in generally near fine condition. The Wilder Award is a bronze medal awarded to an author or artist by the Association for Library Service to Children, a division of the American Library Association, for excellence in children's literature. *From the Estate of Garth Williams.*

Est.: $600-up
Start Bid: $300

36490 **Garth Williams. Three Preliminary Drawings for Illustrations in Laura Ingalls Wilder's *On the Banks of Plum Creek*, 1953.** Pencil on tracing paper. Three sheets, two measuring approximately 9 x 6 inches (one in landscape), and one measuring 9 x 11.75 inches. Includes two versions of the frontispiece/title page opening, with fold down the middle by the artist, and a slightly different version of the illustration of the covered wagon and dugout

house that faces page one. **All are signed in full by Garth Williams.** All generally fine. *From the Estate of Garth Williams.*

Est.: $400-up
Start Bid: $200

36491 **Garth Williams. Ten Sheets of Original Spot Illustrations for Laura Ingalls Wilder's *On the Banks of Plum Creek*, 1953.** Pencil on paper. Ten sheets, measuring approximately 9 x 6 inches, containing seventeen charming tiny drawings. **All initialed by Garth Williams.** Even though these appear in a little folder with Williams' notation "Not for publication," these appear to be the originals reproduced exactly in the book as spot illustrations decorating chapter headings. All in generally fine condition. *From the Estate of Garth Williams.*

Est.: $400-up
Start Bid: $200

36492 **Garth Williams. Fifteen Rough Sketches for Illustrations in Laura Ingalls Wilder's *On the Banks of Plum Creek*, 1953.** Pencil on paper. Fifteen sheets of varying sizes, most being 8.5 x 5.5 inches. Includes a preliminary drawing of the cover art, **signed in full by Garth Williams**. All other smaller sketches are **initialed by Williams**. All in generally fine condition. *From the Estate of Garth Williams.*

Est.: $400-up
Start Bid: $200

36493   Garth Williams. Twenty-One Rough Sketches for Illustrations in Laura Ingalls Wilder's *On the Banks of Plum Creek*, **1953.** Pencil on paper. Seventeen sheets of varying sizes, most being 8.5 x 5.5 inches. All **initialed by Garth Williams**. All in generally fine condition. *From the Estate of Garth Williams.*

Est.: **$400-up**
Start Bid: **$200**

36494   [Aubrey Beardsley]. Two Art Bindings, including: *The Early Work of Aubrey Beardsley.* [and:] *The Later Work of Aubrey Beardsley*. Both published in New York by Dover Publications in 1967. Reprints. Two quarto volumes, bound by Eric B. Rasmussen in full morocco, with inlays in black, brown, green, and orange, and with lettering and decorative devices in gilt. Patterned endpapers. Original wrappers bound in; also bound in at the end of each volume is a handwritten note on the binding techniques employed by the binder. The volume of *Early Work* housed in a custom full leather slipcase. Both fine.

Est.: **$600-up**
Start Bid: **$300**

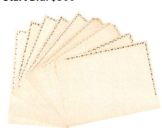

36495   [Californiana]. Will Bradley. Collection of Nine Manuscript Borders and Assorted Ephemera. Housed together in a blue half-leather slipcase and chemise. **Includes nine original manuscript borders designed and drawn by Will Bradley,** one with manuscript notations along the bottom edge.

Three examples have a small piece of the top left corner missing, with soiling to one. In addition to the borders, the chemise contains a Typed Letter Signed from Lewis Allen to Bradley soliciting an article on fine printing for the Book Club of California, a sampling of prospectuses, several small Christmas greeting cards address to or designed by Bradley, two pamphlets on the book arts, and a disbound publication called *Vogue Ornaments*. A note inside the box reads, "Lot of material by, about, & from the library of Will Bradley."

Est.: **$600-up**
Start Bid: **$300**

36496   [William Everson]. Walt Whitman. *American Bard. Being the Preface to the First Edition of Leaves of Grass Now Restored to Its Native Verse Rhythms and Presented as a Living Poem.* [Santa Cruz]: The Lime Kiln Press, 1981. **First edition, one of 115 copies signed by Everson, this being copy number 88.** Folio. [40] pages. Woodcuts by Everson. Publisher's half mottled gray pigskin over raw Indian silk boards, spine lettered in gilt. Fine. With the original prospectus laid in.

Est.: **$600-up**
Start Bid: **$300**

36497   William Everson. *A Man Who Writes.* Northridge, California: Shadows Press, 1980. **First edition, one of 26 lettered copies, this being copy "R".** Oblong quarto.

[28] printed on rectos only. With signed limitation page inserted at rear. Publisher's quarter black glossy morocco over green cloth boards, spine lettered in gilt, slipcase. Fine.

Est.: **$600-up**
Start Bid: **$300**

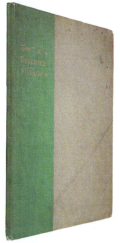

36498   [Elbert Hubbard]. Oliver Goldsmith. *The Deserted Village.* By Oliver Goldsmith, to which is prefaced some notes concerning a Little Journey to "Sweet Auburn" as written by Elbert Hubbard. East Aurora, New York: Roycrofter Shop, 1898. First edition, **number 291 of 470 copies signed by Hubbard** on the limitation page. Quarto. 56, [57-58, blank] pages. Publisher's green cloth over gray paper boards with gilt titles to the front board. Hand-illuminated initial letters. Minor wear and staining to the covers. Corners exposed. Ownership inscription to the front flyleaf. **Elbert Hubbard's bookplate affixed to the front pastedown.** Near fine.

Est.: **$600-up**
Start Bid: **$300**

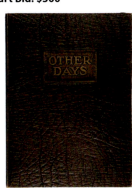

36499   Herschel C. Logan, woodcuts. Everett Scrogin, text. *Other Days in Pictures and Verse.* Decorations by C. A. Seward. Kansas City: Burton Publishing Co., Publishers, [1928]. **Number 0 of 100 De Luxe edition copies signed by Logan, Scrogin, and**

Seward on the limitation page. Quarto. With twelve original woodcuts tipped in opposite the text. Publisher's brown textured and padded cloth with gilt titles on the front board. Silk endpapers. Top edge and fore-edge gilt. Bottom edge uncut. Minor edge wear to the boards. Mild white soiling to the covers. Near fine. **Herschel Logan's own copy, with his bookplate affixed to the verso of the front free endpaper.**

Est.: **$600-up**
Start Bid: **$300**

36500   [Miniature Books]. [Alfred Mills, designer]. *Pictures of English History, In Miniature.* London: Printed for Darton, Harvey, and Darton, 1815. First editions of these charming books. Approximately 2.5 x 2.25 inches. Two small quarto volumes. Extensively illustrated with engravings. Bound in contemporary full red straight-grain morocco. Covers ruled in blind, spines ruled and lettered in gilt. Front board of Volume I nearly detached, some rubbing to volumes. Overall, very good.

Est.: **$600-up**
Start Bid: **$300**

36501   Christoph Ernst Prediger. *Des in aller heut zu Tag ublichen Arbeit wohl anweisenden accuraten Buchbinder und Futteralmachers...* Ansbach, Frankfurt and Leipzig, [n. d., 1741?]. Two octavo parts in one. [xvi], 266, [8, Register and Errata leaf] pages. With engraved frontispiece bound as [viii] plus twenty engraved plates (bound in no discernible order, with plate numbers 9 and 13 repeated). Section title as page 223, reckoned in the pagination.

Contemporary calf with four raised bands. Moderate wear to the boards, with the rear joint split, and the spine coming loose as a result. Short split to front joint. Foxing and toning throughout. Light staining. Renewed fore-edge to plate one. Two large fore-edge chips to two leaves. Large fore-edge marginal chip to the second leaf of the Register. A good copy of the oldest German technical book on book binding.

Est.: $600-up
Start Bid: $300

36502   Francesco Algarotti. *Opere del Conte Algarotti.* *Cavaliere dell'ordine del Merito e Ciamberlano di S. M. il Redi Prussia.* Livorno: Marco Coltellini, 1763-1765. Approximately 7 x 4.25 inches. Eight small octavo volumes. Portrait frontispiece in Volume I, engraved title pages in each volume. Text in Italian. Contemporary full vellum, spines stamped and lettered in gilt. Very minor rubbing, a few small spots. An excellent set of Algarotti's works on fine arts and philosophy. **From the library of legendary eighteenth-century English actor, playwright and theater manager David Garrick, with his large bookplate on the front pastedown of each volume.**

Est.: $600-up
Start Bid: $300

36503   Countess Laura di Barezia. *La Sposa Cristiana Ossia La Donna Second oil Cuore di Dio Nella Famiglia e Nel Mondo.* Milano: Casa Editrice Bietti, [n.d., circa 1911]. Twelvemo. 432 pages. Ornately embossed metal covers and spine panel. Silk moiré endpa-

pers. All edges gilt. Old tape repair on page 59, else a beautiful little book in fine condition.

Est.: $600-up
Start Bid: $300

36504   Amable Bonnefone. *L'Annee Chrestienne,* ou l'Abrege de la Vie des Saincts. Paris: Chez Pierre de Bresche, 1645. Septiesme Edition (seventh edition). Approximately 5 x 3 inches. Two small octavo volumes. With an engraved frontispiece in Volume I. Beautifully bound by Le Gascon in contemporary full burgundy morocco, covers elaborately ruled in gilt with gilt floral cornerpieces and central floral motif, spines elaborately ruled, tooled, and lettered in gilt in compartments, five raised bands, gilt board edges. Some wear to spines (Volume I has some tears to spine) and bindings, bookplates. Contemporary ownership inscription in both volumes. Overall, a very good and striking set. Housed in turquoise clamshell case.

Est.: $600-up
Start Bid: $300

36505   Edward Bulwer Lytton. [*Works*]. Boston: Dana Estes, [n.d., ca. 1900]. Warwick Edition, one of 1,000 numbered copies, of which this is number 44. Thirty-two octavo volumes. Illustrated with frontispieces and full-page plates. Publisher's half olive levant morocco, gilt. Spines uniformly sunned to brown, some rubbing and minor wear to bindings. Overall, very good.

Est.: $1,000-up
Start Bid: $500

36506   Thomas Carlyle. *Works.* London: Chapman and Hall, 1885-1888. "The Ashburton Edition." Complete in seventeen octavo volumes. Publisher's half brown crushed levant morocco over marbled boards, spines ruled in black and gilt and lettered in gilt in compartments, five raised bands, top edge gilt, marbled endleaves. Spines somewhat worn, front joint of Volume I cracking, some wear to bindings. Good.

Est.: $600-up
Start Bid: $300

36507   S. F. A. Caulfeild and Blanche C. Saward. *Encyclopedia of Victorian Needlework.* New York: Dover Publications, 1972. First Dover edition. Two quarto volumes. Extensively illustrated. **This copy bound in a beautiful and unique hardcover binding of elaborate, multi-colored needlework on blue cloth.** Original wrappers bound-in. Spines very slightly sunned. A superb copy. Housed in custom slipcase.

Est.: $600-up
Start Bid: $300

36508   [Miguel de Cervantes Saavedra, Alain Rene le Sage, Mendoza-Mateo Aleman, contributors]. *Spanish Romances.* New York: Worthington Company, 1890. Twelve octavo volumes. Contemporary half brown calf over marbled boards, spines tooled and lettered in gilt in compartments, five raised bands, top edge gilt, marbled endpapers. Some wear to joints, spines and corners, some rubbing. Good.

Est.: $600-up
Start Bid: $300

36509   [Roger de Coverly, binder]. **Rev. John Bathurst Deane.** *The Worship of the Serpent Traced Throughout the World.* London: J. G. & F. Rivington, 1833. Second edition. Octavo. xvi, 476 pages. **Beautiful, full morocco binding by Roger de Coverly,** with an elaborately-tooled spine featuring a serpent design wrapping itself around gilt titles, single-rule borders on the covers, and gorgeous gilt inner dentelles. Marbled endpapers. All edges gilt. Small impression to the front cover. Spine sunned. Very minor rubbing to the bottom corners. A sumptuous binding in near fine condition. Roger de Coverly was one of the most accomplished English binders during the latter part of the 1800s. He bridged the gap between two incredible binders in their own right, first as an apprentice to Zaehnsdorf in 1845, and then as master to T. J. Cobden-Sanderson in 1883-84.

Est.: $600-up
Start Bid: $300

36510   Étienne Deville. *La Reliure Française, II. - Le XVIIIe et le XIXe Siécle.* Paris: Les Édition G. Van Oest, 1931. First edition. French text. Octavo. 48 pages. Thirty-two plates. Beautifully rebound by Rasmussen in full calf with inlays of morocco. Marbled endpapers. Hand-laced headbands. Top edge gilt. Minor sun fading to spine and a portion of the rear board, else a gorgeous binding in fine condition.

Est.: $600-up
Start Bid: $300

36511 **[Fore-Edge Painting].** Henry Southgate [editor]. *Many Thoughts of Many Minds.* London: Charles Griffin and Company, 1867. Later printing. Octavo. 682 pages. **With a fore-edge painting depicting two hunters in the woods with their kill.** Contemporary full tan morocco with brown inlay. Gilt titles and decoration. Marbled endpapers. Binding is lightly rubbed and soiled. Shows a few scuffs and some sunning to backstrip. A very good copy.

Est.: $600-up
Start Bid: $300

36512 **[Fore-Edge Painting].** Edmund Spenser. *The Faerie Queene: Disposed into Twelve Bookes, Fashioning XII. Morall Vertues.* London: Routledge, Warne, and Routledge, 1865. New edition with a glossary. Twelvemo. 820 pages. **With a fore-edge painting, split horizontally, one half of the fore-edge depicts a bust of Edmund Spenser, the other half a gentle knight.** Contemporary full purple morocco with gilt ruling and titles. Lightly rubbed and scuffed with mild sunning to backstrip. A very good copy.

Est.: $600-up
Start Bid: $300

36513 **David Hume. *The History of England,*** from the Invasion of Julius Caesar to the Revolution in *MDCLXXXVIII.* Philadelphia: Printed for Robert Campbell, 1795-1796. [Together with:] T[obias] Smollett and Others. *The History of England,* from the Revolution to the End of the American War, and Peace of Versailles in 1783. Philadelphia: Printed for Robert Campbell, 1796-1798. A New Edition of both titles. Together, twelve octavo volumes. With frontispiece portraits in

each volume. Uniformly bound in contemporary full tree calf, spines ruled and numbered in gilt, burgundy gilt morocco lettering labels. Some wear to spines, a few headcaps chipped, a few joints cracked, some wear to boards, previous owner's ink signatures on title pages (and occasionally the front free endpaper), some foxing and browning in text. A good set.

Est.: $800-up
Start Bid: $400

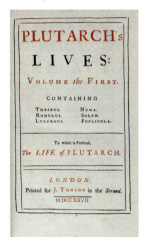

36514 **Plutarch. *Plutarch's Lives.*** London: J. Tonson, 1727. [Together with:] Plutarch. *A Supplement to Plutarch's Lives.* London: John Gray, 1737. Together, nine octavo volumes. Illustrated with engraved frontispieces and plates and with title pages printed in black and red (except the *Supplement* volume). Uniformly bound in contemporary full paneled calf, covers double-ruled in blind with blind floral cornerpieces, burgundy gilt morocco lettering labels, five raised bands. Spines a bit worn, most labels chipped or missing entirely, joints tender or starting, front pastedown in Volume I and Volume VIII loose, bookplate and previous owner's signature in each volume. Good.

Est.: $600-up
Start Bid: $300

36515 **[Ramage Binding].** Carrie Brooks Sheldon. *A Summer Across the Sea.* N.p.: Privately printed for Carrie Brooks Sheldon and Her Friends, Christmas 1905. First edition. **Inscribed by the author** (signed with her initials). Square octavo. 114 pages. Illustrated with photographs by Walter Brooks Sheldon.

Exquisite *art nouveau* custom binding by Ramage of London in full salmon-colored crushed morocco, with black and green leather onlays and gilt stamping; doublures of similar design, with triple gilt borders, and ivory silk moiré endpapers. Top edge gilt; fore-edge rough, bottom edge trimmed. Bookplate to first blank page. Fine. A travel diary of the author's trip to Europe in the summer of 1901 in a stunning art binding.

Est.: $600-up
Start Bid: $300

36516 **Sir Walter Scott. *The Poetical Works of Sir Walter Scott Baronet.*** Edinburgh: Cadell, 1830. Eleven octavo volumes. Engraved title-pages, frontispiece portrait in Volume I, and a few volumes with plates inserted. Bound in contemporary full green straight grain morocco, covers decoratively ruled in gilt, with gilt floral cornerpieces, spines elaborately tooled in gilt, with brown and burgundy gilt morocco lettering labels, four raised bands, gilt board edges and turn-ins, marbled endleaves. Some wear to spines and corners, some rubbing to panels, gilt on board edges rubbed, bookplate in each volume. A very good set.

Est.: $600-up
Start Bid: $300

36517 **Sir Walter Scott. *Waverley Novels.*** London: Merrill and Baker, [1893]. Beaux-Arts Edition, one of 500 numbered sets (#163). Thirty octavo volumes. Publisher's binding of half burgundy levant morocco, gilt. Some rubbing to bindings, spines slightly sunned, a few spines with minor damage, Volume I has cracked hinges. Very good.

Est.: $600-up
Start Bid: $300

36518 **[Sir Walter Scott, subject].** John Gibson Lockhart. *Memoirs of the Life of Sir Walter Scott.* Boston: Houghton Mifflin, 1901. Large Paper Edition. Ten octavo volumes. Illustrated with plates and frontispieces. Volume I has a hand-colored and illuminated uniform title page. Publisher's three-quarter green levant morocco, gilt. Spines sunned, some moderate rubbing and soiling. Still, near fine.

Est.: $600-up
Start Bid: $300

36519 **William Shakespeare. *The Works of Shakespear.*** In which *The Beauties observed by Pope, Warburton, and Dodd, are pointed out. Together with The Author's Life; A Glossary; Copious Indexes; and, a list of the Various Readings.* London: A. Manson, R. Dilton, et al.: [n.d., ca. 1720]. Eight twelvemo volumes. With frontispiece in Volume I. Contemporary full calf. Volumes uniformly rebacked in nineteenth-century brown morocco, brown and burgundy gilt morocco lettering labels, tooled in gilt in compartments, five raised bands, corners reinforced with later brown morocco. Some wear to spines, some rubbing, previous owner's neat ink inscription on title-pages. Overall, near fine.

Est.: $600-up
Start Bid: $300

36520 **Voltaire. *The Ferney Edition of the Works of Voltaire.*** Paris: E. R. Dumont, [1901]. One of 190 numbered copies (#36). Forty-two octavo volumes. Illustrated with frontispieces and full-page plates. Publisher's half brown levant morocco over marbled boards, spines tooled and lettered in gilt in compartments. Some wear and scuffing to spines and corners, front joint of volume XXX just starting. Good.

Est.: $600-up
Start Bid: $300

36521 **[Books About Books].** *The Book Lover's Almanac.* New York: Duprat & Co., 1893-1897. First editions of these charming almanacs. Approximately 7 x 5 inches. Five octavo volumes. With illustrations, full-color plates, and articles by various authors. Bound in publisher's various cloth or wrappers. Some minor wear. Overall, a fine set of these handsome books. Chemised in slipcase.

Est.: $600-up
Start Bid: $300

36522 **[Bookbinding]. Leon Gruel.** *Manuel Historique et Bibliographique de L'Amateur de Reliures.* Paris: Gruel & Engelmann, 1887 (Volume I) and Gruel and Leclerc, 1905 (Volume II). Number 856 of 1,000 copies, and one of 700 printed on Velin de Rives paper (Volume I); number 678 of 700 copies, and one of 600 also printed on Velin de Rives paper (Volume II). 188; 187 pages. Profusely illustrated with 140 plates, mostly colored. Custom three-quarter dark green morocco with five raised spine bands and gilt spine titles. Original wrappers bound in. Moderate rubbing and abrading to the edges. Spines sunned. Minimal, very occasional foxing. Two bookplates to each pastedown. A wonderful pair of books in very good condition.

Est.: $600-up
Start Bid: $300

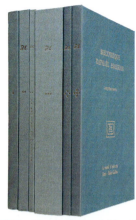

36523 **[Bookbinding]. [Auction Catalogue].** *Bibliotheque Raphael Esmerian.* Paris: Georges Blaizot and Claude Guerin, 1972-1974. First edition of this massive auction catalogue. Five parts in six folio volumes, complete. Profusely illustrated in black and white and mounted full-color plates. Publisher's full turquoise cloth, front covers and spines lettered in gilt. Spines slightly sunned. A fine set. The auction for this enormous collection took place over two years, and was one of the greatest collections of fine and unusual bindings, manuscripts, and illustrated books ever assembled. This beautifully illustrated set is an excellent reference guide for French bindings.

Est.: $600-up
Start Bid: $300

36524 **[Bookbinding]. Marius Michel.** *La Reliure Française depuis l'invention de l'imprimerie jusqua la fin de XVIII Siècle par MM. Marius Michel, Relieurs-Doreurs.* [bound with:] *La Reliure Française commercial et industrielle depuis l'invention de l'imprimèrie jusqua nos jours ...* **Paris: Damascène Morgand & Charles Fatout, 1880-1881.** First editions. Two folio volumes bound in one, with the original gray printed wrappers bound in with their respective volumes. 12.5 x 8.75 inches. [4], 144 and 139 pages. Profusely illustrated, including color and folding plates showing examples of bindings, decoration, ornamentation and lettering. Green buckram with leather spine label lettered in gilt, now

somewhat rubbed and worn. Light foxing in places, but generally very clean. An attractive copy in very good condition.

Est.: $600-up
Start Bid: $300

36525 **[Bookbinding].** *Catalogue de reliures du XVe au XIXe siècle, en vente a la librairie Gumachian & Cie.* Paris: [n.d., ca. 1910]. Limited to 1,000 copies. Quarto. Vi, [182] pages. A catalog of 398 bindings and books on binding. 135 full-page plates, some in color. Three-quarter crushed green morocco over marbled boards, with original printed wrappers bound in. Some discoloration to leaves at center margin, but the plates themselves are in very good condition. Bookplate of The Rasmussens, California bookbinders. This is catalogue XII of the firm of Gumuchian & Cie.

Est.: $600-up
Start Bid: $300

36526 **[Bookbinding]. W. Salt Brassington, editor.** *A History of the Art of Bookbinding With Some Accounts of the Books of the Ancients.* London: Elliot Stock, 1894. First edition. Quarto. xvi, 277 pages. Illustrated with numerous

engravings and photographic reproductions of ancient bindings in color and monotints. Publisher's green pictorial cloth featuring a stag being pursued by dogs. Floral endpapers. Top edge gilt, all other edges untrimmed. Modest shelf wear to boards. Contents clean. A very good copy.

Est.: $600-up
Start Bid: $300

36527 **[Bookbinding]. R. R. Holmes.** *Specimens of Royal Fine and Historical Bookbinding, Selected from the Royal Library, Windsor Castle.* London: W. Griggs & Sons, 1893. First edition. Approximately 14.5 x 10.5 inches. Large quarto. [4], v, [1, blank], 16 pages. With inserted frontispiece of the Royal Library, and 152 lithographed plates of bindings. All text pages are lithographed as well (the frontispiece is the only leaf in the book that is not a lithograph). Publisher's full red cloth, elaborately stamped in black, blue and gilt, spine lettered in gilt, lithographed endleaves. Spine sunned and soiled, some soiling and rubbing to covers, plates 47-51 are loose, yet present. A very good copy of a beautiful book of English royal bindings.

Est.: $600-up
Start Bid: $300

36528 [Bookbinding]. Roger Devauchelle. *La Reliure en France de ses origines a nos jours.* Paris: Jean Rousseau-Girard, 1959-1961. First edition of this huge work on the history of French binding. Three quarto volumes. Text in French. Each volume as issued with unbound, uncut signatures, and extensively illustrated in black and white and full color. Housed in original wrappers, glassines and slipcases. Minor wear to a few glassines. An excellent copy of this rare and desirable set.

Est.: $600-up
Start Bid: $300

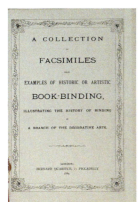

36529 [Bookbinding]. Two Nineteenth-Century Books on Bookbinding Published by Bernard Quaritch, including: *A Collection of Facsimiles from Examples of Historic or Artistic Book-Binding, Illustrating the History of Binding as a Branch of the Decorative Arts.* London: Bernard Quaritch, 1889. 29 pages of text plus 103 superb plates in gold and color by Griggs. [and:] *Examples of the Art of Book-Illumination During the Middle Ages.* London: Bernard Quaritch, 1889-1892. No text. 113 plates in gold and color by Griggs. Some original wrappers bound in. Two large octavo volumes. Both volumes bound in matching three-

quarter green morocco over green cloth with gilt spine titles. Top edges gilt. Bindings worn, shaken and cracked in places, noticeably in Volume I, in which the binding is broken about a third of the way through the book. Some preliminaries loose in each volume. Two bookplates to each pastedown. Occasional minor foxing. Overall, both volumes in very good condition with stunning color plates.

Est.: $600-up
Start Bid: $300

36530 [Bookbinding]. L. Derome. *La Reliure De Luxe Le Livre et l'Amateur.* Paris: Édouard Rouveyre, Éditeur, 1888. First edition limited to 900 numbered copies. French text. Octavo. 246 pages. 65 plates under captioned tissue guards with designs by J. Adeline, G. Fraipont, C. Kurner, and M. Perret. In a stunning Rasmussen fine binding of green leather lavishly accented with gilt with titles and rules stamped in gilt on the spine in five compartments between five raised bands. Marbled endpapers. A fine copy of this marvelous work which discusses fine book binding.

Est.: $600-up
Start Bid: $300

36531 [Bookbinding]. Georges Andrieux. *Bibliotheque de Mr. P[aul]. M[arteau]...Reliures de Van West.* Paris: Exposition, 1934. Two octavo volumes in one. 59;

91 pages. Custom full dark brown morocco with gilt spine titles and five raised spine bands. Gilt inner dentelles of alternating half-moon and arrow designs with black inlaid corner pieces. Marbled endpapers. Original wrappers of each volume bound in. Housed in a custom marbled paper slipcase. Minor rubbing to the covers, bookplate to verso of front free endpaper, gift inscription to the half-title page of Volume I, else a fine copy. **With four original bookplate engravings for Paul Marteau, two signed by the bookplate artist**, laid in.

Est.: $600-up
Start Bid: $300

36532 [Bookbinding] [Bible in French]. *Le Nouveau Testament, C' est a dire, La Nouvelle Alliance de nostre Seigneur Jesus Christ.* Charenton: Pierre des-Hayes, 1656. [Bound with:] [Bible in French]. *Les Pseaumes de David, Mis en rime Francoise.* Charenton: Anthoine Cellier, 1661. Approximately 5.75 x 3 inches. Twelvemo in sixes. [2], [174]; [116] pages. Beautifully bound by Anthoine Ruette, the binder to the king (1640-1650) in contemporary full burgundy morocco, covers elaborately ruled and paneled in gilt, spine elaborately ruled and tooled in gilt, five raised bands, gilt board edges and turn-ins, all edges gilt. Some wear and chipping to spine, some wear to boards, holes on boards from where clasps were fixed. Overall, very good. It is unclear if this is a binding made for the king. Gruel, *Manuel de L'Amateur de Reliures*, p. 160.

Est.: $600-up
Start Bid: $300

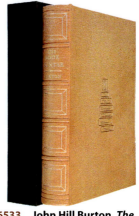

36533 John Hill Burton. *The Book-Hunter etc.* Philadelphia: Robert A. Tripple, 1881. Copy number three of a limited edition of only twenty-seven large paper copies. Octavo. xvi, 396 pages. Beautifully bound by Rasmussen in tan leather with a stacked book vignette in blind on the front board and titles and rules stamped in five compartments between four raised bands on the spine. Top edge gilt, all other edges untrimmed. Decorative endpapers. A stunning example of a fine binding in excellent condition and housed in a matching custom slipcase.

Est.: $600-up
Start Bid: $300

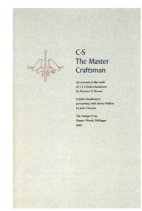

36534 [Doves Press]. [T. J. Cobden-Sanderson]. Norman H. Strouse and John Dreyfus. *C-S. The Master Craftsman.* Harper Woods, Michigan: The Adagio Press, 1969. **Number fifty of seventy-five copies containing a quarto leaf on vellum, in this case a vellum leaf from a Doves Press printing of John Keats's poems, and a Doves Bible leaf on paper.** Folio. 54 pages. Publisher's white leather backstrip over patterned paper boards with gilt spine titles. Minor scuffing to the rear joint. Lightly rubbed corners, else a near fine copy. Also includes a reproduction photograph of Emery Walker and T. J. Cobden-Sanderson and an "epilogue to the publication of C-S The Master Craftsman" titled "A Letter from Stella" from the Adagio Press in 1971.

Est.: $600-up
Start Bid: $300

36535   [Doves Press]. T. J. Cobden-Sanderson. *The Journals of T. J. Cobden-Sanderson. 1879-1922.* London: Richard Cobden-Sanderson, 1926. Number 514 of 1,050 limited edition sets. Two octavo volumes. [xii], 400; [xii], 437 pages. Portrait frontispiece in Volume I. Publisher's sturdy black cloth with gilt titles. Original printed dust jackets. Minor edge wear to boards. Sunning to jacket spines. Near fine condition. **Loosely inserted in Volume I are two Autograph Letters Signed by T. J. Cobden-Sanderson,** with the original mailing envelopes. In one letter, dated 1911 and headed "The Doves Press, Hammersmith," Cobden-Sanderson discusses at some length a commission to bind a book at Doves for a customer named James Blake. Transcripts of the letters by Newbegin's Books in San Francisco are included. **Also laid in are a Doves Press prospectus and a pamphlet printed at Doves Press entitled, "The City Planned."**

Est.: $600-up
Start Bid: $300

36536   [T. J. Cobden-Sanderson, Dard Hunter, et al.]. *The Miscellany.* Volumes One, Two and Three. Kansas City: 1914-1915 (Volumes One and Two) and Cleveland: 1916 (Volume Three). Twelve parts total (four parts to each volume). Saddle-stitched and/or stab-sewn in the original printed wrappers. Housed together in a custom green half-leather drop-down box with gilt spine titles. Minor toning and edge wear to some wrappers. Light sunning to the box spine. Near fine condition.

Est.: $600-up
Start Bid: $300

36537   Walter Crane. *Of the Decorative Illustration of Books Old and New.* London and New York: George Bell and Sons, 1896. First edition, **number 44 of 130 copies printed on Tall Japanese Vellum.** Octavo. xii, 336 pages. Publisher's white wrappers. Uncut and mostly unopened. Original printed paper dust jacket. Housed in a custom brown half-leather slipcase and cloth chemise. Very short fore-edge marginal tears to three leaves and the rear cover. Binding cracked in some places. Some offsetting to the jacket from the chemise. Spine toned. Light sunning to the box slipcase spine. Very good condition.

Est.: $600-up
Start Bid: $300

36538   [Hübel & Denck, publishers]. Fourteen Issues of *Monatsblätter für Bucheinbände und Handbindekunst,* **Circa 1924-25.** Leipzig: Hübel & Denck, 1924-25. German text. Octavo. Each issue contains on average 28 pages. Illustrated, with many tipped-in examples. Seven issues from 1924; and seven from 1925. Printed wrappers. Fine condition. Housed

in a custom folding case. Each issue is a treasure trove of information for fine book binding.

Est.: $600-up
Start Bid: $300

36539   John Andrews Arnett [pseudonym of John Hannett]. *An Inquiry Into the Nature and Form of the Books of the Ancients*: with a History of the Art of Bookbinding.... London: Richard Groombridge, 1837. First edition. Twelvemo. iv, 212 pages. Illustrated with numerous engravings. Color frontispiece with gilt highlights. Index. Contemporary full calf. Joints rubbed, boards with a few scars and scrapes. Front hinge cracked but binding still quite sturdy. An attractive little book in better than very good condition. An important work on the subject, by the author of the landmark *Bibliopegia.*

Est.: $600-up
Start Bid: $300

36540   [Baron S. de la Roche Lacarelle Auction Catalog]. *Catalogue des Livres Rares et Précieux Manuscrits et Imprimés Composant La Bibliothéque de Feu M. Le Baron S. De La Roche Lacarelle.* Paris: Charles Porquet, 1888. First edition. Octavo. xv, 190 pages. Many illustrations, some folding, some color. Top edge gilt other edges untrimmed. Marbled endpapers. Three quarter morocco and marbled boards. Titles and decoration stamped in gilt in six compartments between five raised

bands. The catalog contains 540 items listed and described for auction. Boards worn at the edges and joints. Contents with occasional light scattered foxing, else very good.

Est.: $600-up
Start Bid: $300

36541   [Mortimer Schiff Auction Catalog]. *Sotheby & Company Catalogue of A Selected Portion of the Famous Library Formed by the Late Mortimer L. Schiff, Esq.* London: Sotheby & Company, 1938. Three octavo volumes. 1-152 pages with fourteen plates in color and thirty-two in monochrome; 153-308 pages with fourteen plates in color and twenty-four in monochrome; 309-554 pages with nine plates in color and thirty-two in monochrome. Printed paper wrappers. All catalogs in fine condition and housed in a custom clamshell case. Schiff's collection of 2,493 items consisted mainly of fine bindings, rare engravings, illustrated books and French literature. The auction was conducted in March, July and December of 1938 and offers a glimpse into the golden age of book collecting.

Est.: $600-up
Start Bid: $300

36542   W. R. Tymms and M. D. Wyatt. *The Art of Illuminating as Practiced in Europe From the Earliest Times.* London: Published by Day and Son, Limited, [n.d., circa 1866]. Octavo. 96 pages. 95 chromolithograph plates. Publisher's original brown embossed cloth with gilt stamped titles and decoration. Modest wear to the extremities of the boards, else a clean copy in very good condition.

Est.: $600-up
Start Bid: $300

36543 **[Type Founding].** *American Specimen Book of Type Styles.* *Complete Catalogue of Printing Machinery and Printing Supplies.* [Jersey City, New Jersey]: American Type Founders Company, 1912. First edition. Large octavo. 1,306 pages. Profusely illustrated with type designs, ornaments, printing equipment, and much, much more. Publisher's red cloth with black titles. All edges red. Minor rubbing, abrading and staining to the cloth. Spine sunned. Binding a bit shaken. Minor thumb-soiling to text. An overall very clean copy of this massive work in very good condition.

Est.: $600-up
Start Bid: $300

36544 **Large Photo Album Containing 350 Bookplates.** Mostly personal, engraved armorial bookplates, but with a smattering of institutional and/or personal *ex-libris*. Most plates appear to be English, Scottish or Irish in origin. Some toning to some plates, but largely they are in very good or better condition.

Est.: $400-up
Start Bid: $200

36545 **William Anderson.** *Pictorial Arts of Japan. With a Brief Historical Sketch of the Associated Arts, and Some Remarks upon the Pictorial Art of the Chinese and Korean.* Boston: Houghton, Mifflin, and Company, 1886. First edition. Approximately 16.25 x 11.25 inches. xx, 276 pages. Complete with eighty plates and their descriptive tissue guards. Sixteen of these plates are chromolithographs. All plates and text are loose, as issued. With wrappers, paper chemises, all housed in four cloth portfolios as issued by the publisher. Portfolios are decoratively stamped in black and lettered in red and gilt. Some rubbing and wear to portfolios, some wear and tear to wrappers and tissue guards. Overall, a near fine set. From the library of Canadian railway magnate Sir George Stephen, with his bookplate in each portfolio.

Est.: $600-up
Start Bid: $300

36546 **[Architecture].** *The International Competition for a New Administration Building for the Chicago Tribune MCMXXII Containing All the Designs Submitted in Response to the Chicago Tribune's $100,000 Offer Commemorating Its Seventy Fifth Anniversary, June 10, 1922.* [Chicago: The Tribune Company, 1923]. First edition. Approximately 12.25 x 7.5 inches. Quarto. [xiv], [104], [568] pages. Collation includes a total of 290 plates, some double-sided, including frontispiece. Publisher's full burlap binding, brown morocco gilt lettering labels on front cover and spine, decorative paper endleaves. Mild browning to spine, else a fine copy. Architect John A. Nyden's copy, with his bookplate (he designed the Victory Monument in Chicago in collaboration with sculptor Leonard Crunelle).

Est.: $600-up
Start Bid: $300

36547 **[Walter Crane, subject].** **P. G. Konody.** *The Art of Walter Crane.* London: George Bell & Sons, 1902. First edition, one of 100 copies on Arnold's handmade paper, this being number 11. Approximately 14.25 x 11.25 inches. Large folio. xiii, [1], 147, [1] pp. Eight photogravure plates, twenty-four color plates, sixty-six monochrome plates, two facsimile leaves, and numerous illustrations in the text. Title printed in red and black. With a tipped-in slip indicating that Crane only helped supply art and research, but had no hand in writing the text. Publisher's beige cloth backstrip over green cloth boards, boards decoratively stamped in gilt, spine lettered in gilt. Spine a bit browned with some mild wear, some rubbing and soiling to boards, some foxing to endleaves, a few gutters a bit overopened. Still, a near fine copy of this rare title.

Est.: $600-up
Start Bid: $300

36548 **[Cut-Paper Pictures].** **[An Album of 32 Cut-Paper Pictures].** [N.p., n.d., ca. 1878]. Album is approximately 7.25 x 4.5 inches. Octavo. The silhouettes are in various colors and mounted onto leaves of various colors. [112] pages present. There are some pages with ink notes, shorthand notes in pencil, and an original drawing in ink of "Lord Somnoddy", and a penciled inscription on the verso of the front free endpaper dated 1878. Contemporary half black straight-grain morocco over straight-grain paper boards. Covers and spine ruled in gilt. Binding worn and chipped, some pages loose, some pages missing. An unusual example of cut paper silhouettes (scenes include a squirrel at a tree, a bull and dog fighting, two shepherds and their flock, and birds on trees).

Est.: $600-up
Start Bid: $300

36549 **[Salvador Dali, illustrator].** *The Autobiography of Benvenuto Cellini.* Translated by John Addington Symonds. Garden City: Doubleday & Company, Inc., 1946. **Number 572 of 1,000 numbered copies signed and dated by the artist** on the limitation page. [x], 442, [4, colophon, flyleaf] pages. Publisher's blue cloth with gilt titles and decorative stamping. Housed in the publisher's slipcase. Minor wear and tape repairs to the slipcase, otherwise a fine copy.

Est.: $600-up
Start Bid: $300

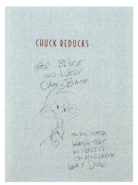

36550 **[Original Drawing]. Chuck Jones.** *Chuck Reducks.* [New York]: Warner Books, [1996]. First edition, first printing. **Signed and inscribed by Jones on half-title page with original drawing.** Quarto. 286 pages. Publisher's binding and dust jacket. Fine.

Est.: $600-up
Start Bid: $300

36551 **Maurice Leloir. Original Watercolor of a Mounted French Officer on a Battlefield.** [N.p., n.d., ca. 1910]. A handsome and vivid watercolor of an officer (probably a nobleman) mounted on a horse, with two cannons in the background. Painted on board. Image size approximately 19.25 x 26. 25 inches. One six-inch scuff mark on the right side. Overall, near fine. Matted.

Est.: $600-up
Start Bid: $300

36552 **Pierre de Nolhac.** *Le Trianon de Marie-Antoinette.* Paris: Goupil, 1914. One of 500 numbered copies (this being number 209) on handmade Arches paper. Large quarto. 182 pages. With 55 lithographed illustrations throughout (four in full color). Original wrappers bound in publisher's deluxe binding of full red morocco, cover elaborately ruled in gilt with *fleur-de-lys* gilt corner-pieces and gilt central armorial stamps, spine tooled, ruled, and lettered in gilt in compartments,

five raised bands, gilt board edges and turn-ins, top edge gilt, marbled endleaves. Spine slightly darkened, some rubbing to spine and mild wear to joints and edges. Still, near fine.

Est.: $1,000-up
Start Bid: $500

36553 **[Northwest Native American Art].** *Amerika's Nordwest-Kuste; neueste Ergebnisse ethnologischer Reisen; aus den Sammlungen der koniglichen Museen zu Berlin.* [America's Northwest Coast; Recent results of an Ethnological Expedition; from the Collection of the Royal Ethnological Museum of Berlin]. Berlin: A. Ascher & Co., 1883. First edition. Elephant folio. 15 x 20 inches. [4], 13, [1] pages, [13] leaves, [13] leaves of plates. Complete. Preface by A. Bastian. Text in German. In original quarter maroon cloth and printed paper-covered boards portfolio. Overall soiling and chipping to the boards and edges, portfolio in fair condition, internally good or better, with moderate toning and light fraying to the edges of some of the letterpress leaves and plates. Internal plates are clean and bright. A beautifully printed portfolio with five full-color lithographic plates and eight black and white gravure plates depicting various Native American masks, dress, and sculpture; each plate is preceded by a leaf with descriptive letterpress text. Very scarce.

Est.: $1,000-up
Start Bid: $500

36554 **[Norman Rockwell, illustrator]. Thomas S. Buechner.** *Norman Rockwell: Artist and Illustrator.* New York: Harry N. Abrams, Inc., Publishers, [1970]. First edition, **designated "I/57" of 1,100 copies signed by Rockwell and Buechner** on the limitation page. Folio. 328 pages. Profusely illustrated with color and black-and-white reproductions of Rockwell's work. Publisher's full blue leather with gilt spine titles and blind-stamped title to front cover. Marbled endpapers. Housed in the original matching slipcase of blue leather over marbled paper. Trivial wear at the spine ends and corners. Minor wear to the slipcase. A beautiful and substantial production, in fine condition, and essential to any Rockwell collection.

Est.: $600-up
Start Bid: $300

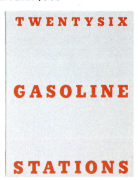

36555 **Edward Ruscha.** *Twentysix Gasoline Stations.* [Alhambra: Cunningham Press], 1969. Third edition, one of 3,000 unnumbered copies. Octavo. Unpaginated. Illustrated with photographs of gas stations. Publisher's white wrappers with titles in red. Glassine dust jacket. Light bumping to top corner. Short tear to the rear panel of the glassine. Light chipping at spine ends. A near fine copy.

Est.: $800-up
Start Bid: $400

36556 **Arthur Szyk. [***Visual History of Nations***].** A collection of 11 heliochrome lithographs, **eight of which are signed by Szyk, and five are signed by the publisher, Kasimir Bileski.** [Winnipeg:] 1946-1947. Fine. Some minor rubbing. Approximately 11.5 x 10 inches. This includes the entire completed output of the planned stamp album of 60 planned illustrations commissioned by Bileski to commemorate the founding nations of the United Nations (Szyk had only completed 9 nations and a print entitled "Airmails of the World" before his sudden death in 1951. The completed prints are Great Britain, Poland, U.S.S.R., France, Israel, Canada, The United States of America, China (two copies included, one unsigned), Switzerland (unsigned), and Airmails of the World (unsigned). With 9 tissue guards, two of which are printed.

Est.: $600-up
Start Bid: $300

36557 **[William] Trusler.** *Hogarth Moralized; A Complete Edition of All the Most Capital and Admired Works of William Hogarth.* London: John Major, 1831. Octavo. 293 pages. Illustrated with copper engravings. Contemporary half leather over marbled boards. Minor rubbing and abrading with front hinge cracking at tail. Bookplate. Foxing to page edges and preliminaries, and lightly scattered throughout. Very good.

Est.: $600-up
Start Bid: $300

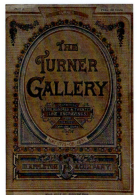

36558 J. M. W. Turner. *The Turner Gallery. Containing One Hundred & Twenty Line Engravings from His Most Celebrated Works.* New York: D. Appleton & Co., [1880]. First American edition. In the original forty parts, with wrappers. Bound into four folio volumes. With 120 steel engravings. Library binding of full blue cloth, spines lettered in gilt. Library markings on spines, library bookplate on front pastedowns. Still, a fine set with magnificent engravings.

Est.: $600-up
Start Bid: $300

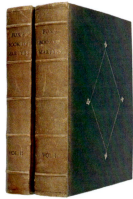

36559 John Fox. *The Book of Martyrs,* or, *Christian Martyrology: Containing an Authentic and Historical Relation of Many Dreadful Persecutions Against the Church of Christ...* Liverpool: Printed by Nuttall, Fisher, & Dixon, 1807. Two large octavo volumes. [viii], x, 11-612; [iv], 580 pages. Engraved frontispiece and nine engraved plates in Volume I; engraved frontispiece and twelve engraved plates in Volume II. Handsome custom full green crushed morocco binding with five raised spine bands and gilt spine titles. Diamond-shaped decorative tooling to the boards with floral cornerpieces. Blind-stamped dragon centerpieces to the rear covers. Spines noticeably sunned. Light edge and corner wear. Contemporary ink gift inscription to the recto of the frontispiece in Volume I. Small corner loss

to the bottom of A2 in Volume II. Minor scattered foxing and toning. Very good condition.

Est.: $800-up
Start Bid: $400

36560 *The Holy Bible Containing the Old Testament and the New, Newly Translated out of the original Tongues and with the former Translations diligently compared and revised by his Majestie's special command.* [Amsterdam?]: 1708, 1707. Folio. With the additional general engraved title showing Moses, Aaron and a view of London. 710, 108, 248, 59 pages. With four engraved folding maps by Visscher and Moxon, the first of which shows California as an island. Elaborately blind-stamped full leather binding with the remnants of clasps. Unevenly toned textblock, with minor loss to the margins of some leaves. Gutter stain through the first 170 pages. Rear endpaper detached. Very good. Apocrypha inserted between the Old and New Testaments. And with the following bound after the New Testament: *The Whole Book of Psalms: Collected into English Meeter,* by Thomas Sternhold, John Hopkins, and others. London: Printed for the Company of Stationers, 1702. Herbert 897.

Est.: $600-up
Start Bid: $300

36561 [Joseph Priestly's copy]. *Sammelband of Eighteenth Century Religious Texts.* London: 1793. Twelvemo. Contemporary half leather with marbled boards. Rubbing and abrading to extremities with splitting joints. Inscriptions. Good.

Est.: $600-up
Start Bid: $300

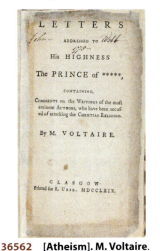

36562 [Atheism]. M. Voltaire. *Letters Addressed to His Highness The Prince of *****,* Containing, Comments on the Writings of the most eminent Authors, who have been accused of attacking the Christian Religion.* Glasgow: R. Urie, 1769. First Scottish edition. Twelvemo. [4], 152 pages. Contemporary mottled calf boards rebacked with modern leather and red morocco spine label with gilt titles. Boards well worn with rubbing with some loss, most notably at rear. Title page and final page of text have fill at margins. Pages toned with browning at edges. Generally very good.

Est.: $600-up
Start Bid: $300

36563 Joannes Blaeu. *Suchuen Imperii Sinarum Provincia Sexta.* [Amsterdam: n.d., ca. 1655]. Hand-colored map of the Suchuen province of China, from *Novus atlas sinensis a Martino Martinus.* In generally good condition with a crease down the center, some toning and soiling, a few short tears. Measures 20 x 24 inches.

Est.: $600-up
Start Bid: $300

36564 Nicolas Sanson d'Abbeville. *Mappa Mondo o Vero Carta Generale del Globo Terestre.* Roma: 1674. Italian edition of the original French map of 1651. Hand-colored map depicting the world in two hemispheres. Generally very good condition with some creasing down the center and some toning and wear to edges, and what appears to be a light ink sketch on the lower right side. Measures 19 x 24 inches.

Est.: $600-up
Start Bid: $300

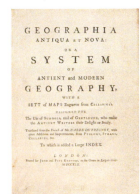

36565 L'Abbé du Fresnoy. *Geographica Antiqua et Nova: or a System of Antient and Modern Geography, with a Sett of Maps Engraved from Cellarius. Designed for the Use of Schools, and of Gentlemen, who make the Antient Writers their Delight or Study.* London: John and Paul Knapton,

1742. First edition of this English translation. Approximately 10 x 8 inches. Quarto. [xii], 157, [1, blank], [37, Index], [1, publisher's catalogue]. **With all 33 fold-out maps inserted throughout.** Bound in later niger morocco, front cover paneled in blind, spine ruled and lettered in gilt. Front hinge cracked, some wear to binding, title-page mounted on tissue to repair some holes, final leaf similarly mounted with tissue (publisher's catalogue text is a bit light due to being covered with tissue). Some soiling in text, generally maps are quite clean. Overall, a good copy.

Est.: $600-up
Start Bid: $300

36566   Henricus Hondius. *Asia recens summa cura delineata.* [Amsterdam: 1631]. Taken from the *Novus Atlas* of 1631. Hand-colored map depicting all of Asia as well as a cartouche and a vignette depicting Asian people. In good condition, with a crease down the center with a short tear to the lower edge, toned, soiling on edges. Two pages of Latin text on verso. Measures 20 x 23.25 inches.

Est.: $600-up
Start Bid: $300

36567   J. T. Lloyd. *Lloyd's Official Map of the State of Virginia.* New York: J. T. Lloyd, 1862. 46" x 30". A large linen-backed folding map first issued in 1861, then 1862, and last issued in 1863 taken from Boye's map of 1828 and extensively revised. Each county is in color. This version was intended for use by Union military officer's and bears the printed notation "This is the only map used to plan campaigns in Virginia by Gen. McClellan". The map is mounted in embossed brown cloth covers measuring 4.5" x 7.25", and the front board is titled in gold *Lloyd's $100,000 Topographical Map of Virginia.* This copy has contem-

porary ink notations on the front pastedown indicating battles and movements corresponding to marks on the map. The front board is detached but the map remains in very good condition.

Est.: $800-up
Start Bid: $400

36568   Guglielmo Sansone. *l'Asia.* Roma: 1677. Hand-colored map showing Asia from India to Japan, including the Philippines, Borneo, Sumatra and Java. In good condition, with a crease down the center, the lower right corner missing (not affecting image), and some general toning and light soiling. Measures 19 x 24.25

Est.: $600-up
Start Bid: $300

36569   Guglielmo Sansone. *l'Africa.* Roma: 1677. Hand-colored map depicting the entire continent of Africa. In very good condition with a crease down the center, some toning and mild wear to edges, and some mild soiling to lower left corner. Mounted and matted. Measures 19 x 24 inches.

Est.: $600-up
Start Bid: $300

36570   Guglielmo Sansone. *l'America Meridionale.* Roma: 1677. Hand-colored map depicting the entire continent of South America. In very good condition

with a crease down the center, some mild toning and light wear to edges. Measures 19 x 24 inches.

Est.: $600-up
Start Bid: $300

36571   Guglielmo Sansone. *l'Europa.* Roma: 1677. Hand-colored map depicting the entire European continent. In very good condition with a crease down the center, and some mild toning and soiling, and some mild wear at edges. Measures 19 x 24 inches.

Est.: $600-up
Start Bid: $300

36572   Guglielmo Sansone. *Russia Bianca e Moscovia.* Roma: 1678. Hand-colored map depicting Russia. In very good condition with a crease down the center and some toning and minor soiling at edges. Measures 19 x 24.25 inches.

Est.: $600-up
Start Bid: $300

36573   Giacomo Cantelli da Vignola. *Asiae Minoris.* Roma: 1686. Hand-colored map depicting Asia Minor, including Cyprus, Rhodes, and Greece. In very good condition with a crease down the center, some mild toning and rubbing to edges. Measures 18.75 x 24 inches.

Est.: $600-up
Start Bid: $300

36574   Giacomo Cantelli da Vignola. *La Gran Tartaria.* Roma: 1687. Hand-colored map depicting Northern China. In very good condition with a crease down the center and some mild toning and wear to edges. Mounted and matted. Measures 18.75 x 23.5 inches.

Est.: $600-up
Start Bid: $300

36575   Giacomo Cantelli da Vignola. *Isole dell' India cio e le Molucche le Filippine e della Sonda.* [N.p.]: 1683. Map depicting Borneo, New Guinea and the Philippines. In good condition with upper right corner and left edge restored, creased down the center, and some wear, soiling and toning to edges. Measures 19 x 23.75 inches.

Est.: $600-up
Start Bid: $300

36576   Giacomo Cantelli da Vignola. *Natolia Detta anticamente Asia Minore.* Roma: 1686. Map depicting Turkey and Cyprus. In very good condition with a crease down the center and some toning and light soiling near the edges. Measures 18.75 x 24 inches.

Est.: $600-up
Start Bid: $300

36577   Giacomo Cantelli da Vignola. *Tartaria d'Europa ouero Piccola Tartaria.* Roma: 1684. Hand-colored map depicting Eastern Europe. In very good condition with a crease down the center and some toning and mild wear to edges. Measures 19 x 24.25 inches.
Est.: $600-up
Start Bid: $300

36578   D. Huntington. *Lady Washington's Reception.* A charming hand-colored engraving of a reception hosted by George and Martha Washington. [N.p., n.d., ca. 1850]. With some toning, thumbsoiling, and marginal damage not affecting image. Very good. Measures 28 x 39.5 inches. Included is a key to the people depicted.
Est.: $600-up
Start Bid: $300

36579   [Illuminated Manuscript]. Persian Illuminated Manuscript. [N.p., n.d.]. Two leaves taken from a book, on one sheet. The images on the recto are of a nobleman and a noblewoman, both illuminated in colors. Approximately 10.5 x 9 inches. With two pages of Arabic script in double columns on verso, edged in gilt. Sheet has torn crease down the center, several small holes and worm damage, a few stains, and general wear. Good. Matted, framed and glazed on two sides to facilitate viewing of both sides.
Est.: $600-up
Start Bid: $300

36580   [Illuminated Manuscript]. Persian Illuminated Manuscript Leaf. [N.p., n.d.]. A beautiful illumination featuring a nobleman surrounded by six female servants in a handsome room overlooking a river or lake, illuminated in colors. Approximately 10.25 x 5.25 inches. With Arabic script on the verso, in black and red inks. Minor wear to edges, else fine. Matted, framed and glazed on two sides to facilitate viewing of both sides.
Est.: $600-up
Start Bid: $300

36581   Abraham Ortelius. Hand-Colored Engraved Title-Page from *Theatrum Orbis Terrarum.* [Antwerp, n.d., ca. 1775 or 1789]. Handsome engraved title-page to a later edition of Ortelius' majestic work, with vibrant hand-color. In good condition with some toning, wear and chipping to edges, some foxing and light offset, and a previous owner's ink signature at top. Dedication text on verso. Mounted and matted. Measures 17 x 12 inches.
Est.: $600-up
Start Bid: $300

36582   Giovanni Battista Piranesi. *Carcere oscura con Antenna pel suplizio de malfatori.* [N.p., n.d.,1743]. From *Prima Parte de Architetture e Prospettive* [1743]. In good condition with foxing and soiling, and lower corner of sheet a bit upbraided (not affecting image). Measures 21 x 15.5 inches.
Est.: $600-up
Start Bid: $300

36583   Georg Matthaus Seutter. *Sphaerae Artificiales.* [N.p., n.d., ca. 1700]. Hand-colored engraving depicting three globes - celestial, terrestrial and a navigation globe. In very good condition with some toning, minor soiling and a short tear to upper margin. Mounted on cardboard. Measures 8.25 x 12 inches.
Est.: $600-up
Start Bid: $300

36584   Douglas Carruthers. *Unknown Mongolia.* Philadelphia: J. B. Lippincott, 1914. First American edition. Two octavo volumes. Illustrated, with many fold-out plates, including four large maps. Publisher's bindings. Covers and extremities worn. Spine and edges darkened somewhat with some light fraying to spine ends. Front hinges broken with rears starting. Half titles loose with front free endpaper missing in volume two. Mild toning to page edges and a few maps. Bookplate on reverse of front free endpaper. Laid-in typed period letter from a Consul General S. J. Fuller regarding travel in region. Otherwise, generally very good.
Est.: $600-up
Start Bid: $300

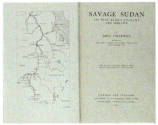

36585   Abel Chapman. *Savage Sudan. Its Wild Tribes, Big-Game and Bird-Life.* London: Gurney and Jackson, 1921. First edition. Octavo. xiv, 452 pages. With 30 full-page plates inserted throughout. Publisher's full green cloth, Covers and spine stamped in gilt. Some rubbing and minor wear, neat gift inscription from one British officer to another, dated "Khartoum/1922". Near fine.
Est.: $600-up
Start Bid: $300

36586   E. Demidoff. *A Shooting Trip to Kamchatka.* London: Rowland Ward, 1904. First edition. Octavo. 302 pages. 113 illustrations, 5 photogravures, and 2 maps, one in rear pocket. Recased binding with publisher's cloth laid on original beveled boards and spine. Cloth slightly soiled with wear at extremities. Original endpapers have been reinforced. Some occasional light foxing to plates and toning to maps. Very good.
Est.: $600-up
Start Bid: $300

36587   A. St. H. Gibbons. *Exploration and Hunting in Central Africa, 1895-96.* London: Methuen, 1898. First edition. Octavo. 408 pages, 40 pages of publisher's catalog dating from December 1897. Illustrated, with large fold-out map. Publisher's binding. Boards and extremities worn with slight bubbling to covers. Corners bumped. Hinges starting. Page edges lightly toned with offsetting to front endpapers from previously laid-in item. Small tear at map hinge. Otherwise, very good.

Est.: $600-up
Start Bid: $300

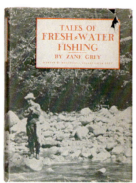

36588   Zane Grey. *Tales of Fresh-Water Fishing.* New York and London: Harper & Brothers Publishers, 1928. First edition. Octavo. 277 pages. With one hundred illustrations from photographs taken by the author. Publisher's green cloth with titles stamped in gilt. Pictorial endpapers. A handsome copy in very good condition and retaining the original dust jacket. The jacket is worn along the edges and is missing a small portion at the top corner.

Est.: $600-up
Start Bid: $300

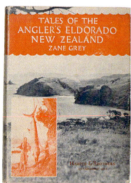

36589   Zane Grey. *Tale of the Angler's Eldorado New Zealand.* New York and London: Harper & Brothers Publishers, 1926. First edition. Quarto. 228 pages. Over one hundred illustrations from photographs taken by the author and from drawings by Frank E. Phares. Publisher's blue cloth with titles stamped in gilt. Pictorial endpapers. Modest shelf wear to the boards. Contents bright. Includes the seldom seen dust jacket which

has some minor wear and scuffing but is generally very good condition.

Est.: $600-up
Start Bid: $300

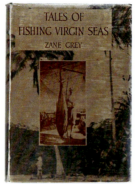

36590   Zane Grey. *Tales of Fishing the Virgin Seas.* New York and London: Harper & Brothers Publishers, 1925. First edition. Octavo. 216 pages. With one hundred illustrations from photographs taken by the author and others; drawings by Lillian Wilhelm Smith. Publisher's green cloth with titles stamped in gilt. Pictorial endpapers. A fine copy in a price-clipped dust jacket which has significant toning to the front panel, else it is in very good condition.

Est.: $600-up
Start Bid: $300

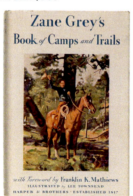

36591   Zane Grey. *Zane Grey's Book of Camps and Trails.* New York and London: Harper & Brothers Publishers, 1931. First edition. **Signed by Loren Grey (Zane's son) on the half-title page.** Octavo. 211 pages. Illustrated with photographs and drawings by Lee Townsend. Publisher's green cloth with titles stamped in gilt. A fine copy in the original dust jacket (jacket has a closed tear on the rear panel), housed in a custom slipcase.

Est.: $600-up
Start Bid: $300

36592   Three Handsome Titles from the *Library of Humorous American Works* **Series.** All books published in Philadelphia by T. B. Peterson, all are twelvemo volumes in the original publisher's lithographed (in gold and colors) wrappers, including: **Frank Forester.** *The Deerstalkers.* [first published 1846, this edition published c. 1855]. 198 pages. Front wrapper with short tear, creased on lower portion, mild rubbing, spine a bit darkened, and lightly chipped, bookplates. Still, near fine. [and:] **Henry William Herbert.** *The Quorndon Hounds.* [first published 1852, this edition published 1859]. 173 pages. Mild rubbing to wrappers and spine. Glue residue on inner front wrapper from bookplate (which is laid-in). Fine. [and:] **Francis Alexander Durivage and George Pickering Burnham.** *Stray Subjects Arrested and Bound Over.* [first published 1848, this edition published, c. 1858]. 199 pages. Mild rubbing to wrappers and spine, glue residue on inner front wrapper from missing bookplate. Fine. **An unusually bright set of these charming books.** Housed in custom-made chemise and slipcase.

Est.: $600-up
Start Bid: $300

36593   P. F. H. Baddeley. *Plates. Whirlwinds and Dust-Storms of India. An Investigation into the Law of Wind and Revolving*

Storms at Sea. London: Bell and Daldy, 1860. First edition. Oblong format. Seventeen of nineteen plates (the "Description of Plates" calls for twenty plates but plate nineteen is not listed). Missing plates three and six. Original brown cloth with blind stamped decoration and titles stamped in gilt. Spine re-backed. Boards worn at the extremities. Scattered foxing throughout. Ex-library copy with a few ink stamps and bookplate on the front pastedown, else good condition. Extraordinarily rare in any condition, this volume contained the plates which accompanied the volumes of text.

Est.: $600-up
Start Bid: $300

36594   Thomas Bartholin. *De Unicornu Observationes Novae. Secunda edition Auctiores & emendatiores editae a Filio Casparo Bartholino.* Amstelaedami: Henr. Wetstenium, 1678. Second edition. Latin text. Twelvemo. [xiv], 381, [15] index pages. All wood engravings present as called for. Contemporary vellum with a repair to a portion of the front board and spine. A remarkably sound copy, internally clean and in very good condition. The horn of the unicorn was thought to have pharmaceutical properties and Bartholin's book expounded on the subject.

Est.: $1,000-up
Start Bid: $500

36595 Edward, Earl of Clarendon. *The History of the Rebellion and Civil Wars in England. Begun in the year 1641.* *With the precedent passages, and actions that contributed thereunto, and the happy end, and conclusion thereof by the King's blessed restoration, and return upon the 29th of May, in the year 1660.* Oxford: Printed at the Theater, 1702-[04]. First edition of this massive and definitive history. Approximately 18 x 11.5 inches. Three folio volumes. [4], xxiii, [1, blank], 557, [1, blank]; [16], 581, [1, blank]; [22], 603, [1, blank], [21, index], [1, blank] pages. With all three engraved frontispiece portraits; two out of three half-titles (Volume III lacking half-title); and engraved printer's devices, sectional vignettes, and historiated capitals. Uniformly bound in nineteenth-century half brown levant morocco over marbled boards, spines ruled in blind and lettered in gilt in compartments, five raised bands. Some rubbing to bindings, joints a bit worn (yet quite solid for such large volumes), Volume I has a tear to the lower margin of page 383, Volume II has some light dampstaining to the lower corners of several pages, and Volume III has short tears to the lower margins of pages 333 and 563 (none of these textual problems affect text). Overall, a very good set. "It is composed from material written at different periods and in widely different circumstances and it remains a classic work. It is also an important contribution to the art of biography and autobiography, and memorable for its portraits of figures as Falkland, Godolphin, Laud, and Strafford" (Drabble and Stringer, *The Concise Oxford Companion to English Literature*, 111). "One of the handsomest books hitherto produced in England" (Barker, *The Oxford University Press and the Spread of Printing*, 28).

CBEL 1680. Lowndes II, p.466.
Est.: $1,000-up
Start Bid: $500

36596 Johannes Baptista van Helmont. *Ortus medicinæ. Id est, initia physicæ inaudita. Progressus medicinæ novus, in morborum ultionem, ad vitam longam.* Lyon: Jean Baptiste Devenet, 1655. Fourth collected edition, edited and published posthumously by Helmont's son, Franciscus Mercurius van Helmont. Approximately 13.5 x 8.25 inches. Quarto. [22], 487, [1, blank], 192, [57, indices], [1, Approbationes] pages. With engraved title-page. Contemporary full mottled calf, rebacked in brown calf, six raised bands. Binding worn, first several leaves a bit tattered, upper corner of page 145 in the second part is missing (not affecting text), a few ink notes and blots throughout. Overall, a good copy. Helmont (1577-1644) "devoted his life to exploring the first principles of nature through chemistry. He is best remembered as the discoverer of gas [derived from the Greek 'chaos'], a term he coined to described the 'specific smokes' that remain after the combustion of solids and fluids; among the gases he identified were carbon dioxide, carbon monoxide, chlorine gas and sulphur dioxide" (Norman Library). *Ortus medicinæ* "is our chief source for the discoveries of Helmont with regard to the chemical nature of living processes" (*Printing and the Mind of Man*). *Opuscula medica inaudita* (the second part of this book), originally published as a separate work in 1644, contains reprints of Helmont's treatises on the stone, on fevers, on the errors of humoral pathology, and on the plague. Garrison and Morton 665. Norman Library 1048. *Printing and the Mind of Man* 135. Waller 4307 and 4306. Willems 1066 and 1067.

Est.: $600-up
Start Bid: $300

36597 Helvetius. *De l'Esprit.* Paris: Chez Durand, 1758. [Bound Together With:] **Helvetius.** *Mandement de Monseigneur l'Archeveque de Paris.* Paris: Chez C. F. Simon, 1778. First editions (second issue of *l'Esprit*). Approximately 10 x 7.25 inches. Quarto. [4], xxii, 643, [1, approbation]; [4, Condamnation et Prohibition]; 28, [3, Extrait des Registres de Parlement], [1, blank], 31, [1, blank] pages. Contemporary full mottled calf, spine tooled in gilt, gilt red morocco lettering label, all edges stained red. Spine worn, front joint cracking, some wear to corners. Still, a very good copy. This book was condemned by the church as a sacrilegious defense of atheism, and was denounced by both Louis XV and Parliament. However, this work was a landmark in the development of utilitarianism, and influenced both Jeremy Bentham and John Stuart Mill.

Est.: $600-up
Start Bid: $300

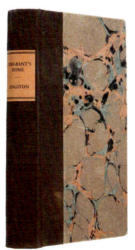

36598 William H. G. Kingston. *The Emigrant's Home; or How to Settle. A Story of Australian Life For All Classes at Home and in the Colonies.* London: Groombridge & Sons, 1856. First edition. Twelvemo. ix, [3], 238, [2] publisher's catalog pages. Recent binding done in an attractive contemporary style with marbled papers over boards and cloth backstrip. Replaced endpapers and pastedowns. Some child's scribbling in pencil on the fly-leaf and title page. Uniform toning to pages with additional light scattered foxing, else a very good copy of this scarce early work on Australia.

Est.: $600-up
Start Bid: $300

36599 Richard Payne Knight. *A Discourse on the Worship of Priapus, and Its Connection With the Mystic Theology of the Ancients, To Which Is Added an Essay on the Worship of the Generative Powers During the Middle Ages of Western Europe.* London: Privately printed, 1894. Limited edition of 500 large paper copies (three hundred for England; two hundred for America). Octavo. xvi, 254 pages. Thirty-nine plates plus "The Witches' Sabbath". Publisher's original maroon cloth re-backed with a portion of the original spine laid down. Boards worn at the extremities, still a very good copy of this rare work.

Est.: $600-up
Start Bid: $300

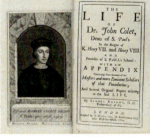

36600 [Samuel Knight]. *The Life of Dr. John Colet, Dean of S. Paul's in the Reigns of K. Henry VII and Henry VIII.* London: Downing, 1724. First edition. Octavo. 494 pages with Table, Index, and Subscribers List at rear. Contemporary calf, recased. Good.

ESTC T92619.
Est.: $600-up
Start Bid: $300

36601 **William Marsden.** *The History of Sumatra, Containing an Account of the Government, Laws, Customs, and Manners of the Native Inhabitants, With a Description of the Natural Productions, and a Relation of the Ancient Political State of That Island.* London: Printed for the author and sold by Thomas Payne and Son, et al., 1784. Second edition. Quarto. xii, 373, [6] index pages. Large engraved folding map of the Island of Sumatra utilized as the frontispiece. Contemporary leather binding with titles and decoration stamped in gilt between five raised bands on the spine. Boards moderately worn at the edges, spine ends and joints. Front hinge cracked but the boards remain firmly connected to the textblock. Endpaper and map signature detached. Contemporary bookplate on the front pastedown. Contents bright and the volume is in generally very good condition.
Est.: $800-up
Start Bid: $400

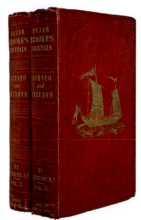

36602 **Captain Rodney Mundy.** *Narrative of Events in Borneo and Celebes, Down to the Occupation of Labuan: from the Journals of James Brooke, Esq.* London: John Murray, 1848. First edition. Two octavo volumes. 385, 395 pages. With 19 plates (including 6 tinted lithographs), five fold-out maps (one hand-colored), and a 16-page publisher's catalogue. Publisher's full red cloth, covers decoratively

stamped in gilt and blind, spines lettered in gilt and stamped in blind. Some light wear and sunning to spines, some rubbing to boards, hinges starting (yet still solid), some minor foxing to plates and maps. Previous owner's neat signature on front pastedowns. Still, a bright, near fine copy.
Est.: $600-up
Start Bid: $300

36603 **Plutarch.** *The Lives of the Noble Grecians and Romans... Translated...into English by Sir Thomas North.* London: Printed by Abraham Miller, 1657. Folio. [14], 1031, [1, The Printer to the Reader], [22]; [2], 76, [34, Table] pages. Engraved title inserted at front (dated 1656). Title-page printed in red and black. Bound in contemporary full brown calf, covers ruled in gilt and blind. Rebacked in modern brown morocco, gilt. Some wear to contemporary boards, some foxing in text, small burn mark on page 565. One page of contemporary ink notations (page 1), and some assorted ink notes throughout. Previous owner's ink stamp on page 1 and printed title-page. Very good. Wing P2633.
Est.: $600-up
Start Bid: $300

36604 **Henry Shaw.** *Dresses and Decorations of the Middle Ages.* London: William Pickering, 1843.

First edition. Large paper copy. Two quarto volumes. [94; 118] pages. Ninety-three plates, many hand-colored, some heightened with gold or silver. Full red morocco boards, inexpertly rebacked with red leatherette. Gilt lettering and faux raised bands to spine. Gilt turn-ins and beautiful gilt *fleur-de-lis*-patterned gauffred edges. Marbled endpapers. Boards with soot damage to edges of boards; light discoloration to front board of Volume II. All hinges strengthened with heavy clear plastic tape. Pages with foxing, plates rarely affected. Both volumes tight and sturdy. In overall very good condition. A lovely collection of plates.
Est.: $600-up
Start Bid: $300

36605 **Sir Harry Smith.** *The Autobiography of Lieutenant-General Sir Harry Smith.* New York: E. P. Dutton & Company, 1902. Reprint after the first edition issued the previous month. Two octavo volumes. With portraits and illustrations. 382; 434 pages. Portrait frontispieces, illustrations, maps. Beautifully half bound in deep red levant over red cloth, with oval pictorial gilt-stamped cloth insets to front board of each volume. Foxing to frontispieces and illustration pages. Pages with minor toning. A lovely tight set in fine condition. Lieutenant General Sir Henry George Wakelyn Smith (1787-1860) was a veteran of the Napoleonic Wars and served military positions in South Africa, India, and England.
Est.: $600-up
Start Bid: $300

36606 **Henry M. Stanley.** *The Congo and the Founding of Its Free State, A Story of Work and Exploration.* New York: Harper & Brothers, 1885. First American edition. Two octavo volumes. 528; 483, 12 pages publisher's ads. Fully illustrated, with two large folded maps at rear in pocket of each volume. Publisher's decorative cloth. Covers lightly rubbed at extremities with hint of dampstaining to front board and top edge of Volume Two. Pages lightly toned throughout. Rear endpaper of Volume One has creased torn bottom corner. Maps somewhat toned with tears at creases. A better than very good set.
Est.: $600-up
Start Bid: $300

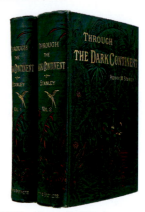

36607 **Henry M. Stanley.** *Through the Dark Continent, or The Sources of the Nile Around the Great Lakes of Equatorial Africa and Down the Livingstone River to the Atlantic Ocean.* New York: Harper & Brothers, 1878-1879. Early American editions. Two octavo volumes. Illustrated, with a large folding map in rear pocket of each volume. Publisher's binding. Covers and extremities lightly rubbed with shelfwear. Hinges starting. Light toning to page edges. Maps have light toning and a few small tears at folds. Both very good or better volumes.
Est.: $600-up
Start Bid: $300

36608   [Virgil]. Publius Virgilius Maro. *Bucolica, Geogica, et Aeneis.* London: A. Dulau & Co., 1800. Approximately 10.25 x 6 inches. Two quarto volumes. [iv], 246; [iv], 276 pages. With fifteen full-page engravings inserted throughout. Contemporary half brown morocco over brown cloth boards, spines ruled in black and lettered in gilt in compartments, five raised bands, marbled edges. Bindings worn, some toning and thumbsoiling in text, some dampstaining to plates. A good set. "The paper and printing [of this edition] are extremely elegant" (Ebert)

Est.: $600-up
Start Bid: $300

36609   Avery Allyn. *A Ritual of Freemasonry, Illustrated by Numerous Engravings With Notes and Remarks. To Which is Added a Key to the Phi Beta Kappa.* Boston: John Marsh and Company, 1831. First edition. Octavo. 302 pages. Numerous plates, possibly engraved by D. C. Johnston. Contemporary leather with titles stamped in gilt on a red morocco spine label. Modest wear to the boards. Significant foxing throughout, marginal stain affecting a small portion of the first third of the book though not affecting text, small portion at the top of the title

page excised though not affecting text, otherwise a sound, tight copy in very good condition.

Est.: $600-up
Start Bid: $300

36610   [American Humor]. A Volume of Three Mid-Century American Humorous Works, including: **George M. Wharton. *The Portfolio of a Southern Medical Student.*** Philadelphia: Lippincott, Grambo & Co., 1851. 181 pages. Illustrations by Croome. Wright II, 2692 [bound with:] **H. N. Moore. *Fitzgerald and Hopkins; or Scenes and Adventures in Theatrical Life.*** Philadelphia: S. G. Sherman, 1847. 166 pages. With four of the five called-for illustrations. Wright I, 1911. [bound with:] **"Everpoint."** [**J. M. Field**]. ***The Drama in Pokerville; The Bench and Bar of Jurytown, and Other Stories.*** Philadelphia: Carey and Hart, 1847. 200 pages. With four of the eight called-for illustrations by F. O. C. Darley. Wright I, 953. All first editions. Twelvemo. Spine rebacked with period morocco label with gilt titles laid on. Original full calf period boards. Covers and extremities somewhat worn. Corners bumped and abraded. Slight lean. Some toning and foxing throughout. Some chipping, light folds, and small tears to page edges. First few pages have chipped loss at edges. Moderate dampstaining and toning to rear text. Generally, a very good copy of this interesting collection.

Est.: $600-up
Start Bid: $300

36611   [John H. Amory]. *Old Ironside. The Story of a Shipwreck.* Boston: James B. Dow, 1840. Later edition. Twelvemo. 144 pages. Illustrated with numerous full-page plates. Ribbed full cloth with stamped borders on covers and insignia on rear. Gilt-stamped front titles. Covers and extremities

rubbed with minor loss at spine head. Some toning and foxing throughout. Very minor nibbling to rear hinge and pinholes at joints. Spot of soiling to one page. Fore-edge with slight indent. Otherwise, generally very good.

Est.: $600-up
Start Bid: $300

36612   [Anonymous]. *Eccentric Biography, or Sketches of Remarkable Characters, Ancient and Modern.* Boston: Nathaniel Balch, Jr., 1825. Early American edition. Eighteenmo. 213, iii contents pages. Frontispiece illustration of Hopkins and Guy engraved by D. C. Johnston. Contemporary paper over boards with paper title label mounted to the spine. Moderate wear to the spine ends with general wear and scattered soiling to the boards. Contents with some light scattered foxing, else a sound copy indeed, in very good condition.

Est.: $600-up
Start Bid: $300

36613   W. P. Bartlett. *Happenings. A Series of Sketches of the Great California Out-of-Doors.* Porterville: privately published by the author, 1927. First edition. **Inscribed by the author on the front free endpaper.** Octavo. 267 pages. Publisher's cloth with titles stamped in gilt on the spine and front board. A few scattered stains to the boards, else a fine copy.

Est.: $600-up
Start Bid: $300

36614   Frank Bellew. *Bad Boy's First Reader.* New York: G. W. Carleton & Co., Publishers, 1881. First edition. Twelvemo. 44, [2] publisher's catalog pages. Printed wrappers. String bound. Wrappers detached; small section of front wrapper detached but present. Former owner's name in ink on the front wrapper. Contents sound and in very good condition. Bellew was an American artist and illustrator who was the first to portray the figure of Uncle Sam.

Est.: $600-up
Start Bid: $300

36615   William H. Bell. *The Quiddities of an Alaskan Trip.* Portland: G. A. Steel & Co., 1873. First edition. Oblong octavo. Sixty-seven un-numbered pages including sixty-one numbered lithographs on thirty-one rectos. Publisher's green cloth with a comic vignette of a bear and eagle ringing a bell stamped in gilt on the front board. Endpapers and pastedowns replaced. Re-backed using a portion of the original spine panel. Contents with occasional scattered foxing. Boards worn at the extremities, still a very good copy of this quite rare comic look at a soldier's travels to Alaska.

Est.: $600-up
Start Bid: $300

36616   [Slavery]. [George Bourne]. *Picture of Slavery in the United States of America.* Middletown: Edwin Hunt, 1834. First edition. Eighteenmo. 224, (1) pages. Frontispiece and ten additional engravings depicting scenes of slavery. Contemporary cloth over thin boards with paper spine title label. Covers rather worn and soiled with some dampstaining and slight bubbling to cloth. Some abrading to spine ends and corners. Lightly faded spine with some splitting and somewhat rubbed sunned label. Moderate foxing and light toning throughout. Front endpapers have some writing and small ink spots. Light dampstaining at fore-edge and top corner through first thirty pages. A few middle signatures slightly proud. A better than good copy. Sabin 6921.

Est.: $600-up
Start Bid: $300

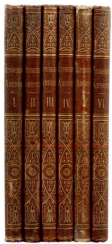

36617   William Cullen Bryant, editor. *Picturesque America.* New York: D. Appleton and Company, 1872. Two volumes in six, complete. Folio. Numerous steel- and wood-engraved plates. Publisher's brick red cloth decoratively stamped in gold and black. All volumes (except Volume IV) with cracked hinges; Volume V loose. Volumes rubbed and with general shelf wear, a few with minor fraying to cloth. Volume I with a few minor dampstains to textblock, Volume V with ink splotches to rear board and splitting to front joint. Plates generally fine. Overall, a very good set, sumptuously illustrated. Uncommon in a six-volume set, usually seen in two, and occasionally four, volumes. BAL 1732.2. Sabin 62692 (the two-volume edition).

Est.: $600-up
Start Bid: $300

36618   Geoffrey Gambado [pseudonym for Henry William Bunbury]. *An Academy For Grown Horsemen.* Philadelphia: Published by M. Carey, 1813. First and only American printing. Octavo. [2] publisher's announce-ment,50, [16] publisher's catalog, 12 catalog pages. 12 engraved plates by William Charles after Bunbury. Publisher's paper over boards. Boards soiled and worn at the extremities. Contents toned with scattered light to moderate foxing. Contemporary owner's name in ink on the front free endpaper. Contemporary soldier's ownership stamp and label on the front board.

Est.: $600-up
Start Bid: $300

36619   [George P. Burnham]. *Gleanings from the Portfolio of the "Young 'Un." A Series of Humorous Sketches.* Boston: R. B. Fitts & Co., 1849. Second edition. Twelvemo. vi, [5]-142 pages. Illustrated by Hitchcock. Modern half-leather over marbled boards. New endpapers. Top edge gilt. Light toning throughout. Illustrations uniformly toned. Minor spotting to fore-edge. A few mar-gin tears at front. Otherwise, near fine. Scarce. Wright I, 461a.

Est.: $600-up
Start Bid: $300

36620   [Humor]. [W. E. Burton]. *Burton's Comic Songster: Being Entirely a New Collection of Original and Popular Songs…* Philadelphia: Kay & Troutman, 1846. Thirtytwomo. 320 pages. With Twelve engravings. Full mottled leather with morocco spine label and gilt titles. Very light abrading to spine ends and corners. Light toning and foxing throughout. Otherwise, near fine.

Est.: $600-up
Start Bid: $300

36621   [F. O. C. Darley, illustra-tor]. W[illiam] E[vans] Burton. *Waggeries and Vagaries. A Series of Sketches, Humorous and Descriptive.* Philadelphia: Carey & Hart, 1848. First edition. Twelvemo. 192 pages. With eight original illus-trations by Darley. Library binding. Typical light wear and markings to covers. Lacking original wraps. Front hinge split with rear begin-ning, though still rather tight. Preliminary blank has inch-long closed tear and paperclip imprint to top edge. Occasional light ton-ing and foxing to text and illustra-tions. Some offsetting and darken-ing to images. A few small tears to page edges. "A difficult book to find in any condition." This being a better than very good copy. Wright I:466. Hamilton 1599.

Est.: $600-up
Start Bid: $300

36622   John W. Carter. *The World's Wonder, or Freemasonry Unmasked.* Madisonville: Johnston & Edwards, 1835. Octavo. xii, [13]-286, [2, Contents leaf], [48, 24 plates] pages. Leather backstrip over marbled boards with blind-stamped spine titles. Heavily worn and abraded binding with partially split joints. Staining to preliminary and end leaves. Foxing throughout. Very good.

Est.: $600-up
Start Bid: $300

36623   [Lydia Marie Child, editor]. *The Oasis.* Boston: Benjamin C. Bacon, 1834. First edi-tion. Sixteenmo. xvi, 276 pages. Fourteen engravings including the vignette on the title page and fron-tispiece. Publisher's pictorial cloth. Joints cracked and repaired but the boards remain firmly attached. Contents with occasional light to moderate foxing. Still, all things considered, a very good copy of this scarce work. Child was an early abolitionist and the stories she ed-its in this volume would likely not have been happily read in some quarters.

Est.: $600-up
Start Bid: $300

36624 **[George Clarke, publisher].** *The Life and Sketches of Curious and Odd Characters.* Boston: Published by George Clarke, 1833. First edition. Sixteenmo. 192 pages. With twenty-four wood engravings. Original paper over boards with cloth backstrip. Titles printed on the front board in black. Moderate wear to the extremities of the boards with additional toning and scattered soiling. Contents uniformly toned with light to moderate scattered foxing, else a very good copy of this quite rare work. Sabin 41032.

Est.: $600-up
Start Bid: $300

36625 **Herman Thwackius [pseudonym for Jonas Clopper].** *Fragments of the History of Bawlfredonia: Containing an Account of the Discovery and Settlement of That Great Southern Continent; and of the Formation and Progress of the Bawlfredonian Commonwealth.* [Baltimore?]: Printed for the American Booksellers, 1819. First edition. Octavo. 164 pages. Publisher's paper over boards. Boards worn and scuffed. Spine worn and exposed. Front board partially detached. Contents toned with light to moderate scattered foxing. Still, internally sound and worthy of conservation. Early work of American political and social satire.

Est.: $600-up
Start Bid: $300

36626 **[Anti-Jacobin]. [William Cobbett]. Peter Porcupine. [The Bloody Buoy].** *Die Blut-Fahne ausgestecket zur Warnung politischer Wegweiser in America...* Reading: Gottlob Jungmann, 1797. First German translation for Pennsylvania Dutch community. Octavo. [x], 198 pages, [2]. With three of the four engravings, lacking frontispiece. Period full calf with two reinforcing tabs across spine and boards. Morocco spine label with gilt titles. Covers and spine very well rubbed and somewhat abraded. Front board detached but connected by bottom tab, rear joint and hinge starting. Slightly cocked. Missing preliminaries, frontispiece and title pages. Moderate toning, foxing, and thumbsoiling throughout. Text block bumped at bottom corner with some lightly folded corners at top. Occasional chipping, small tears and margin loss at page edges. Previous owner's name to front pastedown. A good copy of this scarce text. Sabin 64160.

Est.: $600-up
Start Bid: $300

36627 **[Anti-Catholic]. [Captivity Narrative]. [Rosamond Culbertson].** *Rosamond: or, a Narrative of the Captivity and*

Sufferings of an American Female Under the Popish Priests, in the Island of Cuba with a Full Disclosure of Their Manners and Customs, Written by Herself. With an Introduction, by Samuel B. Smith... Pittsburgh: John Sharp, 1848. Later edition. Twelvemo. 240 pages. Two engraved frontispieces. Library binding with gilt spine titles. New endpapers. Light toning and foxing. Light dampstaining to head to text block throughout. Very good.

Est.: $600-up
Start Bid: $300

36628 **[D. C. Johnston, illustrator]. Mary Curtis.** *Memoirs of a Country Doll. Written by Herself.* Boston and Cambridge: James Munroe & Company, 1853. First edition. **Inscribed by the authoress.** Twelvemo. 82 pages. Illustrated by D. C. Johnston. Full publisher's cloth with blind-stamped borders and decoration. Gilt-stamped titles to front cover. Covers light rubbed. Extremities show shelfwear and minor loss at corners and spine. Slightly cocked. Text block shifted with signatures somewhat proud. Contents clean and tight. Minor offsetting of plates. Protective tissues intact. A better than very good copy of a scarce beautifully-illustrated book.

Est.: $600-up
Start Bid: $300

36629 **General G. A. Custer.** *Wild Life on the Plains and Horrors of Indian Warfare.* St. Louis: Sun Publishing, 1883. Early edition. Publisher's light brown cloth. Covers lightly worn and rubbed, especially at spine and corners. Front hinge broken and a bit loose, rear hinge starting. A good copy.

Est.: $800-up
Start Bid: $400

36630 **R. Dagley, illustrator.** *Death's Doings; Consisting of Numerous Original Compositions in Prose and Verse. The Friendly Contributions of Various Writers; Principally Intended as Illustrations of Thirty Plates, from Designs by R. Dagley.* Boston: Charles Ewer, 1828. From the second London edition with considerable additions. Two octavo volumes. 1-232; 233-472 pages. Thirty copper plates illustrated by Richard Dagley. Contemporary half binding and marbled paper over boards. Marbled endpapers. Titles stamped in gilt on the spine. Modest shelf wear to the extremities of the boards. Scattered light foxing throughout, else a very good set.

Est.: $600-up
Start Bid: $300

36631 **[F. O. C. Darley, illustrator]. [William Tappan Thompson].** *The Chronicles of Pineville: Embracing Sketches of Georgia Scenes, Incidents, and Characters.* Philadelphia: Carey & Hart, 1845. Later edition. Twelvemo. 186 pages. Illustrated with twelve original engravings by Darley. Crudely bound in wrappers with handwritten titles. Chipping and small tears to extremities. Front cover has moderate stain which continues through to preface. Torn top corner of preliminary. Cocked. Light foxing and toning throughout. Some dampstaining to rear cover, fore-edge and top corner. Front signature sprung, loose, and somewhat proud. Housed in a simple fixed paper chemise within custom cloth wraparound boards with gilt titles on a morocco label. A good copy of a scarce Georgia title.

Est.: $600-up
Start Bid: $300

36632 [F. O. C. Darley, illustrator]. [D. Corcoran]. *Pickings From the Portfolio of the Reporter of the New Orleans "Picayune:"*... Philadelphia: Carey and Hart, 1846. First edition. Twelvemo. 216 pages. Illustrated by Darley, lacking one plate. Half leather over marbled boards. Well rubbed covers and abraded extremities. Spine head cracked at joints. Pages toned and foxed. Ownership signatures. Good.

Est.: $600-up
Start Bid: $300

36633 [F. O. C. Darley, illustrator]. [F. A. Durivage and George P. Burnham]. *Stray Subjects, Arrested and Bound Over*: Being the Fugitive Offspring of the "Old 'Un" and the "Young 'Un," That Have Been "Lying Bound Loose," and are Now "Ties Up" for Fast Keeping. Philadelphia: T. B. Peterson and Brothers, [1848]. later edition. Twelvemo. viii, (2), [19]-199 pages. With eight original illustrations, from designs by Darley. Library binding with original illustrated wrappers bound in. Covers ribbed and lightly worn. Minor abrading to spine ends and corners. Slight fading to spine. Ex-library with typical wear, labels, and markings. Bookplate noting "From the

library of Talcott Williams, Director of the School of Journalism, 1912-1919. Very light toning and wear. Generally near fine. Scarce in original wrappers. Sabin 92751.

Est.: $600-up
Start Bid: $300

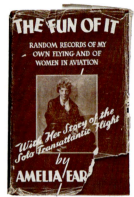

36634 Amelia Earhart. *The Fun of It. Random Records of My Own Flying and of Women in Aviation.* New York: Brewer, Warren & Putnam, 1932. Third printing. **Signed by Earhart on the front free endpaper.** Octavo. 218 pages. With thirty-one illustrations and complete with the small phonograph recording of a portion of Earhart's address in London, May 22, 1932. Publisher's brown cloth with titles stamped in white. The book is in very good to fine condition; the jacket has suffered loss to the front panel and the edges are tatty and worn.

Est.: $600-up
Start Bid: $300

36635 [American Independence]. William Emmons. *An Oration and Poem Delivered July 4, 1826, Being the Anniversary of American Independence.* Boston: Published by the author, 1826. First edition. Octavo. 16 pages. Quarter leather with cloth over boards. Gilt titles on spine. Pamphlet with original wrappers bound in. Binder's blanks both before and after text.

Covers lightly soiled and rubbed, particularly at spine. Hinges starting. Wrappers slightly browned with three tears on fore-edge, two repaired with tape on reverse and two with small paper fill. Reverse shows owner's signature and five small spots on wax on inside edge, presumably where missing D. C. Johnston illustration was tipped in. Pages lightly toned and foxed. Spots of light dampstaining to head of the majority of pages, rear wrapper, and tail of the title page. Generally very good. Sabin 22533.

Est.: $600-up
Start Bid: $300

36636 *The Every Body's Album: A Humorous Collection of Tales, Quips, Quirks, Anecdotes, and Facetiae.* Philadelphia: Charles Alexander, 1836. First edition. Two octavo volumes. Contemporary half leather with rubbing and abrading to extremities. Pages with foxing and edge wear. A few leaves detached. Illustrated. Overall good.

Est.: $600-up
Start Bid: $300

36637 [Humor]. [William Croome, illustrator]. Falconbridge. *Dan Marble; a Biographical Sketch of that Famous and Diverting Humorist,* with Reminiscences, Comicalities, Anecdotes, etc. etc. New York:

Dewitt & Davenport, [1851]. First edition. Twelvemo. xvi, [13]-235 pages. Illustrated by William Croome and others. Modern rebacked cloth spine with paper label over period marbled boards. Boards and corners somewhat rubbed with minor loss. New endpapers. Ex-library with typical stamps, markings, and wear. Light toning to page edges and illustrations. Occasional light foxing and soiling. Light creases to corners. Very good. Scarce. Sabin 23722.

Est.: $600-up
Start Bid: $300

36638 Henry J. Finn, editor. *American Comic Annual.* Boston: Richardson, Lord & Holbrook, 1831. First edition. Twelvemo. 220 pages. Illustrated by D. C. Johnston. Original pictorial boards and morocco backstrip. Titles stamped in gilt on the spine. Modest wear to boards with scattered light to moderate foxing to the contents, else a near fine copy. This annual, of which no other volumes were published, contains some of the most interesting work of Johnston who has been called "the American Cruikshank."

Est.: $600-up
Start Bid: $300

36639 [Nathan Daboll]. Edmund Freebetter. *The New-England Almanack; And Gentleman's and Lady's and Diary, for the Year of Our Lord Christ 1777.* New-London: Printed and Sold by T. Green, [1776]. First edition. Twelvemo. [24] pages. Handstitched self-wrappers. Rubbing and soiling to covers. Vertical creasing to leaves. Small hole in last two leaves, affecting a few words of text. Minor chipping and small tears around edges. Some corners creased. Very good. Drake 310. Evans 14724. Trumbull 224.

Est.: $600-up
Start Bid: $300

36640 **[Humor]. [Philip Morin Freneau].** *The Cabinet of Momus; a Choice Selection of Humorous Poems*... Philadelphia: Mathew Carey, 1809. First edition. Twelvemo. viii, 136 pages. Embellished with Six Engravings. Period full calf with morocco spine label with gilt titles. Slight rubbing to covers and extremities. Bottom edge, spine tail, and corners have abrading and wear. Very minor predation to front joint and front free endpaper. Light toning to pages with minor foxing at endpapers. Poem tipped in facing title page. Previous owner's name and notes at front and rear, with occasional marginalia. Few pages of front signature a bit proud. A very good copy of a scarce early example of American Humor. BAL, Vol. 3, p. 253. Shaw & Shoemaker 17136.

Est.: $600-up
Start Bid: $300

36641 **Lewis H. Garrard.** *Wah-To-Yah, and The Taos Trail; or Prairie Travel and Scalp Dances, with a look at Los Rancheros from Muleback and the Rocky Mountain Campfire.* Cincinnati: H.W. Derby, 1850. First edition. Octavo. Viii, 349 pages. Attractively bound in black morocco, lettered in gilt. Some pages slightly browned or soiled, a few occasional chips to the edges, else a very good copy.

Est.: $1,000-up
Start Bid: $500

36642 **Frederick Gerstacker.** *How a Bride Was Won; or, A Chase Across the Pampas.* New York: Appleton, 1869. First American edition. Octavo. 274, 6 advertising pages. Publisher's binding with light rubbing and abrading to extremities. Illustrated. Very good.

Est.: $600-up
Start Bid: $300

36643 **Barry Gray and John Savage.** *Ale: in Prose and Verse.* New York: [Privately printed for friends of the John Taylor & Sons Brewery by] Russell's American Steam Printing House, 1866. First, and presumably only, edition. Octavo. 97 pages. Frontispiece and thirteen plates, some by McNevin and some engraved portraits of various brewery scenes and buildings. Publisher's soft brown cloth covers with gilt titles on the front cover and quadruple-ruled blind borders to both covers. Housed in a red cloth slipcase and chemise with a gilt-lettered morocco spine label and gilt spine stamping. Minor fraying to the cloth edges. Short tear to the cloth at the spine head. Binding a touch shaken. A well-preserved, and rare title, in very good condition. A notice from the brewery is tipped-in to the front free endpaper reading, in

part, "This book is not for sale, and only a limited number of copies have been printed for presentation."

Est.: $600-up
Start Bid: $300

36644 **[Humor]. [Frederic Stanhope Hill].** *The Flowers of Anecdote, Wit, Humor, Gayety and Genius.* Boston: Frederic S. Hill, 1831. Twelvemo. 285 pages. With three etchings and a title illustration. Period full cloth over thin boards with paper spine label. Covers rubbed and worn with somewhat soft abraded corners and spine ends. Cloth somewhat rippled. Spine somewhat faded and with minor loss to ends and toned label.. Light toning and foxing throughout with occasional small spots of staining. Pencil notations at rear. Otherwise, a very good copy of a scarce title.

Est.: $600-up
Start Bid: $300

36645 **George Rogers Howell.** *The Early History of Southampton, L. I. New York, With Genealogies.* New York: Published by J. N. Hallock, 1866. First edition. Octavo. 318, [2] publisher's catalog pages. CDV of Howell mounted and used as the frontispiece. Library rebound in brown cloth and containing some library marks in pencil. A few pages loose but the collation is complete. Otherwise an internally bright and sound copy in very good condition.

Est.: $600-up
Start Bid: $300

36646 **[D. C. Johnston]. [Humor].** *The Aurora Borealis, or Flashes of Wit; Calculated to Drown Dull Care and Eradicate the Blue Devils.* Boston: by the Editor of The Galaxy of Wit, 1831. Early edition. Sixteenmo. 216 pages. With fourteen original etchings designed and executed by D. C. Johnston, including frontispiece and half-title. Spine rebacked with period hand-tooled and blindstamped full leather covers. Morocco spine label with gilt titles. Covers and extremities well rubbed with light abrading to corners. Endpapers and page edges toned with some light foxing throughout. A few pages have small tears not affecting text or lightly folded corners. A few signatures proud near rear. A very good copy of rather scarce Johnston book.

Est.: $600-up
Start Bid: $300

36647 **[D. C. Johnston]. Joseph C. Neal.** *Charcoal Sketches; or, Scenes in a Metropolis.* Philadelphia: E. L. Carey & A. Hart, 1838. Early edition. **Original pencil drawing for the plate opposite page 66 laid in. Image measures approximately 4 x 4 inches.** Twelvemo. 222 pages. Illustrations by David C. Johnston. Publisher's patterned cloth with paper spine label. Covers well rubbed and soiled with abrading to spine ends, turned corners and spine label. Slight lean with text block somewhat crimped at bottom. Moderate foxing and toning to pages with a touch of light dampstaining to the bottom edge. Drawing lightly toned with a hint of mat burn. Otherwise, a better than good copy of the author's first book with a wonderful drawing by illustrator D. C. Johnston laid in.

Est.: $600-up
Start Bid: $300

36648   [Humor]. [D. C. Johnston, illustrator]. *The Laughing Philosopher: or Fun, Humour and Wit: Being a Collection of Choice Anecdotes, Many of Which, Never Before in Print, Originated in or About "The Literary Emporium."* Boston: Printed for the Publisher, 1825. First edition. Twelvemo. 216 pages. Some of the earliest published illustrations by D. C. Johnston. Modern full dark blue cloth over thin boards with a morocco label with gilt titles. New endpapers. Pages uncut. Minor toning and foxing with occasional thumbsoiling. First signature a bit overopened, causing a few very minor tears at the gutter. A very good copy of a scarce early edition.

Est.: $600-up
Start Bid: $300

36649   E. Otis Kendall. *Uranography; or, A Description of the Heavens; Designed for Academies and Schools; Accompanied by an Atlas of the Heavens, Showing the Places of the Principal Stars, Clusters, and Nebulae.* Philadelphia: Butler & Williams, 1844. First edition. Octavo. 365 pages. Illustrated. Publisher's printed paper over boards with cloth backstrip. Boards worn and contents with moderate scattered foxing, else a very good copy.

Est.: $600-up
Start Bid: $300

36650   Sampson Short-and-Fat [pseudonym for Samuel Kettell]. *Daw's Doings, or the History of the Late War in the Plantations.* Boston: William White & H. P. Lewis, 1842. First edition. Twelvemo. 68 pages. With several engraved vignettes throughout text. Text block slightly trimmed and rebound in modern blue cloth with titles stamped in gilt on a blue morocco spine label. A very clean copy with only light scattered foxing, but in otherwise very good condition.

Est.: $600-up
Start Bid: $300

36651   [The Star-Spangled Banner]. [Francis Scott Key]. *The Defence of Fort M'Henry.* Contained in *The Analectic Magazine, Vol. IV, November, 1814.* First appearance in magazine form. Octavo. Pages 433-434. Publisher's printed wrappers. Covers lightly rubbed and soiled, with very light dampstaining to rear, not affecting text block. Spine somewhat abraded, with minor loss at head. Some light toning and foxing. Housed in a custom chemise with a half morocco slipcase with gilt spine titles. Generally very good. BAL 11081. Hill, p. 26. Sabin 1358. Sonneck, p. 83. Streeter Sale 1070.

Est.: $1,000-up
Start Bid: $500

36652   [Charles Godfrey Leland]. *Ye Book of Copperhead.* Philadelphia: Frederick Leypoldt, 1863. First edition. Oblong octavo. 30 pages. Twenty-four cartoons with satirical captions followed by verse about the Copperheads. Original printed wrappers. Fine condition. Howes L245; Sabin 39962.

Est.: $600-up
Start Bid: $300

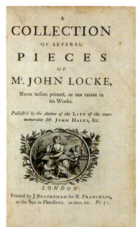

36653   [Carolina Constitution]. John Locke. *A Collection of Several Pieces of Mr. John Locke, Never Before Printed or not Extant in His Works.* London: J. Bettenham for R. Francklin, 1720. Octavo. [62], 362 pages, [22] pages including 1 page of errata and 3 pages of publisher's ads. One engraved plate. Contemporary paneled calf boards rebacked with five raised bands and morocco spine label. Boards somewhat worn. New endpapers and some fill to a preliminary page. Pages toned with occasional foxing and bent corners. Overall, a very good copy. JCB 271. Sabin 41726. Streeter Sale 1119.

Est.: $900-up
Start Bid: $450

36654   [D. C. Johnston, illustrator]. Doctor Ebenezer Mack. *The Cat-Fight; A Mock Heroic Poem. Supported with Copious Extracts*

From Ancient and Modern Classic Authors... New-York: n.p., 1824. First edition. Octavo. 276 pages. Five engravings by D. C. Johnston. Paper spine with label over period paper covered boards. Covers warped and worn with some loss and dampstaining. Spine has some splitting at top of joints. Hinges reinforced. Pages uncut and some unopened. Light foxing and toning with some minor dampstaining. Otherwise, generally very good.

Est.: $600-up
Start Bid: $300

36655   John McLenan. *Bits of Humor.* New-York: Published by M. Smith, 1866. First edition. Quarto. Twenty tipped-in plates by McLenan on the recto of 40 pages. Publisher's green cloth over beveled boards with titles stamped in gilt. Soiling to the boards with some wear at the corners and spine ends. Foxing to the verso of the pages with some scattered light foxing to the plates, else very good. An exceedingly rare work and featuring otherwise unpublished drawings by McLenan.

Est.: $600-up
Start Bid: $300

36656   [Magic]. Harry Hermon. *Hellerism. Second-Sight Mystery, Supernatural Vision, or Second-Sight. What Is It? A Mystery. A Complete Manual For Teaching This Peculiar Art.* Boston: Harry Hermon, 1884. First edition. **Inscribed and signed by the author** on the front free endpaper, dated 1884. Small square octavo. 129 pages. Illustrated. Frontispiece. Original pictorial green boards, stamped in purple. General wear to binding, particularly to spine ends and extremities. Title page detached cleanly and laid in. Contents clean and sturdy. Very good. An early how-to book on "mind-reading," with lists of verbal cues and exercises for two participants. The author's note offers private tutelage in this apparently profitable parlor trick; he is also "prepared to furnish professionals and amateurs with [magical] apparatus of every description at the lowest prices."

Est.: $800-up
Start Bid: $400

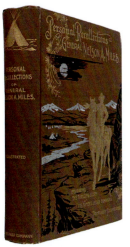

36657   General Nelson A. Miles: *Personal Recollections and Observations of General Nelson A. Miles.* Chicago, New York: The Werner Company, 1896. First edition, second issue. With an autographed card tipped in: "Nelson A. Miles / Major General / Com-(?) US Army." Publisher's pictorial brown cloth, Frontispiece portrait tattered along margin. An excellent copy in near fine condition.

Est.: $600-up
Start Bid: $300

36658   [C. V. Nickerson, illustrator]. *The Humourist; A Collection of Entertaining Tales, Anecdotes, Epigrams, Bon Mots, &tc.* Baltimore: C. V. Nickerson, and Lucas and Deaver, 1829. Early American edition, two volumes in one. Twelvemo. 124; 124 pages. Hand-colored copperplate engravings by C. V. Nickerson. Contemporary quarter binding

with titles stamped in gilt on the spine. Moderate wear to the edges of the boards. Contents with scattered foxing, else a sound copy in very good condition.

Est.: $800-up
Start Bid: $400

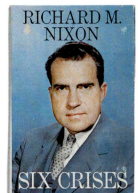

36659   Richard M. Nixon. *Six Crises.* Garden City: Doubleday, 1962. Later edition. **Inscribed by Nixon.** Octavo. 458 pages. Publisher's binding and dust jacket. Cloth very lightly rubbed with some light sunning to top edge. Page edges have light toning. Rubbed jacket has a few scuffs and small tears with toning to rear panel. Price on front flap ripped off. Pencil notes in index. Otherwise, very good.

Est.: $800-up
Start Bid: $400

36660   Hector Bull-Us [pseudonym for James Kirke Paulding]. *The Diverting History of John Bull and Brother Jonathan.* Philadelphia: Published by M. Carey and Son, 1819. Third edition. Twelvemo. 144 pages. Several engraved plates. Contemporary paper over boards. Edges untrimmed. Boards worn at the spine ends and corners. Contents generally clean but a few pages are rather ragged along the edges, else a very good copy.

Est.: $600-up
Start Bid: $300

36661   William T. Peters, illustrator. *The College Experience of Ichabod Academicus; Illustrated by William T. Peters and Dedicated to Their Brother Collegians by the Editors, H.F.P. & G.M.* [New Haven]: [n.p.], [n.d., circa 1849-1850]. First edition. Oblong octavo. Unpaginated. Printed wrappers. String-bound. Wrappers toned with some dampstaining; tatty along the edges. Contents with occasional scattered foxing. A few pages loose, but taken on balance a very good copy of this scarce work. Peters' cartoons follow college students from the freshman year through senior year in serialized form.

Est.: $600-up
Start Bid: $300

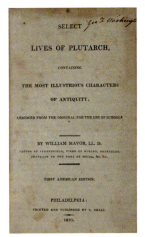

36662   [Plutarch]. William Mavor. *Select Lives of Plutarch, Containing the Most Illustrious Characters of Antiquity; Abridged from the Original for the Use of Schools.* Philadelphia: Printed and Published by A. Small, 1810. First American edition of this abridged version. Approximately 7 x 4.25 inches. Small octavo. [viii], 418 pages. Contemporary full tree calf, spine ruled in gilt, with red morocco gilt lettering label. Some wear to binding, front joint cracking, some dampstaining to text, two leaves (pages 161-164) a bit loose. A good copy. **With the ownership signatures of George F(ayette) Washington, and his son, George F(ayette) Washington, Jr.** on the title page and front free endpaper, respectively. George Fayette Washington was President George Washington's grand-nephew, being the grandson of his brother

Charles, and George Fayette Washington, Jr. was President Washington's great grand-nephew.

Est.: $600-up
Start Bid: $300

36663   [Presidents of the United States]. *The Presidents. The White House Gallery of the Official Portraits of the Presidents.* New York: The Gravure Company of America, 1901. The McKinley Memorial Edition, this is number 518 and is registered to Mrs. Russell Sage (with official bookplate). Approximately 19.75 x 15.75 inches. Folio. [iv], [24] pages. With 24 full-page portraits and descriptive tissue guards inserted. Publisher's three-quarter brown levant morocco over green cloth, front cover stamped and lettered in gilt, wraparound red ribbon. Spine worn, boards detached (as well as worn and soiled), tape repairs to front free endpaper and first blank at gutter. Good.

Est.: $600-up
Start Bid: $300

36664   [F. O. C. Darley, illustrator]. Solitaire. [John S. Robb]. *Streaks of Squatter Life, and Far-West Scenes. A Series of Humorous Sketches Descriptive of Incidents and Character in the Wild West.* Philadelphia: Carey and Hart, 1847. First edition. Octavo. 187 pages. Eight plates by Darley. Distressed marbled boards and morocco spine label with gilt titles. Covers and extremities lightly rubbed. New endpapers. Illustrated half-title and backed frontispiece have some moderate repair to loss at top of gutter. Title page torn with loss at same area. A few signatures standing proud at bottom at rear of text block. Illustrations uniformly toned with some offsetting. Corners of block lightly bumped and rubbed. Generally very good. Hamilton 594. Howes R335aa. Wright I, 2126.

Est.: $600-up
Start Bid: $300

36665   William Russell. *The History of America, From Its Discovery by Columbus to the Conclusion of the Late War.* London: Printed for Fielding and Walker, 1778. First edition. Complete in two large quarto volumes. iv, 596; 629, [1, Errata]. 48 of the 51 maps and plates called for. Full contemporary calf. Spines with five raised bands and two gilt-stamped morocco labels. Leather quite worn, with repairs to joints and spines. Occasional mild foxing and offsetting throughout, but interior generally quite clean. Minor closed tears to a few folding maps and to plates. With engraved armorial bookplate of James Shepherd on front pastedowns; also with his ink name, date Nov. 21st, 1787, and elaborate flourish on front free endpaper of each volume. Very good condition. ETSC T114880. Howes R539 ("aa"). Sabin 74383.

Est.: $800-up
Start Bid: $400

36666   [D. C. Johnston, illustrator]. William Russell. *Rudiments of Gesture, Comprising Illustrations of Common Faults in Attitude and Action.* With Engravings, and an Appendix Designed for Practical Exercise in Declamation. Boston: Carter and Hendee, 1830. First edition. Octavo. viii, 48 pages. Illustrated by D.C. Johnston. Period boards and cloth

spine with paper title label to front cover. Well-worn and lightly soiled with moderate loss and predation to spine and boards. Light foxing and toning throughout. A few very minor tears to page edges. Otherwise, generally near fine.

Est.: $600-up
Start Bid: $300

36667   [Crime]. Henry St. Clair, compiler. *The United States Criminal Calendar:* or An Awful Warning to the Youth of America; Being an Account of the Most Horrid Murders, Piracies, Highway Robberies, &c. &c. Boston: Charles Gaylord, 1835. Third edition. Twelvemo. 536 pages. Fifteen engravings, attributed to D. C. Johnston. Contemporary half leather over marbled boards. Boards and extremities worn. Endpapers and page edges lightly foxed. Minute dampstaining to top edge at rear of text. Some light spotting, minor tears, and thumbsoiling throughout. Two-inch loss at pages 215-216 in outer margin slightly affecting text. Otherwise, very good. Howes S27.

Est.: $600-up
Start Bid: $300

36668   Dick Humelbergius Secundus. *Apician Morsels.* New York: J. & J. Harper, 1829. First American edition. Twelvemo. 212, [2], 2 pages of advertisements. Contemporary quarter leather with paper-covered boards. Rubbed and worn with rear board detached. Soiling and foxing throughout. About good.

Est.: $600-up
Start Bid: $300

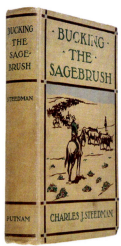

36669   Charles J. Steedman. *Bucking the Sagebrush or The Oregon Trail in the Seventies.* New York and London: G. P. Putnam's Sons, 1904. First edition. Octavo. 270 pages. Illustrated by Charles M. Russell. Folding map. Publisher's illustrated binding. Top edge gilt. A handsome copy with modest shelf wear to the extremities of the boards, else very good condition.

Est.: $600-up
Start Bid: $300

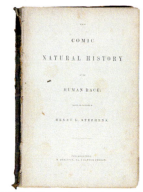

36670   Henry L. Stephens. *The Comic Natural History of the Human Race: Designed and Illustrated by Henry L. Stephens.* Philadelphia: S. Robinson, 1851. First edition. Quarto. 216 pages. Forty lithographic plates by Henry L. Stephens. Contemporary quarter leather and marbled boards. Front board and frontispiece detached. Spine panel cracked. Boards worn at the extremities. Contents with light to moderate scattered foxing. Still, a sound copy of this uncommon work. Copies exist with colored plates, this copy's plates are unadorned.

Est.: $600-up
Start Bid: $300

36671   Wilkins Tannehill. *The Masonic Manual, or Freemasonry Illustrated.* Nashville: Printed by George Wilson, 1824. First edition. Twelvemo. [ii, engraved title or half-title leaf not accounted for in Sabin], [i]-vii, [viii, blank], 412 pages. With six inserted engraved plates. Contemporary full calf with a black leather title label lettered in gilt. All edges yellow. Significant wear to the binding. Spine ends frayed. One-third of the title label missing. Partial vertical split to the spine leather. Heavy foxing throughout. Large damp-stain to the last fifty or so pages. Ownership signatures to each free endpaper. A few leaves with loss to the bottom corner; a few creased. One gathering standing proud. A complete copy in good condition. Sabin 94309.

Est.: $600-up
Start Bid: $300

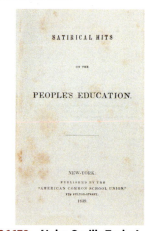

36672   [John Orville Taylor]. *Satirical Hits on the People's Education.* New-York: Published by the "American Common School Union," 1839. First edition. Sixteenmo. [4], 7-98 pages. Eight lithographic plates attributed to Nathaniel Currier. Publisher's brown cloth. Boards moderately water-damaged; front joint with a three-inch split; contents with light to moderate foxing, else a very good copy of this scarce work.

Est.: $600-up
Start Bid: $300

36673   [F. O. C. Darley, illustrator]. [Thompson]. *Major Jones's Courtship: Detailed with Other Scenes, Incidents, and Adventures, in a Series of Letters, by Himself.* Philadelphia: Carey & Hart, 1846. Seventh edition, greatly enlarged. Twelvemo. 200 pages. Twelve plates by Darley. Modern half leather over cloth with gilt spine titles. Covers and spine lightly rubbed. New endpapers. Moderately toned with light foxing and offsetting throughout. Very good copy of a scarce title. Sabin 95543.

Est.: $600-up
Start Bid: $300

36674   [Satire of British and Tories]. John Trumbull. *M'Fingal: A Modern Epic Poem, in Four Cantos.* New York: John Buel, 1795. First illustrated edition with plates and explanatory notes. Octavo. 136 pages. With eight of the nine called-for plates by E.[lkanah] Tisdale. Period full calf with gilt spine ruling and morocco spine label with gilt titles. Covers rubbed and somewhat worn with extremities and edges with minor loss. Corners and spine ends bumped with spine head torn. Front hinge lightly split. Front pastedown shows some light dampstaining and excision. Pages with moderate toning and foxing. A few light markings or small stains present. Minor tears at edges and some light folds or loss to corners. Generally, a very good copy. Evans 29659.

Est.: $600-up
Start Bid: $300

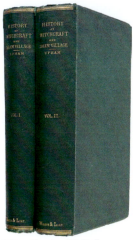

36675   Charles W. Upham. *Salem Witchcraft*, with An Account of Salem Village, and A History of Opinions on Witchcraft and Kindred Subjects. Boston: Wiggin and Lunt, 1867. Large paper edition limited to 50 copies, with Volume I being number 49, and Volume II being number 44. Two quarto volumes. xl, 469; 553 pages. Frontispieces. Fold-out map, illustrations, index. Full green cloth with gilt titles to spines. Both volumes over-opened at limitation page. Volume I with front hinge starting and front joint splitting. Volume II with wear to joints. A tight bright copy in better than very good condition. A scholarly investigation into "the great and awful tragedy." Howes U21. Sabin 98039.

Est.: $600-up
Start Bid: $300

36676   [Anti-Slavery]. Roberts Vaux. *Memoirs of the Lives of Benjamin Lay and Ralph Sandiford*; *Two of the Earliest Public Advocates for the Emancipation of the Enslaved Africans.* Philadelphia: Solomon W. Conrad, 1815. First edition. Twelvemo. 73 pages. Engraved frontispiece. Period tree calf with gilt spine titles on a morocco label and gilt ruling. Covers and extremities rubbed with wear to edges and joints. Corners and spine tail somewhat abraded. Some foxing to endpapers. Mild toning to text. Slight loss across the top of a preliminary leaf; rear endpaper adhered to pastedown.

Bookseller's ticket. Otherwise, a better than very good copy. Sabin 98705.

Est.: $600-up
Start Bid: $300

36677   Sam R. Watkins. "Co. Aytch," Maury Grays, First Tennessee Regiment; or, a Side Show of the Big Show. Nashville: Cumberland Presbyterian, 1882. First edition. Octavo. 236 pages. Publisher's binding. Rebacked, preserving much of the original spine, some rubbing to boards, previous owner's signatures on endleaves, some soiling in text. Overall, very good. Housed in custom full morocco clamshell case.

Est.: $600-up
Start Bid: $300

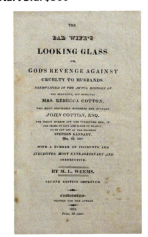

36678   M. L. Weems. Six Titles Bound as a Single Volume. Various: Weems, 1818-1823. All later edition. Octavo. Contemporary half leather over marbled boards. Rubbing and scuffing to extremities with joints beginning to crack. Hinges cracked with foxing to endpapers. Name on front free endpaper. Faint staining along top edge of textblock. Scattered foxing throughout. Occasional pencil notations. Illustrated. Good.

Est.: $600-up
Start Bid: $300

36679   Benjamin West. *The New-England Almanack, or Lady's and Gentleman's Diary, for the Year of our Lord Christ 1774...* Providence: Printed and Sold, Wholesale and Retail, by John Carter, [1773]. First edition. Twelvemo. [24] pages. Hand-stitched self-wrappers. Some edge wear, with minor tears and chips. Noticeable loss to the bottom edge of last leaf. Staining to the cover pages. A few leaves with contemporary marginalia. Very good. Alden 508. Drake 12840. Evans 13075.

Est.: $600-up
Start Bid: $300

36680   Benjamin West. *The New-England Almanack, or Lady's and Gentleman's Diary, for the Year of our Lord Christ 1775...* Providence: Printed and Sold, Wholesale and Retail, by John Carter, [1774]. First edition. Twelvemo. [24] pages. Hand-stitched self-wrappers. Stitching worn away to top third of spine. Foxing and unobtrusive marginalia to a few leaves. Edges lightly worn. Very good condition. On pages 18-21, an aggressively-worded political editorial titled "A brief View of the present Controversy between Great-Britain and America, with some Observations thereon," makes reference to "Taxation and representation," the Boston Tea Party, and "revolution." Alden 530. Drake 12842. Evans 13764.

Est.: $800-up
Start Bid: $400

36681   Benjamin West. *The New-England Almanack, or Lady's and Gentleman's Diary, for the Year of our Lord Christ 1776...* Providence: Printed and Sold, Wholesale and Retail, by John Carter, [1775]. First edition, first state, with "Thomas Church" the last name at the bottom of page 22. Twelvemo. [32] pages. Hand-stitched self-wrappers. Small abrasion hole to the fore-edge margin of the first leaf, not affecting any text. Some browning and foxing. Marginalia to one leaf. A very nice copy in very good condition. Alden 575. Drake 12945. Evans 14619.

Est.: $600-up
Start Bid: $300

36682   Benjamin West. *The New-England Almanack, or Lady's and Gentleman's Diary, for the Year of our Lord Christ 1777...* Providence: Printed and Sold by John Carter, [1776]. First edition. Twelvemo. [24] pages. Hand-stitched self-wrappers. Minor foxing to some leaves. Moderate edge wear, with minor chipping and a

few tiny tears. A clean copy in very good condition. Alden 632. Drake 12849. Evans 15216.

Est.: $600-up
Start Bid: $300

36683   [Book of Common Prayer in Mohawk]. [Rev. Eleazer Williams, V. D. M., translator]. *The Book of Common Prayer According to the Use of the Protestant Episcopal Church.* New York: Protestant Episcopal Tract Society, 1853. [Bound with:] **[Psalms and Hymns in Mohawk]. [Rev. Eleazer Williams, V. D. M., translator].** *Selections from the Psalms and Hymns According to the Use of the Protestant Episcopal Church.* New York: Protestant Episcopal Tract Society, 1853. Both works are "Revised Edition of His Former Translation." Approximately 6.25 x 3.75 inches. Two twelvemo volumes bound into one. 108; 67, [1, blank] pages. Contemporary full brown morocco, covers paneled in blind, with gilt central motif of a cross and a bible, spine ruled in black and lettered in gilt. Light rubbing, else fine.

Est.: $600-up
Start Bid: $300

36684   [Illustrated Year Book]. *The Illustrated Year-Book of Wonders, Events and Discoveries.* *Edited by a Popular Writer.* London: Arthur Hall, Virtue & Co., 1850. First edition. Octavo. [xvi], 336, [16, publisher's ads] pages. With twenty full-page engravings inserted throughout. Publisher's green cloth, covers decoratively ruled and stamped in blind, spine deco-

ratively tooled and lettered in gilt. Spine and edges of covers sunned and mildly rubbed, some mild foxing in text, the contemporary signature of H. A. Middleton on the front pastedown. A fine copy.

Est.: $600-up
Start Bid: $300

36685   Two Hand-Colored Photo Albums, including: *Scenes through the Canadian Rockies.* [and:] *The Grand Canyon of Arizona.* [Brooklyn and Elizabeth, N. J.: C. P. R. News Service and Kolb Brothers, 1911]. Oblong folio albums with hand-colored mounted photographic reproductions: *Canadian Rockies* has twelve (and three loose additional photos), and *Grand Canyon* has eighteen. Both complete. Publishers' string-tied wraps. Some wear. Very good.

Est.: $600-up
Start Bid: $300

End of Session Two

Terms and Conditions of Auction

Auctioneer and Auction:

1. This Auction is presented by Heritage Auctions, a d/b/a/ of Heritage Auctioneers & Galleries, Inc., or Heritage Auctions, Inc., or Heritage Numismatic Auctions, Inc., or Heritage Vintage Sports Auctions, Inc., or Currency Auctions of America, Inc., as identified with the applicable licensing information on the title page of the catalog or on the HA.com Internet site (the "Auctioneer"). The Auction is conducted under these Terms and Conditions of Auction and applicable state and local law. Announcements and corrections from the podium and those made through the Terms and Conditions of Auctions appearing on the Internet at HA.com supersede those in the printed catalog.

Buyer's Premium:

2. FOR AUCTION SESSIONS ON OR BEFORE DECEMBER 31, 2011: On bids placed through Auctioneer, a Buyer's Premium of fifteen percent (15%) will be added to the successful hammer price bid on lots in Arms & Armor, Currency, US Coin, and World & Ancient Coin Auctions or nineteen and one-half percent (19.5%) on lots in all other Auctions. There is a minimum Buyer's Premium of $14.00 per lot. In Gallery Auctions (sealed bid auctions of mostly bulk numismatic material), the Buyer's Premium is 19.5%.

FOR AUCTION SESSIONS ON OR SUBSEQUENT TO JANUARY 1, 2012: All bids are subject to a Buyer's Premium which is in addition to the placed successful bid:

- Fifteen percent (15%) on Arms & Armor, Currency, US Coin, and World & Ancient Coin Auctions lots; except that the World and Ancient Coin Auctions 3003 & 3018 shall have a Buyer's Premium of 19.5%;
- Nineteen and one-half percent (19.5%) on Americana & Political, Civil War & Militaria, Comic, Manuscript, Movie Poster, Space Exploration, Sports Collectibles, Texana, Wine, and Gallery Auction (sealed bid auctions of mostly bulk numismatic material) lots;
- For all other categories not listed above, twenty-five percent (25%) on the first $50,000, plus twenty percent (20%) of any amount between $50,000 and $1,000,000, plus twelve percent (12%) of any amount over $1,000,000 on each lot. There is a minimum Buyer's Premium of $14.00 per lot.

Auction Venues:

3. The following Auctions are conducted solely on the Internet: Heritage Weekly Internet Auctions (Coin, Currency, Comics, Rare Books, Jewelry & Watches, Guitars & Musical Instruments, and Vintage Movie Posters); Heritage Monthly Internet Auctions (Sports, World Coins and Rare Wine). Signature® Auctions and Grand Format Auctions accept bids from the Internet, telephone, fax, or mail first, followed by a floor bidding session; HeritageLive! and real- time telephone bidding are available to registered clients during these auctions.

Bidders:

4. Any person participating or registering for the Auction agrees to be bound by and accepts these Terms and Conditions of Auction ("Bidder(s)").
5. All Bidders must meet Auctioneer's qualifications to bid. Any Bidder who is not a client in good standing of the Auctioneer may be disqualified at Auctioneer's sole option and will not be awarded lots. Such determination may be made by Auctioneer in its sole and unlimited discretion, at any time prior to, during, or even after the close of the Auction. Auctioneer reserves the right to exclude any person from the auction.
6. If an entity places a bid, then the person executing the bid on behalf of the entity agrees to personally guarantee payment for any successful bid.

Credit:

7. In order to place bids, Bidders who have not established credit with the Auctioneer must either furnish satisfactory credit information (including two collectibles-related business references) or supply valid credit card information along with a social security number, well in advance of the Auction. Bids placed through our Interactive Internet program will only be accepted from pre-registered Bidders. Bidders who are not members of HA.com or affiliates should preregister at least 48 hours before the start of the first session (exclusive of holidays or weekends) to allow adequate time to contact references. Credit will be granted at the discretion of Auctioneer. Additionally Bidders who have not previously established credit or who wish to bid in excess of their established credit history may be required to provide their social security number or the last four digits thereof so a credit check may be performed prior to Auctioneer's acceptance of a bid. Check writing privileges and immediate delivery of merchandise may also be determined by pre-approval of credit based on a combination of criteria: HA.com history, related industry references, bank verification, a credit bureau report and/or a personal guarantee for a corporate or partnership entity in advance of the auction venue.

Bidding Options:

8. Bids in Signature® Auctions or Grand Format Auctions may be placed as set forth in the printed catalog section entitled "Choose your bidding method." For auctions held solely on the Internet, see the alternatives on HA.com. Review at HA.com/common/howtobid.php.
9. Presentment of Bids: Non-Internet bids (including but not limited to podium, fax, phone and mail bids) are treated similar to floor bids in that they must be on-increment or at a half increment (called a cut bid). Any podium, fax, phone, or mail bids that do not conform to a full or half increment will be rounded up or down to the nearest full or half increment and this revised amount will be considered your high bid.
10. Auctioneer's Execution of Certain Bids. Auctioneer cannot be responsible for your errors in bidding, so carefully check that every bid is entered correctly. When identical mail or FAX bids are submitted, preference is given to the first received. To ensure the greatest accuracy, your written bids should be entered on the standard printed bid sheet and be received at Auctioneer's place of business at least two business days before the Auction start. Auctioneer is not responsible for executing mail bids or FAX bids received on or after the day the first lot is sold, nor Internet bids submitted after the published closing time; nor is Auctioneer responsible for proper execution of bids submitted by telephone, mail, FAX, e-mail, Internet, or in person once the Auction begins. Bids placed electronically via the internet may not be withdrawn until your written request is received and acknowledged by Auctioneer (FAX: 214-443-8425); such requests must state the reason, and may constitute grounds for withdrawal of bidding privileges. Lots won by mail Bidders will not be delivered at the Auction unless prearranged.
11. Caveat as to Bid Increments. Bid increments (over the current bid level) determine the lowest amount you may bid on a particular lot. Bids greater than one increment over the current bid can be any whole dollar amount. It is possible under several circumstances for winning bids to be between increments, sometimes only $1 above the previous increment. Please see: "How can I lose by less than an increment?" on our website. Bids will be accepted in whole dollar amounts only. No "buy" or "unlimited" bids will be accepted.

The following chart governs current bidding increments.

Current Bid	Bid Increment	Current Bid	Bid Increment
<$10	$1	$20,000 - $29,999	$2,000
$10 - $29	$2	$30,000 - $49,999	$2,500
$30 - $49	$3	$50,000 - $99,999	$5,000
$50 - $99	$5	$100,000 - $199,999	$10,000
$100 - $199	$10	$200,000 - $299,999	$20,000
$200 - $299	$20	$300,000 - $499,999	$25,000
$300 - $499	$25	$500,000 - $999,999	$50,000
$500 - $999	$50	$1,000,000 - $1,999,999	$100,000
$1,000 - $1,999	$100	$2,000,000 - $2,999,999	$200,000
$2,000 - $2,999	$200	$3,000,000 - $4,999,999	$250,000
$3,000 - $4,999	$250	$5,000,000 - $9,999,999	$500,000
$5,000 - $9,999	$500	>$10,000,000	$1,000,000
$10,000 - $19,999	$1,000		

12. If Auctioneer calls for a full increment, a bidder may request Auctioneer to accept a bid at half of the increment ("Cut Bid") only once per lot. After offering a Cut Bid, bidders may continue to participate only at full increments. Off-increment bids may be accepted by the Auctioneer at Signature® Auctions and Grand Format Auctions. If the Auctioneer solicits bids other than the expected increment, these bids will not be considered Cut Bids.

Conducting the Auction:

13. Notice of the consignor's liberty to place bids on his lots in the Auction is hereby made in accordance with Article 2 of the Texas Business and Commercial Code. A "Minimum Bid" is an amount below which the lot will not sell. THE CONSIGNOR OF PROPERTY MAY PLACE WRITTEN "Minimum Bids" ON HIS LOTS IN ADVANCE OF THE AUCTION; ON SUCH LOTS, IF THE HAMMER PRICE DOES NOT MEET THE "Minimum Bid", THE CONSIGNOR MAY PAY A REDUCED COMMISSION ON THOSE LOTS. "Minimum Bids" are generally posted online several days prior to the Auction closing. For any successful bid placed by a consignor on his Property on the Auction floor, or by any means during the live session, or after the "Minimum Bid" for an Auction have been posted, we will require the consignor to pay full Buyer's Premium and Seller's Commissions on such lot.
14. The highest qualified Bidder recognized by the Auctioneer shall be the Buyer. In the event of a tie bid, the earliest bid received or recognized wins. In the event of any dispute between any Bidders at an Auction, Auctioneer may at his sole discretion reoffer the lot. Auctioneer's decision and declaration of the winning Bidder shall be final and binding upon all Bidders. Bids properly offered, whether by floor Bidder or other means of bidding, may on occasion be missed or go unrecognized; in such cases, the Auctioneer may declare the recognized bid accepted as the winning bid, regardless of whether a competing bid may have been higher.
15. Auctioneer reserves the right to refuse to honor any bid or to limit the amount of any bid, in its sole discretion. A bid is considered not made in "Good Faith" when made by an insolvent or irresponsible person, a person under the age of eighteen, or is not supported by satisfactory credit, collectibles references, or otherwise. Regardless of the disclosure of his identity, any bid by a consignor or his agent on a lot consigned by him is deemed to be made in "Good Faith." Any person apparently appearing on the OFAC list is not eligible to bid.
16. Nominal Bids. The Auctioneer in its sole discretion may reject nominal bids, small opening bids, or very nominal advances. If a lot bearing estimates fails to open for 40–60% of the low estimate, the Auctioneer may pass the item or may place a protective bid on behalf of the consignor.
17. Lots bearing bidding estimates shall open at Auctioneer's discretion (approximately 50%-60% of the low estimate). In the event that no bid meets or exceeds that opening amount, the lot shall pass as unsold.
18. All items are to be purchased per lot as numerically indicated and no lots will be broken. Auctioneer reserves the right to withdraw, prior to the close, any lots from the Auction.
19. Auctioneer reserves the right to rescind the sale in the event of nonpayment, breach of a warranty, disputed ownership, auctioneer's clerical error or omission in exercising bids and reserves, or for any other reason and in Auctioneer's sole discretion. In cases of nonpayment, Auctioneer's election to void a sale does not relieve the Bidder from their obligation to pay Auctioneer its fees (seller's and buyer's premium) and any other damages or expenses pertaining to the lot.
20. Auctioneer occasionally experiences Internet and/or Server service outages, and Auctioneer periodically schedules system downtime for maintenance and other purposes, during which Bidders cannot participate or place bids. If such outages occur, we may at our discretion extend bidding for the Auction. Bidders unable to place their Bids through the Internet are directed to contact Client Services at 1-800-872-6467.
21. The Auctioneer, its affiliates, or their employees consign items to be sold in the Auction, and may bid on those lots or any other lots. Auctioneer or affiliates expressly reserve the right to modify any such bids at any time prior to the hammer based upon data made known to the Auctioneer or its affiliates. The Auctioneer may extend advances, guarantees, or loans to certain consignors.
22. The Auctioneer has the right to sell certain unsold items after the close of the Auction. Such lots shall be considered sold during the Auction and all these Terms and Conditions shall apply to such sales including but not limited to the Buyer's Premium, return rights, and disclaimers.

Payment:

23. All sales are strictly for cash in United States dollars (including U.S. currency, bank wire, cashier checks, travelers checks, eChecks, and bank money orders, and are subject to all reporting requirements). All deliveries are subject to good funds; funds being received in Auctioneer's account before delivery of the Purchases; and all payments are subject to a clearing period. Auctioneer reserves the right to determine if a check constitutes "good funds": checks drawn on a U.S. bank are subject to a ten business day hold, and thirty days when drawn on an international bank. Clients with pre-arranged credit status may receive immediate credit for payments via eCheck, personal or corporate checks. All others will be subject to a hold of 5 days, or more, for the funds to clear prior to releasing merchandise. (ref. T&C item 7 Credit for additional information.) Payments can be made 24-48 hours post auction from the My Orders page of the HA.com website.
24. Payment is due upon closing of the Auction session, or upon presentment of an invoice. Auctioneer reserves the right to void an invoice if payment in full is not received within 7 days after the close of the Auction. In cases of nonpayment, Auctioneer's election to void a sale does not relieve the Bidder from their obligation to pay Auctioneer its fees (seller's and buyer's premium) on the lot and any other damages pertaining to the lot.
25. Lots delivered to you, or your representative in the States of Texas, California, New York, or other states where the Auction may be held, are subject to all applicable state and local taxes, unless appropriate permits are on file with Auctioneer. (Note: Coins are only subject to sales tax in California on invoices under $1500 and in Texas on invoices under $1000. Check the Web site at: http://coins.ha.com/c/ref/sales-tax.zx for more details.) Bidder agrees to pay Auctioneer the actual amount of tax due in the event that sales tax is not properly collected due to: 1) an expired, inaccurate, inappropriate tax certificate or declaration, 2) an incorrect interpretation of the applicable statute, 3) or any other reason. The appropriate form or certificate must be on file at and verified by Auctioneer five days prior to Auction or tax must be paid; only if such form or certificate is received by Auctioneer within 4 days after the Auction can a refund of tax paid be made. Lots from different Auctions may not be aggregated for sales tax purposes.
26. In the event that a Bidder's payment is dishonored upon presentment(s), Bidder shall pay the maximum statutory processing fee set by applicable state law. If you attempt to pay via eCheck and your financial institution denies this transfer from your bank account, or the payment cannot be completed using the selected funding source, you agree to complete payment using your credit card on file.
27. If any Auction invoice submitted by Auctioneer is not paid in full when due, the unpaid balance will bear interest at the highest rate permitted by law from the date of invoice until paid. Any invoice not paid when due will bear a three percent (3%) late fee on the invoice amount or three percent (3%) of any installment that is past due. If the Auctioneer refers any invoice to an attorney for collection, the buyer agrees to pay attorney's fees, court costs, and other collection costs incurred by Auctioneer. If Auctioneer assigns collection to its in-house legal staff, such attorney's time expended on the matter shall be compensated at a rate comparable to the hourly rate of independent attorneys.
28. In the event a successful Bidder fails to pay any amounts due, Auctioneer reserves the right to sell the lot(s) securing the invoice to any underbidders in the Auction that the lot(s) appeared, or at subsequent private or public sale, or relist the lot(s) in a future auction conducted by Auctioneer. A defaulting Bidder agrees to pay for the reasonable costs of resale (including a 10% seller's commission, if consigned to an auction conducted by Auctioneer). The defaulting Bidder is liable to pay any difference between his total original invoice for the lot(s), plus any applicable interest, and the net proceeds for the lot(s) if sold at private sale or the subsequent hammer price of the lot(s) less the 10% seller's commissions, if sold at an Auctioneer's auction.

Terms and Conditions of Auction

29. Auctioneer reserves the right to require payment in full in good funds before delivery of the merchandise.
30. Auctioneer shall have a lien against the merchandise purchased by the buyer to secure payment of the Auction invoice. Auctioneer is further granted a lien and the right to retain possession of any other property of the buyer then held by the Auctioneer or its affiliates to secure payment of any Auction invoice or any other amounts due the Auctioneer or affiliates from the buyer. With respect to these lien rights, Auctioneer shall have all the rights of a secured creditor under Article 9 of the Texas Uniform Commercial Code, including but not limited to the right of sale. In addition, with respect to payment of the Auction invoice(s), the buyer waives any and all rights of offset he might otherwise have against the Auctioneer and the consignor of the merchandise included on the invoice. If a Bidder owes Auctioneer or its affiliates on any account, Auctioneer and its affiliates shall have the right to offset such unpaid account by any credit balance due Bidder, and it may secure by possessory lien any unpaid amount by any of the Bidder's property in their possession.
31. Title shall not pass to the successful Bidder until all invoices are paid in full. It is the responsibility of the buyer to provide adequate insurance coverage for the items once they have been delivered to a common carrier or third-party shipper.

Delivery; Shipping; and Handling Charges:

32. Buyer is liable for shipping and handling. Please refer to Auctioneer's website www.HA.com/common/shipping.php for the latest charges or call Auctioneer. Auctioneer is unable to combine purchases from other auctions or affiliates into one package for shipping purposes. Lots won will be shipped in a commercially reasonable time after payment in good funds for the merchandise and the shipping fees is received or credit extended, except when third-party shipment occurs.
33. Successful international Bidders shall provide written shipping instructions, including specified customs declarations, to the Auctioneer for any lots to be delivered outside of the United States. NOTE: Declaration value shall be the item'(s) hammer price together with its buyer's premium and Auctioneer shall use the correct harmonized code for the lot. Domestic Buyers on lots designated for third-party shipment must designate the common carrier, accept risk of loss, and prepay shipping costs.
34. All shipping charges will be borne by the successful Bidder. On all domestic shipments, any risk of loss during shipment will be borne by Heritage until the shipping carrier's confirmation of delivery to the address of record in Auctioneer's file (carrier's confirmation is conclusive to prove delivery to Bidder; if the client has a Signature release on file with the carrier, the package is considered delivered without Signature) or delivery by Heritage to Bidder's selected third-party shipper. On all foreign shipments, any risk of loss during shipment will be borne by the Bidder following Auctioneer's delivery to the Bidder's designated common carrier or third-party shipper.
35. Due to the nature of some items sold, it shall be the responsibility for the successful Bidder to arrange pick-up and shipping through third-parties; as to such items Auctioneer shall have no liability. Failure to pick-up or arrange shipping in a timely fashion (within ten days) shall subject Lots to storage and moving charges, including a $100 administration fee plus $10 daily storage for larger items and $5.00 daily for smaller items (storage fee per item) after 35 days. In the event the Lot is not removed within ninety days, the Lot may be offered for sale to recover any past due storage or moving fees, including a 10% Seller's Commission.
36. The laws of various countries regulate the import or export of certain plant and animal properties, including (but not limited to) items made of (or including) ivory, whalebone, turtle shell, coral, crocodile, or other wildlife. Transport of such lots may require special licenses for export, import, or both. Bidder is responsible for: 1) obtaining all information on such restricted items for both export and import; 2) obtaining all such licenses and/or permits. Delay or failure to obtain any such license or permit does not relieve the buyer of timely compliance with standard payment terms. For further information, please contact Ron Brackemyre at 800- 872-6467 ext. 1312.
37. Any request for shipping verification for undelivered packages must be made within 30 days of shipment by Auctioneer.

Cataloging, Warranties and Disclaimers:

38. NO WARRANTY, WHETHER EXPRESSED OR IMPLIED, IS MADE WITH RESPECT TO ANY DESCRIPTION CONTAINED IN THIS AUCTION OR ANY SECOND OPINE. Any description of the items or second opine contained in this Auction is for the sole purpose of identifying the items for those Bidders who do not have the opportunity to view the lots prior to bidding, and no description of items has been made part of the basis of the bargain or has created any express warranty that the goods would conform to any description made by Auctioneer. Color variations can be expected in any electronic or printed imaging, and are not grounds for the return of any lot. NOTE: Auctioneer, in specified auction venues, for example, Fine Art, may have express written warranties and you are referred to those specific terms and conditions. .
39. Auctioneer is selling only such right or title to the items being sold as Auctioneer may have by virtue of consignment agreements on the date of auction and disclaims any warranty of title to the Property. Auctioneer disclaims any warranty of merchantability or fitness for any particular purposes. All images, descriptions, sales data, and archival records are the exclusive property of Auctioneer, and may be used by Auctioneer for advertising, promotion, archival records, and any other uses deemed appropriate.
40. Translations of foreign language documents may be provided as a convenience to interested parties. Auctioneer makes no representation as to the accuracy of those translations and will not be held responsible for errors in bidding arising from inaccuracies in translation.
41. Auctioneer disclaims all liability for damages, consequential or otherwise, arising out of or in connection with the sale of any Property by Auctioneer to Bidder. No third party may rely on any benefit of these Terms and Conditions and any rights, if any, established hereunder are personal to the Bidder and may not be assigned. Any statement made by the Auctioneer is an opinion and does not constitute a warranty or representation. No employee of Auctioneer may alter these Terms and Conditions, and, unless signed by a principal of Auctioneer, any such alteration is null and void.
42. Auctioneer shall not be liable for breakage of glass or damage to frames (patent or latent); such defects, in any event, shall not be a basis for any claim for return or reduction in purchase price.

Release:

43. In consideration of participation in the Auction and the placing of a bid, Bidder expressly releases Auctioneer, its officers, directors and employees, its affiliates, and its outside experts that provide second opines, from any and all claims, cause of action, chose of action, whether at law or equity or any arbitration or mediation rights existing under the rules of any professional society or affiliation based upon the assigned description, or a derivative theory, breach of warranty express or implied, representation or other matter set forth within these Terms and Conditions of Auction or otherwise. In the event of a claim, Bidder agrees that such rights and privileges conferred therein are strictly construed as specifically declared herein; e.g., authenticity, typographical error, etc. and are the exclusive remedy. Bidder, by non-compliance to these express terms of a granted remedy, shall waive any claim against Auctioneer.
44. Notice: Some Property sold by Auctioneer are inherently dangerous e.g. firearms, cannons, and small items that may be swallowed or ingested or may have latent defects all of which may cause harm to a person. Purchaser accepts all risk of loss or damage from its purchase of these items and Auctioneer disclaims any liability whether under contract or tort for damages and losses, direct or inconsequential, and expressly disclaims any warranty as to safety or usage of any lot sold.

Dispute Resolution and Arbitration Provision:

45. By placing a bid or otherwise participating in the auction, Bidder accepts these Terms and Conditions of Auction, and specifically agrees to the dispute resolution provided herein. Consumer disputes shall be resolved through court litigation which has an exclusive Dallas, Texas venue clause and jury waiver. Non-consumer dispute shall be determined in binding arbitration which arbitration replaces the right to go to court, including the right to a jury trial.
46. Auctioneer in no event shall be responsible for consequential damages, incidental damages, compensatory damages, or any other damages arising or claimed to be arising from the auction of any lot. In the event that Auctioneer cannot deliver the lot or subsequently it is established that the lot lacks title, or other transfer or condition issue is claimed, in such cases the sole remedy shall be limited to rescission of sale and refund of the amount paid by Bidder; in no case shall Auctioneer's maximum liability exceed the high bid on that lot, which bid shall be deemed for all purposes the value of the lot. After one year has elapsed, Auctioneer's maximum liability shall be limited to any commissions and fees Auctioneer earned on that lot.
47. In the event of an attribution error, Auctioneer may at its sole discretion, correct the error on the Internet, or, if discovered at a later date, to refund the buyer's purchase price without further obligation.
48. Dispute Resolution for Consumers and Non-Consumers: Any claim, dispute, or controversy in connection with, relating to and /or arising out of the Auction, participation in the Auction, award of lots, damages of claims to lots, descriptions, condition reports, provenance, estimates, return and warranty rights, any interpretation of these Terms and Conditions, any alleged verbal modification of these Terms and Conditions and/or any purported settlement whether asserted in contract, tort, under Federal or State statute or regulation shall or any other matter: a) if presented by a consumer, be exclusively heard by, and the parties consent to, exclusive in personam jurisdiction in the State District Courts of Dallas County, Texas. THE PARTIES EXPRESSLY WAIVE ANY RIGHT TO TRIAL BY JURY. Any appeals shall be solely pursued in the appellate courts of the State of Texas; or b) for any claimant other than a consumer, the claim shall be presented in confidential binding arbitration before a single arbitrator, that the parties may agree upon, selected from the JAMS list of Texas arbitrators. The case is not to be administrated by JAMS; however, if the parties cannot agree on an arbitrator, then JAMS shall appoint the arbitrator and it shall be conducted under JAMS rules. The locale shall be Dallas Texas. The arbitrator's award may be enforced in any court of competent jurisdiction. Any party on any claim involving the purchase or sale of numismatic or related items may elect arbitration through binding PNG arbitration. Any claim must be brought within one (1) year of the alleged breach, default or misrepresentation or the claim is waived. This agreement and any claims shall be determined and construed under Texas law. The prevailing party (party that is awarded substantial and material relief on its claim or defense) may be awarded its reasonable attorneys' fees and costs.
49. No claims of any kind can be considered after the settlements have been made with the consignors. Any dispute after the settlement date is strictly between the Bidder and consignor without involvement or responsibility of the Auctioneer.
50. In consideration of their participation in or application for the Auction, a person or entity (whether the successful Bidder, a Bidder, a purchaser and/or other Auction participant or registrant) agrees that all disputes in any way relating to, arising under, connected with, or incidental to these Terms and Conditions and purchases, or default in payment thereof, shall be arbitrated pursuant to the arbitration provision. In the event that any matter including actions to compel arbitration, construe the agreement, actions in aid or arbitration or otherwise needs to be litigated, such litigation shall be exclusively in the Courts of the State of Texas, in Dallas County, Texas, and if necessary the corresponding appellate courts. For such actions, the successful Bidder, purchaser, or Auction participant also expressly submits himself to the personal jurisdiction of the State of Texas.
51. These Terms & Conditions provide specific remedies for occurrences in the auction and delivery process. Where such remedies are afforded, they shall be interpreted strictly. Bidder agrees that any claim shall utilize such remedies; Bidder making a claim in excess of those remedies provided in these Terms and Conditions agrees that in no case whatsoever shall Auctioneer's maximum liability exceed the high bid on that lot, which bid shall be deemed for all purposes the value of the lot.

Miscellaneous:

52. Agreements between Bidders and consignors to effectuate a non-sale of an item at Auction, inhibit bidding on a consigned item to enter into a private sale agreement for said item, or to utilize the Auctioneer's Auction to obtain sales for non-selling consigned items subsequent to the Auction, are strictly prohibited. If a subsequent sale of a previously consigned item occurs in violation of this provision, Auctioneer reserves the right to charge Bidder the applicable Buyer's Premium and consignor a Seller's Commission as determined for each auction venue and by the terms of the seller's agreement.
53. Acceptance of these Terms and Conditions qualifies Bidder as a client who has consented to be contacted by Heritage in the future. In conformity with "do-not-call" regulations promulgated by the Federal or State regulatory agencies, participation by the Bidder is affirmative consent to being contacted at the phone number shown in his application and this consent shall remain in effect until it is revoked in writing. Heritage may from time to time contact Bidder concerning sale, purchase, and auction opportunities available through Heritage and its affiliates and subsidiaries.
54. Rules of Construction: Auctioneer presents properties in a number of collectible fields, and as such, specific venues have promulgated supplemental Terms and Conditions. Nothing herein shall be construed to waive the general Terms and Conditions of Auction by these additional rules and shall be construed to give force and effect to the rules in their entirety.

State Notices:

Notice as to an Auction in California. Auctioneer has in compliance with Title 2.95 of the California Civil Code as amended October 11, 1993 Sec. 1812.600, posted with the California Secretary of State its bonds for it and its employees, and the auction is being conducted in compliance with Sec. 2338 of the Commercial Code and Sec. 535 of the Penal Code.

Notice as to an Auction in New York City. These Terms and Conditions of Sale are designed to conform to the applicable sections of the New York City Department of Consumer Affairs Rules and Regulations as Amended. This sale is a Public Auction Sale conducted by Heritage Auctioneers & Galleries, Inc. # 41513036. The New York City licensed auctioneers are: Sam Foose, #095260; Kathleen Guzman, #0762165; Nicholas Dawes, #1304724; Ed Beardsley, #1183220; Scott Peterson, #1306933; Andrea Voss, #1320558, who will conduct the Sale on behalf of itself and Heritage Numismatic Auctions, Inc. (for Coins) and Currency Auctions of America, Inc. (for currency). All lots are subject to: the consignor's rights to bid thereon in accord with these Terms and Conditions of Sale, consignor's option to receive advances on their consignments, and Auctioneer, in its sole discretion, may offer limited extended financing to registered bidders, in accord with Auctioneer's internal credit standards. A registered bidder may inquire whether a lot is subject to an advance or a reserve. Auctioneer has made advances to various consignors in this sale. On lots bearing an estimate, the term refers to a value range placed on an item by the Auctioneer in its sole opinion but the final price is determined by the bidders.

Notice as to an Auction in Texas. In compliance with TDLR rule 67.100(c)(1), notice is hereby provided that this auction is covered by a Recovery Fund administered by the Texas Department of Licensing and Regulation, P.O. Box 12157, Austin, Texas 78711 (512) 463-6599. Any complaints may be directed to the same address.

Notice as to an Auction in Ohio: Auction firm and Auctioneer are licensed by the Dept. of Agriculture, and either the licensee is bonded in favor of the state or an aggrieved person may initiate a claim against the auction recovery fund created in Section 4707.25 of the Revised Code as a result of the licensee's actions, whichever is applicable.

Rev. 12-30-11

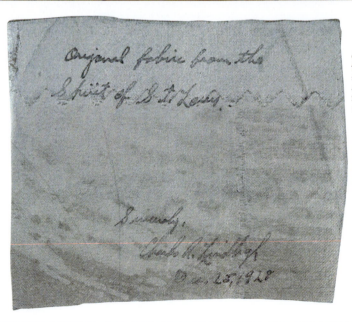

YOUR PERSONAL ONLINE COLLECTION INVENTORY

FREE!

Heritage's new **MyCollection** software is a private record of collectibles that you own, buy, or resell, and it's great for insurance or estate planning.

It's FREE, and...

✦ Stores images, description, and more.

✦ All items bought from Heritage are added automatically!

✦ Items bought elsewhere can also be added

✦ Allows for infinite organization of your collection.

✦ Exports to Excel or to print for easy reference.

✦ You enjoy absolute privacy. Your information will not be shared with, or sold to, any third party for any reason.

✦ Available in all Heritage categories

	Photo (hide)	Your Reference #	Description & Population Data	Your Value / Numismedia Wholesale Ask	Purchase Price	Wantlist Demand	Make Offer to Owner Status
☐ All							
			Total Value: $15,364,067				
			Total purchase price: $18,559,992				
			Total Make Offer Value for items accepting offers: $21,763,751				
☐			1652 SHILNG OAK TREE AU55 NGC Population 15/32 View Auction Prices Realized	Set Value	$8,625		Not Taking Offers
☐			AM PLANT 1/24RL RESTRIKE MS62 PCGS Population 8/6 View Auction Prices Realized	Set Value	$1,265	32	Not Taking Offers
☐			Elephant Halfpenny, LONDON, Thick Planchet, BN MS62 PCGS Population 16/23 View Auction Prices Realized	Set Value	$2,530	31	Not Taking Offers
☐			Elephant Halfpenny, LONDON, Thick Planchet, BN AU55 NGC Population 25/55 View Auction Prices Realized	Set Value	$1,725		Not Taking Offers
☐			1722 Rosa Americana Halfpenny, D:G:REX, BN AU58 PCGS Population 3/8 View Auction Prices Realized	Set Value	$1,840	31	Not Taking Offers

Click on the headings to sort.

But the most exciting thing about the new **MyCollection** software is the ability to receive offers on items you purchased from Heritage at auction, including the ability to set your own "Buy Now" price.

Heritage members now have the opportunity to make an anonymous offer to the buyer of items previously purchased at auction from Heritage, directly through our Auction Results Archives. Heritage manages the transaction, maintaining privacy for both parties. Acceptance of an offer represents agreement with the terms and conditions of sale, including Heritage's commission. This service is free to the buyer (no buyer's premium), includes a 7 day return policy, protects the identity of both parties, and allows offers and counter-offers. If you receive an offer, you will have 72 hours to decline, counter-offer or accept the offer. You are under no obligation until you accept an offer or a buyer accepts your counter offer. You will receive payment for items sold within 30 days of Heritage's receipt of your item.

THE PERSONAL PROPERTY OF JOHN WAYNE auction made history.

Now you can own special Limited Edition mementos to commemorate this amazing event.

STILL AVAILABLE!

A limited number of the Summer/Fall 2011 edition of *The Intelligent Collector* is still available, featuring an interview with John Wayne's son Ethan and select highlights from the historic auction.

Only $15 or FREE with purchase of Catalog or DVD!

A portion of the proceeds from the sales of the library edition catalogs and all profits from the sale of the DVD will benefit the John Wayne Cancer Foundation.

THE PERSONAL PROPERTY OF JOHN WAYNE 300-PAGE SPECIAL LIMITED EDITION ILLUSTRATED AUCTION CATALOG

- Full-Color Photographs
- Descriptions for Over 700 Lots
- More than 300 Pages

SOFTCOVER AUCTION CATALOG — $50

LIMITED LIBRARY EDITION SIGNED BY ETHAN WAYNE HARDCOVER AUCTION CATALOG — $125

THE PERSONAL PROPERTY OF JOHN WAYNE KEEPSAKE COLLECTOR'S DVD

- Family Members Ethan, Patrick, Marisa and Pilar Wayne Reflect on Wayne's Life and Career
- Highlights from the Historic Auction
- Family Home Movies and Rarely Seen Photos

KEEPSAKE COLLECTOR'S DVD — $19.95

Order Your Collectible Auction Catalog, Keepsake DVD, & Magazine Today!

Call 866-835-3243 or visit HA.com/JohnWayne

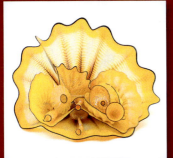

HERITAGE
TEXANA AUCTION
MARCH 3, 2012 | HOUSTON | LIVE & ONLINE

Highlights from our upcoming auction!

[James Fannin] Presentation Cane. Ball-handle is 14K gold decorated with floral scrolls and bears the inscription: *"Wm. L. Hunter/to/E. R. Lane/ I cut this stick/from the grave/of/Col. Fannin."* **Est. $10,000-$15,000** | HA.com/6067-28001

1890 Spring Palace Award Medal *"Awarded to/Houston County"* 2.5 x 4.75 in. **Est. $3,000-$5,000** | HA.com/6067-30001

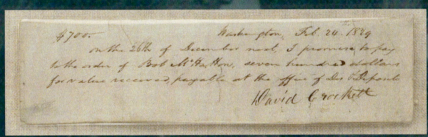

David Crockett Promissory Note Signed *"David Crockett."* One page, 7.75 x 2 in. Washington, February 24, 1829 **Est. $25,000-$35,000** | HA.com/6067-21001

Texas State Historical Association

A portion of all proceeds from this auction will go to benefit TSHA.

For more information contact:
Sandra Palomino | Director, Historical Manuscripts & Texana | 800.872.6467, ext. 1107 | SandraP@HA.com

Annual Sales Exceed $800 Million | 700,000+ Online Bidder-Members

3500 Maple Avenue | Dallas, Texas 75219 | 800-872-6467 | HA.com

HERITAGE HA.com
AUCTIONS

DALLAS | NEW YORK | BEVERLY HILLS | SAN FRANCISCO | PARIS | GENEVA

22753

HERITAGE

Coast to Coast

3 U.S. Locations to Serve You

DALLAS
3500 Maple Avenue
Dallas, Texas 75219

214.528.3500

Hours:
Mon-Fri: 9:00 AM CT - 5:00 PM CT
Saturday: 9:00 AM CT - 1:00 PM CT

NEW YORK
445 Park Avenue (at 57th Street)
New York, New York 10022

212.486.3500

Hours:
Mon-Fri: 10:00 AM ET - 6:00 PM ET
Saturday: 10:00 AM ET - 3:00 PM ET

BEVERLY HILLS
9478 West Olympic Boulevard
Beverly Hills, California 90212

310.492.8600

Hours:
Mon-Fri: 9:00 AM PT - 5:00 PM PT
Saturday: By Appointment

Annual Sales Exceed $800 Million • 700,000+ Online Bidder-Members

HERITAGE HA.com
AUCTIONS

3500 Maple Avenue • Dallas, Texas 75219 • 800-872-6467

DALLAS | NEW YORK | BEVERLY HILLS | SAN FRANCISCO | PARIS | GENEVA

HERITAGE

FINE SILVER & VERTU AUCTION
APRIL 10, 2012 | DALLAS | LIVE & ONLINE

CONSIGN NOW
CONSIGNMENT DEADLINE: FEBRUARY 7

1. A GROUP OF TIFFANY & CO. SILVER AND ENAMEL CIRCUS
   FIGURES DESIGNED BY GENE MOORE
   circa 1990
   Sold for a total of: $68,772
   December 2011
   HA.com/5086

2. A GORHAM SILVER AND MIXED METAL TEA CADDY
   Providence, Rhode Island, 1880
   4-3/8 in. high
   Sold for: $11,950 December 2011
   HA.com/5086*68259

3. A GORHAM COIN SILVER
   FIGURAL CENTERPIECE
   Providence, Rhode Island, circa 1865
   12-5/8 x 11-1/2 x 9-3/8 in.
   Sold for: $5,676 December 2011
   HA.com/5086*68220

4. A LUEN WO CHINESE EXPORT
   SILVER GOBLET
   Shanghai, China, circa 1900
   10 in. high
   Sold for: $3,107 December 2011
   HA.com/5086*68202

5. A RATTRAY & CO. SCOTTISH GOLD PRESENTATION
   CENTER BOWL
   Dundee, Scotland, circa 1931
   7-3/8 x 11-1/4 x 9-1/4 in.
   Sold for: $56,763 December 2011
   HA.com/5086*68199

INQUIRIES: 800-872-6467
Tim Rigdon, ext. 1119 or TimR@HA.com
Karen Rigdon, ext. 1723 or KarenR@HA.com

For a free auction catalog in any category, plus a copy
of *The Collector's Handbook* (combined value $65), visit
HA.com/CATG22753 or call 866-835-3243 and reference
code CATG22753.

HERITAGE HA.com
A U C T I O N S
THE WORLD'S THIRD LARGEST AUCTION HOUSE

23343

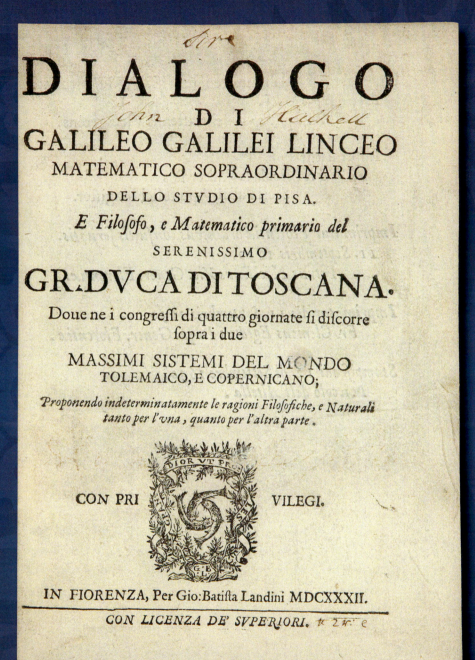

Department Specialists

For the extensions below, please dial 800.872.6467

Comics & Comic Art
HA.com/Comics

Ed Jaster, Ext. 1288 • EdJ@HA.com

Lon Allen, Ext. 1261 • LonA@HA.com

Barry Sandoval, Ext. 1377 • BarryS@HA.com

Todd Hignite, Ext. 1790 • ToddH@HA.com

Fine Art

American, Western & European Art
HA.com/FineArt

Ed Jaster, Ext. 1288 • EdJ@HA.com

Brian Roughton, Ext. 1210 • BrianR@HA.com

Marianne Berardi, Ph.D., Ext. 1506 • MarianneB@HA.com

Ariana Hartsock, Ext. 1283 • ArianaH@HA.com

Kirsty Buchanan, Ext. 1741 • KirstyB@HA.com

Deborah Solon, Ext. 1843 • DeborahS@HA.com

California Art
HA.com/FineArt

Alissa Ford, Ext. 1926 • AlissaF@HA.com

Deborah Solon, Ext. 1843 • DeborahS@HA.com

Decorative Arts & Design
HA.com/Decorative

Tim Rigdon, Ext. 1119 • TimR@HA.com

Karen Rigdon, Ext. 1723 • KarenR@HA.com

Nicholas Dawes, Ext. 1605 • NickD@HA.com

Carolyn Mani, Ext. 1677 • CarolynM@HA.com

Illustration Art
HA.com/Illustration

Ed Jaster, Ext. 1288 • EdJ@HA.com

Todd Hignite, Ext. 1790 • ToddH@HA.com

Lalique & Art Glass
HA.com/Design

Nicholas Dawes, Ext. 1605 • NickD@HA.com

Modern & Contemporary Art
HA.com/Modern

Frank Hettig, Ext. 1157 • FrankH@HA.com

Silver & Vertu
HA.com/Silver

Tim Rigdon, Ext. 1119 • TimR@HA.com

Karen Rigdon, Ext. 1723 • KarenR@HA.com

Texas Art
HA.com/TexasArt

Atlee Phillips, Ext. 1786 • AtleeP@HA.com

Vintage & Contemporary Photography
HA.com/ArtPhotography

Ed Jaster, Ext. 1288 • EdJ@HA.com

Rachel Peart, Ext. 1625 • RPeart@HA.com

Handbags & Luxury Accessories
HA.com/Luxury

Matt Rubinger, Ext. 1419 • MRubinger@HA.com

Historical

American Indian Art
HA.com/AmericanIndian

Delia Sullivan, Ext. 1343 • DeliaS@HA.com

Americana & Political
HA.com/Historical

Tom Slater, Ext. 1441 • TomS@HA.com

John Hickey, Ext. 1264 • JohnH@HA.com

Michael Riley, Ext. 1467 • MichaelR@HA.com

Don Ackerman, Ext. 1736 • DonA@HA.com

Arms & Armor
HA.com/Arms

Greg Martin, Ext. 1883 • GregM@HA.com

Jemison Beshears, Ext. 1886 • JemisonB@HA.com

Cliff Chappell, Ext. 1887 • CliffordC@HA.com

Roger Lake, Ext. 1884 • RogerL@HA.com

David Carde, Ext. 1881 • DavidC@HA.com

Civil War & Militaria
HA.com/CivilWar

Dennis Lowe, Ext. 1182 • DennisL@HA.com

Historical Manuscripts
HA.com/Manuscripts

Sandra Palomino, Ext. 1107 • SandraP@HA.com

Rare Books
HA.com/Books

James Gannon, Ext. 1609 • JamesG@HA.com

Joe Fay, Ext. 1544 • JoeF@HA.com

Space Exploration
HA.com/Space

John Hickey, Ext. 1264 • JohnH@HA.com

Michael Riley, Ext. 1467 • MichaelR@HA.com

Texana
HA.com/Historical

Sandra Palomino, Ext. 1107 • SandraP@HA.com

Jewelry
HA.com/Jewelry

Jill Burgum, Ext. 1697 • JillB@HA.com

Peggy Gottlieb, Ext. 1847 • PGottlieb@HA.com

Movie Posters
HA.com/MoviePosters

Grey Smith, Ext. 1367 • GreySm@HA.com

Bruce Carteron, Ext. 1551 • BruceC@HA.com

Music & Entertainment Memorabilia
HA.com/Entertainment

Margaret Barrett, Ext. 1912 • MargaretB@HA.com
Kristen Painter, Ext. 1149 • KristenP@HA.com
John Hickey, Ext. 1264 • JohnH@HA.com
Garry Shrum, Ext. 1585 • GarryS@HA.com

Vintage Guitars & Musical Instruments
HA.com/Guitar

Mike Gutierrez, Ext. 1183 • MikeG@HA.com
Isaiah Evans, Ext. 1201 • IsaiahE@HA.com

Natural History
HA.com/NaturalHistory

David Herskowitz, Ext. 1610 • DavidH@HA.com

Numismatics

Coins – United States
HA.com/Coins

David Mayfield, Ext. 1277 • DavidM@HA.com
Jessica Aylmer, Ext. 1706 • JessicaA@HA.com
Win Callender, Ext. 1415 • WinC@HA.com
Chris Dykstra, Ext. 1380 • ChrisD@HA.com
Sam Foose, Ext. 1227 • SamF@HA.com
Jim Jelinski, Ext. 1257 • JimJ@HA.com
Bob Marino, Ext. 1374 • BobMarino@HA.com
Mike Sadler, Ext. 1332 • MikeS@HA.com
Beau Streicher, Ext. 1645 • BeauS@HA.com

Rare Currency
HA.com/Currency

Len Glazer, Ext. 1390 • Len@HA.com
Allen Mincho, Ext. 1327 • Allen@HA.com
Dustin Johnston, Ext. 1302 • Dustin@HA.com
Michael Moczalla, Ext. 1481 • MichaelM@HA.com
Jason Friedman, Ext. 1582 • JasonF@HA.com
Brad Ciociola, Ext. 1752 • BradC@HA.com

World & Ancient Coins
HA.com/WorldCoins

Cristiano Bierrenbach, Ext. 1661 • CrisB@HA.com
Warren Tucker, Ext. 1287 • WTucker@HA.com
David Michaels, Ext. 1606 • DMichaels@HA.com
Scott Cordry, Ext. 1369 • ScottC@HA.com

Sports Collectibles
HA.com/Sports

Chris Ivy, Ext. 1319 • CIvy@HA.com
Peter Calderon, Ext. 1789 • PeterC@HA.com
Derek Grady, Ext. 1975 • DerekG@HA.com
Mike Gutierrez, Ext. 1183 • MikeG@HA.com
Lee Iskowitz, Ext. 1601 • LeeI@HA.com
Mark Jordan, Ext. 1187 • MarkJ@HA.com
Chris Nerat, Ext. 1615 • ChrisN@HA.com
Jonathan Scheier, Ext. 1314 • JonathanS@HA.com

Timepieces
HA.com/Timepieces

Jim Wolf, Ext. 1659 • JWolf@HA.com

Wine
HA.com/Wine

Frank Martell, Ext. 1753 • FrankM@HA.com
Poppy Davis, Ext. 1559 • PoppyD@HA.com

Services

Appraisal Services
HA.com/Appraisals

Meredith Meuwly, Ext. 1631• MeredithM@HA.com

Corporate & Institutional Collections/Ventures
Karl Chiao, Ext. 1958 • KarlC@HA.com

Credit Department
Marti Korver, Ext. 1248 • Marti@HA.com
Eric Thomas, Ext. 1241 • EricT@HA.com

Media & Public Relations
Noah Fleisher, Ext. 1143 • NoahF@HA.com

Trusts & Estates
HA.com/Estates

Mark Prendergast, Ext. 1632 • MPrendergast@HA.com
Karl Chiao, Ext. 1958 • KarlC@HA.com
Carolyn Mani, Ext. 1677 • CarolynM@HA.com

Locations

Dallas (World Headquarters)
214.528.3500 • 800.872.6467
3500 Maple Ave.
Dallas, TX 75219

Beverly Hills
310.492.8600
9478 W. Olympic Blvd.
Beverly Hills, CA 90212

San Francisco
800.872.6467
478 Jackson Street
San Francisco, CA 94111

New York
212.486.3500
445 Park Avenue
New York, NY 10022

DALLAS | NEW YORK | SAN FRANCISCO
BEVERLY HILLS | PARIS | GENEVA

Corporate Officers

R. Steven Ivy, Co-Chairman
James L. Halperin, Co-Chairman
Gregory J. Rohan, President
Paul Minshull, Chief Operating Officer
Todd Imhof, Executive Vice President
Kathleen Guzman, Managing Director-New York

U.S. Rare Coin Auctions	Location	Auction Dates	Consignment Deadline
U.S. Rare Coins	Long Beach	February 1-5, 2012	Closed
U.S. Rare Coins	New York	March 8-9, 2012	January 27, 2012
U.S. Rare Coins	Schaumburg, IL	April 18-21, 2012	March 9, 2012
World & Ancient Coin Auctions	**Location**	**Auction Dates**	**Consignment Deadline**
Judean Coin Auction	New York	March 8-9, 2012	Closed
CICF Ancient Coins	Chicago	April 25, 2012	March 6, 2012
CICF World Coins	Chicago	April 26-28, 2012	March 6, 2012
Rare Currency Auctions	**Location**	**Auction Dates**	**Consignment Deadline**
Currency	Long Beach	February 2-3, 2012	Closed
CSNS	Chicago	April 18-23, 2012	March 2, 2012
Fine & Decorative Arts Auctions	**Location**	**Auction Dates**	**Consignment Deadline**
The Estate Auction	Dallas	February 7, 2012	Closed
Illustration Art	Beverly Hills	March 1-2, 2012	Closed
California Art	Beverly Hills	March 20, 2012	Closed
Fine Silver & Vertu	Dallas	April 10, 2012	February 7, 2012
Vintage & Contemporary Photography	New York	May 1, 2012	March 6, 2012
Texas Art	Dallas	May 5, 2012	March 3, 2012
Art of the American West	Dallas	May 5, 2012	March 3, 2012
American & European Art	Dallas	May 15, 2012	March 13, 2012
Modern & Contemporary Art	Dallas	May 22, 2012	April 6, 2012
Illustration Art	Beverly Hills	June 6, 2012	April 11, 2012
Decorative Arts	Dallas	June 12, 2012	April 10, 2012
20th Century Design	Dallas	June 13, 2012	April 11, 2012
Jewelry, Timepieces & Luxury Accessory Auctions	**Location**	**Auction Dates**	**Consignment Deadline**
Fine Jewelry	New York	April 30, 2012	February 27, 2012
Handbags & Luxury Accessories	New York	May 1, 2012	February 29, 2012
Watches & Fine Timepieces	New York	May 21, 2012	March 20, 2012
Vintage Movie Posters Auctions	**Location**	**Auction Dates**	**Consignment Deadline**
Vintage Movie Posters	Dallas	March 23-24, 2012	January 31, 2012
Comics Auctions	**Location**	**Auction Dates**	**Consignment Deadline**
Comics & Original Comic Art	Dallas	February 22-23, 2012	Closed
Music & Entertainment Memorabilia Auctions	**Location**	**Auction Dates**	**Consignment Deadline**
Vintage Guitars & Musical Instruments	Beverly Hills	February 4-5, 2012	Closed
Music, Celebrity & Hollywood Memorabilia	Dallas	March 30-31, 2012	February 7, 2012
Historical Grand Format Auctions	**Location**	**Auction Dates**	**Consignment Deadline**
Rare Books & Autographs	Beverly Hills	February 8-9, 2012	Closed
Historical Manuscripts	Beverly Hills	February 8-9, 2012	Closed
Texana	Dallas	March 10, 2012	January 18, 2012
Arms & Armor	Dallas	Spring 2012	January 15, 2012
NRA Firearms for Freedom	Dallas	Spring 2012	January 15, 2012
Art of the Americas	Dallas	May 5, 2012	March 14, 2012
Americana & Political	Dallas	May 12, 2012	March 21, 2012
Space Exploration	Dallas	May 12, 2012	March 21, 2012
Militaria	Dallas	June 9, 2012	April 18, 2012
Vintage Sports Collectibles Auctions	**Location**	**Auction Dates**	**Consignment Deadline**
Vintage Sports Collectibles	Dallas	April 26-27, 2012	March 5, 2012
Natural History Auctions	**Location**	**Auction Dates**	**Consignment Deadline**
Natural History	New York	May 20, 2012	February 11, 2012
Fine & Rare Wine	**Location**	**Auction Dates**	**Consignment Deadline**
Fine & Rare Wine	Beverly Hills	March 2-3, 2012	January 15, 2012

HA.com/Consign • Consignment Hotline 800-872-6467 • All dates and auctions subject to change after press time. Go to HA.com for updates.

HERITAGE WEEKLY INTERNET COIN AUCTIONS • Begin and end every Sunday & Tuesday of each week at 10 PM CT.
HERITAGE MONTHLY INTERNET WORLD COIN AUCTIONS • Begin and end the first Tuesday of each month at 10 PM CT.
HERITAGE THURSDAY MODERN COIN AUCTIONS • Begin and end every Thursday at 10 pm CT.
HERITAGE TUESDAY INTERNET CURRENCY AUCTIONS • Begin and end every Tuesday at 10 PM CT.
HERITAGE WEEKLY INTERNET COMICS AUCTIONS • Begin and end every Sunday at 10 PM CT.
HERITAGE WEEKLY INTERNET MOVIE POSTER AUCTIONS • Begin and end every Sunday at 10 PM CT.
HERITAGE WEEKLY INTERNET SPORTS AUCTIONS • Begin and end every Sunday at 10 PM CT, with extended bidding available.
HERITAGE WEEKLY INTERNET WATCH & JEWELRY AUCTIONS • Begin and end every Tuesday at 10 PM CT.
HERITAGE WEEKLY INTERNET VINTAGE GUITAR & MUSICAL INSTRUMENT AUCTIONS • Begin and end every Thursday at 10 PM CT.
HERITAGE WEEKLY INTERNET RARE BOOKS & AUTOGRAPHS AUCTIONS • Begin and end every Thursday at 10 PM CT.
HERITAGE MONTHLY INTERNET WINE AUCTIONS • Begin and end the second Thursday of each month at 10 PM CT, with extended bidding available.

1-1-2012

Auctioneers: Samuel Foose: TX 11727; CA Bond #RSB2004178; FL AU3244; GA AUNR3029; IL 441001482; NC 8373; OH 2006000048; MA 03015; PA AU005443; TN 6093; WI 2230-052; NYC 0952360; Denver 1021450; Phoenix 07006332. Robert Korver: TX 13754; CA Bond #RSB2004179; FL AU2916; GA AUNR003023; IL 441001421; MA 03014; NC 8363; OH 2006000049; TN 6439; WI 2412-52; Phoenix 07102049; NYC 1096338; Denver 1021446. Teia Baber: TX 16624; CA Bond #RSB2005525. Ed Beardsley: TX Associate 16632; NYC 1183220. Nicholas Dawes: NYC 1304724. Marsha Dixey: TX 16493. Chris Dykstra: TX 16601; FL AU4069; WI 2566-052; TN 6463; IL 441001788; CA #RSB2005738. Jeff Engelken: CA Bond #RSB2004180. Alissa Ford: CA Bond #RSB2005920. Leo Frese: CA Bond #RSB2004176; NYC 1094963. Shaunda Fry: TX 16448; FL AU3915; WI 2577-52; CA Bond #RSB2005396. Kathleen Guzman: NYC 0762165. Stewart Huckaby: TX 16590. Cindy Isennock, participating auctioneer: Baltimore Auctioneer license #AU10. Carolyn Mani: CA Bond #RSB2005661; Bob Merrill: TX 13408; MA 03022; WI 2557-052; FL AU4043; IL 441001683; CA Bond #RSB2004177. Cori Mikeals: TX 16582; CA #RSB2005645. Scott Peterson: TX 13256; NYC 1306933; IL 441001659; WI 2431-052; CA Bond #RSB2005395. Tim Rigdon: TX 16519. Michael J. Sadler: TX 16129; FL AU3795; IL 441001478; MA 03021; TN 6487; WI 2581-052; NYC 1304630; CA Bond #RSB2005412. Eric Thomas: TX 16421; PA AU005574; TN 6515. Andrea Voss: TX 16406; FL AU4034; MA 03019; WI 2576-052; CA Bond #RSB2004676; NYC #1320558. Jacob Walker: TX 16413; FL AU4031; WI 2567-052; IL 441001677; CA Bond #RSB2005394. Peter Wiggins: TX 16635. (Rev. 5-15-11)